OVERTHROWING
THE QUEEN

CONTENTS

ACKNOWLEDGMENTS

AS PART OF A COLLABORATIVE research project, this book owes a great debt to scores of people, first among them the incredibly generous and trusting people who sat down to talk about their views and experiences with public assistance. My debt to grocery store cashiers, aid providers, volunteers, students, politicians, and community members is immense; all of these men and women were willing to share their views on a sensitive issue that would inevitably be popular with some of their peers and deeply unpopular with others. That debt is multiplied exponentially for the aid recipients who were willing to face the stigma of poverty and welfare in this country and share deeply personal stories of challenges that for many of them continue to this day.

My deep gratitude follows quickly to my coresearchers on this project, beginning with the community partners who added this project to their already overstuffed workload. In Alamance County, there were Linda Allison, Latawnya Hall, Susan Osborne, and Michelle Poole at the Department of Social Services; Nikki Ratliff at the Burlington Housing Authority; first Hunter Thompson and then Kim Crawford at Allied Churches; Tracy Salisbury at the Open Door Clinic; Heidi Norwick and April Durr with the United Way; and Lynn Inman, who works as a housing and mental health specialist. Partners in Guilford County included Robin Britt, Angela Ben-Zekry, Maria Stevens, Brad Huffstetler, Jaye Webb, Wanda Ford, Deborah Willoughby, and Katina Madison at Guilford Child Development; and Sarah Glover, Jennifer Ruppe, and Fanta Dorley at the United Way.

Integral to the research were the Elon University students who conducted interviews: in Alamance County, Jamie Albright, Kristen Bryar, Heather Cassano, Kit Connor, Jessica Elizondo, Greg Honan, Hannah Hyatt, Chelsea McQueen, Caroline Miller, Sophie Rupp, Alex Sherry, Chessa Simpson, Gloria So, Laura Lee

Sturm, and Ben Waldon; and in Guilford County, Sara Blough, Jamie Fleishman, Whittni Holland, Tim Kitslaar, Shenandoah Lucero-Keniston, Citlaly Mora-Hernandez, Olivia Musgrave, Osca Opoku, Alyssa Potter, Jeremy Revelise, Anna Rice, Noah Rossen, Vashti Shiwmangal, Rihana Spinner, and Emily Thomas. Their commitment to careful, ethical fieldwork was inspiring and invaluable.

Aware of my research, numerous family, friends, students, and colleagues forwarded me relevant articles, citations, and examples of welfare lore from social media. The book is stronger for their contributions, and chapter 9, on social media, would not have existed without input from the following people: Bill Barnett, Brooke Barnett, Lily Barnett-Mould, Ben Bridges, Mike Carignan, Hiram Cutie, Eric Eliason, Jessica Elizondo, Di Goldstein, Greg Honan, Jeremy Hunt, Dorry Noyes, and Eleanor Walden. I also benefitted greatly from conversations about relevant theories, sources, and approaches to my work from my colleagues at Elon University, including Steve Bednar, Cindy Fair, Alexis Franzese, Tom Henricks, Jason Husser, Barbara Miller, Aunchalee Palmquist, Ann Cahill, and Toddie Peters, as well as my folklore colleagues scattered across the country, particularly Ray Cashman, Eric Eliason, Bill Ellis, Di Goldstein, Dorry Noyes, Henry Glassie, Pravina Shukla, Jason Jackson, Carl Lindahl, Elliott Oring, Leonard Primiano, Michael Dylan Foster, Lisa Gilman, Greg Kelly, Jennifer Schacker, Caroline Miller, and Ben Bridges. In libraries and archives close to home and across the country, there were a number of incredibly knowledgeable and generous folks who helped me track down materials as diverse as Reagan's campaign speeches, welfare jokes from the 1970s, and the owner of a race horse named Welfare Queen: Pauline Cox at the Memorial University Folklore and Language Archive; Yasmin Golan at the University of California, Berkeley, Folklore Archives; Carrie Schwier at the Indiana University Archives; Jim Sam at the Hoover Institution Library and Archives; Barbara Truesdell at the Center for Documentary Research and Practice; and Teresa LePors, Jamane Yeager, and Lynn Melchor at Elon University's Belk Library. Special thanks to Teresa LePors, who was indefatigable no matter my question and more tenacious than I could have hoped; and to her friend Beverly Brown, who helped scour online horse racing databases in my quest to determine the inspiration for the first known use of welfare queen in print. Deep thanks also to the folks at IU Press and Amnet in helping get this book into print, particularly Gary Dunham, Leigh McLennon, Nancy Lightfoot, David Hulsey, Rachel Stern, Rachel Rosolina, and Stephen Williams.

Last but hardly least, there is my family: Lucille Mould; Rob, Laura, Caroline, and Charlie Mould; Diana, Dave, and Elizabeth Adams; Rob Kleinsteuber; my incredible cadre of in-laws; and my father, Bill Mould, who died during the fieldwork for this book but whose love, kindness, wisdom, and humor I carry with me always. Finally, there are Lily and Jack, who make life so fun and surprising; and Brooke, who makes it all worthwhile.

OVERTHROWING
THE QUEEN

SECTION 1

WELFARE LEGENDS

An American Tradition

ONE

INTRODUCTION

SOME STORIES SNEAK UP ON us; others hit us over the head. This one did both. It was April 2011, and I found myself at a dinner that spanned the white-collar world from the front desk to the corner office. The weather was mild, as it often is in North Carolina in the spring, and we sat outside under a large white tent at tables with starched white tablecloths. The wine and hors d'oeuvres suggested that conversation was meant to be cocktail chatter, but political divisions peeked out from even the most innocuous comments. It was not long before I found myself discussing one of the most contentious issues of the day: health care.

It had been just over a year since US president Barack Obama signed the Affordable Care Act (ACA) into law, and revisions continued to be made. A week earlier, Congress had voted to repeal an unpopular tax requirement tied to the ACA, and Obama agreed to sign it. The mood in Congress and around the country, however, remained divisive. My conversation partner, Janet Haley, was a woman in her sixties who found the ACA abhorrent.[1] After trading views for about fifteen minutes, we stumbled on something we could agree on: that having people use the emergency room as their primary physician was both a bad use of taxpayer money and a bad approach to health. "An ounce of prevention is worth a pound of cure," I offered, hoping that a well-worn proverb might continue to help us find common ground. I was wrong.

"Yes, but"—and now I'm quoting directly from the field notes I took as soon as I could excuse myself from the table:

Poor people will still use and abuse the system when they can. I was in the grocery store not too long ago when the woman in front of me tried to buy dog food with her food stamps. She was wearing a fur coat, polished nails, designer handbag. The checkout girl told her she couldn't do that, and this really made her mad. She huffed and puffed and threw the dog food down and said, "Fine,

3

then he'll eat steak instead." She marched back to the meat counter while we're all standing there, waiting for her. The cashier is looking apologetically at us. And here she comes, sure enough, with two steaks.

Janet followed her story with a litany of beliefs about the poor, the excesses of government programs, and the widespread fraud she believed ran rampant throughout social services programs, ultimately returning to the topic of "Obamacare" to again express her dissatisfaction with the plan.

As I listened, I was struck with how closely her story paralleled a contemporary legend told around the country for at least the past forty years, a story I had heard when I was in high school. The version I remembered was also of a woman trying to buy dog food with food stamps and resorting to buying steaks instead, but I also remembered her climbing into a brand-new Cadillac. These stories described an archetypal figure that has come to symbolize welfare in the United States: the welfare queen.

The welfare system in the United States has always been stigmatized, but not until Ronald Reagan began telling stories of a woman in Chicago with eighty names, thirty addresses, twelve Social Security cards, four nonexistent deceased husbands, and $150,000 in unearned benefits did that system have a name. Not a real name—though the woman in Chicago was based on a real person—but a symbolic one that evoked not just a lack of poverty but also the excessive and unearned wealth of royalty.

As a story, the fraudulent antics of the welfare queen were deeply compelling in the context of current debates about economic justice in a country where the gap in wealth has been growing exponentially. But for Janet, the story was compelling in the context of health care debates specifically and the role of government more generally. Both food stamps and affordable health care were part and parcel of the same system, as were the people who would participate in these programs. The same entitled behavior of the woman in the grocery store was transferrable in her mind to a health care system similarly offered to everyone, deserving or not. For Janet, the story of the welfare queen was not simply a symbol and indictment of the welfare system but of the entire government enterprise.[2]

Her story caught me by surprise. I had thought stories of "welfare queens" and "welfare Cadillacs" had died out in the years since Reagan, when I had heard them as a child. But when I told my friends and colleagues about my encounter, I was surprised to hear many of them either share their own versions of the welfare queen story—albeit with caveats that such stories were rare—or point me to stories in their email boxes or Facebook pages from coworkers, uncles, high school friends, and neighbors. One friend and colleague told of hearing a woman at a you-pick-'em strawberry patch tell a version of the food-stamps-for-dog-food story only a week earlier. Curious interest soon became professional inquiry. This book is the result.

Initial research supported the conventional wisdom that the welfare queen was a bogey created by Ronald Reagan in 1976 for political ends that just never went away. But six years of fieldwork with bus drivers, grocery store clerks, local business leaders, students, and politicians suggested this specter of the social welfare system in the United States was hardly confined to elite political circles, and fieldwork with aid providers suggested the story was far more complex than the simplistic, one-sided, and stigmatizing narrative the welfare queen offered. But most revealing was the fieldwork with aid recipients who relied on public assistance to meet basic needs. Their stories painted a very different picture of welfare in the United States. Together, stories from all these groups form the backbone of this book, competing narratives that diverge and overlap in often surprising ways.

But exploring these stories is not without its downsides and dangers. The welfare queen as a cultural archetype conjures gendered, racialized images of fraud, corruption, laziness, and immorality. Repeating such stories—even to disrupt, dispel, and ultimately displace them—risks further cementing her image in the social fabric and public discourse for generations to come. This is not a new risk for folklorists, who recognize that while many vernacular traditions emerge from artistic impulses toward beauty, joy, friendship, and celebration, others emerge from darker corners of our beliefs and fears that explore racist, classist, sexist, misogynistic, homophobic, xenophobic, Islamophobic, and jingoistic ideologies.

The question of how to write about the stories of public assistance in the United States without reinforcing the very stereotypes that have caused so much damage was one that kept me up more nights than I can count. At its core, it is the same question that corporations face when trying to decide how to respond to an unfounded rumor or legend about their product or politicians face when deciding whether to ignore baseless rumors or come out swinging, though their concerns may be economic and political as much as ethical and moral.

One solution is to humanize participants by describing the mundane, not just the extraordinary (Fine et al. 2003). The solution is a good one for a purely ethnographic project but less effective for a study focusing on vernacular narrative traditions, where cherry-picking the unusual from the usual is a fundamental narrative process. Another solution is to take a performer- and performance-centered approach to analysis that helps lay bare the personal, social, and cultural histories of the storytellers and the myriad factors that shape those stories. Such an approach humanizes while remaining faithful to the narrative tradition. One answer, however, cannot be to ignore the issue. Sweeping an issue under the rug has rarely been an effective strategy for social reform. The spurious legends and stereotypes about aid recipients have not gone away in the world where this book has yet to be published. Nor is it likely that the publication of this book will either single-handedly provide life support for the welfare queen or eradicate her from social memory and discourse for good. The unchecked legend purported as true deserves the trash can if we provide no lens through which to understand it. But when studied in context alongside the stories of real people living with the aid of public assistance, there is room for new understanding.

Although this book is unapologetic in its goal of attacking inaccurate stereotypes about the poor in this country, and aid recipients in particular, it is not inherently partisan. There are inaccurate stereotypes of the poor coming from both sides of the political aisle and everywhere in between. This book is focused just as much on understanding the stories about welfare shared among a group of businessmen who gather weekly to discuss the events of the day as on the stories of the women and men who feed their families with the help of food stamps and who gather each day in GED prep classes to earn their high school degrees. Yet although these narratives traditions are parallel, they are not equivalent. Some stories are based heavily on hearsay, brief observation, and assumption, while others are based on firsthand encounters, embodied experience, and extensive interaction. Balance, fairness, and justice is achieved not by suggesting all views are equal but by evaluating the evidence offered in support for any given story and constructing meaning accordingly.

HISTORY OF THE PROJECT

In folklore, as in anthropology, the lone fieldworker immersed in a community, observing, interviewing, and participating where appropriate, remains the dominant paradigm for fieldwork. However, as scholars have become more sensitive to the power and politics involved in cultural epistemological work, fieldworkers increasingly are engaging in some form of community-based research that centers on collaboration with communities rather than more one-sided endeavors. The research that provides both the foundation and the data for this study is part of a collaborative project that brought faculty, students, and community partners together in an effort to address the stereotypes and perceptions of public assistance in the United States generally and Alamance County, North Carolina, specifically. The project began after I approached leaders in the community who were working on issues of poverty and economic justice—in both government agencies and nonprofits—with the story I had heard at dinner that night in April. Within a month, we had formed a working group that included directors and staff of programs that serve those in need: the Department of Social Services, the Burlington Housing Authority, Allied Churches (which runs a local food pantry, soup kitchen, and homeless shelter, among other services), the Open Door

Clinic (which provides free health coverage for the uninsured), and the United Way. During the next few months, we worked to flesh out the parameters of a project that would examine and ultimately work to dispel the stereotypes and misperceptions surrounding public assistance and the people who receive it. As the director of Elon University's Program for Ethnographic Research and Community Studies (PERCS), I also brought the project to our PERCS committee as a collaborative research project to engage students through both classroom instruction and independent research.

Over the course of the next year, we established a list of ten outcomes: six to serve community agencies and community members, four geared toward academic audiences. Additionally, we determined a time line, submitted grant applications to fund the project, set the structure and learning goals for the service-learning course, received institutional review board (IRB) approval, and developed fieldwork protocols, including interview questions, field note templates, and processes for how to identify and approach participants. Initial conversations helped us establish the nature of our collaboration together. Rather than the model of full participation in all aspects of the project that is typically assumed in the participatory-action research literature, we followed the more expansive lead of community-based research that embraces a division of labor model.[3] Accordingly, I served as the principle investigator for the research and was involved in all aspects of the project; the students served primarily as fieldworkers; and community partners served as project developers, advisers, facilitators, advocates, and researchers in gathering and providing statistical and policy information.[4]

By 2015 we had completed many of the outcomes we set out with and some that emerged in the course of our work, including a presentation for aid providers ("Improving Programming in Public Housing" for the Burlington Housing Authority), a cheat sheet for local politicians and leaders ("Public Assistance in Alamance County at a Glance"), and documents, presentations, and resources for the general public (a "Top Truths about Welfare" document, "Re-Envisioning Welfare in Alamance County" public forum and panel discussion, *Portraits of Hope* traveling exhibit, and the Voices of Welfare website, which has served as a repository for some of this work). There were also scholarly presentations and publications, including two journal articles ("The Welfare Legend Tradition in Online and Off-line Contexts" [Mould 2016] and "Collaborative-Based Research in a Service-Learning Course: Reconceiving Research as Service" [Mould 2014]). In the course of sharing our work publicly, we had begun to garner some media coverage. That is when the executive director of Guilford Child Development (GCD), Robin Britt, heard about our project in Alamance County and wanted to set up a similar project in Guilford County. Britt's focus would be on a new initiative to consolidate programs and provide community members a one-stop-shopping approach to resources such as GED classes, job training, and childcare. A few months later, we were written into a grant with the United Way in GCD's launch of the Family Success Center.[5] Over the course of the summer, we worked to clarify the specific research plan: ensuring that the methods were ethical as well as practical; considering the specific organizational structures and goals of GCD; and developing the questions, processes for data collection, and final outcomes. A year later we had completed our research in Greensboro and submitted a 177-page report to GCD and the United Way, providing both agencies with stories told by their clients about their goals, ongoing challenges, and successes related to working toward self-sufficiency, as well as a qualitative assessment of their pilot project from the perspective of their clients.

The one major outcome left to complete was a book capturing the stories of aid recipients, aid providers, and the general public in order to better understand perceptions and experiences of public assistance. The publication of this book signals the completion of our joint goals. For aid recipients, however, it signals only one more step, albeit hopefully a significant one, toward a more accurate, destigmatized view of welfare in the United States today.

While formal collaboration was established with institutionalized agencies, the primary collaboration of this project has been with women and men receiving public aid. Those relationships often began in institutional settings before developing more informally as recipients introduced us to their friends and family. For example, Nikki Ratliff at the Burlington Housing Authority gave us a calendar of events and classes for their residents and then gave their staff a heads-up that we might be attending. Either I or a student working on the project would then attend the meeting, meet people, explain our project, and follow up with those who expressed interest in talking further. As with all ethnographic fieldwork, we worked carefully to earn the trust of the people with whom we worked. Some of those relationships deepened as we returned again and again over the course of the next few years. In other cases, a single interview was all that was feasible, as with many of the people we met at the homeless shelter, where transience was the norm.

Ever present was the question of whether people were willing to open up fully about such sensitive and stigmatized topics or whether aid recipients, aid providers, and the general public told us only those stories that were most socially acceptable. It is a fair question, but one that must be asked of all qualitative data collection, no matter the topic. Erving Goffman was particularly effective in explaining what so many of us recognize as true in our own lives: that we are constantly negotiating our public personas to portray versions of ourselves that we find most useful, expedient, or socially acceptable (1972). Part of that negotiation involves assessing our audience. To be sure, my identity as a white, male, middle-class college professor affected how people responded to me—not in any singular way but in ways specific to the stereotypes and views each person held about those signifiers. One might assume that people were likely to respond to me in significantly different ways than to student researchers who were younger, more ethnically diverse, or female. Surely these factors mattered. It is certainly true that my Latina students had an easier time establishing rapport with fellow Latinas, though language was clearly one key factor. Yet analysis of the stories told by black recipients to black researchers or Latina recipients to Latina researchers as compared to white researchers reveals no quantifiable difference in the number, type, or tenor of the stories told. Rather, time appears the most reliable indicator of openness. Over the course of an hour, as people warmed up to us, they often told more unflattering stories about themselves or others. With the families we came to know well, an easy conversational flow marked our discussions. But as in all life, we constantly negotiate and renegotiate the boundaries of what we share with others; there is no reason to expect ethnographic interviews would be any different.

One dimension of this process, however, was initially surprising. While some people opened up only after weeks and months of conversation, others like Jashanna Kingston opened up because we did *not* know her well. "I'm a very private person, and the only reason why I'm speaking to y'all is because y'all are strangers. You can talk to strangers better than you can talk to the people that you know." Jashanna highlighted what others told us in various ways: telling their stories, whether under the cover of anonymity or with name and photo attached, could be cathartic, uplifting, and empowering, as well as scary, troubling, and stressful.

METHODS

Folklorists depend most heavily on qualitative fieldwork. Although we did conduct some surveys and can quantify much of our data, the methods of collection and analysis are primarily based on interviews and observation. While I conducted the majority of that fieldwork, as a collaborative research project that involved students, a significant portion of the interviews were conducted by student researchers. Preparing novice fieldworkers for such conversations was neither easy nor quick. The students who conducted fieldwork for this project were members of my Voices of Welfare class, receiving semester-long training and preparation as well as ongoing support. When it was time to head into the field, not all of the students were prepared to speak with aid recipients and navigate the personal and often difficult stories they were likely to encounter. Those students either conducted archival research or worked with less inherently vulnerable populations, such as their fellow students, whom they already knew, or grocery store clerks, bus drivers, community leaders, and aid providers. No matter the group, the same rigorous ethical standards were followed.

In the end, we formally interviewed 138 people—76 aid recipients, 28 aid providers, and 54 nonrecipients. We informally talked to a few dozen more and recorded approximately 1,260 stories.[6] Although students also analyzed their interviews as part of their learning process, I coded and analyzed all of the data myself to ensure consistency, using both Dedoose qualitative software and Excel. Such a large corpus of narratives has allowed me to look for patterns and trends that move the conversation from its qualitative foundation toward something that approximates the quantitative, with numbers and percentages that guide my claims. In some cases, these numbers forced me to rethink initial conclusions based on qualitative analysis alone. For example, qualitative analysis suggested that steak remained the dominant symbol of unearned luxury items enjoyed by the poor. On running the numbers, however, I was surprised to find that drugs and alcohol *far* surpassed steak and similar luxury items, such as lobster and crab legs.

The tendency with such a wealth of data is to place example after example in the text to bolster the argument and make it clear to the reader that I have not cherry-picked the one example that supports a particular point. I have chosen not to do this in order to make the book less daunting, instead providing depth coupled with statistics that suggest breadth.

TERMS AND NAMES: ISSUES OF ETHICS

One term used throughout this book is *welfare*. It is unavoidable when documenting the narrative tradition. The question is whether to use it myself. I have chosen to use *government assistance, public assistance,* and *public aid* in many cases as less loaded but still accurate terms, but I have not shied completely away from the term *welfare* for two reasons. The first is clarity. The subtitle of this book uses the term as an efficient way of describing the contents that follow. The book is not concerned with all forms of public assistance, just the ones people commonly label "welfare." The other reason is that one of the goals of this book is to tackle stereotypes head on. One way to do so is to work to rehabilitate the term *welfare* to return it to its original meaning as a social good focused on well-being. A single book cannot achieve this transformation, but using *welfare* to name public assistance in contexts that highlight positive connotations of well-being is, I believe, a productive step forward in fighting the stigma of poverty and government assistance.

What is unacceptable, however, is to lay this burden of rehabilitation at the feet of the people who are stigmatized by so much of the discourse around public assistance today. Accordingly, the participants' last names have been changed to provide some degree of confidentiality, and, in all but a few cases, their first names have been changed as well. Many of the stories people told describe traumatic experiences of abuse, domestic violence, and insecurities around food, shelter, and family. Even more common were stories of major illnesses that rendered people unable to work, stories that detailed highly personal information about their health. Uncommon, but not nonexistent, were stories about selling food stamps to pay utility bills or rent. Such honesty is crucial for a project such as this, but it comes only with the understanding that people will not be harmed by such admissions. But more than any other one factor, the widespread use of pseudonyms for aid recipients in this book comes because of the incredible stigma that continues to plague not just the public aid system and its recipients but the poor generally.

And yet a few of the families we worked with asked that we use their real first names and, in some cases, their last. Further, some, as with the *Portraits of Hope* exhibit, agreed to use their photos as well. As Karraha explained, "A lot of people write stories about how families and the actual program are successful and stuff, but they never really ask them. And since you guys were willing and wanting to listen, it was like, 'Yeah,' so we can put our story out there the way it should be told." In those cases, we used first names only, respecting their wishes but ensuring some degree of privacy.

While most of the names are not real, the stories are. Further, they are verbatim as they were shared, with a few minor exceptions. I removed the instances of *um* and the many utterances such as *you know* and *like* that so many of us use as verbal filler but that are distracting when transcribed to the page. In a few cases, I removed false starts, keeping only those that suggested a reflective train of thought regarding what was being said. Ellipses indicate pauses or changes of direction, not omitted words. In all cases, I edited lightly with the goal of ensuring as little disruption as possible to the stories as they were shared but recognizing that the shift from the oral to the written requires some adjustment to ensure the stories are read as clearly as they were heard.

STRUCTURE OF THE BOOK

This book is structured like an old grandfather clock losing time. The pendulum initially swings confidently back and forth between aid recipients and non-recipients, section by section, but as the book progresses and the clock winds down, the arc gets smaller and smaller, and the two groups are brought closer and closer together into dialogue. A similar rhythm is established between the topic of welfare and the study of narrative with welfare grabbing the spotlight for the first half of the book and narrative rising to the fore in the second half. At no point, however, are the two rent asunder; welfare narratives cohere in topic and structure to form the core of this book.

Section 1 lays the foundation for the book, exploring the welfare system, narrative scholarship, and narratives of one of the most iconic stereotypes of welfare today: the welfare queen. Within it, chapter 1 begins with data about the welfare system in the United States, followed by definitions and parameters for narrative analysis and the primary genres of this study: personal experience narrative, legend, and the slippery interstitial spaces that link the two. Chapter 2 explores the origins and historical contexts for the welfare queen as political fodder, cultural archetype, and canonical narrative in the popular imagination as constructed through mass media, politics, and the folk tradition. By the end of the chapter, the focus narrows to the structural and thematic parallels with the most widespread master narrative in the United States—the American dream—helping explain the durability of legends of the welfare queen.

Section 2 shifts from the perspectives of politicians, nonrecipients, and the mass media to those of aid recipients and the stories they tell about life with public assistance. Dominating this narrative tradition are origin stories of how people found themselves in need, challenge stories of ongoing hardship, making-ends-meet stories of how they overcome these challenges, and success stories that provide hope for the present and the future. Not surprisingly, these stories are dramatically different from the legends of the welfare queen, but they are not without parallels that challenge easy dualities so often evoked in debates about welfare.

Section 3 swings back to the stories shared by nonrecipients, expanding the image of welfare beyond the welfare queen to encompass the wide range of stories about public assistance and its recipients. The stories are often constructed with little evidence and no firsthand experience with public assistance, though such limited credentials appear to have done little to dampen the tradition. While the topic of public aid is front and center in these chapters, issues of narrative form and performance context are never far from the discussion. Chapter 9, however, follows the topic of public aid out of the face-to-face interactions and into the virtual interactions of the internet and social media and, in doing so, moves beyond narrative to consider other genres of expressive culture that comment on the issue of welfare in the United States.

Section 4 shifts the focus more clearly to the study of narrative. Chapter 10 considers how the narrative tradition is shaped by the available contexts for performance. Chapter 11 examines the various narrative forms people use to talk about public assistance, introducing a doubt-centered approach to the study of legend and an analysis of the unique power of the mostly ignored genre of generalized experience narratives. Chapter 12 brings public assistance back front and center, but narrative still dominates as the book addresses the eternal and infernal question: What do we do about spurious legends? In a world of fake news and alternative facts, chapter 12 considers ways to engage in public debate with the stories told by aid recipients, applying research in legends, rumor management, and confirmation bias to distinguish between strategies that common sense suggests will be effective from those backed by evidence.

NOTES

1. As with the majority of people interviewed in this book, "Janet Haley" is a pseudonym.

2. Cf. Tangherlini (2008), who notes that beggars in nineteenth-century Denmark had become a conceptual category for a more general outside threat (182).

3. For participatory research, see Reason and Bradbury (2008); for community-based research, see Strand et al. (2003, 176, 188–91). For a more detailed description of this project, see Mould (2014).

4. For additional information about this project and the people involved, see the "About Us" section of the website for this project, Voices of Welfare, which launched March 4, 2014. See also Mould (2014), which describes the structure of the university course that introduced students to the project.

5. For local newspaper coverage of the project, see McLaughlin (2015, 2017).

6. These numbers total more than 138 because 5 people were both providers and current or past aid recipients, 11 people were past aid recipients but often shared stories as a non-aid recipient, and 7 people were volunteers who straddled both provider and general public roles (with 3 people filling all three roles). I say *approximately* since there are many ways to identify and define a narrative. Kernel narratives are references to narratives rather than narratives in and of themselves. General experience narratives are often longer but similarly loose in boundaries and form. In other cases, narrators begin a story but then veer into more general discourse. For some folkloric studies, only those narratives that exhibit clear competence in performance as defined and discussed by Dell Hymes (1981), Richard Bauman (1977), and Charles Briggs (1988) earn our attention (see also Mould 2011b). For this project, however, attending to the myriad ways that people attempt to narrate welfare was necessary, leading to blurry and ambiguous boundaries for what to label narrative or not. Accordingly, it is not possible to provide a single finite number of stories studied since some fit one approach to narrative analysis while others fit another.

TWO

—⚭—

THE WELFARE SYSTEM AND NARRATIVE SCHOLARSHIP

"YOU AND YOUR BABY ARE receiving food stamps and Medicaid?" asked the caseworker at the Department of Social Services.

"We both have Medicaid, but I don't have food stamps," replied the young woman sitting on the other side of the desk, bouncing her young son on her knee.

"Why not?"

"Pride," she murmured.

"Sorry, what was that?"

"Pride."

On the otherwise nondescript walls of the caseworker's office in a similarly nondescript hive of offices in the Department of Social Services are two inspirational messages: "Believe. All things are possible if you believe," and "Family. Where life begins and love never ends." The messages are sincere, as is the young caseworker, but they can appear ironic to the women, children, and men who enter these offices looking for help. Confidence and hard work rarely prove sufficient when it comes to making ends meet and family has too often been the cause of hardship, not its cure, for the clients sitting in plastic chairs answering questions about their lives, jobs, and financial challenges.

The young woman seeking help with childcare that afternoon was not the most dramatic counterexample of these inspirational quotes who came in that day, but she fit the bill. The father of her eight-month-old son left her soon after their child was born and moved to Tennessee. She wants to enroll in a police academy training course at the local community college but cannot afford the tuition. She hopes that the money from a new job at a local bar will help her save enough to pay for school, but she cannot accept the job without affordable childcare. It is a catch-22 common among single parents: stay at home and care for your children

14

but have no way to earn income or get a job and spend the bulk of the paycheck on childcare.

Family failed her, and believing in herself has not been enough. But the stigma of poverty and welfare has been a strong deterrent to applying for the help she needs. Pregnant and without health insurance, she was forced to apply for Medicaid. Figuring out a way to pay for training for a career that will provide a living wage pushed her to apply for childcare. But the stigma of using food stamps publicly every time she goes to the grocery store has remained too strong to overcome. Eligible for food stamps but not childcare, she left the office with neither, unsure whether she would be able to afford to accept the job she had been offered.

The stigma that kept her from applying for food stamps might be traced to a person, event, or catalytic moment in her life. But it is reinforced by the deep-seated stereotypes about welfare embedded in the stories repeated in the mass media and by people at every level of society. In these stories, one figure reigns supreme: the welfare queen. Racialized as black, castigated as a single mother, and demonized for her immorality and criminality for committing fraud, the welfare queen is a contender for the most stigmatized scapegoat in US society today.[1] She is lazy but savvy, succeeding in a perverted version of the American dream where *no* work rather than *hard* work is rewarded. As a political bogey, she typically emerges implicitly rather than explicitly, too incendiary to be named outright in public discourse. For example, at the end of November 2017, Donald Trump was touring the country to drum up support for a tax overhaul being debated in Congress, and he evoked a divide between the deserving and undeserving poor: "Welfare reform, I see it, and I've talked to people. I know people that work three jobs and they live next to somebody who doesn't work at all. And the person who is not working at all and has no intention of working at all is making more money and doing better than the person that's working his and her ass off. And it's not going to happen. Not going to happen" (Takersley 2017). Trump did not use the phrase *welfare queen*; even for a president who worries little about offending people with blunt language, the term is political dynamite. But he did not have to. The welfare recipient living a life of ease and luxury on the taxpayer's dime while hardworking Americans struggle to get by forms the core message of welfare queen stories. Folklorists call this type of story a kernel story: a shorthand reference to a narrative quickly recognizable to audiences who can fill in the details for themselves (Kalčik 1975, 7). Trump does not need to use the term *welfare queen*—any more than *Cadillac* or, for many listeners, *black*—but the legendary story is evoked all the same.

That is one story of welfare. But there are millions more. They include the stories of people like the woman too embarrassed to apply for food stamps, who asks that her name not be used to protect her privacy and dignity from a public she has grown to believe cares little about her and those like her. Although hundreds of books have been written about poverty and welfare in the United States over the past fifty years, and dozens have recorded the stories and biographies of people receiving aid, few take seriously Marshall McLuhan's famous dictum that the medium is the message. He was speaking of television, but the claim applies equally to narrative. Stories do not simply reflect our lives; they interpret and shape them. Stories ask us to identify complications, turning points, climaxes, and resolutions. They ask us to identify the unusual, remarkable, and compelling. In other words, stories ask us to cherry-pick details from our lives and the lives of others to create something that can be shared, remembered, and retold with a specific goal in mind: convince a jury, sway a voter, entertain friends and family, scare a college roommate, educate a student, disagree with a neighbor. The list of reasons is long; the list of social contexts, infinite.

If we are to understand how welfare is viewed in the United States, and how those perceptions affect real people and real policy, we have to understand not just the stories that dominate the headlines but the stories told around the kitchen table, at the water cooler, in the barber shop, and on the front porch—stories not just *about* aid recipients but *by* them. Only in understanding how these stories are created, reconstructed, and retold can we hope to distinguish fact from fiction and bogeyman from neighbor and recognize our own complicity in sanctioning some voices while ignoring others.

One method for traversing this quagmire of competing images and claims is by attending to the stories people tell about their experiences with public assistance. But to interpret these stories fully, it is useful to first address some of the basic facts about public assistance in the United States.

WELFARE IN THE UNITED STATES TODAY

Jacques Derrida was right: words fail us, falling apart before our very eyes, often in spectacular ways (1982). A term that in other contexts means prosperity and good health, evokes poverty, crime, fraud, and despair in the context of government assistance (Gordon 1994, 1). The transformation is not complete, however. We continue to speak positively and protectively of ensuring the welfare of our children as a sacred duty. Yet when it comes to speaking of the welfare of our neighbors, and most specifically of our policies to help guarantee it, we make an about-face. As historians of welfare policy have made clear, it has not always been this way.

When the modern welfare state was born with the Social Security Act of 1935, attending to the welfare of the country's citizens was seen overwhelmingly as a noble and necessary job of the government. While Americans have typically continued to favor aiding the poor, they have increasingly demonized the programs that attempt to do so. Like most symbols, however, the relationship between symbol and meaning is not neutral; nor are the basic parameters of the term agreed upon. The confusion over which government programs are considered "welfare" and which escape the tainted designation is part of an even more fundamental confusion over how these programs are administered in the first place. Case in point: the viral photo of a woman angrily holding a sign in protest that reads, "Keep Your Government Hands off My Medicare" (Cesca 2017; Rucker 2017).

The largest government assistance programs are entitlement programs. Entitlement programs provide support regardless of income. Social security, Medicare, and unemployment insurance are well-known examples, providing support to all Americans as long as they have worked in the wage labor force.[2] In this way, we can distinguish between contributory and noncontributory programs. All three of these programs are contributory. Welfare, on the other hand, typically refers to means-tested programs: programs whose eligibility is based on a person's or family's income. Means-tested programs include anywhere from 13 to 126 programs depending on whether reference is made to major umbrella programs or to each line item program that is means-tested or has as one of its goals fighting poverty.[3] Some of these smaller programs (1) are consolidated into larger programs, such as Temporary Assistance for Needy Families (TANF); (2) focus on indirect services, such as job training or education, including Pell Grants or Adult Basic Education Grants; (3) appear as tax credits, such as the earned income tax credit; or (4) are for such a small portion of the population that they are rarely discussed when speaking generally of welfare, such as Senior Community Service Employment. Focusing on the major welfare programs in the United States based on spending provides a more useful picture of welfare as it is often discussed in government and mass media reports. These programs include the following:

- **TANF: Temporary Assistance to Needy Families.** Also referred to as Work First or the Check. Means-tested. TANF provides cash assistance to low-income families with children living in the home. With the passing of the Personal Responsibility and Work Opportunity Reconciliation Act (PRWORA) in 1996, TANF replaced Aid to Families and Dependent Children (AFDC). Exceptions are available, but most recipients receiving TANF must be actively seeking work in the wage labor force. Assistance includes childcare vouchers given to low-income parents to help them work outside the home. Despite having become one of the smallest federal programs, with little name recognition, TANF is what most people are referring to when they say someone is "on welfare."

- **SNAP: Supplemental Nutrition Assistance Program**. Also known as food stamps. Means-tested. Eligibility is based primarily on income but also considers personal resources, citizenship, and work history. SNAP is one of the largest federal welfare programs in terms of budget and people served.
- **Medicaid**. Means-tested. Provides health care for low-income people, including children and people with disabilities. Related programs include the Child Health Insurance Program (CHIP; formerly SCHIP, where the S stood for *State*), which provides federal matching funds to cover uninsured children in families whose income is low but not low enough to qualify for Medicaid.
- **SSI: Supplemental Security Income**. Means-tested. Provides stipends to low-income people who are sixty-five or older, blind, or disabled, to cover basic needs.
- **SSDI: Social Security Disability Insurance**. Entitlement program. Provides stipends to disabled workers who have paid into the Social Security system for at least ten years.
- **Housing assistance**. Also referred to as public housing or section 8. Means-tested. Provides housing for low-income people. Includes a range of vouchers and housing options administered through the Department of Housing and Urban Development (HUD). Some of the most common programs include specifically designated neighborhoods and low-income housing as well as section 8 vouchers that provide subsidies for housing regardless of neighborhood.
- **General Assistance**. Means-tested. Provides direct cash assistance for emergencies, often to pay utility bills. Includes the Low Income Home Energy Assistance Program (LIHEAP), a federal program to assist those with the lowest incomes that pay a high proportion of household income for home energy, and the Crisis Intervention Program (CIP), a federal program to help low-income people pay their heating and cooling bills.
- **Child Nutrition Program**. Means-tested. Provides free or reduced school lunch for children in low-income families. It is a federal program administered by states.
- **WIC: Special Supplemental Nutrition Program for Women, Infants, and Children**. Means-tested. Provides food, health care referrals, and nutrition information to low-income pregnant women, breastfeeding women, and children under five. It is a federal program administered by the US Department of Agriculture (USDA).

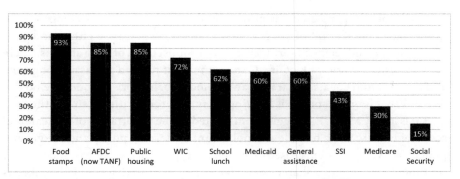

Chart 2.1. Percent of Americans who view a program as part of welfare
(Kaiser/Harvard Survey on Welfare Reform, December 1994). AFDC,
Aid to Families with Dependent Children; TANF, Temporary Assistance
for Needy Families; WIC, Special Supplemental Nutrition Program for
Women, Infants, and Children; SSI, Supplemental Security Income.

These major programs track closely with popular perceptions of welfare. In a 1994
poll, people were asked whether they considered specific programs to be welfare
(chart 2.1). The two programs that polled the lowest for inclusion were the only
two not means-tested: Medicare and Social Security.

The interviews conducted for this book closely parallel these responses, defining welfare primarily as means-tested programs for low-income families. When
people named specific programs, food stamps was by far the most common. This
was true as well of the stories told by both recipients and nonrecipients. Public
housing, disability (SSI and SSDI), and Medicaid followed as common inclu-
sions. Although aid recipients mentioned TANF, nonrecipients either mentioned
older names, such as AFDC, or referred simply to "welfare checks" to describe
the central welfare program that provides direct cash assistance to low-income
families. The top five programs named in our research also match the five programs identified by the US Census Bureau as the major welfare programs today:
TANF, SNAP, Medicaid, SSI, and housing assistance (US Census Bureau 2015).
Medicare and Social Security were never mentioned as part of welfare in the
United States; nor were grants for education or tax credits for low-income families. Accordingly, a suitable operational definition for welfare is the group of
federally funded programs that aid low-income families, particularly with food,
housing, health, and utility bills.

Key Points of Disagreement

One of the biggest problems with stories and debates about welfare is in talking
about aid recipients as if they constitute a single, homogenous group. Can we

imagine a one-size-fits-all description of any group to which we belong? Yet the most fundamental point of disagreement is often pitched as an either/or debate about whether aid recipients are lazy, cheats, promiscuous, or drug abusers. There are bad eggs in every walk of life. Choose the most revered profession or group, and one can find cheats and frauds and immoral behavior. The poor are no different. What is unacceptable is labeling an entire group with the sins of the few.

But is it only a few? The wiggle room created by the uncertainty of the scale and scope of welfare fraud has allowed politicians to develop policy and the general public to develop opinions based on expedience, preconceived ideas, and popular sentiment rather than a shared set of data. The question that should be asked is not whether there are welfare cheats but whether they constitute a significant enough proportion of the group to justify punitive policies and negative public opinions, and whether those proportions are commensurate with other government programs that have eluded such critique. Qualitative interviews about public assistance suggest additional questions that people either believe they have answers to or are searching to address. Those questions can be divided roughly into questions about aid recipients, welfare policy, and deep-seated ideologies about how society operates.

- Aid Recipients
  - Who receives aid? Who *should* receive aid?
  - What are the proximate and ultimate causes of poverty?
  - Is immoral, unethical, or undesirable behavior widespread among aid recipients?
  - What types of fraud are most common in the welfare system, and who perpetrates it?
- Welfare Policy
  - Is welfare a disincentive to work?
  - Is welfare too generous?
  - Is current welfare policy effective?
  - Is welfare policy punitive?
  - Is drug testing justified or cost-effective?
- Ideologies
  - Should federal or state governments address social problems or allow local or private institutions to address such issues?
  - Is poverty primarily a product of individual failings or structural inequities?
  - Can shame and stigma ever be good?
  - Is the American dream possible?
  - Are some people undeserving of aid?
  - Should self-sufficiency be the desired goal for everyone?

      ○ Is wage labor a condition of full citizenship? Is the job of raising children worthy of compensation?

Recognizing that many of these questions cannot be answered definitively, some scholars, bloggers, and pundits have nonetheless taken to the internet to address these questions in an effort to combat stereotypes about public assistance in the United States, often constructing top-ten lists of "welfare myths" that describe beliefs commonly held but utterly false.[4] The lists are valuable assets in efforts to combat widespread stereotypes, but they occasionally fall into a few traps. The most common are card stacking and straw man arguments, but a third—unintentional confirmation—may be the most damaging and insidious. In 2007, a group of researchers took a flyer from the Centers for Disease Control website that was developed for the general public to debunk popular myths about the flu vaccine. The one-page flyer listed six popular beliefs, each one labeled true or false. Three were true; three were false. When people were quizzed on the information right after reading it, they correctly identified the true and false information consistently, with only a few errors. Thirty minutes later, however, they misremembered 15 percent of the false statements as true (Schwarz et al. 2007, 147–48).[5]

But top-ten lists are powerful and memorable in their simplicity and should not be discarded too hastily. By recasting the conversation with a focus on what is true rather than false, including only arguments with well-supported data, and addressing only those issues that appear in contemporary discourse, it is possible to avoid erroneous confirmation, card stacking, and straw man arguments. As part of the Voices of Welfare research project, we created a website with the top *truths* about welfare, which would do just this.[6] A brief survey of these findings, examined in the context of public opinion polls, can provide a useful foundation for assessing and interpreting the stories in this book.

American Perceptions by the Polls

Americans do not fare well when assessed on their knowledge of political issues. Welfare is no exception. When a team of political scientists studied the effectiveness of providing factual corrections to misinformation about welfare, they found that people were wrong about basic welfare facts 66–90 percent of the time. More disturbingly, those who were most consistently wrong were also the most confident that they were right and the least likely to change their views when faced with the facts (Kuklinski et al. 2000).

One way to get a sense of the general opinions about welfare is to consider national polling data. A particularly useful place to start is the Roper Center for Public Opinion Research, which provides a searchable archive of over 23,000 datasets, with polls beginning in the 1930s and extending to today. A search for the key word *welfare* with parameters restricted to the United States returned responses from 1,822 survey questions. The most relevant questions were those that asked people their opinions about who received welfare and why, resulting in 233 questions asked from 1964 to 2016, which reveal an overwhelmingly negative view of welfare and its recipients.

These polls indicate that over the past fifty years, a majority of Americans believe welfare recipients are female more often than male, black more often than white, able-bodied but unemployed, urban more than rural, and have more children to increase their benefits. Further, Americans believe immigrants are more likely to use welfare than natural-born citizens, especially Hispanic immigrants. They also believe, however, that welfare recipients suffer discrimination more than nonrecipients. As for the welfare system, the majority of Americans believe that welfare causes people to avoid work, makes them dependent, and traps them in a life of poverty.

Opinions are more mixed about whether aid recipients have lower moral values than other Americans, choose welfare over work, or receive benefits they are not entitled to, deserve, or need. Americans also express more mixed opinions about aid recipients generally, with sympathies shifting over the years from slightly more negative views before 1995 to slightly more positive in the years that have followed. This shift parallels changes in Americans' opinions concerning why people are in poverty, with more people today believing the majority of the blame lies outside people's controls, when in the past more believed the opposite.[7] How do these opinions stack up to the research? In most cases, not well.

Who Receives Public Assistance?

The biggest recipients are children, followed by the disabled and the elderly. For TANF, 100 percent of aid goes to families with children. For food stamps, 78 percent of all aid goes to families with a child, a disabled person, or an elderly person. For SSI, 86 percent goes to the disabled, with the other 14 percent to the elderly.[8] True to stereotype, the vast majority of single-parent households are headed by women. But unlike those stereotypes, these households are not led by teen mothers with scores of children from multiple fathers. For TANF, the average number of children among aid recipient households is 1.8, less than the national average of 2.4.[9] Further, the vast majority of parents receiving TANF are between twenty and twenty-nine years of age (51.3%) or between thirty and thirty-nine (25.4%); 15.4 percent are over thirty-nine, while only 7.9 percent are under twenty.

Ethnically and racially, the picture is slightly more complicated. Liberals often claim that the majority of aid recipients are white. Conservatives often claim that the majority of aid recipients are black or Latino. Who is right? They both are, depending on the program and depending on total numbers versus percentages

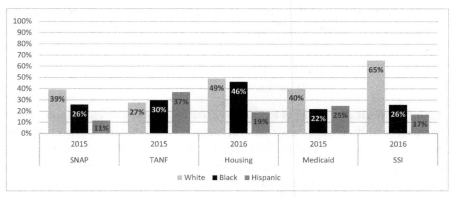

Chart 2.2. Race of recipients based on total count.[10] SNAP, Supplemental Nutrition Assistance Program; TANF, Temporary Assistance for Needy Families; SSI, Supplemental Security Income.

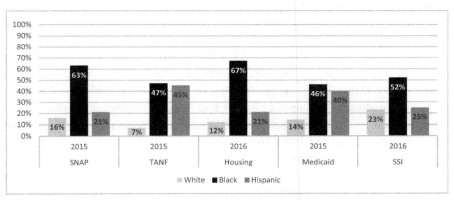

Chart 2.3. Race of recipients based on percent of the US population. SNAP, Supplemental Nutrition Assistance Program; TANF, Temporary Assistance for Needy Families; SSI, Supplemental Security Income.

(charts 2.2 and 2.3). By sheer numbers, whites receive more aid in SNAP, housing, Medicaid, and SSI. Only in TANF benefits do they lag behind. However, such numbers are misleading since there are 249 million whites compared to 43 million blacks and 55 million Hispanics. Normalizing the numbers to compare apples to apples, every column in chart 2.3 should be exactly the same height if all three major ethnic groups were equally represented in welfare programs. But as one can see, that is not the case. Any number over 33 percent suggests the group is overrepresented. Across the board, African Americans appear on the welfare rolls far more often than any other group, while Latinos are overrepresented in TANF and Medicaid. Overall, ethnic minorities are disproportionately represented on the welfare rolls. As one would expect, they are also disproportionately poor. The question is why.

What Are the Causes of Poverty?

Among Americans, answers to this polarizing question often fall into one of two camps: individual blame versus structural inequities. A 2001 poll suggests Americans are almost evenly divided on the question, with 48 percent thinking that people are not doing enough to help themselves and 45 percent blaming circumstances beyond their control.[11] These perceptions represent a significant shift from just a decade ago. In 1994, 53 percent blamed a lack of effort and only 29 percent said circumstances beyond their control.[12] For those who believe the blame falls to the individual, a slew of reasons are given, the most popular being drug abuse, a decline in moral values, single-parent families, and lack of motivation. For those who see structural issues, the top causes are perceived to be high medical bills, low-paying jobs, and poor-quality schools (appendix 1, chart A1.9).

On the "blame the individual" side of the argument, the Moynihan Report published in 1965 has been particularly influential. Drawing partially on research by Oscar Lewis in the barrios of Puerto Rico and New York, the report argued that a culture of poverty had developed among the poor in this country that reinforced antisocial and pathological behaviors. For Moynihan, that culture was specific to African American families and confirmed what many people in the country already believed: that African Americans were poor because of individual choices within a culture that encouraged immoral behaviors, foremost among them helplessness, laziness, and promiscuity, which undermined the traditional family structure seen as the bedrock to American society and success.

Those views have continued today, despite an avalanche of research that highlights structural inequities, some of which are race based, some of which are class based, but all of which make moving out of poverty particularly difficult for low-income families of color. One of the biggest culprits is a lack of capital. Wealth begets wealth. Having the financial luxury to invest, pay large down payments, avoid high interest and loan costs, and move to neighborhoods with good schools and infrastructures translates directly into a greater ability to succeed financially.[13] Analysis by nonpartisan agencies and researchers show that the US financial landscape is strongly influenced by wealthy Americans and that recent legislation and tax policies favor the wealthy. Research has further shown that senators' roll-call votes and federal government policy more closely correspond with the preferences of Americans in the top one-third of income distribution than with those in the bottom two-thirds (Bartels 2008; Gilens 2012). A 2013 article reported that the political views of the top American wealth holders were "more conservative than the American public as a whole with respect to important policies concerning taxation, economic regulation and especially social welfare programs" (Page, Bartels, and Seawright 2003). Economic policies of the past forty years have led to a dramatic increase in the wealth gap in the United States. In fact, the gap between the rich and the poor has never been higher in the history of the United States.[14] An increased wealth gap makes it harder for people to move out of poverty (Corak 2013). The result is generational poverty, where families remain stuck in cycles of poverty without the resources to break out.

Another cause of generational poverty and poverty in general is the lack of a livable wage, forcing many to choose between taking a job while not being able to feed one's family or staying at home and relying on government assistance (Iceland 2006, 78).[15] Further, with no money in the present, families are ill equipped to prepare for the future.

These are problems for all poor Americans, but ethnic minorities in the United States have historically had even less access to wealth than whites. And despite the hope that one can recover from the inequalities of the past in one's own lifetime, research suggests that historical legacies of income inequality are likely to last three to five generations and potentially far longer, as many as three hundred to four hundred fifty years (Clark 2016). Both contemporary and historical issues, such as immigration and slavery, have resulted in a massive head start for the white majority in the United States.

The median net worth of white families in the United States is $113,149, twenty times more than the median net worth of black families, at $5,677, and eighteen times more than Hispanic families, at $6,325 (Kochhar, Fry, and Taylor 2011). One reason for this disparity is historical wealth accumulation: white families have had more time to save money through the generations. When white and black families start off with a similar amount of wealth, their wealth accumulation is fairly similar ($5.19 per $1 income increase for whites, $4.03 for African Americans) (Shapiro, Meschede, and Osoro 2013, 4–5). Just by positioning black and white families at the same financial starting line goes a long way in erasing the difference between the two groups in terms of financial success. But most black families do not start off where white families do, so the reality is far different. One result is that white families in the United States are five times more likely to inherit a sum of money than other ethnic groups. Among those who did receive an inheritance, white families received about ten times more wealth than African Americans. Findings also show that each $1.00 of inheritance added $0.91 to the overall wealth of white families as opposed to only $0.20 to African American families. This is explained by the fact that white families are more likely to add their inheritance to the considerably larger assets they typically start out with, while African Americans are more likely to use new wealth for emergencies and pressing needs (Shapiro, Meschede, and Osoro 2013, 5).

Inequalities in education and employment also affect black families differently than white ones. Education is often assumed to be the "great equalizer." However, as a result of neighborhood segregation, lower-income students—especially students of color—are zoned and confined to failing or inferior schools.[16] This leaves them less academically prepared to both enter and complete college. Even when a young African American student is academically prepared to succeed, the cost of higher education is often far out of reach. The total costs of public universities have risen 60 percent in the last twenty years. Low-income and minority students who do attend college are often either forced to take jobs rather than attend school full time or graduate deep in debt. While debt is a problem that students of all ethnicities may have to face, African American students are more susceptible to it—80 percent of black students graduated with debt as opposed to 64 percent of white students (Shapiro, Meschede, and Osoro 2013, 5–6).

There is a commonly held misconception that minority students receive more than their fair share of college scholarships and financial aid. In fact, students of color are *less* likely to receive both private scholarships and merit-based institutional grants than white students. White students receive more than 75 percent of institutional grants, although they constitute less than 66 percent of the student population. Further, white students receive 65 percent of private scholarship funding, compared to 12 percent for African American students, 8 percent for Hispanic students, and 6 percent for Asian students (Kantrowitz 2011).

As for jobs, unemployment rates are higher for African Americans, and in economic downturns, African Americans are more negatively affected than whites since on average African American families have less substantial nest eggs to draw from (Shapiro, Meschede, and Osoro 2013, 3). Further, research shows that the same accomplishments are rewarded differently depending on a person's race. For example, African Americans with the same college degree as whites earn 20 percent less (Carnevale, Rose, and Cheah 2011, 11). At least part of the reason is access to work appropriate to their skills and training. Even with college degrees, African Americans are more likely to work jobs that require unskilled labor. These jobs not only pay less than careers that call for higher education but also come with hidden costs, like unavailability of health care benefits (Jacobs 2006).

Inescapable, however, is the role that racism plays in this country. A 2018 study conducted by researchers at Stanford, Harvard, and the Census Bureau found that the impact of how black men are treated in this country—the expectations of criminality, the higher incarceration rates for similar crimes, and discriminatory treatment—means that black men starting out in the same financial and family situation as white men fare far worse than their white peers. None of the old tropes held up. These disparities are not about culture. Black women typically avoid the criminalization expectations of black men and do as well as their white peers. Nor are the disparities explained by family structure. Having a father in the home had little to do with either overall income of the household or success rates of children in the home. Racism in the United States against African American men provides the primary explanation for why black families remain poorer than their white or Hispanic peers (Chetty et al. 2018).

Do Most Aid Recipients Work?

Examining two programs most often referenced when discussing welfare—food stamps (SNAP) and TANF—provides a useful picture. In 2016, 31.4 percent of non-elderly adults receiving food stamps were employed, while 25.3 percent were actively seeking work (US Department of Agriculture, Food and Nutrition Service 2017, 64).[17] The other 43.4 percent of recipients were listed as "not in labor force and not looking for work." Such numbers seem to confirm widespread stereotypes until one considers that this 43.4 percent of adults includes single parents and the disabled. Examining the numbers for who must register for work and who is exempt helps clarify. Among food stamp recipients, 30.5 percent are expected to register for work; 68.9 percent are exempt. Among those exemptions, 22.3 percent are for disabled people; the other 46.5 percent include single parents caring for a child either under one year old or under six years old but with no access to childcare, students enrolled in school, people receiving unemployment, and people who are already working over thirty hours a week. In summary then, 99.4 percent of non-elderly adult food stamp recipients are either working, disabled, caring for a small child, or ineligible for work and therefore ineligible for food stamps of their own. The remaining 0.6 percent are listed as "nonregistrant should have registered" for work. The result: barely more than half of 1 percent of recipients should be looking for work but are not.

For TANF recipients, 24 percent of adults receiving aid were employed, 47 percent were unemployed but actively looking for work, and 29 percent were not in the labor force, defined as "not looking for work (includes discouraged workers)."[18] In other words, 71 percent of people receiving TANF benefits were either employed or actively looking for work outside the home.

But what about the 29 percent of TANF recipients who do not have a job and are not looking for one? Among these recipients, 13 percent were exempt from the workforce because of disabilities. That leaves 16 percent (US Department of Health and Human Services, Office of Family Assistance 2012). The inclusion of "discouraged workers" sheds additional light. According to the US Bureau of Labor Statistics, discouraged workers are "persons not in the labor force who want and are available for a job and who have looked for work sometime in the past 12 months (or since the end of their last job if they held one within the past 12 months), but who are not currently looking because they believe there are no jobs available or there are none for which they would qualify" (US Department of Labor 2016). In other words, the number of people receiving aid who want to work in the wage labor market is probably much closer to 90 percent. That still leaves 10 percent. High costs of childcare, the lack of a living wage, and the lack of transportation help explain this final 10 percent.

These realities are discouraging. But as many aid recipients describe, it is even more discouraging to work a job that does not pay the bills. There is a vast gap between the minimum wage and a living wage. In Alamance County, for example, a living wage for one adult with two children is $24.10/hour, but the minimum wage is only $7.25. To reach even the poverty line, the hourly wage would have to be $8.80.[19] For a single parent, minimum wage can rarely support a family, especially with the added costs of childcare.

Are Welfare Benefits Large Enough to Lead a Life of Luxury?

For many parents, public assistance may be more financially viable than trying to work a low-wage job and pay for childcare. This does not, however, mean that public assistance provides excessive disposable income for luxury items. Eligibility for TANF requires that households be at or below 200 percent of the federal poverty level and have assets of less than $3,000 (NC Department of Health and Human Services, Division of Social Services 2013, 3, 8; Alamance County Community Assessment 2011, 133). This may initially seem generous until one considers that only 15 percent of people who received food stamps in 2010 had an income above the poverty line. Further, in the United States, the average monthly assistance for families receiving TANF was $392 in 2010. Monthly cash payments to families averaged $327 for one child, $412 for two children, $497 for three children, and $594 for four or more children. Many of these families were also eligible to receive food stamps. The average monthly assistance for families receiving food stamps in 2010 was $130. For a single parent raising two children at home, that average was $135 (US Department of Agriculture, Food, and Nutrition Service 2011, 15, 20). Adding the average TANF and average food stamp totals together equals $547 per month, or $6,564 per year for a single parent with two children, barely a third of the poverty level for this size family and less than a sixth of the cost of living in Alamance County, North Carolina (fig. 2.1).[20]

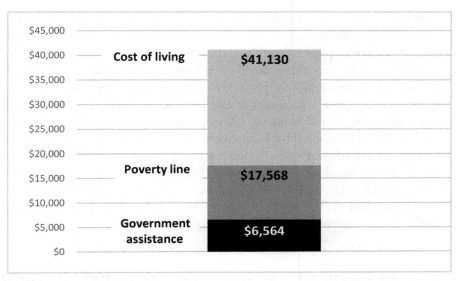

Figure 2.1. Average government assistance for a single parent with two children.

Do Aid Recipients Have Significant Substance Abuse Problems?

Alcohol and drug addictions affect people across the spectrum of American society, wealthy and poor alike. Government reports from 2011 show that the rate of alcohol use was over 10 percent higher for employed people than it was for the unemployed. Further, in 2010, 9.6 percent of full-time employed people used illicit drugs compared to only 2.6 percent of unemployed people. However, *regular* use by the unemployed was double that among those employed full time: 8.4 percent versus 17 percent (US Department of Health and Human Services, Substance Abuse and Mental Health Services Administration 2012).[21] In other words, employed Americans use alcohol and drugs at a far higher rate than the unemployed. But when the unemployed do use drugs and alcohol, they tend to use them more consistently.

For aid recipients specifically, the statistics are mixed. While heavy alcohol use is lower among recipients than the rest of the population (5.9% compared to 6.4%), drug use is higher (9.6% compared to 6.8%) (NHSDA Report 2002). However, if the rate of drug use was reduced to the same level as non-aid recipients, the decrease in participation in aid programs would be approximately 1 percent (Kaestner 1998).

For those who see addiction as a moral failing, alcohol and drug abuse fit neatly into the narrative of the immoral recipient, provoking punitive action. For those who see it as a chemical dependency and disease, such abuse more often provokes efforts of rehabilitation. But rehabilitation is not easily managed, either program-matically or personally, and those challenges are even more difficult for people living at or near the poverty line. From the start, if a person admits to an alcohol or drug addiction, they risk losing their benefits (Metsch and Pollack 2005).[22] Further, even with benefits, the price of rehabilitation can be prohibitive, costing hundreds of dollars a day. Insurance may cover some of that amount, but over 25 percent of Americans do not have health insurance (DeNavas-Walt, Proctor, and Smith 2012). Paying for rehabilitation is often a luxury that Americans in poverty cannot afford. Even with the large percentage of rehab facilities that offer free or reduced costs for treatment, time off from work, transportation, and unsubsidized costs can make treatment difficult to attain and maintain (US Department of Health and Human Services, Substance Abuse and Mental Health Services Administration 2013).

Do Aid Recipients Have More Children to Increase Their Benefits?

Women receiving aid have fewer children than women who are not receiving aid (Handler and Hasenfeld 2007, 53). Further, according to a study done before lifetime caps were placed on TANF, the longer women were on welfare, the less likely they were to have a child (Rank 1989).

Yet the image of large families on welfare persists, often coupled with the assumption that women have more children simply to increase the size of their benefits (appendix 1, chart A1.1). As early as 1959, an editorial in the *Daily News*, published in New York City, claimed, "Ladies have babies by assorted gentlemen so as to keep the relief checks growing fatter each year" (Martin 2012). In a 1995 poll, 72 percent of Americans thought that women on welfare have more children so they can receive more money "often"; 24 percent said "not often" and 4 percent said they "did not know." "Never" was either not an option or not a response (*Los Angeles Times* Poll, October 1995). These perceptions dropped by 2001, but more than half of Americans (57%) continued to believe women see children as a meal ticket, despite research to the contrary.[23]

Women have children for many reasons. Some pregnancies are intended; oth-ers are not. For those that are intended, women negotiate a number of complex factors to reach their decision to have another child.[24] Finances can be one of them, but typically in terms of whether a person feels they can afford to have another child.[25] Of all the factors at play, there is no research that indicates women have children expecting to improve their financial situation.

Yet the stories stick because of a parallel belief that welfare pays handsomely. Again, a look at the numbers suggests otherwise. With the welfare reforms of 1996, a woman who gets pregnant while receiving TANF funds cannot apply for TANF funds for that child.[26] Having more children, therefore, does not reap larger TANF benefits for people already receiving such aid. For women who are *not* already receiving TANF but who are considering applying, each additional child adds very little. In North Carolina, for example, an additional child would provide an average of just $28 more per month.[27] Food stamps, on the other hand, could provide somewhat more of an increase. Because the government wants to ensure that children are properly fed, additional children could raise a family's SNAP benefits by $159 per month. Such an increase hardly outweighs the cost of a newborn, however. For families in the lowest income bracket, the USDA estimates that a single-parent family will spend an average of $10,129 per child per year, or $844 per month.[28]

Further, if women were motivated by increased benefits to have more children, we should expect to see a correlation between benefit levels and birth rates among poor women. But studies show no such correlation. Further, we should see higher birth rates among aid recipients in states that provide relatively higher benefits. But again, we do not. Finally, as benefits drop, so should birth rates among aid recipients. We see no such drop (Sawhill 1995).

What Are the Levels of Fraud in the Welfare System,
and Who Perpetrates That Fraud?

The conversation about welfare fraud tends to focus on recipient fraud. Policies and reforms have been guided by the assumption that aid recipients are cheating the government and living lives of luxury as a result. Highly publicized cases of recipient fraud have helped fuel these beliefs. Public opinion similarly assumes widespread fraud among aid recipients, with well over half of Americans believing such cheating is a serious problem (appendix 1, chart A1.8).

Here again, however, the reality is far different. The vast majority of improper payments within major welfare programs is administrative, and far lower than public opinion would suggest. For food stamps, the USDA reported a drop in the trafficking of food stamps from 4 percent in 1998 to around 1 percent in 2013. Trafficking describes people selling their food stamps for ineligible goods, services, or cash. There is also fraud incurred by people applying for and receiving aid by falsifying their applications. This is included under "improper payment," which, in 2016, was estimated at between 3.2 percent and 5.8 percent. These numbers are misleading, however, as they include improper payments due to clerical errors within government agencies as well as accidental errors made by recipients. According to congressional testimony on July 6, 2016, "in fiscal year 2013, USDA reported that 62.44 percent of errors were because of administrative errors by the state agencies, and 37.27 percent of errors were because of recipient errors. Some of the errors may be attributable to recipient fraud; however, the magnitude of such program abuse is unknown" (US Government Accountability Office 2016, 8).

In other words, if all of the recipient errors were intentional acts of fraud, the fraud rate would still only be 1.1–2.1 percent. Accordingly, the estimates of 1 percent of fraud for trafficking likely parallels the fraud rates for application.

Estimates of fraud for other welfare programs are similarly difficult to distinguish from waste and error but include comprehensive estimates of 6 percent for CHIP, 9 percent for Medicaid, 4 percent for rental housing assistance programs, 8 percent for SSI, and 4 percent for WIC (Deloitte Consulting 2016).[29] As with food stamps, clerical and administrative errors account for the vast majority of improper payments.[30] In medical programs, dollar for dollar, the fraud that does exist is overwhelmingly perpetrated by doctors, medical equipment providers, patient recruiters, pharmacy owners, and home health care providers, not aid recipients (US Department of Health and Human Services, Office of Inspector General 2017).

Summary

All in all, people of color are disproportionately represented for reasons tied heavily to structural inequalities and generational poverty. The vast majority of aid recipients are working, trying to find work, disabled, or caring for a child. Substance abuse is a problem among all socioeconomic groups in the United States, including aid recipients, but those numbers are well below common assumptions. There is no evidence that women have more children to increase their welfare checks, and the math makes it clear such plans would be foolhardy at best. Aid benefits are far from generous and come nowhere near the poverty line or the cost of living, much less a life of luxury. And finally, official fraud levels are low among recipients, with the bulk of fraud in the welfare system perpetrated by providers, not recipients. Armed with this background context, it is possible to more effectively interpret the narrative tradition.

GENRE AND NARRATIVE

When Janet shared her eyewitness account of a woman buying steaks for her dog on food stamps, she shared it as part of a political argument against safety-net programs, such as welfare, Obamacare, and Medicaid. But she shared it in the form of a story. It is one thing to say that 90 percent of Americans believe the poor should be helped, but only 40 percent believe the current welfare system is effective in doing so. But it is another thing altogether to ask how people came to those views and how and when they apply them. The concept of cognitive dissonance makes it clear that we can hold multiple, competing views at once, deploying them in different contexts as we find useful and appropriate. What are those circumstances, for example, that allow us to turn a blind eye to the poor despite our professed commitment to aiding them? When do the stories of the welfare queen impede our charitable nature?

The concept of genre provides an avenue for exploring these questions. We create and experience a comedy differently than a drama, a lecture differently than a story, and a legend differently than a first-person account. In addressing how we come to know what we know about welfare, we must attend not just to contextual data, such as source and setting, but also to the forms of communication that distinguish argument from statistics from story. A focus on genre orients analysis to how we communicate in culturally specific, recognizable forms and how those forms shape the information we hear, remember, and share.

Only a few years ago, I might have said simply that this book is about the stories we tell about welfare in the United States and left it at that. In fact, that is exactly what I did in my study of narratives of personal revelation among Latter-day Saints. But in the past decade, narrative has become one of the hottest buzzwords of the social sciences—an exciting turn of events but one that necessitates a brief orientation to how this study approaches narrative since it differs from these new approaches in a few important ways.

Culling through scholarship from literature, linguistics, folklore, sociology, and communication, definitions of narrative emerge with some stable and consistent but rarely uncontested characteristics. As an initial, operational definition, narratives index or describe a past event; provide a sequence of action; include elements of orientation, complication, and resolution; and are structured with a beginning, middle, and end. They include plots, characters, settings, and actions. Structured as bounded events, narratives can be retold in new settings.[31]

However, scholars in political science, economics, and sociology have also embraced a broader definition of narrative so that one can speak of the Cold War narrative, the War on Terror narrative, and the Rise of China narrative (Hodges 2011; Miskimmon, O'Loughlin, and Roselle 2014). Such narratives can operate like a constellation of smaller stories of individual events, but they can also be divorced from any actual events or any vernacular articulations of those events and instead describe the overarching account constructed by academics. In this way, for some social scientists, narrative analysis need not be grounded in specific past events but instead can find actors, settings, complications, and resolutions in ideology rather than action. Nor do they need to reference narratives constructed by the actors they are studying, operating instead either as heuristics or as the scholar's own metanarrative.[32]

The field of folklore, on the other hand, considers the formal qualities of genre to be of central importance. Commentaries and conversations are not structured as narrative; nor are arguments, essays, statistics, or reports. Form impacts function and vice versa. It is the formal qualities of narrative that make it so compelling, recognizable, and memorable and provide clear boundaries so it can be decontextualized from one setting and retold in another. Folklorists' attention to genre in this way is one of the field's significant contributions to the social sciences.

The stories in this book hew closely to this approach to narrative, but, as with most social phenomena, related forms emerge in contexts that demand attention as part of a coherent and holistic analysis. In particular, a variety of narrative forms emerge in conversations about public assistance, foremost among them canonical narratives, master narratives, hegemonic narratives, and counternarratives. While these terms are applied inconsistently across and within disciplines, operational definitions for each can be drawn from a review of scholarship in folklore, anthropology, sociology, law, philosophy, critical race theory, and political rhetoric.

Canonical narratives are widespread stories widely recognized within a culture or society as the dominant or authoritative version of events (Polletta 2008). In the strictest formal sense, master narratives are not narratives at all but rather a constellation of ideas that serves as a comprehensive explanation for a historical event, historical trajectory, or cultural phenomenon and adopts the view of those in power, often in terms of colonization. Master narratives are never performed but rather serve as the foundation for specific stories that are (Adair 2000; Delgado 1995; Lyotard 1984; Polletta 2006, 2008; Scott 1990). Hegemonic narratives adopt a similar but not identical view from a position of power by assuming a natural order to support the status quo (Bell 2003; Ewick and Silbey 1995). Although the two terms are often used synonymously, I use hegemonic narrative to describe master narratives that are performed. In this way, *hegemonic* serves as a qualifier for a narrative to describe its relationship to power. Counternarratives are those stories that oppose master and hegemonic narratives of a culture or society (Bell 2003; Delgado 1995, 64). Such stories are often shared by or express the views of marginalized groups and individuals.

THE BOUNDARIES OF LEGEND

The legend, like narrative, enjoys a simple definition in the vernacular, a complex one in academia. In contemporary English usage, there are three primary kinds of legend. There is the celebrity, as when we slap the label of "legend" on James Dean, Miles Davis, or Marilyn Monroe. There is the historical story, such as the tales of King Arthur, that claims historical basis even though authentication is difficult. And there are the urban legends that people dismiss as false: too good to be true, but fun to tell all the same. The first is easily written out of this study, but the other two share common traits: they are stories that are supposed to be true but may not be. King Arthur legends are set far enough in the past as to typically leave a question mark around the truth. But when people label a contemporary story a legend, they invariably mean it is not true. The question mark is removed; the lie exposed. Just as no one describes one's own religious belief system as myth, no one calls the stories one believes to be true a legend. In vernacular usage, legend equals false, the same wholesale fate that *folklore* and *myth* typically get. "That's just a myth," or "That's just folklore"—both mean that's not true.

Not surprisingly, folklorists define folklore and myth without any such dismissive exclusions. Some of the stories we tell are true; some are not. Both can be part of oral tradition and part of the study of folklore. Myths may make claims to historical truth that cannot be supported by the scientific method, but most articulate sacred truths evaluated on a different set of criteria from such simple dichotomies of true or false. Academic definitions of legend similarly refuse the label false. Beyond that, definitions can get muddy. If there is one constant in legend scholarship, it is that there is no definitive definition for a legend. Elliott Oring summarizes this state of affairs through the questions that remain unanswered, including whether legends are narratives or formless, true or false, negotiated, traditional, different from anecdotes and personal experiences, part of a specific communicative channel, or a way to parse ambiguous situations (Oring 2008, 127–28).[33] Gillian Bennett and Paul Smith ([1996] 2011, xxii–xxiii) provide an even more extensive list of questions about legends. Implicated in this list are definitions that focus on form, function, style, content, belief, process of transmission, and performance. Scholars have also suggested temporal orientation as significant. Early definitions relegated the legend to the past (Thompson 1946, 8), while more recent definitions embrace the *contemporary* legend that is believed to have occurred recently with the possibility of occurring again soon (Georges 1971; cited in Lindahl 2011, xii).

Despite folklorists' nuanced consideration of the complexity of etic genres, operational definitions for contemporary legends do exist.[34] Bennett and Smith reference Alexander Woolcott's afterthought of a definition buried in a footnote in his book *While Rome Burns* by noting, "In three neat sentences he thus anticipates three criteria nowadays usually considered to be basic to the genre: the conception of contemporary legend as an 'emergent' form; the 'friend-of-a-friend' authenticating ploy; and the impossibility of either effectively challenging or establishing an originating event" (Bennett and Smith 2011, xxviii). A more common starting place for many folklorists, however, is Gary Alan Fine's 1992 definition:

> Recognizing the impossibility of presenting a fully acceptable definition, and hoping for a plausible one, I propose that a "contemporary legend" is a narrative that a teller presents to an audience in the context of their relationship. The text

> is an account of a happening in which the narrator or an immediate personal contact was not directly involved and is presented as a *proposition for belief*; it is not always believed by speaker or audience, but it is presented as something that could have occurred and is told as if it happened. These occurrences are notable happenings of the kind that are allegedly "strange but true." The content of the narrative involves events that happened in contemporary society and depicts persons, relations, organizations, and institutions that are recognized by narrator and audience to characterize the modern world. (Fine 1992, 2; emphasis in original)

Fine raises the question of belief, arguing later that stories must be both plausible and credible even if they are not necessarily believed to be wholly or even partially true (29). The issue of belief lies at the heart of the legend, not as a requirement but rather as a question mark. I join many scholars in arguing that a key criterion of legend—even *the* key criterion—is whether the truth of the story is debated.[35] "For there to be legend, there must be *someone* who fundamentally doubts the truth of the legend account" (Oring 1990, 164). Without this doubt, the story can more accurately be labeled as any of a number of other nonfiction genres, including news story, anecdote, and personal experience narrative.[36]

In chapter 8, I revisit current definitions of legend and suggest a recentering of our study on issues of doubt as much as truth. For now, it is sufficient to cull the many definitions of legend put forth not just by folklorists but by scholars from fields as diverse as literature and psychology and provide my own operational definition for contemporary legend based on the study at hand. While contemporary legends may not always be shared in narrative form, for example, this study is particularly interested in storytelling. Accordingly, contemporary legends in the welfare tradition are stories of past events that are plausible even if not believed that raise some degree of doubt by storyteller or audience, that happen most often to someone else, and that occur in multiple versions with reoccurring motifs and themes. As with any living tradition, such stories must be relevant to storyteller, audience, or both and convey a particular worldview, often moral or ideological in nature.

WELFARE LEGENDS: IN SEARCH OF A FOLK TRADITION

The original legend of the welfare queen was created from the intersection of news story, stump speech anecdote, and mass media news coverage. Chicago newspapers provided the story, Ronald Reagan gave it a national audience, and the mass media helped ensure its long life. But stories of welfare fraud were hardly new. Reagan's welfare queen built on a pattern already established in the media. Repeated in stump speech after stump speech around the country by an increasingly recognizable and charismatic actor turned politician, however, Reagan's story caught fire. Combined with the sensational and catchy *welfare queen* moniker, the anecdote became one of the most recognizable stories of Reagan's tenure in politics. More importantly, the story became part of the cultural zeitgeist, so recognizable by audiences that simply repeating the name or echoing the concept could evoke the story. And yet, a glaring omission exists. If the story had truly become part of the cultural fabric of American society, if the story was recognized easily at the merest mention of a name, where was the story in the folk tradition?

Gary Alan Fine appears to be the first folklorist to take up the topic of welfare legends as part of a widespread folk tradition in his 1992 book *Manufacturing Tales: Sex and Money in Contemporary Legends*. Fine references the welfare Cadillac legends that complement Reagan's welfare queen by depicting a person on welfare indulging in the extravagances of material wealth, whether through outright fraud or broken government policy.

> Narratives about the "Welfare Cadillac" implicitly reflect the frustration that the middle class have with their own stultifying work life and pose the question whether they might do better striving less and being sharper. The persistent fear of the middle class is that both the upper and lower class are happier than they are and have an easier life. The protagonist of the Welfare Cadillac legend—the person who picks up a welfare check in a Cadillac—melds upper and lower class in a figure who lives off the sweat of others. This narrative is complex in the way its themes reflect social order. That the car is a Cadillac suggests to some tellers and audiences that the welfare cheat is Black—perhaps an entrepreneur in the underground economy, such as a pimp or drug dealer. The meaning of the legend can be that the eligibility for welfare is not checked sufficiently or that benefits are set too high. In either case there is an implicit criticism of government programs. (Fine 1992, 8)

Fine references these legends again when he teams up with Patricia Turner in their 2001 book *Whispers on the Color Line: Rumor and Race in America*. Again, stories are mentioned generally, referencing the mass media and generalized beliefs, but not oral or vernacular traditions (Fine and Turner 2001, 121). The simplest answer to my question "Where is the welfare queen in the folk tradition?" is that she is assumed to be everywhere but noted and analyzed nowhere. Why this should be the case both illuminates trends in current folklore studies as well as challenges in how we have approached the study of contemporary legend.

Apart from the obvious difficulties of recording oral narratives in their natural contexts, there are two specific issues working against efforts to record stories of welfare queens and Cadillacs: one methodological, one ideological. Methodologically, folklorists typically rely on qualitative methods. Such methodology is particularly well suited to studies of small groups in bounded interactions. Considering Dan Ben-Amos's often-cited definition of folklore as "artistic communication in small groups" (1971, 13), such a methodology has served the field well. In terms of the study of legend, this approach is successful when we study the ghost stories at a local university (Tucker 2007), the rumors and legends about Church's fried chicken told by African Americans in Philadelphia (Turner 1993), or the legends shared among Katrina survivors about why their neighborhoods were hit hardest (Lindahl 2012). As a primarily humanistic rather than social scientific enterprise, this approach is extremely useful for giving voice to small, identifiable groups, but it is less effective for corralling traditions that are assumed to extend more widely, like many contemporary legends are assumed to do.

Second, as folklorists who heed Warren Roberts's call to attend to the 95 percent of people who are not recorded in history and whose daily lives of expressive culture would otherwise go unrecognized and undervalued outside their communities, folklorists are used to studying narratives that operate in opposition to hegemonic stories shared in the media or among majority populations: legends that position the people in opposition to the government, big business, and scientific thinking. Welfare legends strike out on both counts. First, they are assumed to be everywhere, shared not within a *particular* group or community but widely throughout the country. Second, they support a hegemonic view where the poor are castigated as lazy and immoral, thereby justifying an economic system that requires no revisions to close the disparity between the haves and the have-nots.

However, it is dangerous to ignore hegemonic legends that aim to justify the status quo, especially if our more common studies of counternarratives depend on them as foils. Although folklorists have paid little attention to welfare legends, we have addressed widespread legends about AIDS, satanic cults, organ theft, and vaccination. Strategies for recording and analyzing oral folk traditions include enlisting student researchers, surveying friends and acquaintances, combing through archives, searching mass media publications, scouring the internet, and targeting groups connected to the topic of the legend at hand. This study employs all of these strategies and also identifies natural discourse communities that have no obvious connection to welfare but instead represent "the general public." Accordingly, this study is informed not only by the stories told by aid providers who process welfare applications, grocery store cashiers who handle electronic benefit transfer (EBT) purchases, and politicians who shape welfare policy but also friend groups who talk about local and world issues that run the gamut but might on any given day include discussions about poverty and welfare.[37]

Those stories are part of a deep legacy of antipoor sentiment in this country. To understand today's stories, then, we must step back in time to consider key moments in the development of the narrative tradition of welfare in the United

States. And no moment is more crucial than Ronald Reagan's initial failed run for the White House.

NOTES

1. See Adair (2000), Boris (2007), Gilens (1996, 1999), Gilliam (1999), Hancock (2004), Hays (2003), Lubiano (1992, 336), Ortiz (2003), Seccombe (2011), and West (2002), many of whom note that the immorality of the welfare queen is often cast as sexual promiscuity.

2. There are exceptions; for example, spouses may have access to these programs and funds based on the work history of their spouses.

3. Robert S. Pfeiffer, creator of the Federal Safety Net website, identifies thirteen major welfare programs (2018). Robert Rector, senior research fellow in welfare studies at the conservative Heritage Foundation, compiled a list of 79 programs for his testimony before the House of Representatives Committee on the Budget on April 17, 2012. A week earlier on April 11, Michael Tanner, director of health and welfare studies at the libertarian Cato Institute, published a policy paper identifying 126 welfare or antipoverty programs.

4. This use of the term *myth* fits comfortably in vernacular usage but runs counter to how folklorists use the term: as sacred or revered stories of how the world came to be and operates today.

5. See also Nickerson (1998) and chap. 12 for a more thorough discussion of confirmation bias and memory.

6. See Voices of Welfare (2014b).

7. See appendix 1, as well as charts 2.1, 3.1, and 7.1 and figs. 3.2 and 3.3, for polling data. See also MacLeod, Montero, and Speer (1999, 175), NBC News (2014), and Population Reference Bureau (2002).

8. See table 7.A1 in Social Security Administration, Office of Retirement and Disability Policy (2017a).

9. The average number of children for TANF households in 2013 was 1.8 (Falk 2015, 5, table 1). The closest stats to 2013 for national averages for number of children in a family was from 2015 (Livingston 2015).

10. The percentages do not add up to 100 percent for two reasons: Latino people may identify additionally as white or black, causing some total percentages to exceed 100, and because other ethnic or racial categories are not represented in these charts since the numbers are so small, causing other total percentages to drop below 100. Those categories include Asian, American Indian or Native Alaskan, and Native Hawaiian or Pacific Islander. Data for both chart 2.2 and chart 2.3: 2015 population stats, Statistical Abstracts of the United States (2015); 2016 population stats, US Census Bureau (2016); US Department of Agriculture, Food and Nutrition Service (2011). This report is the most recent in a series of annual reports providing information about the demographic and economic circumstances of

SNAP households. In fiscal year 2015, as in prior years, nearly two-thirds of SNAP participants were children (44%), elderly (11%) or disabled non-elderly adults (10%). The average monthly benefit received by SNAP households was $254 (US Department of Health and Human Services, Office of Family Assistance 2016, table 10; US Department of Housing and Urban Development 2018, HUD statistics). Medicaid data: US Department of Health and Human Services, Centers for Medicare and Medicaid Services (2015; Medicaid Eligibles/Demographics, Table I.17). For SSI data, see Social Security Administration, Office of Retirement and Disability Policy (2017b, 3.10–3.12).

11. Henry J. Kaiser Family Foundation (2001).

12. CBS News/*New York Times*, December 1994. Roper Center for Public Opinion Research, iPOLL.

13. Voices of Welfare (2014a).

14. For a compelling illustrated viral video on wealth inequality in the United States, see Politizane (2012).

15. See also Living Wage Action Coalition (n.d.). A livable wage is enough to support the earner and her or his family the "most basic costs of living without need for government support or poverty programs."

16. The funding of schools through property taxes helps to perpetuate this inequality.

17. The report refers to households without a job-eligible adult as "nonparticipating household head," noting noncitizens as an example (32). The year 2016 was chosen as it was the most recent report at the time of writing.

18. The year 2009 was chosen because it was the most recent year that the employment rate was broken into employed, unemployed but looking for work, and unemployed not looking for work. For comparison, however, in 2016, the employment rate of TANF recipients was significantly higher than in 2009 or 2010 at 28.2 percent (US Department of Health and Human Services, Office of Family Assistance 2010, table 30). Numbers were current as of August 24, 2010; those numbers have dropped a bit for 2010 when 22.3 percent were employed (US Department of Health and Human Services, Office of Family Assistance 2012).

19. The Living Wage Calculator was developed by Dr. Amy K. Glasmeier at MIT. Online calculators are updated regularly. Alamance County data can be found at Living Wage Calculator (n.d.).

20. For poverty thresholds for 2010, see US Census Bureau (2018). In the early 1990s, Kathryn Edin and Laura Lein made similar computations and found the gap similarly wide (1997). By 2010, when Edin and her coauthor H. Luke Shaefer revisited the numbers and the people struggling to survive in the United States, they found that one in twenty-five families with children were living on less than $2 a day per person, an astounding increase in deep poverty in the United States that emerged directly from the 1996 Welfare Reform Act (PWRORA) (2015, xvii).

21. These statistics are based on self-reports from 153,873 people. For a complete explanation of sampling procedures, see pp. 109–13.

22. See also Pollack et al. (2002).

23. A poll conducted jointly by National Public Radio, the Harvard University Kennedy School of Government, and the Henry J. Kaiser Family Foundation indicated that 57 percent of Americans believe that welfare encourages women to have more children (Henry J. Kaiser Family Foundation 2001).

24. "Preconception desire for pregnancy was related to a woman's values and goals (including goals for marriage, desire for family, and beliefs about the importance of family), preparation and readiness (including employment, career development, financial preparation, emotional preparation, and readiness of other children), relationships with others (preeminently the partner and his desires, but also extended family and friends), prior experiences with pregnancy and family, experiences in her family of origin, and expectations for a pregnancy. We found that preconception desire for pregnancy arises from a complex interaction between long-term goals and values and current circumstances, and therefore it changes with time" (Stanford et al. 2000, 185).

25. See the Child Timing Questionnaire developed by Miller and Pasta (1994) and discussed in Miller (1994, 12).

26. According to the NC TANF State Plan, "a family cap on assistance is in effect. This means that a family's Work First Family Assistance cash payment or Work First Benefits will not increase when a child is born ten (10) months after a month in which a family received cash assistance" (NC Department of Health and Human Services, Division of Social Services 2013).

27. These amounts are updated periodically and vary slightly depending on the number of people in the household. Thirty-six dollars is the increase from a two-person household to a three-person one. The increase varies for each additional member, never more than twenty-seven dollars but as low as thirteen dollars (NC Department of Health and Human Services, Division of Social Services n.d.).

28. These numbers are based on a survey by the US Department of Agriculture, with numbers updated to 2015 dollars using the Consumer Price Index (Lino et al 2017).

29. This source is an online interactive chart compiled from dozens of government reports.

30. PaymentAccuracy.gov (n.d.). PaymentAccuracy.gov is an official website of the US government, developed after the passage of the Improper Payments and Elimination and Recovery Act of 2010.

31. See Bal ([1985] 2009), Bruner ([1986] 2009), Freytag ([1863] 1968), Labov and Waltezky (1967), and Polletta (2006, 8–11).

32. When William Foote Whyte famously declared that the groundbreaking ethnography *Street Corner Society* (1943) is as much his interlocutor Doc's story as his own, he is expanding narrative not only to include the entire ethnography but

to suggest that his articulation mirrors what the people in his community would have written had they done so instead of him.

33. For other scholars who have highlighted the difficulty of a definition for legend and contemporary legend specifically, see Bennett and Smith (2007, xvi–xviii; 2011, xxii) Dégh (2001, 44–45), Main and Hobbs (2007, 41, 49), and Turner (1992).

34. Etic genres are identified by terms that are applied across cultural boundaries, such as *folktale*, *legend*, and *myth*. They can be contrasted with emic genres, which are identified by terms specific to a culture group such as *shukha anumpa* stories among the Choctaw Indians in Mississippi (Mould 2004) or the *caso* among Mexican Americans in Texas (Graham 1981).

35. Not to be confused with whether the narrator believes the story.

36. Folklorists have pointed out that, too often, the person expressing doubt is the scholar rather than audience members, locating the power of generic designation outside the performance context (see Mould 2018). In chap. 11, I suggest that a fruitful reorientation of legend scholarship is to place doubt at the center of our analysis.

37. I explore these strategies in depth as well as explain in greater detail the benefits of conducting fieldwork with "irrelevant" natural discourse communities in Mould (2016). I developed the list of five common strategies for data collection by analyzing the following works of key legend scholars in the field: Bennett and Smith ([1996] 2011), Brunvand (1981, 1984, 1986a, 1989, 2001), Campion-Vincent (2005), Dégh (1995, 2001), Ellis (2003, 2009), Fine (1992), Fine and Ellis (2010), Fine and Turner (2001), Frank (2001), Goldstein (2004), Kitta (2013), Langlois (2005), Nicholaisen (1992), Smith (1992), and Turner (1987, 1993).

THREE

—ᴡ—

BIRTH IN A NATION

RONALD REAGAN: THE GREAT COMMUNICATOR

Rarely can we point to the moment when a legend is born. Not so for the welfare queen. The year was 1976. Gerald Ford was president despite having never campaigned nor been elected to either the vice president or president positions he held. Spiro Agnew's resignation as vice president in 1973 vaulted Ford into the number two spot, followed only a year later by Richard Nixon's resignation, which launched Ford into the Oval Office. The Republican Party was not unified behind Ford, however, and so, by the fall of 1975, the Hollywood actor and California governor Ronald Reagan entered the race as the sole Republican challenger to Ford.

Reagan hit the campaign trail with a story that he would repeat hundreds of times in stump speech after stump speech, a story that has been referenced hundreds of thousands of times by politicians, journalists, and the American public in the years since. It was a story about a woman in Chicago: "There's a woman in Chicago. She has 80 names, 30 addresses, 12 Social Security cards and is collecting veterans' benefits on four nonexisting deceased husbands. And she's collecting Social Security on her cards. She's got Medicaid, getting food stamps, and she is collecting welfare under each of her names. Her tax-free cash income alone is over $150,000" (*New York Times* 1976a, 15). This version, taken from a stump speech in February 1976 in New Hampshire, has become the standard version of Reagan's welfare queen story. In the end, Reagan lost the nomination to Ford through a ballot vote on the second to last day of the Republican National Convention. Yet while he lost the race, neither he nor the welfare queen narrative he helped create and disseminate disappeared from politics or from the stories shared by Americans across the country over forty years later.

43

Sitting in her office at the Alamance County Department of Social Services, Kate Garnett recounts the story of Reagan's welfare queen while talking about her job as a caseworker. Many of the details have shifted, but not only does Kate attribute the story to Reagan, she recognizes the ongoing process of naming new welfare queens from the rare but dramatic stories reported in the news.

> If you'll remember the Reagan era, just before Clinton, there was that big FOAF [friend-of-a-friend legend] of the welfare queen of this woman that might have lived in Michigan or Detroit or wherever that had six Cadillacs and two homes, and she made seven thousand dollars in benefits, and she had all these children, but we could never pin this person down, right? They kept putting this out there that this person existed, but we couldn't find her.
>
> I was reading an internet story where they actually found one person who had seventeen aliases and had that similar story, but it certainly wasn't epidemic. It certainly wasn't across the nation. And it was somebody who just happened to fit the FOAF. And the way that it had been portrayed is that this goes on everywhere. So, there was that sliver of truth.

So how did we get to this point, with a story so powerful it is being retold over forty years later and a character so memorable and recognizable that she remains a household name?[1] One answer lies with Reagan, though he has been given both too much and not enough credit for creating the welfare queen. He didn't coin the term *welfare queen* and does not appear to have even used the term until after the mass media had cemented the connection (Levin 2013). Nor did he invent the stereotype of the lazy, fraudulent aid recipient. The building blocks for the welfare queen were already well established in American culture by the time Reagan burst onto the scene.

But he *did* use the story incredibly well politically—so well, in fact, that twenty years later, Bill Clinton, a Democrat, signed into law a welfare reform act based on assumptions that had been firmly established with the welfare queen story. And Reagan *did* tell a number of other stories about welfare, both before and after the welfare queen, that have also stuck with us, shaping popular perceptions of public assistance and its recipients in the United States today.

Looking closely, we see that the story of the welfare queen was an example of both trickle-down and bubble-up storytelling and that Reagan was planted firmly in the same folk tradition as his voters.[2] This is why the other answer to the question of how the welfare queen remains alive and well today must be searched for not solely among political elites or even the mass media but among us all, among the folk. Accordingly, tracking Reagan can provide insight into not only the development of the welfare queen by an elite political figure but also a folk tradition that has been assumed to exist but has never been fully documented and analyzed.

WILL DIVORCE FOR WELFARE

Let us begin by going back another ten years or so to 1964. In that year, Reagan had never held public office much less run for it, yet he had firmly established himself as a politically active celebrity: a Hollywood actor who regularly threw his support behind candidates and issues. Initially that support was for Democrats with liberal views. In 1948, he appeared on stage with Harry S. Truman during a campaign speech in Los Angeles. In the years that followed, Reagan remained active politically, both personally as well as through his job as a motivational speaker for General Electric. His political views, however, began to shift so that by 1952 he was supporting Republican Dwight D. Eisenhower and Richard M. Nixon in 1960. It was not particularly strange, then, when Republican presidential candidate Barry Goldwater asked Reagan to tape an endorsement speech for a paid political telecast called "Rendezvous with Destiny" that aired on October 27, 1964. The destiny established that night was not Goldwater's, however, but Reagan's. Political historians point to this speech as the moment when Reagan was vaulted into national prominence within the Republican Party. Within a year he was running for governor of California, winning the job with two campaign promises: "to clean up the mess at Berkeley," by which he meant antiwar and antiestablishment student protests, and "to send the welfare bums back to work" (McKee 2014, 33).

The fight against welfare abuse was a successful rallying cry for Reagan in his first political race and every one after. Pithy slogans were powerful, but so were his stories. In 1964, in the televised speech that became so famous it earned its own name—"A Time for Choosing" or just "the speech"—it was a woman in California rather than Chicago: "Not too long ago, a judge called me here in Los Angeles. He told me of a young woman who'd come before him for a divorce. She had six children, was pregnant with her seventh. Under his questioning, she revealed her husband was a laborer earning two hundred and fifty dollars a month. She wanted a divorce to get an eighty dollar raise. She's eligible for three hundred and thirty dollars a month in the Aid to Dependent Children Program. She got the idea from two women in her neighborhood who'd already done that very thing" (Reagan 1964).

What appears to have begun as a story shared around the office and among friends and family to let off steam and marvel at the unusual, outrageous, or unbelievable ended up being broadcast to millions of Americans. Soon, that work story of one unusual case became for Reagan and many of his supporters the typical face of welfare. The fact that the story fell not as a seed among the rocks but into fertile soil was certainly due in part to contemporary political concerns about government waste and increases in welfare spending (cf. McKee 2014, 33;

Neubeck and Cazenave 2001) and in part to stories splashed across national magazines and newspapers decrying welfare abuse.

DETROIT CRACKS DOWN ON RELIEF CHISELERS

How much of the tax money in your town goes to shameless cheats who claim charity they don't need? Detroiters took a close look at their relief rolls and uncovered some facts that shocked the state and will shock you too. (*Saturday Evening Post*, December 10, 1949, 19)

WHEN IT PAYS TO PLAY PAUPER

(*Nation's Business*, September 1950, vol. 38, p. 29)

WELFARE: HAS IT BECOME A SCANDAL?

- In California, a salesman collected $820 in jobless pay over 21 weeks, although he was earning $88 a week as a salesman.
- In Oklahoma, 125 women, each of whom had eight or more illegitimate children, drew aid-to-dependent-children grants.
- In Washington, D.C., a husband-wife team collected $1,650 in unemployment compensation, although they were fully retired Federal employees on a monthly pension of $480.
- In New York City, a woman collected relief checks while hiding a hypodermic needle in her brassiere. For two years, she used relief money to buy narcotics.
- Throughout the nation, a large number of people drew doubled Social Security benefits by fraudulently using two names and account numbers.

(*Look*, November 7, 1961, 31–33)

CHILDREN WITHOUT FATHERS: THE SHOCKING TRUTH ABOUT THE AID TO DEPENDENT CHILDREN WELFARE PROGRAM

(*Reader's Digest*, November 1961, 72–80)

With sensational headlines that assured readers they would be shocked by what followed, magazine articles in the years leading up to Reagan's speech often trotted out individual aid recipients as examples of the abuses assumed to be rampant. In the *Look* magazine story, editors pulled out four specific stories (and one generalized one) to print in large font as the subtitle for the article, spotlighting these stories both as a compelling hook for the reader and clear evidence that the answer to the headline's question was a resounding yes. The Detroit "chiseler" story is equally sensational in its headline and subtitle, leading the reader into the story to meet eighteen aid recipients whose stories are meant to shock—as the subtitle promises—as well as persuade.

The stories of these individuals are framed as unacceptable, the tone of the articles critical and in many cases derisive and caustic. The few accompanying photos provide a face and a name to the otherwise abstract fear and outrage at widespread fraud that takes money out of the pockets of hardworking Americans and hands it over to immoral, undeserving "chiselers." The rhetorical power of these stories is clear: tangible, specific, and indisputable support for the belief that the welfare system is rife with cheats and must be overhauled. Reagan's stories in 1964 and 1976, then, simply built on a pattern already gaining traction in the media.

Less easily tracked is the oral tradition. What were people saying at the water cooler about welfare? What were the stories about aid recipients shared among family and friends over dinner? The judge who called Reagan provides a glimpse, and half a century of folklore research into how and why legends are shared makes it clear that there is often a vibrant feedback loop between mass media and folk traditions (Mould 2011a, 327–80; see also Brunvand 2001; Dégh 1994). What we know is that Reagan's story from 1964, heard from a judge in Los Angeles, lodged within the folk tradition so that sixty years later a version of it was still being told in Alamance County, North Carolina.

Inside the small, dark bar, the air was stuffy, the blanket of music and conversation pervasive. It was a favorite hangout of student fieldworker Caroline Miller. Over the past few months, she had become acquaintances with all the regulars, including Silas Matthews, a forty-nine-year-old white working-class man whose politics veered toward the libertarian. As an excuse to escape the heat and noise, Caroline invited Silas outside into the cool of a southern November evening to share his views about welfare.

> I heard about the old story that Ronald Reagan spoke of before he was elected. And it was the welfare queen. And it was the woman who goes to . . . She's divorcing her husband. She has five kids, she's in California, and the judge asks her—and it's a black woman—and the judge asks her, "Hey, why are you divorcing your husband?"
>
> And she goes, "Well, I just want a divorce because he don't bring no money home, but if I go on welfare with my five kids, I will be making so much, X amount more than what he's bringing."
>
> So, they make more money being on welfare than flipping burgers. Having three kids, they can make more money by being on welfare.
>
> And it's a cycle. And they are teaching people who are on welfare; they get together and help newbies—the new ones who are getting on the system—and help them say the right words to say the catch words the key words to speak so you can get this stuff.
>
> You know it's wrong. I don't believe you should be, if you are on Medicare or, I mean, if you are on welfare or something like that, you should only be on it for a certain amount of time, a year or two, and then you are off it, and you are out and gone. You can't be on it for another five years and let people become so poor that they are willing to do anything to make money.

The story he shares repeats the key elements of Reagan's story—the woman divorcing to get more money from the government, the local grapevine that teaches people how to game the system—as well as details like the fact that she was from California that we might not expect to have remained. But there are also a few new details that were not part of the original. The most obvious is the moniker of the "welfare queen." There is no reason Silas should not apply the term. The *welfare queen* was intended to describe a vast contingent of welfare chiselers.

More troubling in Silas's narrative is the explicit addition of race. As with his story about Linda Taylor, Reagan did not mention the race of the woman seeking the divorce, but Silas understood her to be black. The race of the woman could have been added into the narrative tradition at any point in the intervening years, including by Silas himself, but the possibility that Reagan's stories were racially coded, whether intentionally or not, seems clear from how people responded to his story. Drew Lewis, described as the Republican National Committee's "top operative" during the 1980 campaign, argued that their job as a party was to correct the image that Reagan was "flinty-hearted and would kick all the blacks off welfare" (Raines 1980). Contributing to the general racialization of welfare at the time was the disproportionate representation in the mass media of welfare recipients as black, the increase in access to welfare by African Americans thanks to the civil rights movement, the racially charged congressional hearings that Senator Robert Byrd from West Virginia held on welfare fraud, and Daniel Moynihan's 1965 influential report that laid the groundwork for the pathologizing of the poor and the critique of welfare that was titled "On the Negro Family: The Case for National Action."[3] While Reagan may not have labeled the woman in Chicago as black, journalists did when they named her Linda Taylor. In any case, the story entered a public discourse that regularly pictured welfare recipients in image and word as black.

THE WELFARE QUEEN

Ten years later, another story caught Reagan's ear, this time not from a work colleague but from the news. Whether an aide or friend directed him to the story or he found it himself, the pattern of narration once again mirrors the folk tradition where stories from the news retold by cab drivers, stockbrokers, and neighbors are reshaped in the oral tradition with shifting meanings and details. This was the famous "woman from Chicago" story. Reagan adapted the story of Linda Taylor both to his own understanding and view of welfare programs in the United States, as well as to his specific political agenda. True to oral performance, the story shifted slightly in each retelling. By October 1976, months after acceding the nomination to Ford, Reagan revisited the story in a radio address to the nation:

I said I would update my story of eighty names and thirty addresses. Here goes.

The trail extends through fourteen states. She has used a hundred and twenty-seven names so far, posed as a mother of fourteen children at one time, seven at another, signed up twice with the same caseworker in four days, and once while on welfare, posed as an open-heart surgeon complete with office. She has fifty Social Security numbers and fifty addresses in Chicago alone, plus an untold number of telephones. She claims to be the widow, let's make that plural, of two naval officers who were killed in action. Now the Department of Agriculture is looking into the massive number of food stamps she's been collecting. She has three new cars, a full-length mink coat, and her take is estimated at a million dollars.

I wish this had a happy ending. But the public aid office according to the news story, refused to cooperate. She's still collecting welfare checks she can use to build up her defense fund.[4]

Reagan continued to avoid using Taylor's name, but for perhaps the first time publicly, he adopted the moniker that journalists had been using both for her and Reagan's story: "the welfare queen." But if Reagan didn't coin the term, who did?

According to Barry Popik, contributor to the *Oxford English Dictionary*, the term *welfare queen* first appeared in print as the name of a racehorse in the Charles Town, West Virginia, race charts printed in the *Washington Post* on September 1, 1973 (fig. 3.1).[5] It is unclear how her owner C. L. Ray came up with the name, but a year later the term appeared in newspapers again, this time applied to Linda Taylor, who would eventually be remembered as the original welfare queen described by Ronald Reagan.[6] "'Welfare Queen' Jailed in Tucson" touts the headline of the *Chicago Tribune* story by George Bliss that ran on October 12, 1974, followed by the opening line of the story: "Linda Taylor, the 47-year-old 'welfare queen,' was being held in a jail in Tucson, Ariz., Friday at the request of Chicago police in lieu of a $100,000 bond." Subsequent stories in the *Chicago Tribune* over the next few months continued to refer to Taylor as the "welfare queen," at which point the term stuck and got picked up by other publications.[7]

By the time Reagan hit the campaign trail in January 1976, Linda Taylor was already known as "the welfare queen." Reagan did not mention Linda Taylor by name or the term *welfare queen*, but journalists quickly picked up on both in their reporting after the *New York Times* (1976a) formally connected the two with its headline "'Welfare Queen' Becomes Issue in Reagan Campaign," at which point the term "went viral" and shifted from Linda Taylor to Reagan's politicized bogeywoman. From there, *welfare queen* entered the American lexicon as a generic term for anyone committing welfare fraud and became the most pervasive image of public assistance, shaping popular perception and public policy (Coughlin 1989; Hancock 2004; Hays 2003).

Charles Town Race Charts

WEATHER—CLEAR TRACK— FAST

1—$2,000, 4½ furlongs, :54⅗.

Horse	PP	¼	Str.	Fin.	Odds
Welfare Queen	1	1hd	2hd	1nk	$1.40
Countess G.	8	33	33	2hd	3.00
Fine Jim	3	2½	1hd	32½	10.30
Just Got Married	4	52	4hd	41	4.00
Get Ahead Suzy	7	71	6½	52	18.20
Dawn Bolero	6	8½	81	61½	16.20
Rollin Boy	9	4hd	53	73	57.80
Apollo's Luck	10	6½	71	81	28.40
Rollin Boy	9	4hd	53	73	57.80
Roman Choice	5	10	10	93	33.50
Out Of Bourbon	2	93	9hd	10	16.20

Welfare Queen (Shuk) 4.80 3.20 3.00
Countess G. (Williams) 3.60 2.80
Fine Jim (Nuckols) 4.20

2—$2,100, 6½ furlongs, 1:23⅕.

Horse	PP	¼	½	Str.	Fin.	Odds
dq-N' O' Neil	4	1hd	1½	11	11½	13.00
Royal Pack'	3	64	3hd	2½	22½	5.40
Night Crawler	6	4½	51½	51½	35	38.50
Frieda's Fro'	1	2½	44	41	41	7.20
Clems Moll	2	72	7½	7½	51	32.50
Send Me	8	5½	21	33	63½	1.00
Slash's Image	7	8	8	61	75	3.30
Big Hans	5	3w	62	8	8	15.40

dq-Disqualified and Placed Fourth.

Royal Package (Dupuy) 12.80 6.80 5.00
Night Crawler (Williams) 23.60 12.60
Frieda's Frolic (Dalgo) 5.40

DAILY DOUBLE (1-3) PAID $32.40

EXACTA (3-6) PAID $319.40

3—$1,600, 4½ furlongs, :54⅘.

Horse	PP	¼	Str.	Fin.	Odds
Sidewinder	7	3hd	31½	11½	$1.70
Lou Lander	4	21½	11½	22½	4.50
On The Sun	3	42	43	31½	11.10
Eksanepp	5	81	7½	41	4.70
Perrys Daisy	2	1	2hd	52	14.90
Small Crasher	8	5½	51	6hd	6.60
Polly Pop Up	1	61½	6hd	71	8.70
Eskimotive	9	71	83	83½	18.20
Irish Amber	6	9	9	9	20.20

Sidewinder (Dalgo) 5.40 3.60 3.20
Lou Lander (Martin) 4.80 3.60
On The Sun (Dupuy) 3.40

TRIZACTA (7-4-3) PAID $248.60
31-TICKETS

4—$1,800, 4½ furlongs, :54.

Horse	PP	¼	Str.	Fin.	Odds
Black John	7	21½	11½	13	$ .60
Moulik	4	31½	31½	2no	11.80
Mountain Mamma	1	6½	4½	34	7.00
Grovie's Star	2	41½	51½	41½	13.10
Chanook	5	1½	2hd	51	28.60
Mischevious Miss	8	7½	71	6hd	8.60
Wyane's Chance	3	8	8	73½	6.70
Welfare King	6	5hd	61	8	19.80

Figure 3.1. First known publication of the term *welfare queen* (*Washington Post*, September 1, 1973, p. D10).

Yet before credit or blame can be levied on journalists for introducing the welfare queen to the American lexicon or Reagan for making it a household term, we cannot ignore the possibility of an earlier vernacular usage that may have prompted one thoroughbred owner to name his horse Welfare Queen. After all, before there was a welfare queen, there was a welfare king.

In the December 10, 1949, edition of the *Saturday Evening Post*, the writer Rufus Jarman reported on welfare "chiselers" in Detroit, citing John E. O'Connor as one of the most notorious of these cheats, having already been dubbed by newspapers as "Detroit's 'Welfare King.'" A father of fourteen, his crime was an inability to support his children, a fact that landed him in jail numerous times and many of his children into juvenile homes. Jarman was not the only "welfare king" to appear in the newspapers. A closer look at the newspaper clip that announced the racehorse Welfare Queen's win reveals another horse that raced that day: Welfare King. To what extent "welfare kings" or "welfare queens" were in the common vernacular is unknown. What is clear is that the stereotype of welfare recipients committing fraud was already well established by the late 1970s when the *welfare queen* became a household term.

Why does the name matter so much? Because it codified a story into an easily remembered term, one that could pack the entire story into a single, memorable phrase. In fact, the welfare queen appears in the mass media most often as a kernel narrative, presumed to be so well known it need not be fully articulated to be understood. The power of the kernel narrative is that it mirrors the work of narrative more generally to capture a coherent plot with vivid details that can be easily remembered and boils it down even further, making it more economical, memorable, and transportable.

ORANGE FOR VODKA

Reagan's first story of welfare fraud in California came from a friend, out of the oral tradition and back into it. His second story about the woman in Chicago came from the news but lodged firmly in the oral tradition, as well as the public consciousness. Both stories continue to be attributed to Reagan but have also spawned variants and joined other versions in the oral tradition as we will see in later chapters. His third story—the "Orange for Vodka" story—continues to be told today as well but is rarely attributed to Reagan by contemporary storytellers, suggesting the folk tradition has superseded the need for historical antecedent and presidential authority.

The story first came to light when fellow Republican Bob Packwood complained to a *New York Times* reporter of Reagan's use of spurious anecdotes in conversations with senior Republican leadership:

Senator Bob Packwood, Republican of Oregon, says he is sometimes dismayed in meetings with President Reagan because the President responds to the concerns of Republican leaders "on a totally different track."

   For example, Mr. Packwood said, Pete Domenici of New Mexico, the chairman of the Senate Budget Committee, might note at a meeting that "'we've got a $120 billion deficit coming,' and the President says, 'You know, a person yesterday, a young man, went into a grocery store and he had an orange in one hand and a bottle of vodka in the other, and he paid for the orange with food stamps and he took the change and paid for the vodka. That's what's wrong.'

   "And we just shake our heads." (*New York Times* 1982)

The story was published on March 2, 1982, under the headline "Reagan's Concept of America Hurts Party, Packwood Says." Despite being buried on page D22, the story got picked up by newspapers around the country and ultimately led to a series of questions during a House nutrition subcommittee meeting about the veracity of this story. In her testimony, Assistant Secretary of Agriculture Mary C. Jarratt referred to the story, saying, "We will try to find the source of the story. It's unfortunate if the President was misinformed." She went on to explain that food stamps cannot be used to buy alcohol and that the most change one can receive from food stamps was from a dollar, concluding, "It's not possible to buy a bottle of vodka with ninety-nine cents." Most damning, perhaps, was her final critique: "Examples in the extreme do not represent a constructive approach to the issue." Democrat representative Frederick W. Richmond also responded to the story, voicing a concern held by many of his Democrat peers: "'If there is a major fraud for us to focus upon,' Mr. Richmond said, 'it is the fraud upon the public of repeating untrue stories. We don't need to change the program to counter these myths. We need to stop the storytellers'" (Pear 1982a).

   Stopping the storytellers would prove to be a tall order. Evidence from the oral tradition suggests Reagan was not the only one telling these stories. Once again, he served less as an originator of legends and more as a prominent mouthpiece for them. Growing up in the 1970s, Andrew Bennett spent time in group homes until he was emancipated at eighteen and found himself on the street with little financial or emotional support. Food stamps helped. But he also saw how they could be abused: "Back in the day when you had paper money, you just went into the store with a dollar [food stamp coupon] and you buy a little Hershey or tootsie roll, which was like three cents. And you got a bunch of change back. And you can go and buy yourself a beer. And that's how it was done way back then." Tracy Salisbury was a checkout clerk and saw the same behavior:

   When I was a teenager, I worked at a local grocery store. And it was back when people had the paper food stamps.

And I still hear people talk about this to this day. But they could literally come through with a dollar food stamp and buy a candy bar. Back then the candy bars were fifty cents or less. Well, you could give them change as long it was under a dollar, so they would come by and buy a candy bar and get the change, and they would keep going through different lines buying something that was under a dollar to get the change. Then they would either buy a forty of malt liquor or cigarettes or whatever.

So I think that's what some of that comes from. And I witnessed that myself because it drove us crazy. We would be like, "I can't believe . . ." But you couldn't not do it because that's the way the law was set up.

And I think those debit cards have helped a lot with that.

Reporting at the time when Reagan was telling this story, *People* magazine referred to the story as "a familiar anecdote" (Bachrach 1982). The reactions from Bob Packwood, Mary Jarratt, Frederick Richmond, and even Reagan's own deputy press secretary suggest the same.[8] The story effectively provided vivid details to a claim he had made a few months earlier during his State of the Union speech where he declared that "virtually every American who shops in a local supermarket is aware of the daily abuses that take place in the food stamp program." He seemed to be referencing stories he told back in 1976 on the campaign trail alongside the Linda Taylor story about working people who were outraged as a "strapping young buck" ahead of them in the grocery line bought T-bone steaks with food stamps (Nordheimer 1976). Once again, a story of welfare abuse was shared widely by the president of the United States, ensuring that the fraud of a few would be understood as the norm of the many.

Today, the "Orange for Vodka" story is one of the most common stories told about welfare fraud—second only to another story in Reagan's repertoire of stories of people buying steaks with their food stamps (Lopez 2014)—with one important revision: the alcohol (or cigarettes or lottery tickets) are purchased with a separate wad of cash. With the introduction of the Electronic Benefits Transfer (EBT) card, change is no longer given at all. The critique however, remains, indicting the aid recipient twofold: first, for how they spend their money, and second, for having money at all. According to these stories, people should not buy luxury items like alcohol if they receive government assistance. Second, if they *do* have disposable income to afford alcohol, clearly they are not as needy as they say they are and should have their food stamps revoked (see chaps. 7 and 8 for versions of these stories). Accordingly, today's stories neatly address the flaw of Reagan's original story, allowing the outrage to continue unabated.

WADING INTO DEEP WATERS

Reagan's stories of the immoral, unethical, and illegal activities of aid recipients were shared at a moment when antiwelfare sentiment was deepening. Despite the fact that Americans have consistently supported the idea of government assistance for the poor (cf. Page and Shapiro 1992, 124), the 1960s revealed a growing distrust of welfare programs that even in the middle of Lyndon B. Johnson's War on Poverty compelled him to lament, "The welfare system pleases no one" (Kohler-Hausman 2017, 121–22; citing Michelmore 2012, 76). Two historical trends help explain this growing dissatisfaction: one racial, one criminal.

First, during the 1960s as more and more African Americans migrated to the North to escape the Jim Crow South and the civil rights movement grew, assistance programs began to open up to previously excluded racial minorities (Kohler-Hausmann 2017, 129–30; Quadagno 1994, chap. 3; Trattner 1974, chap. 14). The result was that welfare began to be seen less as a program for white widows, children, and disabled workers and more for single black, and eventually Latina, women. The Progressive Era push in the 1920s for mothers' pensions, by assigning value to the work of women raising children in the home, was being replaced with the view that wage labor was more important than childrearing. Second, as Martin Gilens has shown in his influential book *Why Americans Hate Welfare*, the belief that the ranks of aid recipients were filled with cheats and chiselers was growing thanks to anti-welfare-fraud campaigns of the 1960s and 1970s at the state level: "During the same period that anti-fraud rhetoric and campaigns escalated, the public faith in welfare declined dramatically. Where 60 percent of poll respondents supported more public support for welfare in 1960, only 20 percent did in 1973. Where a plurality in 1961 thought the state invested 'too little' in welfare, the plurality in 1977 thought the state spent 'too much.' By 1976, 85 percent of a poll agreed that 'too many people on welfare cheat by getting money they are not entitled to'" (Kohler-Hausmann 2015, 766).

Julilly Kohler-Hausmann provides the political context for this shift and for Reagan's views on welfare by considering the welfare reform debates during Nixon's presidency. Where Nixon's Family Assistance Plan would blur lines between wage earners and single parents to provide a minimum family income and exponentially expand the welfare rolls, Reagan's plan would shrink them by defunding programs and denying benefits to previously eligible families (Kohler-Hausmann 2017, 134–40). The picture that emerges is a political landscape with policy recommendations that swung wildly from inclusion to exclusion over the course of a decade, with aid recipients increasingly blamed for their circumstances. Even Nixon, who was trying to pass legislation that would help erase stigmatizing boundaries among the poor, employed political rhetoric that played to the us-versus-them, deserving-versus-undeserving rhetoric that would become a hallmark of Reagan's stories: "It is incredible that we have allowed a system of law under which one person can be penalized for doing an honest day's work and another can be rewarded for doing nothing at all. . . . The person on welfare can often have a higher income than his neighbor who holds a low paying job" (Nixon, quoted in Kohler-Hausmann 2017, 139). The sentiment would be echoed with eerie similarity by Donald Trump almost forty-five years later as he began to float his own ideas about welfare reform.[9]

THE IMPACT OF A STORY AND AN ARCHETYPE

In the context of growing antiwelfare sentiment, a folk narrative tradition that traded in welfare abuse stories, and newspaper stories that cataloged abuse, Reagan's story rose to the fore. Opinions about welfare have waxed and waned, but the welfare queen has endured. A number of scholars have attempted to explain these shifts in opinion. Martin Gilens has provided the most extensive explanation through his analysis of public opinion polls, finding that while age, marital status, family income, political ideology, party affiliation, and views about individualism are all statistically significant predictors of opposition to welfare spending, two factors outpace the others by three and four times the others: whether people believe blacks are lazy and whether people believe aid recipients are undeserving (1999, 93). In terms of race, these findings extend beyond welfare spending. When people were asked about black aid recipients, their views were consistently more negative than when asked about whites, up to four times more negative (100).

But what triggers these stereotypes? Why would these views wax and wane over time? Gilens suggests it is all about the economy. By tracking changes in per capita gross domestic product (GDP) with the tendency of people to blame the poor for their circumstances rather than forces beyond their control, Gilens concludes that when the economy declines, so does criticism of welfare recipients (1999, 48–49). At first glance, one might assume this trend can be attributed to the fact that more people find themselves out of work and in need of help during recessions. However, opinions of the poor, the middle class, and the wealthy all shift in similar ways (49–52). Rather, it appears that in times of economic prosperity, jobs are assumed available to all, leading people to assume that if you are poor, it is because you do not want to work, but that in times of economic depression, even hard workers may find themselves unemployed. Gilens's hypothesis is based on a narrow window of time, however, and for more than half of the duration, opinion does not track as it should. He explains the lengthy anomaly of the 1980s, when public opinion should have been much more negative than it was, by arguing that people were well aware that the prosperity of the 1980s did not "trickle down" to the poor as Reagan predicted it would, creating more sympathetic views of aid recipients than per capita GDP would suggest (49).

A different but not contradictory explanation can be drawn from the research conducted by Robert Shapiro and John Young comparing changes of attitudes

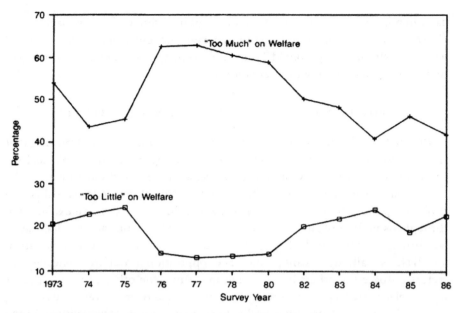

Figure 3.2. Liberal rebound in opinion toward welfare spending (Shapiro and Young 1989, 62).

about welfare spending between 1973 and 1986 (1989, 62; see fig. 3.2). The authors include the graph as evidence of a "liberal backlash" in opinion about cuts to welfare spending once Reagan took office: "Coinciding with the rhetoric and policies of the Reagan administration and especially with the recession, public support for maintaining and expanding government assistance rebounded since the early 1980s, and Americans rejected further cuts in social welfare programs" (Shapiro and Young 1989, 61). When Reagan entered office in 1980, he had strong public support for two issues he had campaigned on: increased funding for the military and decreased funding for welfare. Over the course of his term, he watched that support dwindle. Why? Had people stopped listening to him now that he was president, as George Edwards's hypothesis of the impotence of the bully pulpit might suggest (2006)? A more defensible conclusion is that people were responding to what Reagan did in his first few years in office and adjusting their assessment accordingly. He passed the largest peacetime increase in defense spending in US history and "sharply reduced or eliminated welfare benefits for the 'working poor'" (Edwards 2006, 54–57; see also Pear 1982b; Mink and Solinger 2003, 441). What was too much in 1980 before Reagan's cuts was too little in 1982 after them. In this way, Reagan was too successful in his initial efforts rather than not successful enough.[10]

The rejection of "further cuts in social welfare programs" is part of the backlash Shapiro and Young identify. But what of the rhetoric of the Reagan administration? It would be naive to suggest that the story of the welfare queen single-handedly transformed Reagan's proposals as a candidate into policy as president. Too many factors are involved in the passage of legislature and the shaping of public opinion. However, some of the most negative views about welfare policy, spending, and recipients accompany those periods when Reagan was most actively telling his stories about welfare. For example, negative views about welfare spending dropped from 1973 to 1974, increased modestly from 1974 to 1975, and then shot up from 1975 to 1976 to peak a year later before declining over the next seven years. In 1974, the *Chicago Tribune* broke the story of Linda Taylor, calling her the "Welfare Queen." By January 1976, Reagan was telling the welfare queen story at campaign stops across the country. The year that Reagan was hitting town after town with a stump speech that vilified welfare recipients was the same year that saw the most dramatic increase in beliefs that the government was spending too much on welfare and led to the most negative views of welfare in at least a dozen years. For example, Americans were polled in 1969, 1971, and 1976 and asked whether they thought people on welfare cheated the system. In 1969, 71 percent of people said yes; in 1971, the number had dropped to 62 percent. But in 1976, the number had jumped to 85 percent.[11] Correlation is not causation, but Reagan's stories certainly found fertile ground among the American public and may have helped till the soil.

Returning to the survey of opinions on welfare spending and expanding the scope to the present, another trend appears (chart 3.1). The most negative views of welfare spending appear twice: once when Reagan was telling his welfare queen stories and again as Republican legislators were preparing a welfare reform bill that, after vetoing the first two, Democrat president Bill Clinton signed into law in 1996. As Ange-Marie Hancock argues in her analysis of news stories and congressional debates during 1995 and 1996, the figure of the welfare queen was evoked repeatedly in characteristic, if not in name, by legislators on both sides of the aisle (2004, 93).[12] Focused on the welfare queen as a newly packaged archetype of long-standing stereotypes of the single, poor black mother, Hancock derived fourteen characteristics identified in the scholarship of this figure and used them to code a random selection of 149 news stories about welfare and 81 congressional debates. The characteristics included the following: drain national resources, *overly fertile, *don't work, lazy, cross-generational dependency, *single-parent family, drug users, *crime, *teen mothers, duration of welfare, *culture of poverty, *illegitimacy, system abusers, inner-city residents. She found that seven of the ten most frequent characteristics commonly attributed to welfare queens appeared in both the mass media and congressional debates (Hancock 2004, 94; marked here

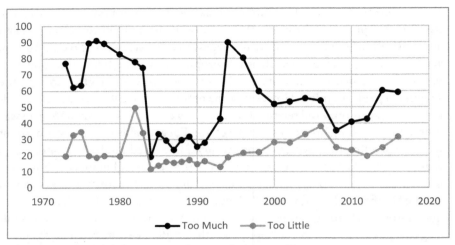

Chart 3.1. Are we spending too much or too little on welfare?
Opinion on welfare spending, 1973–2016.

with an asterisk). More importantly, she found that these fourteen characteristics informed the policy options discussed during debates, in particular recommendations for workfare (56 mentions), state rather than federal programs (37),
family caps (32), regulating teen pregnancy (26), paternal involvement as through
marriage or child support (18), time limits (16), and eligibility for immigrants (12)
(see Hancock 2004, 74).

Her work suggests three important issues to consider. First, the stereotypes
associated with the welfare queen clearly influenced policy proposals, debates,
and legislation. It is not a stretch to suggest that the vivid stories that conveyed
those stereotypes contributed to these policies. Second, if Hancock is right that
"the term *welfare queen* simply gives a name to long-standing beliefs regarding
single, poor African American mothers" (2004, 57), we must view Reagan's story
in a new light, giving credence to claims that although Reagan never mentioned
race, audiences interpreted the story as describing African Americans. In this
way, Reagan's stories could activate existing racist assumptions about black
women, thereby feeding a virulent and damaging stereotype for not only the
poor but for black women as well. Third, in focusing solely on the poor African
American mother, Hancock's analysis overlooks the men implicated in Reagan's
stories and the oral tradition more generally. If one adds the characteristics of
aid recipients drawn from Reagan's stories and not just stereotypes of poor black
women, the only two policy recommendations that Hancock found had no correlation with the welfare queen stereotype in mass media coverage—revising,
reducing, or eliminating the food stamp program or cutting Medicaid (74)—are

both explained by stories in the broader narrative tradition. Reagan's "Orange for Vodka" story, however, perfectly aligns with such a recommendation, as do the numerous related stories about people buying steak, crab legs, or other luxury items with food stamps. Though less common, stories of able-bodied men claiming disability to avoid work help explain the proposed cuts to Medicaid. So although the welfare queen archetype can explain some of the policy recommendations, the broader narrative tradition is needed to explain others.

Further, it is clear that welfare legislation has been regularly proposed—and in some cases, passed—that responds directly to many of the unproven accusations about the poor made in these stories. The connection between the narrative tradition and public policy is often impossible to ignore. In 2016, just before the House of Representatives voted to cut food stamp funding by 5 percent, Republican representative Tim Huelskamp from Kansas declared, "You can no longer sit on your couch or ride a surfboard like Jason in California and expect the federal taxpayer to feed you" (Delaney 2013). Huelskamp was referring to the unemployed musician Jason Greenslate, dubbed "the Food Stamp Surfer," who was profiled by Fox News surfing and buying sushi and lobster with his EBT card. Like Linda Taylor, Greenslate was used as a poster child for welfare rather than an anomaly. Similar responses have come from state legislators, such as Republican state senator Patty Ritchie, who proposed legislation so that food stamps could not be used to buy lobster, steak, or energy drinks (Fox News Insider 2016).

Such proposals are not new. Just after Reagan's unsuccessful bid for president when he introduced the welfare queen to the nation, Jimmy Carter signed the Food Stamp Act of 1977. One of the provisions debated but ultimately eliminated from the final bill was a provision that limited the types of foods that could be purchased, excluding those with low nutritional value (Caswell and Yaktine 2013). More recently, President Trump's budget proposal released on February 12, 2018, suggested limiting half of a family's benefits to boxes of food selected by the government, a restriction dramatically out of step with both food and nutritional decision making as well as the Republican platform that professes greater personal liberties and freedoms from government control (Dempsey 2018).

In the end, antiwelfare stories reflect as much as create the atmosphere for such policies. What is clear is that they are a vibrant part of this perception loop that has a very real influence on policy and people.

THE WELFARE QUEEN TODAY

In 1985, the American Enterprise Institute teamed up with the *Los Angeles Times* to conduct an opinion survey on poverty. In 2016, they revisited that survey, asking many of the same questions. Overall, views of welfare and poverty have

Question	1985	2016	Change
Overall, do you think most poor people are hardworking . . .	50%	65%	+15%
. . . or do you think most poor people do not work very hard?	25%	21%	−4%
In general, do you think that welfare benefits give poor people a chance to stand on their own two feet and get started again . . .	19%	35%	+16%
. . . or do you think they make poor people dependent and encourage them to stay poor?	59%	54%	−5%
Do you think that most poor people who receive welfare benefits prefer to stay on welfare . . .	63%	61%	−2%
. . . or would rather earn their own living?	25%	36%	+11%

Table 3.1. Shifts in views of welfare and the poor from 1985 to 2016. (Interactive charts comparing the two surveys can be found online; see Lauder and Lauter 2016).

not shifted dramatically, but when they have, it is toward a more positive view (table 3.1). In 1985, people were more likely to think that poor people did not work very hard, that welfare benefits encouraged dependence, and that welfare recipients preferred welfare to work than they are today. Despite these gains, opinions remain intensely negative, particularly in terms of welfare. Only 21 percent of people today think the poor do not work hard, but almost three times that number think people on welfare prefer it to work, and more than twice as many think welfare encourages dependency. This view aligns with decades of research that suggests the American public agrees the government should take care of the poor but cannot agree on how to do it. The collateral damage falls at the feet of welfare recipients.

Political rhetoric during presidential elections has remained particularly negative. John Blake summarized examples from the 2012 Republican primaries in his CNN article "Return of the Welfare Queen": "While campaigning in Iowa, Santorum said 'I don't want to make black people's lives better by giving them somebody else's money.' He later said he didn't mean to say black people, but meant people. Romney has repeatedly said that Obama wants to transform America into an 'entitlement society.' Gingrich has attracted the most attention for his language. He called Obama a food-stamp president, questioned poor children's work ethic, and said poor people should want paychecks, not handouts" (Blake 2012). One could add Mitt Romney's "forty-seven percent" rhetoric to this list, as well as Paul Ryan's more recent "makers and takers" (Liasson 2017).

Outside of election years, the welfare queen and other welfare chiselers remain popular figures in the mass media from both the political right and left. On the one hand, conservative politicians, pundits, and news outlets most often evoke the archetype of the cheating aid recipient through coded language to justify policy in ways mirroring election years. However, periodically, the welfare queen gets updated with a new case of fraud to maintain the archetype as real. While Linda Taylor may never be dethroned, her court expands every few years, most recently with Jason Greenslate, "the Food Stamp Surfer."

On the other hand, there is the use of the welfare queen by liberal pundits to bludgeon conservatives and Republicans whenever policies are proposed to cut social welfare programs, pointing to the welfare queen as the political right's biggest lie. A particularly common move is to highlight the hypocrisy of demonizing the welfare queen while handing out billions in corporate subsidies, tax breaks, and bailouts (chap. 12). In either case, the welfare queen as term and narrative evokes a deeply damaging stereotype that has moved far beyond her humble beginnings as a single case in Chicago. The study of how legends work can help explain why.

Legends provide socially acceptable ways to express anxieties, fears, or desires.[13] Legends of stolen kidneys provide tourists a way to discuss anxieties around travel abroad, and legends about needles infected with HIV hidden in movie theater seats, gas pump handles, and ball pits provide people a way to discuss their uncertainty about the spread of AIDS. Legends continue to be told as long as the anxieties, fears, and desires that power them remain. Accordingly, stories of the welfare queen are far less effective at tracking fraud than tracking fears about fraud. Consider the shifts in public perception about welfare, whether during economic recessions, policy debates, or changes in funding. Instances of fraud do not wax and wane during these periods, but anxieties about who is getting assistance and why does. In this way, welfare queen stories tell us far more about the general public than about aid recipients or the welfare system.

The anxieties expressed in stories about welfare are explored in depth in the chapters in section 3 and include economic justice, morality, race, and immigration. Running throughout all of these anxieties is a sense of the loss of power and an unfair economic system in a world of limited good. In what is conceived of as a topsy-turvy world, hardworking taxpayers struggle while lazy freeloaders enjoy lives of luxury. These anxieties, coupled with close attention to genre and the structure of these narratives, reveal yet another reason stories of the welfare queen remain so pervasive in American culture. Virtually detail for detail, the welfare queen and her story stand in direct opposition to the most fundamental cultural myth of this country: the American dream.

THE AMERICAN DREAM

The American dream forms the bedrock of national ideology in the United States, shaping norms for social, economic, political, personal, and cultural identities and values. At its core are values of independence, equality, hard work, and moral-ity. The result? Financial success and personal happiness. Although the Ameri-can dream has meant different things to different people, shifting according to individual circumstances as well as historical epochs and tracking important changes in social and political ideology, its basic tenets remain recognizable.[14] The story typically begins with a person of humble beginnings who faces chal-lenges in life due to their relative poverty, but by working hard and making good and moral choices in life, the individual gains both personal and financial success. Even before the term *American dream* was coined, the story had been captured and codified by Horatio Alger Jr. in 1868 in his Ragged Dick book series and by numerous bootstrap stories that followed. Although Alger's stories remain the quintessential American dream narratives, few readers know or remember that the protagonist succeeds not simply by hard work and moral strength but by good luck and wealthy benefactors. In the original Ragged Dick story, for example, young Dick is helped by Mr. Greyson, who invites him to church; Mr. Whitney, who gives him five dollars, a small fortune at the time for a young and often home-less shoeshine boy that allows him to rent his first apartment and open a bank account; and Mr. Rockwell, who gives him a new suit and respectable job after Dick saves his son from drowning. Good luck and generous benefactors have disappeared in more recent articulations of the American dream. Hard work and moral fortitude alone are expected to be sufficient.

The American dream is a story for every American citizen, as well as those yearning to become one. Although Alger's protagonist Ragged Dick is native born, the American dream has a common immigrant version, one held by hopeful migrants around the world. The key symbol of this story is the Statue of Liberty, the motto is that the United States is "the land of opportunity," and the ethos is that nothing except your own work ethic can hold you back or keep you from suc-cess. A meritocracy without hierarchies of class continues to entice immigrants to the United States, particularly in countries where opportunities for work and financial stability seem impossibly out of reach.

Increasingly, however, attainment of the American dream has seemed impos-sibly out of reach as well. The wealth gap that has exploded in the past decade has made it more and more difficult for a family to survive on a single income. With-out a college degree, many feel the American dream is increasingly out of reach. Over the past two decades, faith in the American dream has slowly declined, with fewer people believing they can get ahead with hard work and more people believ-ing such determination is simply not sufficient to guarantee success (fig. 3.3). Unequal access to education, job opportunities, and capital has led many people to question the promise of the American dream. For millennials—the genera-tion of Americans born between 1977 and 1994—the loss of faith in the American

Does Hard Work Lead to Success?

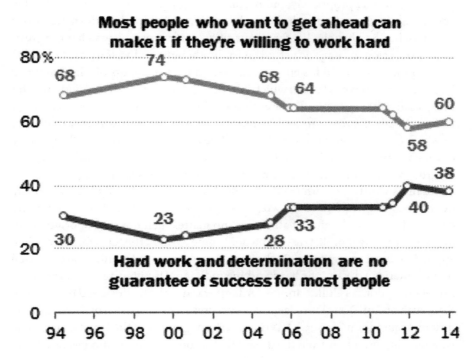

Most people who want to get ahead can make it if they're willing to work hard

80%···74···

68   68
                                                  64
                                                                        60

60 ···

                                                              58

                                                              38
40 ···

      30   23   33   40
20   23   28

Hard work and determination are no guarantee of success for most people

0
      94   96   98   00   02   04   06   08   10   12   14

Survey conducted Jan. 15-19, 2014. Q44a.

PEW RESEARCH CENTER/USA TODAY

Figure 3.3. Does hard work lead to success? Fluctuations in belief that hard work is sufficient to get ahead, 1994–2014 (Pew Research Center 2014).

dream is even greater, with 49 percent believing it is viable and 48 percent who do not, statistics tied to a leveling off of financial growth and the inability to achieve greater success than their parents (Bump 2015).[15]

These two components of the American dream—hard work as the only requirement for success and the promise of greater wealth with each successive generation—have been central parts of the dream since the term was first coined in 1931. Like the welfare queen, the American dream as a concept is an old one, but as a term, it has a more recent and identifiable origin. Convinced that no one would shell out hard-earned money for a book about a dream, James Truslow Adams's editor refused to allow Adams to title his book *The American Dream*. Adams acquiesced but used the term over thirty times in the book that would be published both appropriately and prophetically as *The Epic of America* (Cullen 2004, 3–4). In his preface to the book, Adams wrote "of that American dream of a better, richer, and happier life for all our citizens of every rank which is the greatest contribution we have as yet made to the thought and welfare of the world" ([1931] 1941, vii–viii). In his epilogue, he reminded his readers of "the American Dream, that dream of a land in which life should be better and richer and fuller for every man, with opportunity for each according to ability or achievement. . . . It is not a dream of motor cars and high wages merely, but a dream of a social order in which each man and each woman shall be able to attain to the fullest stature of which they are innately capable, and be recognized by others for what they are, regardless of the fortuitous circumstances of birth or position" (404).

Adams's words are both ironic and prescient. In describing the ideal dream, he refers to the "welfare of the world," employing the term *welfare* as a positive concern for the well-being of all people, no matter their country of origin, with no hint of the anger or distrust that would come to mark the term for many when applied to social programs to aid the poor. And yet even in this initial articulation of the American dream, the hardworking individual is pitted against a system to protect the poor. As Cullen argues, "Adams was deeply disillusioned by Franklin Roosevelt and his New Deal, feeling they represented a betrayal of American traditions of autonomy" (2003, 4). Written at the beginning of the Great Depression, Adams's *Epic of America* and the dream that stood as its foundation were a direct indictment of the welfare state. Ultimately, that indictment would be captured as a story: the legend of the welfare queen.

The two narratives are built on deep-seated assumptions about work, morality, and success making comparison dramatic in its contrast (fig. 3.4). Charted structurally, one can see where the two narratives diverge (table 3.2). If the welfare queen story were a simple negative reflection of the American dream story, it would pose no threat, reinforcing rather than challenging the fundamental cultural myth of the American dream. Such a story would end with the person living in dire poverty with no one to blame but themselves. But the welfare queen story concludes with the same success as the American dream; in fact, the life of luxury is even more explicit for the welfare queen than the American dream. In the American dream, the protagonist has his own home and an increase in disposable income for a relatively comfortable life. In the welfare queen story, however, the protagonist has fur coats, expensive jewelry, designer clothes, and luxury sedans. So while the American dream tells us that with hard work and strong morals, working independently we can establish a stable life, achieve marital bliss,

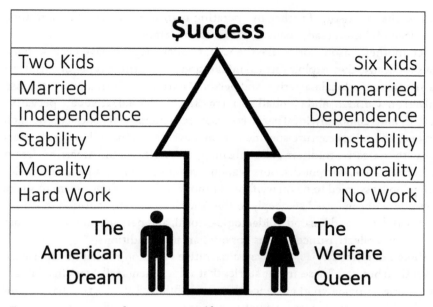

Figure 3.4. American dream versus welfare queen narratives.

Structure	American Dream	Welfare Queen
Orientation	Humble circumstances	Humble circumstances
Complicating Action	Go to school, hard work, strong moral compass	Drop out of school, no work, immoral behavior
Climax	Gain stability, become independent, get married, have two children	Lose stability, become dependent, do not get married, have six children
Resolution	Earn financial wealth and live a life of luxury	Handed financial wealth and live a life of luxury

Table 3.2. Comparisons of the narrative structures of the American dream and the welfare queen.

and become wealthy, the welfare queen story tells us that the reverse is true—that with no work, loose morals, and dependence on the government, we can live a life of luxury. Such a story is cultural blasphemy.

In their book *Made to Stick*, Chip Heath and Dan Heath argue that stories are inherently "sticky" or memorable and that we can increase that stickiness by ensuring the stories we tell have a simple idea, concrete details, resonate emotionally, and fit within a frame we understand (2007). The welfare queen story has all of these characteristics. Further, by operating as an anti–American dream story, these legends have a ready-made frame for interpretation.

Yet another reason stories like the welfare queen legend have been so tenacious is because they exploit vertical integration among three types of narrative: master narrative, local narrative, and personal narrative (Corman 2013; see also Halverson, Corman, and Goodall 2011, 179–82). Master narratives are pervasive spatially and temporally, local narratives capture contemporary social events, and personal narratives capture specific personal events. As the following chapters reveal, the narrative tradition of welfare integrates all three: the American dream master narrative, current discourses about welfare policy, and personal stories with people assumed to be on welfare. It is no wonder we cannot seem to shake the welfare queen—tied so deeply to the American dream, captured in simple and vivid detail, and located in ideological, local, and personal contexts—from neither our collective unconscious nor our narrative traditions.

There are other stories, however, a narrative tradition rooted in experience rather than hearsay. These are the stories that aid recipients tell. Stark in contrast, their stories provide vivid evidence that the politicized stories that have dominated public discourse require drastic revision.

NOTES

1. While this book is focused on the vernacular tradition, it is worth nothing that "the welfare queen" has also resurfaced recently in popular culture on the Netflix show "GLOW: Gorgeous Ladies of Wrestling," initially playing to, and then critiquing, the stereotype. The fictionalized series purports to tell the behind the scenes story of the nonfiction wrestling show of the same name from the 1980s, although the original GLOW did *not* include a wrestler named "the Welfare Queen."

2. When the White House director of communications David Gergen was asked about Reagan's story about children in a wealthy neighborhood getting free school lunch, he responded, "He heard it at a dinner party'" (Green and MacColl 1983, 12).

3. See Gilens (1999, 102–32) and Neubeck and Cazenave (2001, 96–110). The impact of the Moynihan Report (as it is more commonly referred to) cannot be underestimated, spawning a national debate about a "culture of poverty" (see Small, Harding, and Lamont 2010). It should also be noted that scholars regularly accuse Reagan of racially coding his stories and comments. Ian Lopez tackles the issue head on in his book *Dog Whistle Politics*, finding ample evidence for such accusations (2014, 55–76). See also Kohler-Hausmann (2017, 5) and Ortiz and Briggs (2003). I address the issue of racial codes in more depth in chap. 7.

4. Audio recording of the radio address is housed in the Hoover Archives, Ronald Reagan Radio Commentary Sound Recordings 1976, box 4. In the address, and for this first time on record, Reagan adopts the term "the welfare queen." Introducing the story with background on aid providers, he says, "They had been touting controls which they said made welfare fraud a minor problem when the welfare queen, as she's now called, suddenly burst onto the scene." For an audio clip of the speech, see On the Media (2013). For additional versions of the story from 1976, see the version from New Hampshire quoted earlier, as well as a version from January told in Asheville, North Carolina (Levin 2013, with complete audio "Ronald Reagan Radio Commentary Sound Recordings" 1976, 76–03).

5. Popik, on his blog, traces the history of the term and includes the first known published record (the racehorse name), where the *Oxford English Dictionary* does not (2006). Both, however, highlight the next use: the 1974 *Chicago Tribune* article that calls Linda Taylor a "welfare queen" (Bliss 1974); and "welfare queen," under the entry for "welfare," in the *Oxford English Dictionary* (2014).

6. Despite combined efforts from the Elon librarian Teresa LePors and her friend and horse racing aficionado Beverly Moore, we were not able to find the barn or a living person to explain how the horse had been named.

7. See, for example, the story in *Jet Magazine* titled "Alleged 'Welfare Queen' Is Accused of $154,000 Ripoff" (1974).

8. Reagan's deputy press secretary Peter Roussel was reported as saying, "He did not know where the President had read or heard the anecdote about food stamps and vodka. However, he said that the President would not tell such stories 'unless he thought they were accurate'" (Pear 1982a).

9. See chap. 1 for Trump's quote. Nixon's comments were in a speech on welfare reform at the Republican Governors Association on April 19, 1971. Both men ignore the domestic work of parents in pitting these two groups against each other.

10. Robert Shapiro, collaborating this time with Benjamin Page, revisits these data, arguing, "The economic stringencies of the 1970s, and conservative interpretations thereof, caused a dip in desires for government spending on welfare, redistribution, medical care, the cities, and minorities—though not (appreciably) on education or social security. Later, when the economy entered and then recovered from the 1981–1982 recession and the Reagan administration was seen as cutting appropriations to the bone, public sentiment for more spending rebounded" (Page and Shapiro 1992, 136).

11. Appendix 1, chart A1.8: "Do people on welfare cheat the system?"

12. Hancock refers to the figure of the welfare queen as a public identity, more coherent, complex, and stable than a stereotype (2004, 15–16). In keeping with a folkloristic approach, I use the term *archetype* to situate the figure of the welfare queen within a body of scholarship that recognizes how a character and motif that can be deployed in narrative, as well as other traditional forms of communication, including jokes, cartoons, and memes. Although past folklorists have studied

archetypes as psychological universals in the way that Carl Jung originally developed the concept, my use here follows a more generic approach as a recurring type constructed culturally rather than psychologically.

13. See Best and Bogle (2014), Brunvand (1981), Ellis (2003), Guerin and Miyazuki (2006), Kitta (2012), and Rosnow (1991), among others.

14. See, in particular, Cullen (2004) and Walker (1983).

15. Bump (2015) cites Harvard University Institute of Politics (2015).

SECTION 2

INSIDER VIEWS
Aid Recipients' Stories

FOUR

—ᴍ—

ORIGIN STORIES

NEVER NAMED FOR CONFIDENTIALITY REASONS, the pseudonymous Lilly Gibbs is nonetheless a legend at the Open Door Clinic (ODC). Tiny but powerful, Lilly has faced incredible challenges but tackles them with a determination that has awed the staff at the clinic, which offers free health care to people who cannot afford insurance but are ineligible for Medicaid. Within days of beginning her volunteer work, student researcher Jamie Albright had heard stories of this dynamic woman, so she was not surprised when she sat down with staff member Lorrie Carter and the first story Lorrie told was about Lilly.

> My first interaction was with a patient that . . . I hadn't been there probably two weeks, and she was waiting on labs. And she stopped me and asked me if I knew how long it would be because she had to get home before it got dark because she didn't have any power, and she needed to be able to see to get to her bed.
>
> I think that was the most difficult thing.
>
> I went home and cried just because the realization of that was, I think, very difficult.

Lorrie told a story about Lilly, but the structure of the narrative makes it clear that the protagonist is Lorrie. Lilly's complication is unresolved. Did she get home before dark? Did she get to bed? Did she ever get her lights turned back on? Lorrie does not tell us. Rather, the story revolves around her own awakening.

Newly employed when she met Lilly, Lorrie did not know what to expect at her job or the scope and scale of the need she would encounter. "It's been a life-changing experience for me," she explained, "because I think that before I came, I didn't realize that a free clinic like this existed. And when I came, I didn't realize what all it involved and what all we did and how many people we helped. And then to get to hear some of the stories of the people that didn't have power and just trying to get by from day to day and not having the money to pay their bills and things like that made me realize how fortunate I am myself even though I don't have a lot of money. So it's been life changing."

It is not long, however, before Lorrie returns to Lilly, prompted by a question about the stories that she shares outside of work. Again, Lorrie does not hesitate.

Well, we had one patient that when she first came . . . It's the same patient that said that about the lights. When she first came, I think she weighed seventy-something pounds. She has diabetes, severe diabetes.

And now I think she weighs a hundred and thirty pounds. She's doing great. And I always tell her that she looks great.

She's living in the Burlington Housing.

At one time she was really upset about having to turn in paperwork. I brought her back, and I talked to her, and she was crying because she was going to be evicted, and she had lost her unemployment. And at that time, it was when the unemployment . . . They weren't going to be able to get the unemployment anymore. She was just despondent and didn't know what she was going to do. We tried to give her some numbers to help her. And she's had a substance abuse problem as well, but she is doing well and as far as I know not using, taking very good care of herself, and gaining weight, and living in the Burlington Housing.

I think she by far is my most favorite story. And I tell that just because I feel like that is what we do. We are helping people. At the end of the day I don't think it's about who's on what drugs and who's what color. At the end of the day it's that they need help, and that's what we're here to do is help them. That's what it's about. And a lot of these patients have been helped.

Lorrie does not tell Lilly's story. She tells her story with Lilly in it. For aid providers, a client's success is also the program's success. Tracy Salisbury, the executive director of the ODC, tells a similar story, with a similar conclusion. Frequently called to speak to donors and benefactors and community partners about the work they do at the ODC, Tracy has a storehouse of stories about the successes they have achieved. Again, Lilly's story looms large among them.

And then we do have one diabetic patient that I can tell you is a success story. She came in as a referral from the hospital. Severe diabetic. She weighed eighty-some pounds. She was abusing cocaine.

And she is still a patient of ours; she started about three and a half years ago. She is clean. And she was pretty much homeless; she got evicted from her home. But she is clean. She is doing what she should for her diabetes. She's up to a hundred and thirty pounds. She goes to church every Sunday. We call her our poster child.

It is not by accident that both aid providers mention Lilly's weight and details of her medical history. Their positions at a health clinic inscribe relevance to some factors over others. The same is true structurally, as they both highlighted her transformation: life before the ODC and life with the ODC. Stories shared by aid providers are crucial to the public debate about welfare. Cast within an institutionalized system and normalized to contemporary social and cultural values, these stories operate as critical counternarratives to the legends of the welfare queen. In fact, Tracy suggests a direct contrast between the two by calling Lilly their "poster child." If Linda Taylor is the poster child of fraud and failure, Lilly Gibbs is the poster child for integrity and success.

Replacing a negative symbol with a positive one can feel satisfying after decades of vicious stereotyping, but both risk manipulation: one heralding the worst of the worst as the normal, the other idealizing the best of the best. Yet that is not what Lorrie and Tracy have done. Their stories present a woman who gets frustrated, even angry, who does not always see the light at the end of the tunnel. In other words, their favorite client is not a saint but a complex human who is eminently relatable and determined in ways most of us only wish we were.

When Jamie sits down with Lilly, we understandably hear a different story. In fact, we hear several stories as Lilly casts her past through the details of her life in multiple ways toward multiple ends. Significantly, the first story she tells is her climb out of homelessness rather than her initial descent.

> Well, at one point in the past, I lost a home; I did not have a car; I did not have a job; and again I started just walking to East Park Baptist Church. I had a house on Main Street, and I was living on unemployment from a previous job in Greenville, North Carolina, and until that ran out, that's how I was taking care of the house.
>
> But after then, I lost everything. I got to the point, was at the point, whereas I could not pay the rent anymore, did not have lights. I heated by kerosene for a whole winter. And it was my puppy and I at that time.
>
> So during my struggles or living with kerosene and candles and stuff, I start attending East Park Baptist Church, visiting, just trying to get Christ in my life. And as things progressed and I made the decision that that's what I wanted to do, I dedicated myself to life and Jesus and joined East Park Baptist Church.
>
> And along the way . . . We have a great congregation there. And within this congregation, we have missionaries; we have the women's auxiliary; we help people in the community and abroad. And people within the congregation, there's a doctor, there's a lawyer, there's a nurse, and other members that help that really get them on their feet. And of course we work with people at Allied Churches. So they helped me a long way as far as food and shelter and helped me get my car on the road. I did get my driver's license!
>
> And you know these people within this congregation have helped me, too. It was a little struggle, a little inch at a time, but each step paid off, and here I am today with everything that I really need, really.

And so now, after I left that house, I had to go to the shelter because I didn't have a choice, and I stayed at a shelter for only about a month. But meanwhile, the few things that I did have left in the household the church stored . . . in the church for me, as far as my belongings . . . stored in the church until I got out of the boarding house. I was there for about . . . being there over on Davis Street . . . it was less than a year maybe. And then through Alamance Transit Authorities, we have affiliates there, one of my members is a director of that as well, so that was my transportation to get to and from the doctor's and places I needed to go here in Alamance County.

I finally did land a job. Well, right now like I said, I work at Mercantile Outlets. You're not really learning anything; you're not going anywhere, but it's a job. A year and two months, and it has been rough. [Laughs] It has been rough. But I still have to look back and say, "Lord, I thank you."

It's not a whole lot of money and no benefits or anything to that nature. And healthwise it was good to have some job and have some income coming in. And healthwise I have progressed. I have enough income now . . . The church helped me land the house that I'm in now. I have my own house, and now the income that I do have helps, pays my bills, and keep me going. But I'm not satisfied. [Laughs] I'm reaching higher.

Lilly tells her story as a tale of religious redemption, using passive voice to skip the factors that led to her poverty. She mentions neither the mental abuse from her husband nor the alcohol and drugs that she used as an escape. While Lorrie and Tracy tell the beginning and the end and skip the middle, Lilly skips the beginning and dives into the middle, where the story turns around and her descent becomes an ascent. In this way, all three women tell success stories, focusing on the areas of success most relevant to them. But the darker story of her past eventually emerges as she warms up to the audio recorder and the idea of exploring her past in full measure.

"What doesn't kill you makes you stronger," Jamie summarizes after Lilly recounts her struggles to find a home and a job.

"Oooh girl," Lilly exclaims. "Repeat that one more time!"

Lilly laughs, wiping away tears she has shed only moments ago, tears that threaten only a moment later when she remembers her father's clock that she lost when she became homeless or when she points skyward toward heaven, pining: "My dad and mother, brother, sister gone. But we are going to meet back up there." She crosses her arms over her chest defiantly. "But it's not my time yet."

There were times, however, when she wondered if that time was near.

I wasn't able to work. With me, what was going on, I was not able to work, with my health and transportation and other things set me back. And I had a personal . . . I was living with someone. I had a bad relationship problem too, and then I lost everything I had. My little Avon business where I was living with a man in Greenville, and—oh boy—that was the worst five years of my life. [Shakes her head] The first two, fine. After then . . . And I mean he caused a lot of my dilemma too, with how I was living in this relationship. I am trapped. And it wasn't good. And I mean he done something to me mentally and physically. I was asking the Lord, "Please, get me out of this."

But it cost me everything I had. I lost a house, stuff in storage. He right there with me but he didn't care. Here I am. All I went was to work and come back, and . . . everything in the book except myself.[1]

At one point it got physical on my side, too. I had to fight back the best way I could. But you know I was going through something.

And it got to the point, where, finally, Alliance One, which, to my processing, it was the dust and smoke that was that part of that place that gave me bronchitis; it was just a job. And there is no cure.

From an abusive husband to health risks at work, Lilly narrates overlapping challenges that piled up around her.

As she shared her stories, Jamie maintained her side of the conversation, sharing a story about a woman she met the previous week who was with a man who was nice at first, then abusive, and then got hooked on drugs. Lilly recognizes the similarities but focuses on the contrasts.

He didn't do drugs and stuff like that. He was just mean and evil and considered himself . . . As I met him, he was a preacher!

He keep me down. And people in the community . . . Behind my back you want me laying over, living with you, but then again on the outside he's around in the community—"Oh, I'm everything in the book." But then the people in the community saw me like that. They didn't see what was going on inside that trailer, either. I finally got myself on my feet. Let me tell you what happened to me. It was supposed to have been a visit. I finally got the car that I drive now, and I was going to finally get away from him that weekend. He didn't take me nowhere. All my check went to his gas, and cooking and cleaning. I was like a little slave. But I said that visit, when I set foot here, back in Burlington from Greenville, I got out at the convenience store out here on Highway 49, the first person that I saw was Aretha Stacks.

And I got out and see, me not knowing now, living with him I didn't know I was as sick as I was. I fell out [tears up] at that store. I got out, I was going to go in the store, and that was it. I went to that hospital. I mean, I fell out at in the store. This is when I found out, you know, "You have diabetes." And here I wasn't getting . . . It was just all out of control. I said, "I'm getting smaller, stressed, diabetes and all this." My sugar was over four hundred and something. Here I am, how long, the period, how many months I have been trapped in that house with him, living like this, getting smaller and smaller and smaller? Oh yeah, he be like, "It's drugs, it's alcohol, it's this." I'm sick.

I did not know I was that sick. I was living in that situation. There I am, wouldn't even take me to the clinic or doctor, but then again, I didn't know. I couldn't tell people.

Again, back to that testimony. And I come here to visit. And me in that situation that I was in, sugars was four or five hundred. There was no one even knowing that I had the diabetes, not on no medication, no kind of medical care. I could have blacked out or anything on that highway at any moment. But you know, I felt good and everything else I did right now. But it was just the Lord drove that car home. It could've happened at any moment in time. [Tears up] Here I am, doing fifty or sixty, driving, trying to be happy and struggle along, but I was going through a lot of stuff. And then when I did fall out, and oh, I got to the Alamance Regional ... whew. [Crying]

You have to go back to even better [inaudible]. I don't even know. At the weight that I was, and things went down from there to there to there. But you know I never made it back and never, one, never thought about it.

But these things have happened in my life to get me away from him. Because he was killing me, slowly. I mean, really. I was so close to being, just falling out, dying somewhere, and ain't nobody never knew. [Sniffles] Never knew.

I was ran down and about to be ran out. [Laughs] I was about to be toes up. Very close to that situation. And death. I was just about dead.

It wasn't my time. But I say, Jesus, he can guide me home. But what did it cost me? Everything. All I had was the clothes on my back and a suitcase for a change of clothes that weekend. That's what it cost me. Everything else was a loss [crying], was a loss. Behind different situation.

And no, I'm not going to sit here and say, "No, I didn't drink no beer." I wasn't on no hard drugs. I can honestly say, like I told my congregation and church ... I wasn't on no hard drugs, but yes, I was smoking my cigarettes and drinking my beer, but that was my comfort zone. [Crying, getting tissue]

Oooh, girl.

I was locked in that trailer, imprisoned in that trailer, and go to work and go to house and go to work and go to house, and cuss and all and raise Cain, and it was killing me slowly. It was killing me slowly. It was killing me slowly. I don't know who she was! [Laughs] I know who I am today. That person, I don't know who she was; she was just like a little rat running in one hole, and I didn't care!

Jamie interjected, "So you didn't see the light at the end of the tunnel.

I couldn't see that light [laughs], all these other things. All I could see was the darkness, the despair, and ... [crying] day in and day out. I mean I was living on ... sleeping balled up on the sofa and just one step being out the door. One step from being out the door is what I went through. But you know, no one goes, "It's me, me, me."

But it's all right; it's over. And I'm not going back.

And like I said, if you in the situation ... I do have a job. Whew. And it's going to get better. That's all I can tell you right now.

He got the audacity and say, "Oh, hey, how you doing? I'm fine."

And I'm, "Fine."

He finally found a way to call me and stuff like that. He called me time and time, on the holidays, you know: "I'm doing this."

"Good for you."

But then again on the same token to say, he finally getting in contact. "I'm doing just great. You don't bother me. A whole lot better without you," is what I wanted to say. [Laughs]

Again, Jamie offers her perspective, noting that someone once told her that happiness and healthiness is the best revenge.

That's right. You can't tell him the things he did to me. So he's doing a whole lot better. Whew. It was rough.

No, it's all right. I have not sit here and told you anything that's not true, just like I said with East Park Baptist Church. We are in this covenant with them, and there is not anything that I did not express to them yet. They knowed I was drinking and this and that, and you know, I had a DWI . . . I had some charges because I had my little experience with other things. I'm not going sit here and tell you I never smoked crack, because I did. You know . . . What could I do? [Crying] What could I do? It's not like I was out there, doing drugs every night and all. I was at the point where that was the only happiness I got. To cope. That's what I did.

Lilly goes back to those dark days, suffering as she does so. The memories are painful, but the joy at the end is real; she has come out the other side stronger.

Despite the emotional roller coaster, her stories are symmetrical, finding coherence in a life that was anything but. Her first story begins with her jobless and homeless and ends with the attainment of a home and employment. Her second starts and ends with her husband, structurally highlighting the antagonist of the story. Both end in stability and contentment, but they tell very different stories along the way. And the emotional impact is acute. Having dived back into the cause of her homelessness, the defenses she has set up begin to crumble. In her first story, there is no mention of alcohol and drug abuse. In her second, she admits there was some alcohol abuse. By the time she revisits her redemption through Jesus Christ in her third story, her trials are bared wide.

Her stories begin in the artificial context of an interview but end in the natural context of religious testimony. "Just like I said with East Park Baptist Church," she says, repositioning her story within the context of past narrations. The story is a confession, as well as a plea for understanding.

That understanding is often in short supply in the oral tradition of welfare in the United States. Just as Lorrie, Tracy, and Lilly focused on the most relevant parts of her story to craft their own, so too do people across the country, either hearing what they want to hear and dismissing the rest or never hearing the full story in the first place. It is not hard to imagine what those other stories might sound like. In fact, Lilly hints at them in her own story. Her husband is telling stories about her behind her back, and the people in the community believed him. "They saw me like that," she says, never describing what "that" was but pointing later to her drug and alcohol abuse. But she adds, "They didn't see what was going on inside that trailer, either."

Without a view "into the trailer," past experiences can be skewed, conveying only a part of the story and leading to damaging and erroneous conclusions. With some selective tweaking, Lilly's story could be recast as a familiar tale of welfare abuse where people use government funds to support alcohol and drug addictions. The malleability of narrative coupled with the shifting sands of perspective allow for a single story to be shaped to support existing political ideology and confirm what we want to believe.

Perspective matters. Rhetorical goals matter. Context matters. Conflating the stories we hear and retell with those shared directly from personal experience is to mistake the photo for the object. Those new "photos"—stories derived from stories—are powerful cultural creations and important parts of a narrative tradition that require careful analysis. But assuming they are the same is to assume we are hearing directly from recipients when in fact we are continuing to speak for them.

The stories in this book explore the wide range of narratives told about welfare in the United States. The stories in this section of the book, however, move beyond initial assumptions and cursory public glances at poverty and welfare and into the homes and lives of aid recipients for a perspective so often ignored in public debates and private conversations across the country. These are not the stories constructed by aid providers, politicians, and neighbors; those stories appear elsewhere in the book. Nor are these the reconstituted narratives constructed by well-meaning scholars who search for a coherent narrative to tell, replacing messy personal stories with tidy biographies.[2] Rather, these are the stories of aid recipients told in their own words. This simple move—of listening to people's stories as they tell them—provides a glimpse into the artistry, beliefs, and complexity of thought that people engage in to make sense of their lives and the world around them. To be sure, the hand of the author is hardly absent. I have relied on interviews and field notes to identify which narratives to include, in what order, to illustrate what point. I have suggested ways these stories might be interpreted. Such is the task of academic work. The difference is that these stories are not a means to an end—data to derive some larger meaning—but the focal point of study.[3]

SHARING ONE'S STORY

Jada Whittle didn't know she was looking for help until help found her. The messenger? A story.

I didn't know about this program until me and my mom was coming past Alton Street, and we seen the News 2 out there. And we stopped and asked the security guard what was going on. He tell us it's an open house, a seminar that they're having. So we parked and we went in.

And there was one of these guys that was speaking, was telling about how him and his wife had become more successful when he enrolled in Child Development up here on Alton Street. And Mr. Robin Britt, he was there as a speaker. And he was introducing all the classes and everything that was going on up there at the Child Development through the Goodwill. And we sat there; we attended that seminar up there. And I said, "Hey, this sounds like something that . . ." Because actually, I found myself being at the . . . There's nothing else to do.

Jada had just moved back to Greensboro and was living with her mom, trying to get her life back on track after losing her only son to terminal illness and her husband to divorce when their marriage slowly fell apart under the strain of their loss. Finding Guilford Child Development (GCD) just as it was kicking off a new program to consolidate resources for families to help them back on their feet felt like divine providence to Jada.

And so that's how we found out about all this. And so I enrolled. I kept up with Jaye.[4] And I was in the first graduation class. And then I turned my sister and my niece onto it. And I also be talking to a lot of girls out here in the streets about the program and how they got the day care downstairs for your child while you attend class upstairs. And it's free of charge.

Because I have been where they've been. Like I said, it's not always been Goody-Two-shoes with me. I have been where they're at now and have overcome.

Jada describes herself as an ambassador, sharing her story with young women whom she sees making some of the same mistakes she made when she was younger. It is the same role that Justin Shepard played the night Jada and her mother were driving past Guilford Child Development. In fact, it is a role Justin has filled a number of times, often with his wife Karraha, sharing their story to shed light on the challenges faced by so many in our communities today.[5] Justin and Karraha are often chosen to speak not because they have already achieved success but because they are working hard to do so.

Settled into the overstuffed sofa of their living room, their daughter Lotus wedged between then, Justin and Karraha describe how they share their story in these contexts.

We usually tell them where we were when we first came into the program, some of the different things that are offered, and then I give some of my experiences on to the things that I've participated in.

After, I'd go into that a bit and then I just encourage folks, like, "If you know somebody that needs it . . ." I encourage them to get them there, just so they can be around folks and get that exposure to different situations and different ways of thinking. A lot of time, some people don't realize that they're burning until somebody's trying to put them out.

The metaphor of the lobster in the boiling pot is an apt one for the people Justin, Karraha, and Jada are trying to reach through their stories. Things start getting bad, but you adapt. Things get worse, you keep adapting. But then, before you know it, you're in way over your head with no way out in sight.

> **Justin:** When we first came into the GCD program, we were just getting into a place here.
> **Karraha:** Newlyweds. New parents because she had just . . . She was born what? How old was she? Was she just under one, wasn't she?
> **Justin:** When we got here? Yeah.
> **Karraha:** Yeah, she was just under one.
> **Justin:** She was probably about eight months or something.
> **Karraha:** Eight months, we had just gotten married recently.
> **Justin:** I had just lost a job in like a day.
> **Karraha:** Yeah, he had it for a day, and then we lost the job.
> **Justin:** It was a trial thing with a food service company. The owner said, "No, you're not going to work out." "OK." Nothing happened, but OK, cool. Whatever, it's cool. I'm glad I'm not there.
> **Karraha:** We got in, we had no money, just married, just had a baby, and the office was like, "You guys owe us three hundred dollars for this month, three hundred dollars for last month," and I was like, "Woah, Wait."

Karraha and Justin describe finding GCD and signing up for classes. They conclude by noting, "We have a story, we persevered, and we prayed, and we stayed on our knees and kept working, and we're here, and we've been doing honestly, and we're here. All of us are ready for that next level, we know we are. We are all ready for that next level. We're ready to buy the house and set all the studs in rooms and everything. It's just getting that bridge from here to there right now."

The "right now" is half of a two-bedroom duplex in a public housing community in Greensboro. In a year, they will have moved to a rental home in High Point, closer to Justin's new job, with a backyard, a driveway for their newly purchased car, and a spot for a garden. For now, the plants are in small pots on the shared front porch and the dreams of greater independence and self-sufficiency clouded with the challenges of the past and present.

Chatting casually in their living room, they share some of the more dramatic moments in their lives.

We went out of town to see my mother-in-law for her birthday and took her out to dinner. About time we were riding back home, I started losing feeling in my toes, and I'm like, "Justin, something is wrong."

The next morning, my face started dripping, and I said, "Justin, something's really wrong."

So we go to the hospital and look, "Oh, there's nothing." They sent us home.

I went online and did some research, and I said, "Baby, all my symptoms really sound like this." We go back to the hospital, and they were like, "Oh yeah, you have Bell's palsy."

But by that time, I lost complete feeling and nerve control of my face, and I couldn't even smile.

Newborn baby, she hadn't been latching. I was just going from baby blues going through Bell's palsy. I was so . . . so . . . And we're rushing. We're going through all this. We're homeless; we're sleeping on floors in friend's houses.

You hear about the humble beginnings and everything. I just didn't expect all of that.

Karraha was the lobster. She found the challenge of being a new mother hard but not insurmountable. Not having her baby latch was stressful, but she managed. She found herself homeless, but again, she persevered. Yet when she began having serious and mysterious medical issues, she finally stood back and realized, in Justin's terms, she was burning. This act of reflection explains why narrating personal stories can be so difficult emotionally. Isolated, the events of one's life may seem manageable; aggregated, they can be overwhelming. Karraha sets out to tell a single story of medical trauma, but the story is inseparable from the larger context of challenges she faced.[6] Stories are not merely records of past events but of the significance of those events. The act of storytelling encourages Karraha to reflect on her experience and its significance. In narrating a single vivid event, she connects the dots; narrating the star, she reveals the constellation.

The act of storytelling can be an act of discovery. Coherence and meaning emerge in the telling. This explains why some scholars have argued that the story comes before the event, that only in narrating our lives do we make sense of them (Bauman 1986; Mink 1978). Retelling a story in new contexts can encourage new interpretations. In many cases, those contexts are informal and spontaneous. But aid recipients are occasionally asked to "tell their story" for public audiences. The request asks people to construct a meaningful path through significant events in their lives, creating a life story.

There are *stories of life* that describe a distinct, bounded event and the *life story* that draws together multiple stories to seek coherence across a lifetime. The life story has been a useful abstraction for oral historians and those studying written autobiographies, but the general lack of a performance context outside the academic interview renders it far less useful for understanding how stories are deployed in social contexts.[7] Yet as Karraha's summation hints, there *are* life stories that are performed in the vernacular oral tradition. This is what Justin and Karraha do for the United Way and Guilford Child Development. It is also what Lynn Burke does, having made a side job of sharing her story with groups and organizations. Over the course of about forty-five minutes, Lynn weaves together a series of personal stories to tell a larger life story of how she got pregnant at eighteen, ended up in jail for writing bad checks, and almost lost her children before she turned her life around with the help of aid agencies and family.

Lynn Burke is unusual in having the platform to share her life story at such length and for so many disparate audiences. Justin and Karraha are part of an only slightly larger group of aid recipients who are given a microphone to share their stories to agency boards, community leaders, and the local media. More often, aid recipients draw stories together into larger wholes in small settings, formal and informal, in conversations with aid providers and among peers.

One might imagine that life stories emerge most frequently and naturally in reflecting on the past. But the opposite is as often true. Imagining the future encourages people to reflect on the past and seek coherence across individual stories. In doing so, past events can take on new meanings and significance.

Delia Taylor works over forty hours at a big-box retail store in Greensboro, fitting in job training classes to help her move out of the low-wage job that does not provide medical benefits for her or her daughters. Reflecting on her experiences with public assistance, she starts with her first use of food stamps.

> I have gotten food stamps since I was in college because I've been on my own since I'm nineteen.
>
> So when I moved down here, I stayed with my brother for maybe about, I'd say, about eight months, and then I got my own place. With the food stamps, you can get them as a student based off your income.
>
> And then my daughter, she came along about four of five years later. So what I did was based off of that.
>
> It just helps. It doesn't completely cover food costs because I do work, I've always worked, so it does help me. And then with covering her costs, I also did Work First for a while, and it actually tapped me into Goodwill and a lot of community projects. And I do a lot of community service and met a lot of good people like at Goodwill, and I met people at Guilford Child Development. So you know it just kind of helps to make a network with people around the city.

The first complication in Delia's story is being on her own at age nineteen and trying to pay for college. Her solution was to move in with her brother and apply for food stamps. The plan worked until she was faced with another complication: she had a child. She could no longer balance school and parenting. "So what I

did" was drop out of school, the climax of her story. The resolution was supporting herself with additional public assistance. The story paints a life of challenges
faced, challenges met, but only with the help of public assistance and a network
of helpful people and agencies.

A few months later, when I asked her where she saw herself in a year, she revisited this moment in her life, again looking for areas of coherence and resolution
but finding new ways to think about the past.

> I have a medical background. When I was in high school, I took a vocational
> medical-assisting program for two years, so I can draw blood, do EKGs. I've
> worked in OSU University Hospital. I've worked in many different areas. But
> when I moved to North Carolina at nineteen out of high school, they're like,
> "That's not considered college credits, so you'd have to go to a two-year program.
> And at the time, out of state was so expensive. I couldn't afford it right away.
>
> And life happens. Maybe a couple years later—when I had started my classes,
> I had all my prereqs ready—my mother passed. Found out I was pregnant. Life
> happens. I've had just-to-get-by jobs. I don't have a problem with working. I love
> working. But now I'm to the point ... My girls are getting ready to go on to the next
> phase. I got one going to pre-K; I've got one, she's on her last year of elementary. I'm
> just ready to get a job that's paying a little bit more, be a little bit more comfortable,
> looking at wanting to buy a house, just do better for my girls and myself.
>
> I took a medical billing and coding quick jobs course. At the time, Walmart didn't
> really want to work with me too much, so it was hard to concentrate in the class. I did
> really well up until the very last maybe few months of the course and just missed it by
> a hair, but then I realized it was boring because it was something where you sit down
> and you're looking at a computer all day. I've been on my feet—let's see ... I've been at
> Walmart since 2009, so I'm used to moving around, being hands on, and then I have
> more like hands-on experience, like lab work and patient care, so I'm just like, maybe
> if I get ready to go back, it will be something like that. Maybe baby steps, start with
> maybe nurse's assistant or something like that, CNA. Then I wouldn't mind being a
> medical assistant again, and sit in a doctor's office is nice. Heavy duty is hospital work.

Life happens. It is the refrain that explains the detours in her life. But in imagining her future, she reimagines her past. The medical work that was irrelevant in
a story that ended with public assistance is of vital importance in a story that
ends with a medical career. This move is not insignificant. Again and again, as
aid recipients imagined their futures, they reflected on their pasts and presents.
In this way, the narrative tradition mirrors research about short- and long-term
thinking, where the pressure to meet basic needs leaves little room for contem-
plating long-term plans.

Narrative completion where the dreams and hopes for the future resolve current challenges also partially explains the disproportionate number of people

whose dreams for the future involve work with children or in aid agencies. Faced with the challenge of finding childcare for their own children or resources for their families to make ends meet, people imagine resolving these issues not just for themselves but for families like theirs whose lives should not be this hard. To understand the great challenges of the present, one only need listen to what people narrate as their futures.

A SYSTEM OF STORIES

The stories people share about their lives on public assistance are clearly situated according to time and need. There are the challenges that led people to seek assistance in the first place, challenges they continue to face, and strategies for meeting those challenges and achieving success. Ideally, analysis of these stories would be guided primarily by native, or emic, categories named by the storytellers themselves. But other than "success stories," there is no shared lexicon for distinguishing one story from the next. The stories themselves, however, cohere around time and need, as well as topic, theme, and function. While there may be additional textual and contextual factors that could be used to distinguish one type of story from another, these localized patterns provide a viable entry point for analysis.[8]

Articulated as types of stories, there are origin stories that recount how people came to need public assistance, challenge stories that recount the kinds of challenges people continue to face, making-ends-meet stories that describe how people have met those challenges, and success stories that describe how people have moved beyond scraping by and achieved some degree of stability if not complete self-sufficiency. Topically, stories of experiencing stigma emerge as particularly significant challenge stories, while stories of community emerge within stories of making ends meet.

ORIGIN STORIES

In origin stories, people describe how they ended up needing public assistance. Aid recipients most often share their origin stories in institutionalized settings. During the process of applying for aid, people meet with caseworkers and explain their situation. These dialogues may be formal, bureaucratic, and follow the script of the aid questionnaires, but they can also be more conversational as caseworkers establish trust with their clients. More often, however, aid recipients share their stories with each other. The setting is again institutional—soup kitchens, homeless shelters, drop-in centers, and nonprofits—but the stories emerge informally.

One can expect these stories—personal experience narratives from people who have to justify their need in formal situations and often have to justify their

Causes of Need	# of Instances	% of Total
Housing	126	98%
Employment	104	81%
Broken Home	101	79%
Education	74	58%
Health Issues	60	47%
Alcohol / Drug Abuse	47	37%
Mental Health	36	28%
Domestic Abuse	35	27%
Single Parenting	33	26%
Childcare	32	25%
Jail/Prison	26	20%
Teen Pregnancy	24	19%
Divorce	22	17%

Table 4.1. Causes that led to seeking aid, derived from analysis of 128 origin stories.

worthiness in informal ones—to be sanitized and idealized. No doubt some are. But as the stories reveal, many aid recipients are incredibly candid about the difficult challenges they have faced and the difficult choices they have made. Those challenges include the usual suspects—loss of job, major illness, lack of education and transportation, teen pregnancy and single parenting, divorce, addiction, and domestic abuse (table 4.1)—but stories provide crucial context for understanding how these factors can catch people unaware, unprepared, and without the scope or depth of resources to weather them.

These factors intersect and overlap in the lives and stories of recipients, but some cohere into larger categories:

- **employment**: inability to find work, insufficient hours, unaffordability and undesirability of outside childcare, challenges of single parenting
- **health**: accidents at work, chronic health problems, deteriorating mental health due to extreme stressors and alcohol and drug addiction
- **housing and unstable home life**: cycle of poverty, insufficient resources, and domestic abuse leading to a lack of self-confidence, constant relocation to escape the abuser, and loss of housing, support, and capital
- **education**: incomplete education due to a lack of support or stability in the home or teen pregnancy

Employment

Bradley Jewell is a college-educated, former US Navy pilot who is divorced with children but lives on his own. He owned his own business before the recession hit but has struggled to rebound.

> A few years ago, I had my own business. I was doing pretty well at it, and, then, of course, the economy tanked. People just couldn't afford repairs anymore. So, it took every penny I had just to keep my doors open. I lost everything I had.
>
> Trying to find work nowadays is a major pain in the butt. You're either overqualified, underqualified, too old, or . . . you know. They find out that you're homeless, and they don't want to hire you.
>
> My main thing is just trying to find work. I don't drink. I don't do drugs. I don't have a criminal record. So, it's like, "What's the deal?" That's the reason that I'm in this situation right now.

According to national polls and local fieldwork, the most common misperception about the poor is that they are uninterested in working. The reality is far different (chap. 1). For many single parents, the cost of childcare makes work financially unfeasible, especially with the kinds of low-wage jobs for which many would be eligible. Add to that the problem of consistent and affordable transportation—not only to and from work but to and from childcare and then work—and wage labor outside the home becomes extremely difficult to manage logistically or financially.

Lack of employment, like loss of housing, is an effect as often as a cause of poverty, although they fuel each other in a vicious cycle. As Bradley notes, loss of a job led to his homelessness, and now his homelessness has made it difficult to find a job.

Health

More often, an accident, major illness, or deteriorating health are traced back as the cause of job loss, whether that illness is one's own or one's child. Peyton Carlton's troubles started when he got laid off from his job. With no prospects in his field, he enrolled at Guilford Technical Community College (GTCC) to get retrained in appliance repair. But just when he finished, he had a stroke and found that no one wanted to hire someone whose health remained questionable. Serena Borden found herself in doctor's offices and hospital rooms so often for her son's asthma that she lost her job. Louise Howard lost two jobs in quick succession after trying to manage the care of one daughter with cerebral palsy and a range of mental and emotional disorders and another who tried to commit suicide. Bethany Chance finally had to stop working after her second son was diagnosed with autism, making the care of her children a full-time job even as they reached school age.

In other cases, an injury or health issue can be serious enough to remove a person from the workforce entirely. Pat Jackson hurt her back while working at a big-box store. She kept working, as she had for thirty years, but the pain grew worse, and when she finally sought medical treatment, the damage had been done. Davey Cannon's problems began with his back as well, but he soon found out things were far worse than he imagined, diagnosed with a degenerative joint disease that has left him in a wheelchair. Jeffrey Thornton has faced debilitating physical and psychological issues but has had little success getting the help he needs. The same was initially true for his brother.

> My brother, he has one leg, and he applied for disability, and they turned him down. . . . On his letter, they said that the situation would not last more than a year.
> So we went up there, and we took him up the Social Security board, and we asked what was going to happen to his leg. It'll grow back? [Laughter]
> So the fellow automatically done a review with him and set the things back in.

Jeffrey's ailments are less obvious, and his efforts to get disability are still in limbo. He has been turned down twice for disability, despite having asthma, emphysema, chronic obstructive pulmonary disease, and congestive heart failure, as well as being diagnosed as bipolar with social anxiety and severe depression.

For Tracie Rutherford, it was the systemic stress from trying to make ends meet as a single parent that contributed to her psychological breakdown. Mental health issues were also at the root of Sharleen Sands's inability to complete high school and subsequently her inability to find a job to support herself. The same was true for Kimberly Harris, who was diagnosed with bipolar disorder after a nervous breakdown. For Diane Clemens, her physical illness caused her to suffer mentally as well; Diane sought therapy for her depression. Jada Whittle turned to drugs. Her addiction took a terrible toll on her health until she finally became clean and sober almost two decades ago. However, new, unrelated health problems emerged more recently. She was forced out of the workforce and her health deteriorated quickly. She passed away in June 2016.

Carla Robinson's story is more common: it was not an addiction of her own that made it difficult to make ends meet but of her husband.

> Right now it's myself and my three kids. I actually am married. My husband is in prison. So he is a big part of why we are now here. My husband and I actually have been married for three years, like two weeks ago. Two weeks ago, it was our three-year anniversary.

But my husband is an addict. Shortly after we got married, I actually had a full-time job. I was making good money. We had our own place. And his addiction just progressed and got a lot worse.

Over time, more or less anything that we had of value he has taken and sold and is gone. I mean it's everything. So I lost my job last year in March due to . . . With his addiction, there would be times he would disappear in the middle of the night. Take the car and be gone. And I would have the kids, and I would either struggle to find some way to get to work, or I would end up taking the kids to work with me. Because at that time I just had the two boys. And so eventually it just caused so many problems, or he would come to my work, and there was a lot of arguing, a lot of fighting there at work. So I ended up losing my job.

Then around March of last year, right before I lost the job, him and I had gotten into an argument. And I'm not an addict, so I don't understand. So I would just get so overwhelmed and mad that I ended up . . . I had to hit him. And I ended up hitting him, and he called the police, and I was put in jail for a weekend.

I've never been in trouble before in my life.

So that was a part of losing my job.

But at that point he realized that things had gotten out of hand. DSS [Department of Social Services] had become involved with us. And they said that because it seemed like his addiction was getting worse, they were going to require him to go to treatment and complete treatment. If he didn't, then I basically had the option of choosing my husband or my kids.

So he was looking into treatments and then up and disappeared one day with a guy's car.

Let's see, that was . . . OK. So after I had went to jail in March, I spent forty-eight hours there. I came back. He had gone into an Oxford House. So at the time that he was at the Oxford House is the time that I had lost my job. So he was doing well at the Oxford House. That's a sober-living facility. Had a curfew, had a job. They did drug testing.

He was doing really well. But he left early because I was at risk of losing our apartment because I was not working and my unemployment was not paying. . . . It wasn't enough to pay the rent and all the bills. So he left the Oxford House and came home. So in May we actually found out that I was pregnant with her [gestures to her daughter]. And by June, June was the point that he had taken the guy's car. He had started using again. He relapsed. He was gone for a week. And this is after the DSS had told me that I could lose my kids.

So when he left for that week, when he disappeared for that week, I knew that he was not going to treatment. So I started packing my kids up. I packed everything up, and I talked to family and friends. I put everything into storage.

And I got a phone call about five days later, and he had totaled the guy's car going about a hundred and twenty-something miles an hour and was in the hospital at Wake Forest. And they didn't know what, why, how he was even alive.

So I went and I got him. He came home for one day. And I told him that we . . .
When he come home, everything was packed. I mean, I had my stuff packed,
and we were leaving. And so he got mad, and he got up, and he walked out the
door with a backpack of clothes and left.

And I didn't know where he was at for a week. And finally got a phone call
that he had been arrested.

So he has been locked up since July fifth of last year.

So at that point the kids and I were basically homeless. We stayed with friends
and family. So that was the beginning of July. So from July until November we
were pretty much homeless.

So then I had looked into housing. And that was when I got into housing. And
that was a struggle getting in here. At the time that they went to do my references,
the apartments that I had lived in prior had told them, you know, "Her husband is
a big problem." And they'd given me a bad reference. And I had to go in. I had to go
in and request to have a hearing. And then I had to sit down with the assistant. I can
see her face. But I can't think of what her name is. She was very nice. I sat in with her
and Lisa Murray. I had to sit down, and basically, I went in prepared to beg basically
and talked to them about the situation and explained the situation. And basically
had to convince them to let us come and move in. So they gave me some stipulations
regarding him and everything, but then that was how I . . . finally got in here.

So it was hard. It was hard.

Carla grew up middle class. Homelessness, poverty, and addiction were not part
of her childhood. She had created a successful career path for herself, eventually
working in management. But her choice in partner threatened everything she had
worked for. Now, with public housing offering her some semblance of stability,
she is hoping to rebuild her life as a single parent.

Housing and Unstable Home Life

One of the most common causes of poverty described in origins stories revolves
around spouses that disappear, divorce, or can no longer provide income. Etta
Washington was married and pregnant with their first child when her husband
began cheating on her. She tried to work it out, but ultimately he left her, leaving
her to figure out how to raise a child as a single parent with no support network.
April Ayers's husband was a hard worker and built a stable home for his wife and
three children. But he had come into the country illegally and, unable to apply
for a green card, was deported. Serena was married and working in the military
when she had her three children. But after her divorce and injuries that put her
on disability from the military, she found herself stuck: overqualified for half
the jobs that were open and underqualified for the rest. She found jobs, but her
daughter's acute asthma, which required hospitalization, forced her to miss too

many days at work. She eventually found a job as a caseworker for the Department of Social Services, but she continues to need help with medical bills for her asthmatic child.

Single parenting, separation, and divorce—creating unstable and untenable family dynamics—are common in origin stories. The same is true for domestic abuse. Lisa Waterman describes being thrown out of the car by her husband. He was sent to jail, but she found herself struggling to find a job and pay the bills. Martha Sadler's fourth marriage is a happy one, but the first three were decidedly not. By her third marriage, the years of physical and emotional abuse had eroded her sense of worth.

> My third husband, I put up with him cheating, alcohol, beating. I had no self-respect. I been stepped on so many times I let him step on me. I fought back the first two times, and then I didn't the third time.
>
> I put my foot down the day he laid his hands on my baby. He grabbed my baby by the throat and was strangling him. And I liked to beat him to death. But his mom came in the house. My baby ran down to his gramma's, his mom came into the house, and I literally was sitting on his neck choking the life out of him. I had done beat him to a pulp. And she looked at me and said, "Martha, he's not worth it."
>
> I said, "You're right." I crossed the street and called my mom and had her come get me.
>
> I've had my head split open; I've been beat with a weed eater while it was running, fractured wrist, cracked ribs. I was beat with a clothes hanger while I was asleep. [Sighs] I was beat while I was pregnant, and I put up with it.
>
> You can beat me all you want, but don't put your hands on my kids. I'm glad it ended. It taught me what I can do, what I can't do. What I will put up with, what I won't put up with. And what nobody should put up with.

Martha made sure that the cycle of abuse stopped when it reached her children. Christie Huston's mother attempted the same.

> I remember being in Wilson, North Carolina. My mom never let men put their hands on me. We had went to church one Sunday morning, and we were coming back. There's a railroad track you got to cross to get back to the house from the church. My shoe got caught in the train tracks, and the guy that she was talking to or whatever got an attitude and was like, "I'm going to whoop her when we get home." My mom was like, "No, you not." So he beat my mom instead.
>
> That's what I had to deal with. They were not allowed to touch me, so she endured what I wasn't going to. I started to remember things like that younger. When you focus on things like that, you don't really pay attention to the welfare and stuff until your lights get cut off or you got to run a kerosene heater in the house because there is no heat.

Her mother was successful when it came to stopping her boyfriends but not when it came to stopping herself from perpetuating the abuse, often physically punishing Christie when she stepped out of line. Christie's biological father was also abusive. As the oldest of his children, Christie often found it necessary to go back home to try to protect her stepsiblings.

> I chose to just be with mom and not have to go through that. I have a half sister and a half brother. My dad was an abusive father, so I would go there to protect them. TJ wasn't here yet. Annie, I knew . . . I was growed. I didn't want her to have to go through that, so I would go down there just to make sure she didn't have to go through what I knew was going on, when doors get slammed and you hear yelling and cussing and screaming. I just held her. That's all I could do. I'm a child myself; what am I supposed to do? My sister still to this day will ask me, sometimes we sit out and we talk, and she'll be like, "Sis, I wish you never had to leave me." I tell her, "It's not that I was leaving you. It's just that I had to go be safer myself." She left home as soon as she could, eighteen. I'm pretty sure my brother is going to; he's giving my dad hell.

Escaping domestic violence often means leaving everything: one's family, finances, support networks, and homes. Bouts of homelessness, couch surfing, and living in substandard housing are common, leading to generational poverty difficult to break out of.

Education

Lack of sufficient education to attain a job that pays a living wage appears again and again in these origin stories but rarely as the ultimate cause. Rather, poor health, an unplanned pregnancy, lack of resources, or family troubles result in dropping out of school. Jashanna Kingston's story is similar to many.

> I started school at GTCC, and I actually had to drop out. I couldn't . . . I didn't further my education. I didn't even think about it because I had my two children to think about. And it was hard because I didn't have no one to babysit my children. And that was my biggest thing, my biggest problem with not being able to further my own education is I was always putting my kids needs before mine.

Jashanna put her kids first. For Betsy Maller, it was her husband's health that derailed her education, forcing her to drop out of school to care for him after he was hit by a train. For Christine Evered, it was her father's failing health that forced her to give up her college education, coupled with the bullying of her older brother, who kicked her out of the house when their father was too feeble to intervene. Challenges overlap or accumulate until holding everything together becomes impossible.

In origin stories, however, these overlapping factors often get reduced to just two in a version of "Sophie's choice": education or employment, long-term investment or short-term survival. The rational choice for many is to conclude that education is a luxury they cannot afford. A few, however, fight the odds and maintain an eye on the long game. This was the hope of recent immigrant Eliza Nguyen.

> Well, I was in Vietnam, so I went to school from first grade or kindergarten, I don't remember, till sixth grade. And then, when I came here, I was too old to get into middle school, so they put me in high school. I was almost too old for high school, too. But I told my sponsor who took care of us when we first came to America, I told him that I wanted to go to school and finish high school and get some sort of certificate or a diploma. I don't even know what the diploma was before. So I told him that I don't want to go to work yet.

Eliza "did not want to go to work yet" because she knew that her options for employment would be drastically reduced, and the likelihood that she would get stuck in a minimum wage job would be high, making self-sufficiency difficult if not impossible.

BAD LUCK OR BAD CHOICES

The vast majority of origin stories focus on obstacles outside one's control: cutbacks at work, unforeseen illnesses, complicated pregnancies, abusive spouses, impoverished parents, and lack of capital and resources. Where the personal experience narrative tradition assumes bad luck, the legend tradition assumes bad choices. Some personal experience narratives, however, include both, where one bad choice sets off an avalanche. Bethany Chance describes herself as young and irresponsible.

> I worked briefly after we had our first baby, and we were so stupid and young. We lived with his parents. We didn't have a lot of bills, and I worked briefly there until we split. We had a long, drawn-out history. And then we got back together and stayed together, and he grew up.
> I worked when he left me the last time, and I was seven and a half months pregnant with Amaya, and he walked out, and I had to pay all the bills and everything like that. And I was working twelve-hour shifts, seven days a week.
> And then we got back together, and I quit working, because I had to be put on maternity leave, because I was pregnant with Kayla. And I went back to work at the same place after I had him [gestures to her son]. I worked there for almost a year, and then I was subsequently fired. And that was a long, drawn-out history because I stood up and did the right thing, but that's neither here nor there.

She pauses deciding whether to tell the story of her firing or not. She decides against it. "We had to move when I lost my job because we couldn't keep up the rent and the car payment and everything on just his income." So they moved back in with her husband's parents.

> I haven't really worked since because my older boys have special needs, and they're both on the autism spectrum. We have to do a lot of therapies. We spent the first year of his life running—well, actually a couple years into his life—running back and forth to doctors in Chapel Hill. And he had two surgeries before he was two. And I haven't really worked a job since just because I feel I needed to be home. Me and my husband are pretty much on the same page with that. He's been the only one that works.
>
> Now, I do photography, and I do cakes on the side to bring in extra income here and there, but he's the main one that brings home. But having five kids in and of itself in today's economy is extremely difficult.

Michael Caster had had a few beers and was playing with his kids on a trampoline when he fell and broke his leg. Uninsured and unable to pay for proper treatment, his leg was set poorly and left him with a permanent limp. He is no longer able to hold the restaurant and factory jobs he once did, all of which require standing for significant amounts of time. Not able to afford a car, Michael had used a bicycle to get to work, but his injury made that no longer possible. Eventually, Michael's drinking got worse, and he lost his home.

Mary Barker has worked all her life, but the road hasn't been easy: "I've had a lot of struggles. I've had struggles with drugs, alcohol." She tried to get clean and found a rehabilitation center that would take her without insurance. But her employer was unwilling or unable to allow her extended absences from work and fired her. To care for her children, she has given up on rehab and gone back to work, a decision that haunts her every day.

The legend tradition finds it easy to excoriate someone for drinking too much, experimenting with drugs, or getting pregnant while still in school, yet national statistics make it clear that these "bad choices" are made no more often among the poor than among the middle class and wealthy (chap. 1). Living close to the poverty line where actions can have severe consequences does not magically make a person more moral or responsible than anyone else. The difference comes in the degree to which a person can recover from a bad choice. With sufficient income, legal charges can be fought, treatment can be sought, new mouths can be fed, and education can be continued. Without such capital, a single mistake can be devastating, economically as well as legally.

HIDDEN CHALLENGES

In these origin stories, people rarely identify deeper, structural causes for their poverty, at least not explicitly. Rather, their stories are narratives of individual challenge. On the one hand, this helps humanize poverty and the people who struggle to make ends meet. On the other, it masks the larger patterns of inequality that perpetuate poverty. The evidence is there, however, as analysis of these stories reveals.

Michael Caster, Betsy Maller, Diane Clemens, Pat Jackson, Kimberly Harris, and Davey Cannon all note how a medical issue sent them into a financial tailspin. Their stories are personal, but the larger problem of access to affordable insurance and health care emerges as a recurring systemic problem. Peyton Carlton, Bradley Jewell, and Etta Washington describe being unable to find work, particularly after the recession in 2008. Such stories point the finger at the economy, but underlying many of these stories is a lack of education and training that would prepare them for a wider array of jobs. Susan Phillips, Christie Huston, Jada Whittle, Delia Taylor, Karraha Shepard, and Louise Howard describe growing up in poverty, and while they do not draw an explicit connection between the lack of capital, resources, and opportunities as a child and their inability to become economically self-sufficient as an adult, their stories highlight the difficulty of "pulling yourself up by your bootstraps." Poverty begets poverty. This phenomenon has less to do with theories of a "culture of poverty" propagated in the 1960s that continues to inform policy today than with the fact that the next generation of aid recipients started with so little—little material wealth and little social capital.

Part of the inability to see the structural inequities that compound individual challenges comes from living too close to the problem. But another is the tunnel vision caused when forced to live day to day and week to week rather than year to year. Figuring out how to pay a utility bill before the heat gets turned off can make it difficult to think about how to save for the inevitable moment when the furnace gives out. Sharleen Sands wants to go back to school to become a nail technician, but she is wary of getting ahead of herself. "I haven't decided as far as what schools I'm going to go. I just want to get through with what I'm getting through now because it seems like when I start planning stuff, it doesn't go through as planned. It's more short-term goals right now than long term." Christie Huston concurs: "I don't really do long-term goals."

The inability to plan for the long term is not an irrational characteristic of people living in poverty but rather a rational response to a lived context where long-term rewards have been few and far between (Mullainathan and Shafir 2013). In poverty, putting out fires and indulging in short-term satisfactions are both rational and deeply human.

The narrative tradition captures stories of these challenges as well. As the stories in the following chapter reveal, many of the same factors that led to the need for public assistance in the first place continue to plague aid recipients in their daily lives.

NOTES

1. Gibbs is referring to an earlier moment when she describes her ex-husband calling her every insult in the book, none of which she felt applied to her. She uses the phrase again, as quoted later in this chapter.

2. For a critique, see Titon (1980).

3. Amy Shuman points out the problem of reproducing and retelling other people's stories, an act that risks appropriation, which can "deny, obliterate, and obscure the voices of the person who suffer the experiences," suggesting that the process of recontextualizing a narrative for a new audience can create a semantic gulf that is difficult to bridge and causes alienation (2005, 147). Presenting narratives verbatim as told, with information about the contexts within which they were shared, helps mitigate against this danger, even if it can never truly overcome it.

4. Jaye Webb is a coach at GCD and assistant director of the Family Success Center there.

5. For example, they were the only family spotlighted in the news story about the kickoff of the new Family Success program (Powell 2015).

6. In this way, these stories are intertextually linked, creating a web of meaning that extends to other performances and other stories (Bauman 2004; Mould 2008).

7. In his chapter "Life History: A Constructed Genre," William Schneider highlights the constructed nature of the life history, citing David Dunaway's tripartite system that establishes a continuum between the scholar's construction of the life story based on interviews and other data and the "oral memoir" where the person's voice and own stories are heard, with minimal context added by the scholar for clarification (2002, 112). See also Cashman (2016), Pentikäinen (1980), Sawin (2004), and Titon (1980).

8. In *Choctaw Tales*, I discuss a tiered approach identifying an emic system of narrative genres within a particular culture group (Mould 2004, 38–60). I have applied a similar approach here, though one that depends more heavily on the back end of the process: considering the sheer number of stories that cohere according to topic, theme, character, style, and function.

CHALLENGE STORIES

DURING A FINANCIAL LITERACY CLASS at Guilford Child Development one morning, the teacher was discussing the benefits of budgeting in order to pay utility bills and still have money at the end of the month for food. One woman spoke up: "My light bill was two hundred and ten dollars last month. This month, it was three hundred and fifty-eight dollars. I can't pay that." Her classmates murmured assent, looking to their teacher hopefully. He responded with a story.

> Well, I grew up in rural North Carolina, raised by my grandmother. We had an air conditioner, but my granny never would turn it on. "Too expensive," she always said.
>
> Except on Sundays. She'd turn on the air conditioner, and—oh, boy—it felt so good. But only on Sundays. We used to look forward to Sundays.

The woman crossed her arms and stared back at him unimpressed. A few minutes later, she spoke again.

> My son breaks his toy, and he expects me to buy him another one. I'm like, "I ain't got no money."
>
> He says, "Yeah, I've seen some money."
>
> "Well, that money was here, but now it's gone."

The room erupts. The laughter is genuine, but so is the concern.

In challenge stories, people describe facing many of the same challenges they described in their origin story. Rather than being the straw that broke the camel's back, these challenges continue to hold people's heads underwater. What a person hoped might be an isolated incident emerges as an ongoing problem. The loss of a spouse or getting pregnant out of wedlock often means a life of single parenting. The diagnosis of a chronic health problem can mean a life of sporadic, part-time work or permanent disability. The loss or lack of a car means transportation can be a permanent challenge, especially in towns without public transportation. Dropping out of school can mean a life of limited job opportunities at low wages. And for single parents, the ever-present hardship of finding quality childcare looms as a constant challenge to maintaining a job.

As with origin stories, institutionalized settings are common for such stories because they justify in stark relief a person's ongoing need. One of the most common settings for challenge stories is when recipients return to social services offices for recertification interviews to be able to continue their assistance. In these meetings, clients explain their current circumstances, what they have been doing to try to make ends meet, and what challenges they continue to face. Rather than single-episode events, most clients share generalized experience narratives of typical events that recur again and again: of not being able to get to work because the car broke down; of applying for another job only to never hear back or be hired for a week until the background check reveals a past criminal charge and they get fired; of recurring medical issues that have kept them bedridden.

While some of these stories are clearly narrated again and again as crystallized narratives, most are what might be termed *short shelf-life stories*. Such stories capture the current challenge a person is facing, only to be replaced by another story a week later. Such stories are typically situated temporally in the here and now. "Everything is out of whack right now," explains Delia Taylor. "Like my rent's gone up, food stamps have gone down, and now they've cut hours because we've got extra people in the bakery now, and it's a slow bread season, because I work on the bread-wrapping side. My hours have gone from . . . Maybe I was getting like forty hours a week to maybe twenty, so it's just a struggle right now."

Because challenge stories are rooted in the present, the complication, rather than a climax or resolution, retains the focus. Life and narrative blend; only in hindsight will it be clear whether the climax has occurred or is yet to come with more challenges on the way. They are interstitial narratives of imbalance in between hoped-for moments of stability.[1]

Despite their instability—both in content and performance—challenge stories serve clear functions according to context. In institutional settings, they serve the instrumental goal of justifying need. Among family, friends, and acquaintances, however, they serve expressive and affective goals, when they are shared at all. Unlike origin stories that capture a one-time moment of crisis, challenge stories describe an ongoing struggle. One defines a moment; the other can define a life.

Aid recipients vary widely on if and when they share their stories of struggle. For some, stigma keeps them silent, even among family. "My pride jumps in," notes Elliott Dunn, explaining that he would rather sit in the dark with no electricity than tell his family he needed help. Matt Putnam voices a similar concern, fearing people would look down on him, as does Leslie Forester, who worries that even people in similar situations would view her poorly: "I just don't want people, even homeless people, to judge me." The exceptions for some are strangers. Jashanna Kingston explains, "I'm a very private person, and the only reason why I'm speaking to y'all is because y'all are strangers. You can talk to strangers better than you can talk to the people that you know."

Other recipients keep their stories to themselves for fear of burdening or boring people with their trials and tribulations. Louise Howard fears it will become tiresome to others. Christie Huston says, "People done been through enough with me. I don't feel like I'm the only person in the world that needs doggone help." Michael Caster explains, "I don't go out and grab a loudspeaker and start telling everybody, 'This is me. This is what happened to me.'" Besides, says his friend Andrew Bennett, "everyone has the same story anyway." He does not mean that literally, but he recognizes that the same challenges come up again and again, year after year. The details vary; the plot is depressingly familiar.

Still others, however, take a different approach to "the same story" phenomenon, seeing an opportunity to commiserate, empathize, and support each other. Tamera Dean has a sister going through many of the same problems she is facing. They talk regularly on the phone, share their stories, and offer support to one another. Eliza Nguyen does the same in a more limited fashion with her classmates in her GED class, as do they. "The whole class actually. . . . We talk about it when we have problems, if we're comfortable enough to talk about it. But they're not going to force you to talk about it. You can talk, just to let it out. They do listen, I mean, especially the teacher. She listens to our problems really good. She would give advice and stuff and numbers and phone numbers that you can call." Not only does Eliza feel better sharing stories of her challenges to an empathetic group, but she benefits in direct, material ways from her teacher's advice. Feeling better is powerful in and of itself as well. "Sometimes just being able to sit and tell somebody about it gives me relief, eases my mind," explains Lilly Gibbs. "I can go home and go to sleep without tossing and turning. Because I feel better I've emptied my mind out, and it gives you that space."

Complaining can serve that function too, and some of the challenge stories women tell happen in spaces where laughter serves as catharsis. After GED class one day, some of the students sat chatting and laughing during lunch. When I asked if I could join them, a chorus of yeses also included Etta Washington who laughed, warning me, "We're having women's gossip." The stories were funny, biting, and tongue-in-cheek. Although some stories were humorous anecdotes about their teachers, husbands, boyfriends, or children, others were less jovial tales of failing their GED or yet another utility bill that went unpaid.

Finding money to cover one's bills is the most basic and common challenge people face and sits at the heart of many of the challenge stories people tell. Further, finding work and maintaining good health emerge here as they did with origin stories, but daily challenges of single parenting, quality childcare, reliable transportation, and navigating the bureaucracy of government offices are perennial themes that defy easy resolution.

SINGLE PARENTING

For single parents, providing a stable home for their children is one of the most common challenges in their stories. Despite working hard to create positive home environments for their children, many women nonetheless feel guilty for not being able to provide more stability or a father figure for their sons. Carla Robinson describes this guilt, as well as the frustration at the double standard of her child's father's family.

> I feel like my child don't deserve the treatment that he receives as far as his dad's side of the family is concerned. So when they reach out to me, I don't know if it's just because they want to know if he's OK just so they can sleep good at night. Because nobody calls, nobody, none of them. They don't do nothing.
>
> And I know that it ain't really his parent's job, but I feel like when he was locked up and his daughter was born, and she needed things or whatever, they did it. They did everything. Bought food, milk, pampers, whatever she needed, and I didn't get nothing.
>
> Not that I really cared. I didn't really care about that stuff. I just wanted my son to have a father because our dad wasn't there really growing up.

Carla goes on to describe her biggest barrier to reaching her goals: childcare. And it's not just her. "I'm speaking for everybody around here again. Obviously, we don't have the money. We can't go out and pay for day care. We can't afford that. That's a luxury. And so it's hard because then it's like you can't work if you have to come up with childcare. You can't pay for childcare if you can't work. So what do you do?"

> And then, with Social Services, they have the option to do day care vouchers, but that's been cut. Like the funding for that has been cut. And so the waiting list at this point is two years long.
>
> So when they took him off of the vouchers, they told me I could go back on the waiting list. He'll be three in, like, two weeks. Two years, he'll be in kindergarten.

She pauses to allow the math to sink in before referencing a story that explains why, even with vouchers, having someone else watch her children makes her nervous.

You can't leave your kids at home. You don't want to just go take them to anybody, you know. You don't want to do that.

I mean, for me anyway, I don't trust a lot of people with my kids. I think, and this is from my personal experience, I had a lot of bad things that happened with my own husband. I sit here, and I think about it, the fact that my almost three-year-old is still alive and wasn't killed in the car with my husband. So why? You know? This is my husband. This is his [pointing to her son] dad. If I can't even trust him to go to him, how do I just pick somebody else to go trust and to stay here?[2]

WELFARE POLICY, BUREAUCRACY, AND RED TAPE

It is the rare government agency that gets showered with praise for efficiency and a personal touch. Efforts to shrink the government have led to political rhetoric that has enshrined the belief that government agencies and many of their employees are ineffective at best, corrupt at worst. The government, its programs, and Democrats are favorite scapegoats in stories about welfare (chaps. 7 and 8). Further, welfare is often singled out for particular abuse and scorn as part of a wholesale condemnation of entitlement programs and aid recipients. The narrative tradition of aid recipients diverges from such blanket critiques but primarily in tone and content rather than valence.[3] Most recipients express gratitude and appreciation for a system that helps ensure they have food and shelter and basic necessities. But recipients do not forfeit their dignity at the door when applying for aid, and although Ayanna Spencer frames her comments with the caveat that she appreciates the help she gets, the stories about the welfare office are dominated by tales of long waits and unfair policies.

I know sometimes they're a little slow, but I can't . . . Beggars can't be choosy.

So sometimes they're a little slow when you're needing help or answering the phone. And then when I go to social services to sit, sometimes I sit for hours before I get to see anyone.

I went to social services one time, and I sat in there . . . I got there around eight o'clock. And I sat in there until twelve o'clock and hadn't been seen yet. And then I got a call that my daughter was sick. I had to leave. So, I was just like, "Oh my God."

Delia Taylor describes the frustration of negotiating a ride to keep an appointment, only to arrive and find out the aid provider had canceled.

I hadn't met my Step Up coordinator, my new one, this whole year. And I still have yet to see her face. We correspond through emails and phone calls, but she and I was supposed to meet, and it was right after the ice storm. I went to her office, and she wasn't even there. I found out that she was out sick. Somebody could have called me or emailed me. I had to get a ride all the way over here. This was early day, where I have to work later. I could have been in bed asleep.

The same thing with NC Works. I traveled all the way to High Point because the lady that I started with, she moved to High Point, but I liked her so much, I started going to High Point. Found my way there, got there, and got all the way into her office, and nobody was there because she had an allergic reaction to something, and nobody called me to tell me, "She's canceling all her appointments today. You don't need to come." I'm just like, "Do you know how long it took us to find this place?"

Unreliable transportation or the lack of it altogether exacerbates these problems, but the most common complaints are tied to the bureaucracy of the system, including long waits, denials, and complicated paperwork requirements. Justin and Karraha Shepard describe a typical visit to the welfare office and the homeless shelter:

> **Karraha:** Yeah, there's usually a runaround, but I guess, for a while now, it's all right, because Justin just kind of stays up on it all the time, but if I need to get in contact with caseworkers or anything like that, it's a runaround. And I don't like that. I've been on three or four hours straight, waiting for someone to come to the phone, and it's just not worth it. You get there, and you're sitting forever.
>
> **Justin:** Most of the time if you really, really need to get something done with them, you have to go there and get in their face. I don't mean to be disrespectful or anything, but they need that presence of "Hey, there's an issue, and you need to address it right now."
>
> **Karraha:** Yeah, and I guess, for us, because they tried to put us on a whole workforce program and everything and, like, "Here's a free check; just tell us you put in applications."
>
> "I don't want the free check; I just need the assistance."
>
> Because at the time we were homeless, and all I'm thinking about is, "I want someplace warm for her to be." And they're like, "No, you two are married; we have to separate you. You have to go this way." Or "You can't go with her; she's not a certain age." Or "You can't be admitted because you're not pregnant anymore."
>
> It's like, every up and down, you make too much, or you make too little, so you can't get in it. It's just a runaround. I want so badly for her to never have to experience this in life ever, but I swallow my pride and swallow our pride and go in there and do it because we need it, you know.

"You make too much or you make too little," Karraha says. The phrase captures the trap that many recipients describe in their stories of living with the help of public assistance.

One Dollar Too Much

"I worked all my life to have something. And then when I'm not able to work, I'm penalized," begins Elliott Dunn.

> One time for me, I was laid off. And I had the same part-time job that I have. And I went to apply for unemployment, and they said, "Well, unemployment is more than what you're doing."
>
> But I said, "It's not as much as I was working per week." So I asked, "Now if I quit my part time job, I can draw unemployment?"
>
> And they told me, "Yeah." [Raises eyebrows]
>
> Even this past time, when I did draw unemployment, they deducted from what I was making on my part-time job. But first time they said, because my part-time job was only like a dollar or two more than what they say, "Well, you can make three hundred dollars and then still draw." But I was making . . . the cutoff line was three hundred dollars, and I was making three hundred and five dollars. I said, "If I quit, then I can draw? Which would pay me what?"
>
> "Four or five hundred dollars a month."
>
> I said, "Well, just pay me the difference!"
>
> I mean, if I'm making three hundred dollars and I can draw five hundred dollars, then just pay me the two hundred dollars.
>
> But they said, "We can't do that."

The complaint that the welfare system, including unemployment benefits, can be a disincentive to work is painted in stark relief in stories like Elliott's. Unlike common criticisms that the disincentive to work is tied to lazy recipients or overly generous benefits, the disincentive described by aid recipients is tied to policies that appear illogical and counterproductive when applied to real people. These stories are so common that they emerge as a recognizable subgenre of challenges stories: the "one dollar too much" story.

"I'm going to say this about welfare. I never say I agree with welfare, I disagree with welfare," James Bryant explains.

> Years ago, my ex-wife went to prison, and I got two of my kids, and I tried to apply for assistance, and they denied me. They said I made one dollar too much.
>
> I thought they were joking. And they were for real. I was like, "Are you kidding me?" And I went on like, you know, my ex-wife getting it all these years when she had the kids, and now I have the kids, and I can't get it. What's the difference than a man getting it and a woman getting it? There's no difference.
>
> I didn't like it. I didn't like it; you know I didn't like it. It pissed me off; it really pissed me off. That's when I went like, "Screw you." I didn't say it like that; I said it with more harsh words.
>
> It's just that I haven't ever cared anything for it. I really haven't. I know it helps people though, sometimes; I know it does. I never cared anything for it, never have. Probably never will.

I mean, I was working two jobs at the time. I just wanted some assistance with day care. But they wouldn't even do that because they said I made one dollar too much a month. Just got to suck it up and go on.

James was homeless for a while and relied on the shelter to help him get back on his feet, but he does not see himself as an aid recipient and does not believe the system works. Like all challenge stories, a satisfying resolution remains just out of reach.

Zero Sum Game

A related problem is the one-to-one policy in adjusting benefits. A raise at work equals a similar reduction of assistance. The result is that there is no financial incentive to work harder and make more money until one moves all the way off public assistance. Lilly Gibbs runs through a litany of examples of when her income has shifted a small amount and her benefits yoyo all over the place, inevitably settling on the lowest level possible, where she can't cover her bills. Louise Howard also describes a history of these moments, narrating her most recent as a way to explain the need for reform

> The system needs to be revised. And I'll tell anybody, "Do not get on these public assistance programs if you don't have to be, because you are going to be put in a box because you can't make a certain amount of money; you can't have a certain amount of things."
>
> I'm wondering what's going to happen with my food stamps and whatever that I'm getting right now once I have to report that I got a 2012 Jeep Cherokee that I needed and got to pay a three-hundred-fifty-dollar car payment.
>
> This is very discouraging. I can't tell you how discouraging I have felt. I have cried. Every time when I get a job, start another job, and I know I got to report that income. And what they do is they go by when I had to report this job. And the people at grant housing said, "Well, because you have a certain amount of hours, that you have a patient, then you have pay."
>
> But my patient just got moved, so my income is not going to be the same. And the housing guy just said, "Well, we can't keep adjusting the rent."
>
> They're supposed to adjust my rent.
>
> And so, this month's paycheck is not going to be last month's paycheck because I done lost my patient.

As a home care nurse, Louise works steadily when she has a patient with chronic illness, sporadically when she is needed for temporary health emergencies. As patients' conditions change, so do their needs, and they may be transferred for greater or less care. The result is an unpredictable income. She feels that agencies are quick to lower her benefits if she seems to be making more money but reluctant to raise them when making less. Others tell similar stories, where rents increase but wages stagnate, or small raises are accompanied by cuts in hours, resulting in lower take-home pay. Louise and so many like her bite the bullet, tighten their belts, and struggle along until they can save enough for their own home, their own car, or tuition for school. In the meantime, the problems these stories describe remain unresolved.

STIGMA STORIES

"Twenty years ago, I was a functioning human being," begins Rick Banks. "I had my own place, two cars and a yard, good job, two jobs. I had all of that, but this is not the same world anymore. I'm not lazy. I don't want free handouts or anything like that. Welfare—it doesn't give you enough where you can enjoy life. It isn't like we're just laying up in Hawaii drinking drinks out of coconuts and looking at pretty girls and things like that. I'm like a pariah in this society, somebody that's the most unwanted. I don't have any money. And when you're associated with a place like this right here"—he sweeps his arm around the homeless shelter where he is currently residing—"a lot of places don't want you around."

For people struggling to make ends meet, stigma is the social force that kicks you when you are already down. As if not being able to feed one's children or maintain a roof over your head is not bad enough, people are vilified, blamed for their lot in life or for having the audacity to ask for help.

In stigma stories, people describe encounters they have had where they were discriminated against or treated poorly because of their use of public assistance. These stories are often set in grocery stores where other shoppers see their EBT cards and leap to judgment. "I use self-checkout now," explains Bethany Chance, "so I don't have to worry about people with judgy eyes watching me."

> Everybody already assumes that because we have five kids they all have different daddies. I can't count the number of times I get asked that. Every day. I go out in public; somebody asks me, "Are all these kids yours? Are you with their daddy? They look like the same father?"
>
> Um-hmm.
>
> And they are like, "Really now?"
>
> And I am like, "Yes, really. They're all mine; me and their dad are married. We know what causes it." [Laughter]
>
> It never fails because I had somebody do it to me. . . . When was it? Last week? Yeah, because we stopped at Walmart on the way to Greensboro; we got to babysit for Uncle John.
>
> And that old man . . . I got stopped by two different people in Walmart before I could get out of the store, and they were like, "Oh, your kids are so cute. Are they yours?"

And then the old man on the way out who was like, "Oh, these kids are so cute; are they all yours?"

And I was like, "Yes."

He is like, "Are you going to have any more?"

And I am like, "No."

And he was like, "Well, that's good."

Well, he asked me how old I was. I was like, "I will be twenty-seven next week."

And he goes, "Well, you don't look it."

And I am thinking, "Well, God, I would hope not. But thank you for your input and your concern there."

Bethany cannot hide her children, but she can hide her EBT card in self-checkout lines. Hiding is a common strategy for avoiding judgment, stigma, and embarrassment.[4] From as early as they can remember, people who grew up in families that needed public assistance recall hiding their addresses and their reduced-lunch tickets as well as they could.

Growing up, people thought it was like leprosy. You don't want to hang around or be around anybody that's like that.

And I would talk to anybody. I would try to be nice to anybody. It didn't matter. And it's like a bad, bad thing growing up.

And when I . . . first got on it, I know I was extremely embarrassed about it and didn't want to talk about it because I knew I didn't want people judging me or looking at me.

Both Leslie Forester and Christie Huston describe poverty and the use of public assistance as a disease, an infection of the body that is contagious and must be washed off.[5] Such views are common, the impact of stigma on psychological and emotional health well documented (Reutter et al. 2009). Stigma can also affect physical health, both at structural and personal levels (Bock 2012, 159; see also Link and Phelan 2001, 2006; Wailoo 2006). For aid recipients, structural devaluation has resulted in policies that are increasingly punitive and restrictive, shrinking aid in terms of both amount and access. Personal devaluation has resulted in people embarrassed to seek the help they need.

Pride is a powerful motivator. As a white man in the South, Elliott Dunn believes he is supposed to be strong, independent, and self-sufficient. To be otherwise is to be pitied or vilified; it is unclear which is worse. Such beliefs are hardly regional. In the documentary film *American Winter* (2013), John (his last name is withheld) admits that he thought welfare was not for people like him. "I finally broke down and went. . . . And this was kind of a prideful thing, but I'd never even had food stamps until a month and a half ago. The food stamps were for people who . . . It was for the needy. I was looking at myself as being kind of like a deadbeat for having to resort to food stamps." When he realized he needed help, his first instinct was to adopt the stereotype rather than revise it; instead of seeing that other recipients might be just like him, he feared he must be a deadbeat like them.

Elliott and John finally broke down and sought aid. Others don't. "I had a next neighbor; she didn't have her GED," Makayla Stirling explains. "I said, 'Hey, buddy, go up there, sign up for the classes. Go and sit up there.' She would say, 'I don't want to go up there and sit up there with all those people.'" And so, their challenges go unmet; their stories go untold.[6]

Strategies for Managing Stigma

There are the practical strategies for managing stigma by trying to avoid it altogether: using the self-checkout at the grocery, hiding the reduced-lunch ticket, keeping to oneself. There are also the psychological strategies for managing stigma that aid recipients are forced to develop. John struggled to manage the stigma of getting food stamps. Over time, he has amended his view of aid recipients as deadbeats. He is working toward a place echoed in the stories of many other recipients like Susan Phillips, a place where public assistance is seen for what it is: help for those who need it. The space between these two points of understanding, however, is an age-old divide between the deserving and undeserving poor so entrenched in American society (chap. 8).

Susan grew up in the South with six siblings. When she describes her childhood, it was full of play: fishing with her dad, climbing trees with her brothers, playing football in the yard. Her family moved around a lot for a series of financial reasons, renting as they went, fighting to stay together. Susan is aware that her family received food stamps growing up but feels like her parents tried to keep that world separate from her life. She has tried to do this same in raising her five-year-old son, but it is difficult. She knows he hears what people say about welfare and the people who rely on it, because she hears it herself daily. Resisting belief in those stereotypes remains hard.

> Oh yeah, I hear it a lot. I believed it because you hear that, "Well, she's getting food stamps, she's lazy." "She's getting this, she's lazy." "She's sitting at home . . ."
> I get food stamps, and I stay in government housing. I'm not at all lazy. It's just hard. I've been trying to get back to work, but now everybody wants you have that GED or that high school diploma. So that's one of the things that pushing me to do what I'm doing.
> Like I said, I don't want to be where I'm at the rest of my life, well, just to say, the projects. There's nothing wrong with them; it's just that I've always wanted my own home, you know? And that's why I'm pushing to do the things that I need to do to get

out. And I don't want to be in that statistic where you're, "She's on food stamps. She's going to be on food stamps all her life."

It's not that; it's just that if I'm not working, and I don't have money coming in, how am I going to feed my child? So I have to do what I got to do. So if that means being on food stamps for a while, then that's what I'm going to do.

Growing up, my mom had to do it, you know? She had five kids. She worked, and my dad worked, and they still couldn't bring things together as to where they didn't need the assistance. And there's still a lot of people out here like that, so I applaud them for getting up and going down there.

Susan recognizes the stereotypes associated with public assistance and the stigma that comes with it. She does *not* want to be another statistic confirming the stereotype. While she is careful not to demonize public housing, she recognizes that others do and strives to get out of "the projects." Her response to the stigma is to let it drive her to do better but refuse to be grouped with those who rely on public assistance for life. Most dramatically, she claims pride in her parents, who defied the stereotypes by both working hard *and* defying the stigma by "going down there" and getting aid. Her parents, and by extension she herself, are to be commended, not demonized, for doing everything they can to care for their children.

The most common strategy in resisting stigma is for people to aver that it does not and will not bother them; nor will it deter them from seeking the assistance they need. Others use humor. In the African American community in particular, humor is a common strategy for deflecting harmful stereotypes.[7] Carla Robinson moves offensively to counter any stigma or stereotyping before it can begin.

So at my church and stuff, I'm very open about my situation. So sometimes when I say it, they're like, "Oh." They're kind of, "Oh, I wouldn't have thought." They're just kind of a little surprised.

So, I mean, nobody has ever treated me bad about it. And I'll joke about it sometimes. Like I joke about us being in the hood. I make jokes because sometimes people, I think once they know, then they don't want to say anything to offend you. So I'm just kind of like, well . . . I'll just joke about it because then it just kind of puts it out there. And then they know.

Less common but equally subversive is Etta Washington's response to a rumor circulating around the internet. "I saw a post on Facebook that said that you're ready to put. . . . See, they're going to start arresting single mothers that are unemployed. And I was like, 'There's going to be a whole lot of people in jail.'" Etta points out the impracticality and sheer ridiculousness of such a policy and the stigma driving it: that single mothers who are home caring for their children are supposed to be criticized, even criminalized, all within the popular political rhetoric of family values and the importance of a parent in the home. "Single mothers are raising their kids by themselves and no help from the fathers. And you arrest me because I don't have a job?"

Yet again we see the power of stigma. Even Etta, defiant in the face of rumor, relies on masking to avoid the constant drumbeat that she is not good enough to amount to anything. "I don't tell nobody. I don't tell a lot of people. Because my kids' father's family, they look down on me as if I'm beneath them because I'm getting assistance." The irony is rich. The stigma reinforced by stereotypes of the lazy, good-for-nothing aid recipient erodes a person's confidence that they can, in fact succeed. Christie Huston is not alone in fighting the urge to just give up. "I would rather come and stay in my house and be sad and know that I don't have it than to keep going around asking people for stuff."

Stories help. The narrative tradition provides space for people to articulate their worth and their refusal to accept social stigma, even if the path to full refutation is a long one. Repeating stories of stigma might seem an exercise is masochism, but the performance of these stories makes clear their function as a palliative strategy to confront stigma and rebuke it.

Not all people experience stigma in the same ways to the same degrees, however. The theory of intersectionality highlights how our multiple identities overlap and affect how we experience a singular phenomenon (see Cho, Krenshaw, and McCall 2013). The stigma of poverty and welfare is levied against people with shared economic hardship, but not consistently or to the same degree. The deserving-versus-undeserving poor trope provides one means of picking and choosing who is stigmatized and who is not (chap. 8). The addition of other stigmatized identities provides another. Martina Morales is Mexican, having immigrated to the United States when she was fifteen to join her parents who immigrated searching for work. As a Latina and an immigrant, she faces discrimination on the basis of her ethnicity, nationality, and gender. In the context of welfare, this is a potent combination. "They say, 'They don't need it. They aren't from this country,' or something like that," says Morales. "I heard when I went to turn in my papers to social services conversations like that."

Together, immigration and welfare form a political powder keg, spawning virulent internet memes and tirades that circulate on email, Facebook, and other forms of social media (chap. 9). April Ayers is white, but her husband is Honduran. She tells stories of the names she is called. "I had a friend, one day going down the road. He looked at me and called me a Mexican lover. The friend of my kids, they are calling me . . . I can't say; he calls me the N word."

The stories she tells about the stigma faced by her children are even worse, if only because they have not built up the defenses that April has constructed as an adult. Her sons are made fun of for their ethnicity, abuse that has been so bad that her oldest son is afraid to go to school. Her daughter is similarly teased, but also for her weight, and April has had to go to the after-school program in her housing community to address bullying. But as April explains, she has dyslexia. "I learn as a second grader. It's hard for me to sit down with my kids and do their homework. It's hard for me to read things and sit down and write a letter to their attorney. It's hard, and it's hard because half the family don't want to have nothing to do with me."

At times, those stigmatized identities are linked rhetorically as well as experientially. When Chad Buckley's parents found out he and his partner, Davey Cannon, were homeless, they drew a causal link between his sexuality and his economic hardship.

> My family found out. I don't know how they found out, but they managed to find out. I haven't heard from them in twelve years since me and him met.
> And it was a big embarrassment because nobody's ever—how do you put it?—looking to get on food stamps or help in general. So they just consider it a big embarrassment. So obviously my "lifestyle" caused it and all that crap.
> So, yeah. Fun, fun, fun.

Chad's parents were drawing on the "gay lifestyle as cause of misery" narrative. It was the same narrative that high-profile televangelists Pat Robertson and Jerry Falwell have used to explain 9/11 and natural disasters, such as hurricanes.[8] The narrative is a familiar one for Chad, who references the larger story with poetic shorthand: "and all that crap." For Chad's parents, being poor is divine punishment for being gay, a clear sign of God's views on homosexuality with one stigmatized identity causing another.

While no two people will share the same lived experiences and therefore will experience stigma differently, analyzing the assumptions made about a stigmatized group provides a window into the pressures individuals feel and the ways in which they respond. Gender, race, and class—the holy trinity of sociological analysis—provide a relevant *etic* framework that captures key demographic assumptions made about aid recipients (chap. 1). The narrative tradition, however, provides an *emic* approach to this analysis that recognizes age and sexuality as relevant factors as well. One need not imagine what those stereotypes, assumptions, and expectations about aid recipients are; narrators identify them in the stigma stories they tell.

The single most common accusation made about aid recipients is that they are lazy. This is true of both men and women. And yet the stigma derived from not meeting social expectations emerges slightly differently for men and women in the stories aid recipients tell. Rick Banks was adamant: "I'm not lazy. I don't want free handouts or anything like that.... It isn't like we're just laying up in Hawaii drinking drinks out of coconuts and looking at pretty girls." He does not need to

say, "People think those of us who receive public assistance are lazy, want handouts, drink cocktails, and chase girls." His rebuttal assumes the initial critique.
This is a common defensive strategy in stigma stories told by men and women.
But the assumptions are different between men and women. Rick assumes his
stereotype as a male aid recipient places him outside the home, unemployed, living high on the hog with government handouts. Female recipients, on the other
hand, hear a different story. "I hear it a lot, so I believed it," says Susan Phillips.
"Because you hear that she's getting food stamps, she's lazy. She's getting this,
she's lazy. She's sitting at home. . . . She's going to be on food stamps all her life."

Men are lazy simply by being unemployed. Women are lazy because they sit
around at home all day. Men *must* be in the wage labor force; women *should* be.
But because women's work is often in the home, the stigma centers around her
being lazy *at home*, when she could be taking care of the house and the children.
Further, there is an assumption that women's laziness is part of a generational
and systemic problem. Women are described as being on welfare all their lives,
not men. Accordingly, women as the primary caregivers become doubly dangerous: establishing a life of dependence not just for themselves but for future
generations.

While women are stigmatized for their role in the family, men are stigmatized
for their lack of one and for selfish, prurient vices. Rick's male aid recipient is
assumed to be drinking cocktails, an image that harkens to the most pervasive
legend about male aid recipients: the man getting cash back from his food stamps
to buy alcohol. The hypersexualized image that links Rick Banks's girl-chasing
stereotype to "young buck" legends is not only gendered but racialized.[9]

Men are also stigmatized for their inability to provide for their families. Elliott
Dunn admits that he rarely shares his story with others because of the stigma
associated with being unable to fulfill his role as breadwinner for the family. The
result is a narrative tradition that is relatively lean when it comes to men's stories
of feeling stigmatized by their dependence on public assistance. The stigma of
poverty silences stories of stigma.

The same should be true for women or anyone stigmatized, but men seem
more fragile in this respect, women more forthcoming. One way men's stories
enter the narrative tradition, however, is through eyewitness narratives, where
they are not the protagonist. Matt Putnam tells the story of his one and only trip
to the welfare office with his father.

> And like so, at that time point was the first time I actually went to a welfare place.
> They were like . . . It was weird because they sit in there, and it was just my dad and
> I. And I didn't say this earlier because I wasn't really warmed up to saying it but . . .
>   So we got in there, and as soon as like my dad handed the paperwork in to qualify
> for welfare, this lady behind the desk kept throwing me coats, throwing me mittens,

throwing me all this stuff that . . . just to like keep me . . . I don't know just like . . . just like regular stuff. Coat, mittens, pants, everything. I mean, I wasn't dressed poorly. I was dressed the way that I was supposed to be.

And as soon as that happened, my dad he brought me out to the car and made me wait there because he didn't like that.

And so that was my first and like really only, truly negative experience of being in a welfare place. And I didn't understand too much as to what was going on at the time. And it was only later that I realized that this is why they were doing it, and this is why my dad pulled me away, because he felt like they were stepping over the line and really taking away from him being able to support us.

Matt was talking with his girlfriend, someone he knew well and trusted, yet he is hesitant to share, noting that he "didn't say this earlier because I wasn't really warmed up to saying it." Matt and his father, both of whom are white, felt the stigma of poverty deeply and personally, his father feeling the sting of not being able to support his family without help. Tia Solomon, who is also white, also felt the sting of stigma deeply and personally, but for different reasons.

Probably about the second time I used my food stamps card, there was a bag boy and he was bagging at Food Lion, and he was pretty cute, and I was like putting my groceries up there, had my little girl in the cart, in the front of the cart. I don't think he saw her at first, but I was putting my groceries up and I went, I scanned the card whenever everything was done. And you could tell that he was well taken care of.

I scanned the card and she was like, "Credit or debit?"

I said, "EBT," which is food stamps. And the guy just kind of looked at me because I'm young, like he just kind of looked at me and walked away to the other cashier. Like at first, he was giving me faces like, "You're cute," and then he seen that I was using EBT and that was a total turnoff.

So, it just kind of made me angry because you don't judge somebody on food stamps. Like if they're on food stamps, they're obviously trying to do something for themselves. But some people have their own outlooks. They just have their own perspectives, but that just kind of made me mad. I just wanted to tell him off, but I was like, "I'm me. I don't care what you think. I'm not going to marry you or nothing."

It bothered me, but it didn't bother me at the same time because obviously he wasn't that good of a person if he's going to turn around when I'm just using food stamps and that just wasn't attractive to him. There's a lot of people that's like that though. A lot of people.

At the same time, the lady asked me if I had an MVP card before I scanned my card and I was like, "No," and he let me use his MVP card.

And then after that [using my EBT card], he was just kind of . . . It was just rude; he was rude.

> But there's a lot of people, like you'll be standing in line, use your EBT, and there's
> people behind you and they'll just kind of like, "You're poor. You're using EBT."

In addition to masking and defiance as a strategy for dealing with stigma, Tia also attempts a more subversive move: turning the tables. *She* is not deficient; the bag boy is. He is not just behaving inappropriately; he "wasn't that good of a person." Nonetheless, she feels the snub personally and responds with a similarly personal attack. Young, white, and single, she imagines herself as an appealing partner. The rebuke she feels from the "cute" and "well taken care of" bag boy seems to catch her off guard.

African American recipients on the other hand appear to be more familiar with such daily microaggressions and acts of prejudice and bias and more often tell stories where the stigma is already firmly in place, perceived structurally as much as personally. The EBT card was confirmation, but their skin color and inability to afford nice clothes were signal enough for people—white people in particular—to dismiss them.

> Well, you can go into a store, and you can see people that's well off, and they
> look at you, and you've got a food stamp card; they look down at you.
>   You have a lot of white folks that's the same way; they feel the same way. You
> in line, you using food stamps, and they look at you and snare their nose up,
> "Oh, why he got food stamps?"
>   Hey, what can you say? That's just the way they feel, so what can we say?

Lamar Reed shrugs off the stigma, believing that things will never change. People think how they want to think, no matter the facts or situation. Where Tia Solomon and Matt's father, who are white, take the affront deeply personally, Lamar recognizes systemic racism. He tries not to let it bother him.

Race is part of the equation. Assumptions about who is needy is another. Makayla Stirling recalls the treatment she receives when people find out she works for UNC Health Care.

> I have went and asked for assistance, and I've had at the Social Service Office a
> lady looked at me and say, "We're not going to give you any assistance; you work
> at UNC."
>   "Well, what does that mean? I got rent to pay. And I pay high gas driving back
> and forth to UNC every day."
>   "Well," it's just like, "no. No, we don't have anything. We don't have any
> benefits, so . . ."

In the documentary film *American Winter*, viewers see the visceral reaction to the stigma felt by a first-time applicant. In the film, however, the stigma comes not from aid providers but from fellow recipients. Pam is white and was middle class, able to afford multiple cars, a home, and a middle-class lifestyle. And then the recession hit, and her husband lost his job. She makes it back to her car and calls her husband, distraught at her first foray into social services.

> I just got out of the place. I've never been so scared and out of place out of my whole life. I just wanted to pull out of there. I did not feel comfortable at all. I am shaking to death. People were talking about me, you know: "Why is she here? Her children are dressed nice, and look at that big wedding ring on her finger. She's obviously married. She's probably doing fine."
>
> It just made me feel so awful and stuff, and I just—oh my god. [Drops her head into her hands] I didn't feel good. [Hands shaking] I don't feel good about it at all.

Tracy Salisbury tells a similar story, feeling out of place and judged for her appearance. "At the time, I was an office manager, so I was probably dressed in more business attire. And walking in there, even the looks that I would . . . It was almost like people were even looking at you. The people, the recipients, were like, 'What are you doing here? Why are you walking up in here?' or, 'Dressed like that and you're trying to get something?'" Tracy, Pam, and Makayla are stigmatized for being too *wealthy*, not too poor, a belief tied intimately to the legend of the welfare queen who claims benefits she does not need.

Stigma bites people coming and going: looked down on for being too poor or demonized for feigning unwarranted need. The stigmatizing stereotypes run so deep that even women like Delia who stand up to such stereotypes and refuse to be made to feel lower than others for relying on public assistance may still be tempted to stereotype and stigmatize others.

> Every once in a while, of course in the break room, sometimes we might watch TV. But now on the holidays, people are talking about, "It's that time of year again," or at the beginning of the month there's a lot of stigma. Because I work in retail. "It's food stamp time; here comes the food stamp people."
>
> I said something to a coworker the other day. I said, "What does that mean?" Because not everybody that gets food stamps . . . not everybody falls into that category. I talk to some people about it, if I'm comfortable or if I feel like they want to put everybody into a box. "Oh, it's food stamp time again; here come the food stamp people."
>
> I'm like, "What does that mean? Not everybody that get food stamps go out and they bring five or six kids and they have four carts of food." I said, "I get food stamps, and I shop just like you do. I might go to the grocery store and get what I need, and then that's it." I'm like, "I use it just like I would my debit card."
>
> They was just like, "I mean I was just saying."
>
> I'm like, "Just saying what?" Because I might get a certain amount, but at the same time I don't have a deep freezer, and I only buy what me and my family need for

maybe a week or two. "I just want to know what that was supposed to mean because I'm one of those food stamp people."

She was just like, "I mean, I was just saying some people do."

I said, "Yeah, some people do, and I'm not going to say that I don't roll my eyes and go like, 'Oh God, here come that lady that comes in here every month and gets four carts of food.' I mean, she might have a big family; she might be helping out a family member." I said, "I've seen everybody's situation, and yet it might annoy me to an extent, but I wouldn't like somebody judging me like you've just judged me."

Origin stories and challenge stories describe some of the darkest moments in a person's life. Fortunately, these stories are paired in the narrative tradition with more positive experiences. Origin stories are resolved with success stories while challenge stories are resolved with making-ends-meet stories, narrative types tackled in chapter 6. The parallelism of the narrative tradition reveals how narrators are able to take experiences that are unsettling, uncomfortable, ambiguous, and traumatic and bring order and coherence through the stories they tell.

NOTES

1. Lack of resolution in life does not necessarily equate to a lack of resolution in the stories themselves. The vast majority of challenge stories are shared with narrative resolutions even when long-term resolutions to the problems themselves remain. As such, these stories meet Labov and Waletzky's criteria for narrative (1967). This is an issue I address in more depth in a paper presented at the 2016 AFS Annual Meeting titled "Refinishing the Story: Transforming Stories of Life into Life Stories," forthcoming from *The Journal of American Folklore*.

2. In chap. 4, Carla shares her origin story, explaining that her husband is an addict and is currently in prison. While she does not elaborate on whether there was a specific incident of her husband caring for or driving their son while under the influence, her fears are clearly not unwarranted.

3. In her study of aid recipients in rural New York, Teresa Lawinski focused on the welfare office as a key site for study, naturally recording a significant number of stories about the bureaucracy of the system. As one might imagine, many of these stories were more explicitly negative (2010).

4. Compare to Erving Goffman's distinction between discredited individuals who belong to a recognizable stigmatized group and suffer accordingly, and discreditable individuals who are susceptible to stigma if their identity was to become known or ascribed, fairly or unfairly (1963, 4, 99–100).

5. For Christie's story, see chap. 11.

6. Diane Goldstein and Amy Shuman describe stories that are expected to receive social sanction as untellable, reserved only for a person's closest family or friends (2012). In Elliott Dunn's case, they may be untellable even in more intimate circles.

7. See, e.g., Dance (1978, 1998), Dundes (1972), Jemie (2003), and Lee (2014, 114).

8. Statements by Robertson, Falwell, and conservative religious leaders claiming a link between human death and disaster and homosexuality are well documented. For a survey of some of them, see Blumenfeld (2016).

9. After attacking Paul Krugman for suggesting that "young buck" was understood in the South as a black man, David Bernstein ultimately admits Krugman was correct, even if he does not admit that Reagan used the term intentionally to race bait (2014).

SIX

MAKING-ENDS-MEET AND ACHIEVING-SUCCESS STORIES

MAKAYLA STIRLING MOVED TO BURLINGTON with her family from nearby Caswell County when she was in high school. After graduation, she moved back and forth between the two places, following available work. When the textile industry faltered and the mills started to close, Makayla worked odd jobs, including as an armed services officer while she trained as a certified nurse's assistant (CNA). She worked as a CNA for a while and eventually got pregnant. So she moved in with her grandmother to help make ends meet. Knowing that she needed to get her own home eventually, she applied for public housing in Greensboro. She moved in but found the rules made it impossible for her to get by.

> So. . . . And I had problems, complications after my first child. I had preeclampsia. My blood pressure was out of the roof. So I was like pretty much on light duty, doctors watching over me, you know, "Don't do any type of strenuous work."
>
> I had to step back from the CNA job. I did like telemarketing then, sitting down every day, sitting on the phones doing outbound calls and things like that.
>
> But the lady who was my caseworker . . . My mother was there like every night. And that's like one of their policies that people can't be there and things like that. And I explained to the lady that my mom was there because I couldn't do anything, pretty much I couldn't lift the couch. I couldn't . . . But she told me, "No, your mother can't be here."
>
> And I told her, I said, "Well, if my mom can't be here, I probably don't need to be here either."
>
> So I moved there in February, and I was out by March.

Makayla's strategy of making ends meet was to rely on family: first her grandmother, then her mother. It also involved relying on public assistance to provide housing. She needed both, but government regulations allowed only one or the other.[1] And so she moved out after only one month. Eventually, she was able to find public housing in Burlington.

> I stayed there and raised my boys. And I worked through Maxim Healthcare for about two years after I got back on my feet and started working after I had my second son. And I worked, worked doing CNA, doing in-home health because it was flexible for me. I could work like ten- and twelve-hour shifts while my kids were at school and things like that in order to make ends meet.
>
> So Burlington Housing had a lot of programs, and every program they would send out paperwork and stuff. And I'd get home, and there'd be something on the door, and I'd say, "Well, I can do that. Self-efficiency? I can do that. I want to learn how to budget." You know what I'm saying? So all of these things that was coming to my door, sitting on my door, I was like, "I can do this. I can do this. I want to know how to do this."
>
> So that's what I started doing. Every meeting that they had, I would just tell them . . . because it's like when you're doing home health type things, it's like freelance work. I can say I'm not coming to work Wednesday, and I don't have to be there. So. . . . And I was like, "I have to leave work at four o'clock because I have a meeting at six o'clock and it was like OK."
>
> So having that freedom within my job allowed me to be able to say, "Oh, I'm going to this meeting today. I'm going to this meeting." So I started reaching out to those meetings and going to those meetings.

In making-ends-meet stories, aid recipients describe how they manage to survive. They typically describe their efforts to find work, do odd jobs, balance budgets, find transportation, feed kids, and find community resources that can provide the crucial bridge to meeting their needs. Family members, public assistance, and hard work are at the center of these strategies and stories. Temporary solutions are found, but permanent stability remains elusive. The stories reveal a balancing act, where solving one problem often leads to another.

Tracie Rutherford tells stories of being able to work with one child but that subsequent children have made that impossible. An obvious outcome of being a single parent is the catch-22 of childcare. Childcare costs are often more than minimum wage, making it financially impossible to get a job instead of staying home to care for one's children. Further, getting a job can lead to a reduction of direct benefits like TANF and food stamps, as well as the loss of Medicaid, leaving families uninsured, a risk that seems irresponsible at best, cataclysmic at worst. But the concerns raised in many of the stories participants tell are not simply economic ones. The deep desire to be good parents, raise their children well, and provide a loving home are at the forefront of these stories. Tracie Rutherford explains her decision to step out of the workforce and devote her time to raising her kids.

I would say with my oldest son . . . He's my first son, and he used to come home from school, and I was always—I'm always willing to learn something, new stuff. So I was always taking somebody's class or something for advancement. And one day he was like, "Mom, when I come home from school, how come you aren't there?"

Because his older sis was there, and I guess the children . . . Siblings are going to bicker, and it was a thing of "Mom, I need you more."

And when he said that, it was like, OK, now I got to figure out a way to be here but keep money coming in the house and keep the lights on and stuff like that.

So that was the one experience with Isaiah that I would say made me like, OK, I need to be home. Because I missed her [oldest daughter] whole, I don't know, I missed the first ten years of her life. So it's like I said, I was working, I was on the go.

With childcare such a deeply and personally felt concern, it is not surprising that some participants describe marriage with sadness when it ends in unexpected divorce and great hope and excitement when it lies on the horizon. The prospects of a committed partner who is able to work outside the home while the other parent stays home to care for the children not only suggests a solution to the catch-22 of childcare but also provides relief from the stress of trying to manage a household by oneself. For Ayanna, the possibility of finishing her degree and moving forward with her career looks feasible for the first time in a long time now that she is engaged. "With me having a little help now with my fiancé, I can focus now. Being a single mom is hard with working and then taking care of your child."

TRANSPORTATION

More mundane obstacles such as a lack of transportation also pose problems, not just for work but for access to education and resources. In Greensboro, where a public bus system is available, most participants can get to work without a car. However, the long hours to get from one point to another if multiple bus transfers are required can make it difficult and time intensive.

Martina Morales described her excitement about getting her son into Head Start but then finding out there was no school bus to get him there. Luckily, she was able to arrange for a ride for him; if she had not, her son would miss out on a crucial opportunity to get the education he needs to succeed. Participants make clear that the opportunities and resources are often available, as long as you can get there. In places without public transportation, cars can become more necessary than homes. Staying in shelters and couch surfing with friends and family can be easier to navigate than finding consistent and reliable rides to work, childcare, and the grocery. But even in areas with public transportation, cost can be prohibitive. Susan Phillips explains:

My son goes to Smile Starters [dentist]. And Monday I had to get him over there. I didn't have the bus fare, so we had to walk. He got out of school, and we walked over there, and we walked back home.

So that's one of the struggles. But I have to do what I have to do. That's why I push myself and push myself the way I do.

Public transportation helps for consistency, but many participants rely on their social networks for more sporadic travel needs. People regularly barter informally with their friends and neighbors, offering help with gas or childcare for a ride. Tracie Rutherford gets a ride with a friend to Graham, where they have an inexpensive meat market, one of the many strategies she employs to make ends meet to feed her family.

I get my stamps on the seventh of the month. There's thirty-one days in the month. I got about four or five people in here to feed. Don't let them have a day off for school or something—that's a whole day's worth of food. I thank God for school because at least they get breakfast and lunch, and all I got to do is worry about dinner. When they're out of school and weekends, girl . . . We got to . . . Boy, peanut butter and jelly can't do enough! You really got to get creative because you only can buy so much.

Like I said, I have the hundred and eighty-four; then I got to take some of my income and slap that on there. I drive all the way to Graham, North Carolina. It's a little meat market. Anyway, it's inexpensive but I have to pay ten dollars for . . .

I have to wait for my girlfriend to arrive with them and use my little bit of stamps to get out there, and I just go just for the meat because it's really inexpensive. I get a five pack of chops for three bucks, and I'm like, that works for me, because I budget and try to preplan my meals, and, you know, you do what you can do to make it work. I got growing boys.

I got one, he can eat a whole Little Caesar's pizza by himself. He's only eight! Somebody should've told me boys are going to do this. They grow, and they eat. The little one, he's still at toddler portions, thank God, but that eight-year-old, he wants man-sized plates and then seconds. It's like, can mom have something to eat? I usually make sure they eat and eat all that they can eat. There are some nights that I go without, but they don't never notice that, but it's OK. I do just to make sure that they're full, you know, and they have what they have.

They have kitchens and stuff where they serve hot food. I know where to go to get the food at; it's just getting there. Again, here we go on our two-bus journey just to get this meal. By the time you get there, you don't even want it no more, and then it's something nasty, and you done went through all of this just to get here, and it's something horrible like, I don't know. They got some questionable meat. It's like cafeteria, you know, in your school. Like, what is this? At least it's something. I get some bread and some sweet tea or something.

Tracie recounts these strategies one after the other, in some cases simply recounting her standard protocol, in others telling generalized experience narratives or recurring events. For those who own cars, the challenge is to keep them road worthy, insured, and with gas in the tank. Christie Huston describes the elation of having a visiting uncle fill up her car with gas.

> Car's on full now because somebody else filled my tank up. I've had that car since tax time, and that car's never been on full. They put twenty dollars in the tank. Gas tank went all the way up to full. I said, "Lord, help me." I was like, "I'm having a heart attack." He was like, "What's wrong with you?" I was like, "She ain't never seen the F. She ain't never seen the F." She be breathing E and will cut off on you and say, "Look, I'm thirsty. We ain't going no more." She gets under a quarter tank of gas, girl, she'll cut off.

The critical need for transportation can lead people into troubled financial waters, affecting short-term decisions, like paying rent, and long-term goals, such as home ownership.

> We make our van payment tomorrow. And then we have one more van payment, and then they're going to redo our loan, and then our van will drop to about two hundred dollars a month. So we're just trying to get to August. If we can just get August, everything will start to straighten out a little bit because we'll have an extra two hundred dollars a month when our car payment changes.
> Because we were tricked.
> Everything was supposed to go on my husband's name, and his dad was supposed to be the cosigner. But no, they put everything in my father-in-law's name. And then told us just to give back our other van because they were going to take it on a trade.
> So we defaulted on an eleven-grand loan because we couldn't keep up with nine hundred dollars a month in car payments plus our rent, and so we're like, "Great."
> So now, that's going to set us back as far as home ownership goes, so that's put us here even longer. So we have to work out that and straighten our credit out. But they're going to take, they said, "Six months," no, "Thirty days late, and we will open everything in your husband's name. Your payment will go to like three hundred and forty-something dollars a month." And I'm like, "OK, that's doable."
> So we pretty much have been toughing it out since February, and it's been really hard.

STRATEGIES

Emerging from these stories is one resounding common theme: family support. Some strategies rely on bartering with neighbors, some with taking advantage of all possible resources available within the community, others with scrimping, saving, and going without. When people *describe* the strategies they have for making ends meet, these are the strategies people mention. But when people *tell stories* of a recent challenge, family emerges again and again as the dominant source for help.

Christie Huston's uncle fills up her gas tank, an unexpected but welcomed surprise that was minor in the grand scheme of things but thrilling at the time and memorable months later. Far more central to her survival, however, is the help her grandparents offered her and her mother when her mother was escaping an abusive marriage. Martina Morales is married, but her husband is often at work and unable to help in emergencies, so she turns to her father, whether to help fix a flat tire or to help pay the utility bills to keep the lights on. Susan Phillips does the same. When Delia Taylor moved from Ohio to North Carolina, she stayed with her brother for a few months until she could find a place of her own. Etta Washington stayed with her sister when her husband left her.

The support of family can have its limits, however. While many people—aid recipient or not—find themselves moving back in with parents during times of transition and need, such arrangements are rarely sustainable. "I was staying at my mom and dad's," explains Davey Cannon. "They had made an apartment, and I was there. And my dad had to have surgery. He was the one that was paying all the bills and everything, you know, my medical bills, my medicine, because without Medicaid, the medicine was straight out-of-pocket, and some of it was very expensive. And he got out of... you know, unable to work, so to make things better, you know, easier, I just come on to the shelter."

Family members appear as one of the best and most consistent support networks available for participants when things get particularly tough. The downside is that if someone moves away from home or becomes estranged from their family, life can become extremely difficult. Paradoxically, stories of receiving aid from family often start with an initial problem in the home. Before Christie and her mother found shelter with her grandmother, Christie Huston's mother struggled to feed her as a baby. When she asked her mother-in-law, who owned a convenience store, for a can of milk, she turned her away. Her mother left with Christie the next day, leaving behind a callous mother-in-law and an abusive husband. Sara Vetter's mother made her daughter think she was developmentally delayed to get disability for her daughter. Only years later when she found herself in need of applying for food stamps of her own did she find out what her mother had done and why. When Ayanna Spencer and her daughter and fiancé had to move out of their apartment, they turned to her aunt and uncle for a temporary place to stay. Yet only hours after moving their boxes into the basement, her uncle came home, changed his mind, and kicked them out.

The popular religious adage "When God closes a door, he opens a window" appears relevant here. When one family member fails to provide the support needed, another often comes to the rescue, as in the case with Ayanna Spencer. Although they were forced to sleep in a Domino's parking lot the night her uncle refused to let them stay, the next day her fiancé's mother took them in despite already having some of her other children's families living with her. She gave Ayanna and her family her own bedroom and let them stay until they got back on their feet a few months later.

Over time, such help can operate as a two-way street, since many participants come from families who are also struggling to make ends meet. Carla Robinson and her sister provide childcare for each other. Etta Washington stayed with her sister when she needed help and then returned the favor when her sister's house burned down. Christie Huston took in her sister and her four kids when they became homeless. Bethany Chance did the same, as well as buying groceries for her mother when she runs out of food.

Unfortunately, sometimes helping family can lead to problems. Tracie Rutherford let her brother stay with her when he had nowhere else to go. The move was a generous one but violated public housing rules, not only because he wasn't supposed to live there but also because he was a drug addict. After a falling out, her brother left but told the public housing authorities that he had stayed with her, getting her kicked out. The impact of helping family was less dramatic for Christie but arguably much more damaging. When her grandfather got sick, she dropped out of high school to take care of him. The impact of not having an accredited high school degree has made it virtually impossible for her to get a job that will pay the bills. Gina Nielson had a job but had to give it up to care for her mother when she got sick.

Fortunately, it is not only family that provides important help in times of need. Social networks help create social capital: the intangible resources people develop among their acquaintances that foster economic, cultural, and personal growth. Social capital is built through relationships marked by trust and reciprocity. The challenge for many low-income families is that social capital is often low or confined to other low-income families with similarly low material and financial capital. However, even small increases in social capital can be productive in helping individuals reach their goals and communities function more effectively.

One avenue for building these connections is through continuing-education classes, such as financial literacy, job preparedness, and GED prep. The primary goal of these courses is individual development and skill building, but an important by-product is the development of horizontal or bonding social capital among peers. Jashanna Kingston notes, "It's like you build a relationship with everyone there. And you get comfortable. And then once you're comfortable, you'll be able to talk more." A stronger community leads to better learning. Etta Washington concurs:

I've made a lot of friends, and I've been keeping up with all of them. We keep close contact. We call each other. They come to the house. I go to their house. Same thing. It's like family. Most of the time we either call each other or text each other.

The first day we usually exchange numbers. The ones that are willing to do it will exchange numbers. If we need help on our homework, we'll call each other, text each other. Whatever we need.

In addition to help on homework, participants create a community in class where they feel free to discuss their day-to-day struggles, both seeking and offering advice to each other. Susan Phillips explains:

Some of the ladies that were in the class with me, I still keep in touch with them from time to time. I've learned a lot. I'm pretty sure a lot of them ... because we in the class and talking to the ladies, we've all had a lot of the same issues. And I didn't know. I thought I was the only one dealing with this and dealing with that. And to talk to those ladies and, "Oh, hey," you know? I learned a lot from them as well. I'm hoping they learned some things from me.

For one thing: how to deal with your children. I hear a lot of the ladies talk about, "Well, my baby did this, and my baby did that," and I'm like, "Oh. Well, my son just did that, so how do I deal with it?" and listen to their stories. Some of the stories they tell me, I apply it to me and my son, and it works for me, you know? Some of the things they say, "Well, try it this way," or, "Try it that way," and it works. So having that connection with other women in the same position I'm in helps a lot.

As participants become friends, social capital grows; so do the ways in which they can help each other. Eliza Nguyen described the emotional support she received from her fellow classmates after sharing stories of the challenges she has faced. Susan Phillips describes the friendly competition among some of her peers as they push each other to complete the four sections of the GED. Etta Washington commented on the power of her peers to motivate her onward: "They also boost my courage," she says. "That made me want to get off of public assistance faster."

The benefits of increased social capital extend beyond the classroom into daily life. Not only do participants share useful information about community resources and parenting; they share childcare and rides. Proximity helps. Social capital built in class supports social capital in neighborhoods.

PUBLIC HOUSING AND THE PARADOX OF COMMUNITY

"Well, I have Etta now," Karraha says, reflecting on the lack of close friends in her immediate neighborhood. "She is the parent committee president, I'm vice president, and she and I have been supporting each other through this since it started. All three of us volunteer a lot and everything. We usually have each other to lean on. That's what I have for encouragement and also to help push her. It's really a push-and-pull kind of relationship. It's really cool."

Karraha settles into her overstuffed sofa, drawing her daughter, Lotus, closer to her. Justin sits on the other side of their daughter, nodding in agreement. "It's all right, I guess," he adds noncommittally. On their front porch, they are growing plants: a zinnia picked out by Lotus, a strawberry plant by Karraha. Despite its small size, there are blooms on the strawberry plant hinting at fruit; the zinnia is farther behind but promises a riot of color when it blooms. Beauty and function. The sloping yard that stretches out from the porch has been recently mowed, as have all the lots in Smith neighborhood where the Shepards live. Kids on bikes and on foot move slowly through the neighborhood in the late afternoon heat of summer. Women hang clothes out on slack lines in backyards with no fences. Empty chairs on front porches hint at a public sociability that emerges at night when it begins to cool off.

The neighborhood, like many public housing communities, is a contradiction even for the people who live there. Karraha and Justin describe their neighborhood with a vague sense of unease, unable to escape the stereotypes of public housing that permeate popular culture. Academics call them "discredited neighborhoods," places that have been stigmatized in the mind without ever seeking evidence of the eye (e.g., Warr 2005). But Karraha and Justin's stories defy their own initial reactions, capturing moments of friendship, community, and trust.

"I don't think it's a bad neighborhood," Karraha says. "I think it gets a pretty bad rep, but it's mostly what you make of the situation." Like the "book nook" they installed so neighbors could exchange books or the community garden that one of the older women in the neighborhood started and maintains with help from the local kids. "It's just a lot of different flowers and cabbage and radish and carrots and beets, and they have the sunflowers," Justin says. "They are already about two, three feet."

> **Justin:** Oh yeah, we have a barter system right now. We have an awesome barter system right now. You have this, we have that. When I put up a fence, we got a dozen of fresh eggs because . . .
> **Karraha:** She has hens.
> **Justin:** Apparently, she has hens, and she just has a whole lot of eggs. We just got eggs.
> **Karraha:** We went over there, and he and Tim were working in the garden. She brought us a bunch of greens. It was just fresh greens and relishes and stuff. I was like, "I don't even know what to do with all this." [*Laughter*]

As with family, social capital is built reciprocally. Justin helps build a fence or work in the garden and gets eggs or vegetables in return. After months of volunteering with the food service company that provided lunches at Guilford Child Development, Justin was hired, providing a job that not only helps his own family but his neighbors as well.

> **Karraha:** We haven't been grocery shopping since. He comes home with huge pans like this [*stretches arms wide*] full of food. Four and five and six of them. Look, we've invested in Ziplock bags, so we've got to bag it all up and give it out.
>
> **Justin:** I watched so much food get thrown out. My fist day I watched them throw out forty-two pounds of greens. Once those leaves cook down, they maybe weigh a quarter of an ounce *maybe*, and this is forty-two pounds of it just thrown away.
>
> **Tom:** So what do you do?
>
> **Justin:** The neighbors get some; some other neighbors over there get some; we take some to church. We just give it to . . .
>
> **Karraha:** We just give it away. We're taking it up to the office. "Here's a pan; just give it to the kids." They don't care. "Take it, because we bogged the refrigerator in."
>
> Our refrigerator, if you open it right now, it's just silver all the way down. And then the freezer was just stacked with Ziplock bags of everything.
>
> We told our friends to come over and go grocery shopping, so we can clear up the freezers. They left with like three huge bags of frozen food, and it was like, "We can't do anything with all of this." There's only three of us. Then a lot of it is meat. So me and her [*pointing to Lotus, since Justin is vegetarian*] have to consume it, and we can't keep that forever.

Abstracted as a place—ideological and geographical—public housing often evokes ambiguous or negative responses from residents echoing the heavy stigma attributed by the general public. But when focused on individuals and relationships, more positive responses emerge. Stories capture both the negative and the positive, but the divide between the faceless neighborhood and the personal relationships within it is repeated in the narrative tradition, helping to explain the contradictory views. Stories about public housing bridge making-ends-meet stories and challenge stories, revealing community to be both antidote and poison.

Delia Taylor recounts her story of leaving town and having her grill stolen but also of getting her daughter together to play with the neighbor's children. Sara Vetter describes people banging on her door at two in the morning having confused her home with her neighbor's, while Carla Robinson shares her story of neighbors who come over and turn off her car lights when she accidentally leaves them on. Small acts of kindness are more common but less memorable and therefore less likely to remain in the narrative tradition. Recent events are narrated but in time drop away from a person's repertoire to be replaced with newer, if still not particularly memorable, examples. Theft and violence, however, are more unusual, dramatic, and memorable.[2] Those stories stick.

"Actually, my house got shot up," Christie Huston begins.

> They don't know why or who it was involving. The police did come out. Luckily, none of the bullets entered our home. They entered the neighbor's residence. One went through the walls and ended all the way up in his laundry room. Luckily, my kids were upstairs sleeping when the accident happened.
>
> We don't know who the people are. I was told that some of them are incarcerated and some of them got right back out. Nothing's happened since then, per se, but that was enough for me. I grew up like this my whole life. I'm almost thirty years old this year, and my mom left and got out of it. My objective is to keep my kids out of situations like that because I had to grow up my whole life like that.

Dehumanized with faceless, nameless actors, these stories feed both the stereotype of "the projects," as well as the us-versus-them divide that separates the deserving from the undeserving, those who see public housing as a stepping stone and those who see it as a finish line, or, as Deborah Warr discovered in her study of public housing in Australia, the "good people" from the "no-hopers" (2005, 294).

Christie Huston's view is fairly bleak:

> I live on public assistance, so it's the projects. You see the same stuff every day. The same way of living every day. It's like a cycle. I feel like they put us there and they leave us there. It's up to us whether we figure out how to climb out of there, or we can live every year and years and years and years. I know some people that have been there for twenty-three years plus. I just don't think it's the best environment for me and the children.

The constant refrain in these stories is fear for the safety of their children. Residents worry not only about random acts of violence but the influences their children are exposed to. Some participants express a sense of hopelessness that can pervade public housing communities that they attribute partly to a perception of government apathy and partly to the lack of autonomy, where space is often shared. Christie Huston explains:

> They put us here, and they leave us here. It's like, "OK, we're going to give you an apartment." Then what? We just live in the hellhole forever like we're reduced? You don't think I want a white picket fence? You know what I'm saying?
>
> I don't have a yard. People don't think that we want stuff like that. They think that because we live over here, we want to live like this.
>
> I hate it. I hate having neighbors that are connected to me.
>
> With my nana and my pawpaw, we lived in a trailer, so the lot, the yard, it was ours. I didn't have to worry about other people playing in my grass and being in my front yard.

I say something now, it'll be like, "This the projects." They can walk wherever they want to out here; ain't nothing you can do about it. Why? It's the projects.

The us-versus-them sentiment is both external and internal, between residents and nonresidents and between "good" residents and "bad." Tiffany Richardson is particularly worried about the bad ones.

If I go outside, I'll speak, but I don't go to their houses. I don't try to . . . I don't need friends; I have sisters. So, it's crazy, because they be trying to act like they my friends and like we cool and no. Like, "You coming outside?"
"No."
I just feel like . . . like my next-door neighbor's son . . . He is bad. He cuss; he's talking about like having a girlfriend and kissing and stuff, and he's four. And I feel like, well, he's getting it from somewhere. I mean, I don't necessarily blame the kid because the kids only do what they see. As much as you allow to. And I don't allow none of that. So it won't go down in my house.
And when they cuss, I make my son come in the house. Because if you even think that you going to be saying any of those words, you're going to be in trouble. So, he just be like, "Mommy, I'm going to go play with my friends."
"Those aren't your friends. I don't want you to have friends that do stuff that you not allowed to do. You need friends that have parents like me."

"Parents like her" are parents who are taking advantage of every opportunity, working hard, saving money, and striving to move out of public housing. It is an ideal reinforced by the policies and ideologies espoused by those in charge of public housing. Homes are intended as temporary and transitional. Programs are set up to provide the skills needed to move up and out. The rationale makes sense, but it risks fueling an ethos that undermines neighborliness. Why invest in friendships, reciprocal relationships, and community building if the goal is to ensure no stable community ever exists?

Ultimately, it is a paradox rather than a contradiction. Safer, tight-knit neighborhoods where people trust and support each other provide avenues for stability and success. Establishing this bonding social capital may seem futile if considering only the friendships destined to be split apart, but the benefits in the short term are great, and the increased possibility for success in the long term, even greater. This is why some people are unwilling to keep their heads down, keep to themselves, and strive to leave as soon as possible. They are not "no-hopers" but rather committed residents striving to make the best of the situation.

The positive stories public housing residents tell about their neighborhoods typically describe neighborly reciprocity, identifying specific people in the neighborhood with whom they trade childcare for rides and groceries for cooking and with whom they share hand-me-downs and leftovers. These stories depict community as a microcosm within the larger geographic boundaries of the neighborhood.

Negative stories, on the other hand, expand out in every way: they are more dramatic, more visceral, and ascribed to the whole community. When Christie recounts the story of shots fired into her house, she situates the story as an exemplar of widespread violence throughout the neighborhood; when Delia describes the stolen grill, she suggests rampant theft. When Jeffrey Thornton describes the sounds of gunfire, it is endemic. The antagonists of the stories are faceless and nameless despite the concrete details of the events. In this way, crimes by unknown perpetrators infect the whole community, casting doubt on everyone, where positive stories about known friends spread trust and friendship in relatively small circles.

The result is that the narrative tradition lends itself to a more negative portrayal of public housing communities despite a more positive portrayal of individuals within them. Jeffrey Thornton attempts to translate the individual efforts to ensure a safe neighborhood into a community-wide ethos when he describes an informal neighborhood watch, but he is one of the few. More often, the individual is the focal point of the good in public housing. That individual is so common as to suggest a localized archetypal character in public housing neighborhoods: the parent to all.

PARENT TO ALL

Pat Jackson sits on her living room couch, crochet needles clicking as she tells stories about her life. Taped to the walls of her home are inspirational quotes: "The only person you should try to be better than is the person you were yesterday," "Life goes on—whether you choose to move on and take a chance in the unknown. Or stay behind, locked in the past, thinking of what could have been," and "God gave you this life because he knew you were strong enough to live it." Piled in a basket beside the television are plastic bags, meticulously sliced into thin strips. She and some of the neighborhood kids will weave them into mats for the homeless, just one of the many activities she does with the children who live near her. "I don't know why, but they play right here," she says and laughs, knowing the answer.

> They want to cook, too, so we've done that. We've got one lady that bakes. So we were going to see if she would show them how to bake. We've even got . . . Now it's a lady next door and she's deaf, and she's learning them how to sign language. So they're working on that. So she's working on them. They go over, and they're so excited; they'd just be running over there to her.

So they're saying we're doing more for our kids and stuff than anybody else is. See, there's no kind of park or nothing else for them to do. So I started thinking of different things to do to keep them occupied, instead of they're out getting in trouble, out in the road, maybe getting hit by a car or something.

That's why I say, one week we do this, one week we do that, keep doing something different because they get bored if you keep doing the same thing.

And the thing about it, the kids got the idea. They're the ones who say, "What if we just pick out something to do every week, and we do something different every week when we come over here?"

And I said, "You know what? That's kind of a good idea." I said, "Well, just write down what you all want to do."

And so that's how we started out doing it.

Some of the things they did were purely for fun, like the movie marathon sleepover.

Well, the youngest I had to sleep over was nine. Really the youngest . . . she came over from next door, she was five years old. [Laughs] She knocked on the door, and she said, "I want to sleep over," so I couldn't say, "No, you can't." So I said, "Come on." [Laughter]

We had all of them on the floor. The youngest ones was in here [the living room] and the older ones in the bedroom, so you know, the youngest ones want to look at different things than the oldest one, because the older ones . . . They was in there looking at that scary movie, and the youngest ones, that wasn't happening. [Laughter]

It worked out pretty good. We had some that was fussing, of course; you've got that many, somebody ain't going to get along.

Other activities are part of Pat's larger goal to ensure the kids set high goals for themselves, like the previous Friday when she took a group of them to Elon University to tour the campus. Fellow Burlington Housing Authority (BHA) resident Makayla Stirling captures the sentiment in the well-worn African proverb: "They say it takes a village to raise a child. That's the God's heaven's truth. It takes people; it takes the village that you're with every day to push you and encourage you to get you where you need to be."

I think the strategies to overcome the roadblocks is being involved in your community. Even before I started back to work, and I was still like go to the meetings that Burlington Housing had to offer and things like that, because they would say, "Well, if Mary needs a babysitter because she's got a job interview Tuesday at eleven o'clock"—you and Mary may never known each other because Mary may stay on this end and you stay on that end, but now you and Mary can meet.

And at the community meetings that they have, you can really get to know people. Because there's a couple people that I didn't know, and then I started back going to community meetings once my classes changed. So I started back going to some of them. But when I first got there, I would go to them all the time, and you would find stuff out like one lady, she said, "I need my blood pressure checked."

I said "Well, OK then, I'll run up through there and check your blood pressure or whatever else."

So you know just who you're around and what you're around who can support you. Somebody may need gas to take their child to day care in the morning, so they can get to work, and you may need a ride to the job interview, so y'all can overcome.

The proverb wears well in deed as well as story. Neighborhood kids move in and out of each other's homes, sometimes as part of play, as often because their parents are heading to work or their grandparents need a break. Homes are permeable and parents willing, but permission is typically sought and granted. More formal arrangements in swapping childcare is also the norm. Such daily arrangements rarely rise to the level of memorable instances worthy of narration, though the social network established within public housing communities is crucial for making ends meet.[3] Other, more dramatic arrangements for childcare, however, do get narrated. Martha Sadler states plainly, "I take in extra kids when their parents can't handle them. Their parents will kick them out, and I give them a place to stay. The last three years I've took in five."

> I've got one that's going in—once he graduates—he'll be going into the army. And one left and went to Virginia and stayed with his aunt, and now he's facing jail time. I've got one that's dropped out of school, one that's got him a job. He finally got him a job; I can't remember where he's working. I just love them. [Laughs]
>
> I've got kids of my own. I had three boys and a girl, and the man I married, he had one child, and I just love them. All the kids around the home call me "Mama." Where I was raised, they still call me "Ma" down there because I been doing it for so long.
>
> The boy that's fixing to join the service? He's eighteen, and I carried him. He wanted to move out. His mama kicked him out, really. He came to me late at night, said, "Ma, can I move in?"
>
> "Yeah, sit you right there."
>
> We went and got his stuff that morning. That afternoon I had him at social services. I said, "If you stay here, you got to go to school." I said, "I can't afford you. I can't afford to feed you; I can't afford to carry you to the doctor. But I will carry you."
>
> It was during the summer, thank God. I carried him to social services and back for the interview. He got his Medicaid card, he got his food stamp card, and he goes to school every day.
>
> But he stayed with me about three months.

Once she starts, the stories of her "children" tumble out, proud of the ones who have done well, saddened by those who went back to broken homes or back to old vices.

I'm being mama bear to everybody else in the neighborhood. [Laughs] There's this boy that lives down the street; he's thirty-six. He comes up, "Ma!" He came the other night; he had a date. [Laughs] He says, "Ma, you got something I could feed two people on?" [Laughs]

So I hooked him up with some hamburger and said, "That's enough for y'all. Your mama got to have some lunch tomorrow."

He said, "Love you, Ma." [Laughs]

Knowing the importance of family as one of the primary safety nets for people living near poverty, it is not surprising that the parent-to-all archetype, phenomenon, and narrative genre encompass relatives as well as neighborhood children.

Back in her darkened living room to escape the heat, Pat continues to knit. Behind her are the photos of her "children." She has two biological daughters who are grown and have given her grandchildren, but the children on her wall are the five additional kids she has raised at some point in their lives. There is her nephew Jaivon, whom she started raising when he was three, even before she had her own children. Her daughters, Jalanda and Quanesha, call him their brother. Then there was Grace. Grace's grandmother and Pat's mother were best friends, and Pat grew up with Grace's mother. Grace's mom became addicted to drugs and went to nearby Durham for treatment. Pat cared for Grace until it became too hard. Grace "would get so mad and tear up my furniture and stuff and just break stuff." Grace's mom ended up doing well, getting sober and custody of her children back, but Grace is in jail. "She and two boys went and robbed somebody, and they killed him." Pat looks back down at her crochet. She admits she wonders sometimes whether there was anything she could have done. Then there was Samuel, her friend's little boy. He died in car crash outside of Atlanta. Pat did not raise Samuel as much as give him and his mother—a close friend of Pat's—a place to stay periodically. But she counts him as one of her own. The photos also include two young boys in red shirts standing against a rustic farm door in a professional studio picture. They are the sons of another close friend who helped Pat get started as a home caregiver.

Pat has been parenting long enough to include multiple generations in her home. In one of the pictures on her wall, Jaivon's son, Khalan, or "Lon," is seen snuggling a stuffed white tiger plush toy. Pat shared joint custody of her grandnephew with Lon's paternal grandmother, Pat's brother's wife. But Lon was upset when Pat moved to Burlington to help care for yet another child, Bree. Like Martha Sadler, Pat has helped raise children with no biological connection. Bree is the daughter of a man Pat used to date. Pat and Bree grew close, going for bike rides and playing in the park. When Pat and Bree's father broke up, Bree asked to move in. Bree's brother was struggling, and home life was rocky with her dad and grandma. Pat has raised her ever since. Someday, Pat says, crochet needles clicking away, she would like to buy a big house and open it to dozens of foster children.

BRIDGING SOCIAL CAPITAL

The bulk of the stories people share about their social networks focus on bonding or horizontal social capital among classmates and fellow aid recipients. But some describe relationships that establish vertical social capital built with staff that led to opportunities difficult to attain otherwise. Susan Phillips describes how the staff at Guilford Child Development helped line her up with the opportunity to shadow a preschool teacher as part of her efforts to pursue a career in education. Justin Shepard recounts the story of how volunteer work earned him a full-time job.

> Right before I got this job actually, everybody that saw me just kept saying, "Man, just stop. Stop helping out." Because I have been helping out at the school since she [Lotus, his daughter] got into school, and I wasn't really expecting them to just give me a job. They didn't just give me a job anyways; I just kept helping out, kept volunteering, and just kept doing it, and everybody was saying, "Just stop. Stop. What are you doing this for? They are just using you."
>
> And then one day I was just going to go home, but I stayed up there and helped out this guy that used to work there and this lady; they were just putting stuff up, like cleaning up, so I helped them out. And she turned out to be the boss.
>
> So had I not kept persevering and kept helping out irregardless, I probably wouldn't have gotten this job. So it was pretty cool for me.

Karraha chimed in, noting that this wasn't a fluke.

> We found out later that essentially that's what most of the employees there came from: they were parents from the center that volunteer their way up into positions to the higher up of the building. But you know it's not something that people actually talk about, so we had no idea.

In the business world, networking is a key means of advancement, but even with such a calculated effort, there is rarely a single, clear, specific goal. Justin's volunteering emerged out of a desire to help and to work. Frustrated with the lack of jobs or the capital to start his own Reiki studio, he hated being idle. Despite the lack of either a calculated plan or specific goal, he built social capital among the staff at Guilford Child Development and the catering company who served them. Social capital became financial capital.

When Makayla Stirling noted that "it takes a village," she wasn't talking about her neighborhood. Rather it was a village of aid providers, coworkers, and family that helped her qualify for a Habitat for Humanity home. She has many stories to tell of being helped, but she returns to one again and again.

When bills were due, and I didn't have no way, I . . . I would come to work some days and would be sad and would look in my locker, and there would be money there. And I didn't say anything to anybody.

And that was like, "OK, I can't give up. I got to keep going. I got to keep going."

And then I got two little boys that's looking in my eyes, and I'm telling them that I got to do this; I'm doing this for us. They're my most . . . That's my biggest motivation right there is to show those two little boys this can be done. It's not where we live; it's how we live. You know what I'm saying? We can do it, you know?"

Unsolicited, a coworker recognized that she was struggling and made a small but significant gesture that did not just help her financially but emotionally. In fact, when she tells stories of calling on Ms. Sabrina and Ms. Shanika at BHA, her sisters, and her coworkers when she is struggling, it is not for financial support but moral support.

For some, work provides the means for making vertical connections that expand their social circle and provide capital that bridges demographic, geographic, and socioeconomic divides. For others, it is church. Lilly Gibbs, Diane Clemens, and Betsy Maller are among many aid recipients who found unsolicited but critical help from the church as an institution, as well as from individual church members. The wider the social network, the greater the social capital, the greater the potential benefit.

NATURAL CONTEXT: EMPATHY, ADVICE, AND INSPIRATION

Making-ends-meet stories provide the fodder for one of the most important and commonly cited functions of personal experience narratives about living near the poverty line: providing empathy, advice, and inspiration to others facing similar problems. It is not by accident that such functions also help build social capital. When shared with aid workers and in interviews with academics and journalists, the tone of the stories is fairly somber. Making-ends-meet stories typically signal scraping by. But performance contexts affect tone and focus, and when making-ends-meet stories are shared with other aid recipients, these stories are often recast as hard-won victories that can provide strategies for others. Listening to the stories closely makes it clear why such a transformation is possible. While the recipient may be depressed about the lack of clear progress, their strength, perseverance, and creativity are nonetheless on display in the story even if they are not brought to the fore. Tracie Rutherford found an out-of-the-way butcher whose prices allow her to serve meat to her children when her budget suggests that should be impossible. Susan Phillips walks her son to the dentist, a miserable task in the southern summer but a testament to the fortitude of doing what needs to be done to care for her child. Jashanna Kingston cuts coupons to stretch her food stamps while Martina Morales takes advantage of the dollar menu at fast-food restaurants to get her kids a treat.

And so men and women share their stories with fellow shelter guests, aid recipients, church members, and neighbors as a humble effort to help those around them with the lessons they have learned over the years, often after frequent failing. Diane Clemens regularly talks to the young women in her church and in her neighborhood about a range of issues including single parenting on a budget, sharing stories of how she made ends meet and how they might do the same. She hopes that her stories spread and that the young women she sees today will find similar ways of balancing work and parenting, even if they don't mirror her path exactly. Gina Nielson tries to provide similar motivation for the women in the shelter where she is staying by sharing her stories of seeking job training. "There's one of them keeps saying that she don't believe she can make it, you know, she's too old. I'm forty-nine, and she's only like forty maybe, early, maybe early forties, and don't think she can, thinks she's too old to learn. I told her she's never too old to learn."

Lilly Gibbs describes her job as a bit of a dead end with low pay and no benefits and declares, "I'm not satisfied. I'm reaching higher." But she recognizes that she's making progress, and her health has improved significantly. "I am a testimony. I am a testimony. So, yes, I talk about it because sometimes people have a tendency... No one just believe anything anyone tell them. But when you can see it for yourself, there's no doubt, and along the way of sharing one's testimony with another person, they may be in a situation or could be in the same fix that I was in."

Lilly hits on a key problem with stories: belief. People who have not lived these experiences can share secondhand stories, but those stories may fall on deaf ears, doubted and ignored. But when people share their own stories, audiences are typically more ready to believe. Aid providers regularly share stories of other clients—without names or revealing details—for the same reasons of inspiration and motivation. Yet not one aid recipient cited a provider as the source of a story that inspired them or stuck with them. Instead, it was the stories of their peers that they remembered, retold, and reflected on.[4]

The one exception is when aid recipients move from one side of the desk to the other and become aid providers. Bernard Faucette had no home or job when he sought help at Allied Churches. He now has both, working at the Drop-In Center to help others in the same situation he was in not long ago. Antonio Wiley heard Bernard's story and holds it up as an example for himself. "I mean, I look at Bernard. He's a success. Because he was once there. That's what motivated me to try, to take it as a chance to make something better of myself, to see him, you know? Because he told me his story."

The rule holds. Bernard is telling his *own* story, not a secondhand story of a client. In sharing his own experiences, he positions himself as a recipient alongside his audience, not a provider separate from the experience. Stories of making ends meet and attaining success shared among their peers are remembered and retold among aid recipients; secondhand stories from aid providers are not.

SUCCESS STORIES

Making-ends-meet stories provide the foundation for one type of success story: one that depicts the life of a person still striving but with lessons learned along the way that can be useful to others. Diane Clemens continues to struggle to adapt to a life on disability, but she shares her stories because she recognizes she has gained some insight along the way that can be helpful to others. While Diane does not believe she has reached "success," in sharing her stories she recognizes that she has been successful. In this way, the act of performance is transformative, turning the stories that describe challenges met into success stories.

Part of this transformative work is done by the narrator in a process of self-recognition, but part is done by the audience. Narrators are all too aware of how much farther they have to go. Audiences, on the other hand, are not weighed down with the larger picture or the memory of the lived experience. They have only the story, which has been shaped to fit narrative convention. Key events are foregrounded; irrelevant parts, ignored. Complications are paired with resolutions, suggesting a coherence that shifts the focus from the ongoing challenge to the strength and perseverance required to meet those challenges. The result is that a speaker may tell a challenge or making-ends-meet story, but the audience may hear a success story. Justin Shepard describes telling stories at the open house about the challenges he faced and the programs he participated in; Jada Whittle describes coming to that open house and hearing him tell success stories. Lilly Gibbs does not see herself as a success, but the aid providers at the Open Door Clinic do. Just as a shift in voice from first person to second or third can mean a shift from a personal experience narrative to a legend, so too can it mark a shift in subgenre from a making-ends-meet story to a success story. In this way, success stories can be created in the hearing, not in the telling.

There is a second type of success story told, one unambiguous in its character or resolution. These are the small success stories that people see in their own lives and prize as trophies of their hard work. This is the story that Etta tells of graduating from her class at the Family Success Center or Delia passing her driver's test and getting a license for the first time at age thirty-three. It is also the story of Makayla Stirling finding a job.

So this Self-Efficiency Program. So I joined that program, and I just kept working at it; I kept working at it. And then Ms. Sabrina, that was her push; she was like, "So, OK you've—" After my first year with her, she's like, "You've conquered this goal."

I had did all my first-year goals. I had found a new job, which my first job had . . . Something happened. I don't know what happened moneywise, and it just dropped, and I was like . . . I went home one day and filled out like thirty applications. And just praying the whole time I'm typing, like, "Please, let me get a job." And I went to Burlington Housing with a stack of applications and stuff that I had printed off of my computer at home, and I was like, "I got to get this stuff faxed. I don't know how much it is going to cost me at the library."

And they was like, "You don't have to go to the library. You can fax everything from right here. All that's free." You know what I'm saying? "You're doing things about yourself. That's what were here for."

So I sit at Burlington Housing, and I kid you not, I had a stack of papers like this. [Indicates a two- to three-inch stack] And I'm like, "OK."

Ms. Nika Triblicker and Shanika Poole-Summers were there, and they were like, "Yeah."

And then I got this job, an awesome job at UNC. It's an endo tech, which is . . . its specialty is endo, but I'm still a CNA, but I'm considered as an endo tech. So I do upper endoscopies, colonoscopies, hemorrhoid treatments, ERCPs, EUS, and things of that sort.[5] So anything with killing colon or digestive cancers, I'm all with it. So . . . which is pretty exciting. Each and every day to know that I'm making a difference in somebody else's family's life to say that this person is going to be cancer-free and things like that. So.

Makayla's success in finding a job starts to move her toward the holy grail of success stories. These are the third and final type of success story: stories of moving from dependence to self-sufficiency, homelessness to home ownership, addiction to rehabilitation, public aid to no aid. These are unequivocal and unambiguous stories of major successes. If small success stories are paired with stories of life, these large success stories are paired with life stories.

Such success stories are typically told either firsthand by former aid recipients as inspiration or second- or thirdhand by current aid recipients as hope. Aid providers who were once aid recipients, such as Bernard Faucette and Parthenia Ingram, share their firsthand stories directly with aid recipients to inspire and motivate. Family members and fellow residents also provide the fodder for success stories, but it is less clear whether they are sharing their experiences as coherent narratives or whether aid recipients who observe their successes are constructing the success story themselves. Like the smaller success stories, audiences may see success where protagonists see the challenges still left to overcome.

Well, when I was in rehab . . . You got the perception within that environment that people think once when they get in a particular situation that when they down and out, they got to stay there.

And I watch my mother come up out of it.

She worked a full-time, part-time job, and she got educated, and she went on. . . . She was an RN for twenty-something years in Winston-Salem.

But I've witnessed people who have come up out of that. So I know for a fact it's not something you have to be stuck in.

And I use that now in my mind-set today where I don't want to be right there, because I know for a fact you can come up out of it.

Gary Duggins looked to his mother and her fight out of addiction and poverty as both inspiration and evidence that his dream of self-sufficiency wasn't a pipe dream. Tia Solomon sees the same in her mother who worked her way "through temp services and got a job and got off EBT and all that, and she's making it." Delois Lacy knows that people can succeed because of people "like my sister. My sister, she was on Bradley Street, and she was on it. She fell down on her luck, lost her job, and she was on Bradley Street for probably . . . It might have been two years, but she went to school, and she worked at the bowling alley, and she worked, and she went to school, and she saved her money. She had to pay rent over there because she was working, but she made it."

The homeless shelter is another place people witness success and where the line between secondhand stories and thirdhand stories blurs and previously attributed stories become legends. Rick Banks remembers a story from the last shelter he was in, retelling it in the shelter in Burlington.

There was a couple that was in Greensboro in the shelter there. They got housing assistance through Greensboro Housing Coalition or something. They ended up getting an apartment. Urban Ministries donated funding to them, and now they're self-sufficient.

So yeah, there's been cases where people have been on welfare and went back to school and got them some skills, and they got off welfare, and they're self-sufficient. Most people who get on welfare that's of working age, they don't stay on it the rest of their life, and I'm not planning on staying on it for the rest of my life if I can help it.

Leslie Forester has also heard success stories at the shelter.

Yeah, I've heard of success stories.

There's a lady in Greensboro, she works at the Interactive Resource Center [IRC]. Her name is Jenny; I can't think of her last name. And she used to be homeless and on drugs, and she got off of all of that. And now she is working as a director of the IRC.

And she gives me confidence, encouragement. She can do it; I can do it. And I'm not even on drugs. I mean, but if she can do this, I can do that.

And there's a lot of people that work here or work at the shelter that used to be homeless, and they're not anymore. And I get courage and strength off of that.

Whether the story comes fully formed from the people themselves or whether other aid recipients are crafting the story through observation, the story's function is clear. In fact, in the performance of most success stories, narrators announce the function at the end of their narrative as a coda. Gary Duggins ends, "And I use that now in my mind-set today." Rick Banks explains, "Most people who get on welfare that's of working age, they don't stay on it the rest of their life, and I'm not planning on staying on it for the rest of my life if I can help it." And Leslie Forester says, "I mean, but if she can do this, I can do that. And there's a lot of people that work here or work at the shelter that used to be homeless and they're not anymore. And I get courage and strength off of that."

In homeless shelters, stories of success are traded like currency, where the payoff is hope, not money. Success stories provide concrete evidence that it is possible to move from poverty and dependence to self-sufficiency and stability. While making-ends-meet stories can provide humble but realistic strategies for survival, this third type of success story provides grand visions of hope for leaving welfare altogether.

REVISITING COMMUNITY IN PUBLIC HOUSING

Throughout section 2, genre and performance context have emerged as crucial factors in understanding the narrative tradition, including why some stories are told while others are not and why some perspectives dominate others despite lived experiences to the contrary. Using stories about public housing as an example, the power of genre and context emerges in stark relief to explain why negative views of public housing can overshadow experiences of reciprocity, friendship, and support. The simple answer is that there are fewer opportunities for sharing positive stories of community. A recap of the dominant genres of narratives told by aid recipients is in order.

- Origin stories describe how a person came to be in need. Complications in life are resolved with the help of public assistance. The stories are shared in institutional settings, formally with caseworkers and informally with fellow aid recipients. These stories are inherently negative, focused on lack and loss.
- Challenge stories have no happy resolution. As narratives, they capture past events with beginnings, middles, and ends, but they

represent ongoing challenges. The negative stories told about public housing fit here.

- Making-ends-meet stories are positively oriented. Complications that set these stories in motion suggest a larger context of difficult, challenging lives, but the stories describe small successes in daily life of making it work. Such stories often describe important reciprocal relationships with family and neighbors, highlighting the importance of social capital. The positive stories told about public housing fit here.
- Success stories are also positively oriented. Success stories describe moving into one's own home and getting off welfare. Although positive for the individual, such stories typically reaffirm a negative view of public housing. If success is moving out of public housing, public housing is positioned from the start as negative, a place to leave as quickly as possible.

Only one of the four genres of narrative can accommodate stories that depict positive views of public housing. Those odds are not great, but they look even worse when considering the performance contexts for aid recipient stories. At aid agencies, people share stories with their caseworkers. These stories fall primarily into one of two categories: challenge stories, where people explain their struggles and needs, and small success stories of finding a new or higher paying job or of the academic achievements of their children. Occasionally, residents will share a making-ends-meet story, but not one that is community focused. The setting calls for individual stories and individual progress.

From time to time, residents are asked to share their stories with a group, such as the Board of the United Way or an open house at an aid agency. The narrative expectation during such formal events is for origin stories, challenge stories, and personal success stories, all of which are either negative (origin and challenge stories) or individually focused (all three types of story). Initially, the same appears to be true in informal settings. Residents often share stories before, during, or after classes. The lunch break during GED classes is a particularly fertile time for storytelling, challenge stories foremost among them. Gathering on front porches at the end of the day is another common context.

And yet, again and again, people describe sharing their stories with other residents and aid recipients in order to provide advice, comfort, and help, and they do so in these small, informal groups with fellow residents. The result is a perfectly circular process when the narrative event matches the narrated event, and both match the community event—in other words, when context, text, and behavior align.

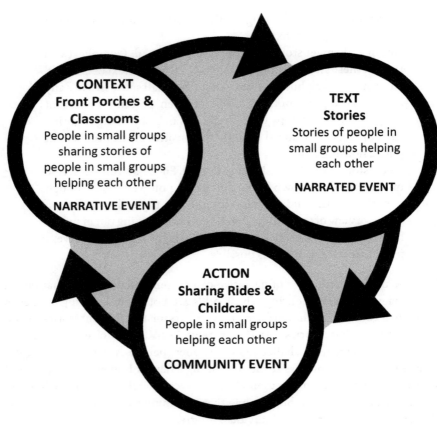

Figure 6.1. Parallels between context, text, and action.

The *narrative* event describes the storytelling context. In this case, people gathered in small groups to share stories of people gathered in small groups to help each other. The *narrated* event is the story itself, describing small groups of people helping each other. The *community* event describes the actions of neighbors gathered in small groups, helping each other (fig. 6.1). It is a self-reifying process. People gather in small groups to share stories that describe people helping each other. Sharing those stories prompts audiences to enact the stories anew by gathering in small groups to help each other. This is ostension at its finest.[6] But as Benedict Anderson has argued ([1983] 1991), communities are imagined, and it seems the imagination has its limits when it comes to beating back the stigma of public housing. A positive sense of community is imagined only as far as it is recapitulated.

Without sufficient genres and performance contexts for stories that highlight the positive dimensions of public housing, negative stereotypes can overshadow positive lived experiences. On the one hand, stories of crime and poor behavior express very real concerns about safety within public housing neighborhoods. On the other, the majority of people living in public housing tell stories of participating in social networks of reciprocity with their neighbors, even if those networks are never expected to encompass the entire geographical space of a public housing development. Considered in context, these stories are subversive, countering the drum beat of the American dream that demands that everyone own their own home and work for themselves in isolation rather than in cooperation with one another. Even if small, the narrative tradition of making-ends-meet stories not only *describes* reciprocal relationships within bounded neighborhoods but also helps to *build* them.

The stories aid recipients tell are not performed in a vacuum. And the stigma of public housing specifically and public aid more generally that recipients confront in their stories is a response not to a historical traditional of welfare queen stories from the past but to a widespread narrative tradition that continues to stereotype the poor today. To fully understand the narrative tradition of welfare in the United States, then, we must temporarily turn away from stories *by* aid recipients and returns to narratives *about* them.

NOTES

1. Eligibility for public housing is based on financial need. No adults are allowed to live in public housing without having their income factored into this equation. Makayla's mother would only be allowed to live with Makayla if she was formally added to the household and had her income factored into eligibility. Such a move would likely make Makayla ineligible for public housing.

2. Both Labov and Waltezky (1967) and Van Dijk (1975) have argued that personal experience narratives must be remarkable in some way—typically unusual, unexpected, or unique. Robinson points out that these qualities are not fixed but depend on the audience, problematizing but not undermining this assumption (1981).

3. This is not to say that stories told only once are not worthy of study, as Amy Shuman argues cogently (2005, 11).

4. This phenomenon can be partially explained by the concept of homophily. Hundreds of studies have shown that people are drawn to, listen to, and respect people who share some fundamental similarity, whether physically, linguistically, behaviorally, or experientially (see, e.g., McPherson, Smith-Lovin, and Cook 2001).

5. With highly technical names for medical procedures, practitioners often use acronyms for shorthand An ERCP is an endoscopic retrograde cholangio-pancreatography, and an EUS is an endoscopic ultrasound.

6. Ostension describes the process of enacting a story in life. See Dégh and Vázsonyi (1983) and Ellis (2003). See chap. 9 for an example of ostension in social media.

SECTION 3

PUBLIC DEBATES

Clash of Cultures

SEVEN

—~m~—

SYMBOLS AND STEREOTYPES

OUTSIDE THE SMALL DOWNTOWN BAR, Silas Matthews launched into his views about welfare, views that would lead to the story he attributed to Ronald Reagan recounted in chapter 3. The first story he shared, however, was more personal.

> Welfare should be like a safety net. When someone is building a high-rise building, they put a safety net around it in case somebody is working and they fall off the building; they are caught by the safety net, and they don't die. The problem is ... The good thing is that the worker gets out of the safety net and goes back to work. The problem with our safety net for welfare is people just stay in the safety net, and it's a career for them, and it's wrong, and it needs to stop.
>
> I have no problem with people who need some assistance and some help to get up and get going, but this career safety net, these career welfare people, it sucks.
>
> I work for a living, and I was going through the grocery line about a month or two ago, and the lady beside me, she was a large African American woman. And I have no problem with that. She paid with her welfare food stamp card, I thought it was, and then she left the receipt behind. And I checked all that out. And she got four hundred and some dollars' worth of food, which I have no problem with them, but she got rib eye after rib eye after rib eye, pork rib slab after pork rib slab, just all this high-dollar meat that I don't even buy for myself. And then when I paid for my ten or twenty dollars' worth of food, she was getting into her Escalade. It was a whole lot nicer than my Ford Focus. And she had these little twenty-inch rims on it. I mean, unbelievable! How are these people getting welfare and dressing better than me, driving cars better than me, got tires better than me, yet I'm paying for their food? I don't understand it. I don't like it. And that's the reason I voted against President Barack Obama, and there you go; I don't like it.
>
> I don't like the fact that this administration is advertising in the country of Mexico to the Mexicans down there this is how you get your welfare benefits, and they are promoting welfare benefits in Mexico. And I'm going that's effed

up! That's effed up! If you are going to do anything, you tell them how to find a job, not how to get freaking benefits so that I can pay for them to get their benefits. All right, peace out; see you, bye. That's what I'm all about.

Silas raced through his views on welfare, his encounter in the grocery store, and his litany of outrages with barely a breath or pause, wrapping up his views as clearly as he began them. Half an hour later, however, he was still talking, sharing stories of his time as an EMT helping uninsured patients, of acquaintances who falsely filed for disability, and even of paying fifty cents on the dollar for food thanks to a desperate aid recipient who needed cash more than he needed his food stamps. As a just past middle-aged white man in the South, Silas's views reflect a common frustration that the lack of one's own economic success is tied to the increased economic opportunities for people of color. These frustrations are not confined to men.

Before the recession, Cindy Powell was making up to $89,000 a year between her photography business and her hair salon. Now she struggles to make $32,000 a year, shifting back and forth between her two businesses based on which is more profitable at any given moment. She works hard but is frustrated that she can no longer afford luxuries like manicures and vacations. Cindy does not receive public assistance but believes she should. In fact, she has applied for aid on multiple occasions, each time being told she makes too much money to qualify. The experience has left her bitter, convinced that if she were black or Hispanic, she would have received aid years ago.

I have people who come in here and sit and brag about how they milked the system, and how they work it, and how they get all this stuff for free, and they have no intention of working.

I bite my tongue. And then I think—when they leave my salon—a few choice swear words. [Laughs]

Just recently I had a girl in here a bit that was bragging that the government is putting her through college, and they've paid for her son to go to day care. But she doesn't take him to day care. Her husband works third shift, so he just stays home, so she has three hundred and forty dollars a month for day care.

They never paid for my day care.

They put her through college, and they didn't put me through college.

If I wanted to go to school now, I'd still have to pay for it. I always overqualify by forty or fifty bucks.

She's married to—I'm not going to lie. She's married to a Mexican. So, she's not Mexican, but she—or a Hispanic or whatever—so she's qualified for that. And I'm like, I bust my butt and work two jobs, but I don't qualify for that? I'm always overqualified; there's always something. I'm always overqualified.

And she wanted to get a job here. I'm not going to give her a job here. I'm irritated that she's milking the system. And she's pregnant again. I'm like, "Let's make another one!" [Laughs]

So I don't know. I know that the government's plan for welfare or what they hoped it was years ago, but it seems like it went just totally off track.

The welfare queen is alive and well in these stories, but the stereotype has expanded. Looking at the stories people tell about aid recipients reveals a new generation of "chiselers" and "young bucks" that reflect a virulent stereotype within the contemporary folk tradition, where race is less often masked through coded language, as typically required in public political discourse, and more often proclaimed explicitly.[1] Alongside the stereotype, however, is also its foil: the hard worker who can't get a break.

Silas and Cindy are unequivocal in their questions about who the real victims are. Why do aid recipients get better food, clothes, cars, even tires than they do? Why do aid recipients get their childcare and college paid for but not them? Silas and Cindy are hardly alone. The aid recipient is so often constructed in contrast to the hardworking taxpayer that it is impossible to discuss one without the other.

In section 2, aid recipients shared stories about their experiences with public assistance. Among those stories were accounts of the stigma they faced in the grocery store, at aid offices, among coworkers and family members, and even from each other. That stigma was not imagined but rather created, honed, revised, and replicated through a deep narrative tradition of welfare in the United States. Having considered the political origins of some of the key *historical* legends of welfare in chapter 3, this section explores the *contemporary* folk tradition, beginning with antiwelfare lore and then shifting to consider countertraditions. The focus remains on narratives but follows the construction of symbols, stereotypes, and stock characters into other folk genres as well.

THE WELFARE CADILLAC

In 1970, *The Porter Wagoner Show* was one of the most popular musical variety shows in the country and would go on to be considered "one of the longest running, most influential, and most successful country music television shows of the late twentieth century" (Darrow 2017). On Saturday, January 24, wedged in between the host's rendition of "I'm Gonna Act Right" and Dolly Parton's "My Blue Ridge Mountain Boy," Guy Drake took the stage and sang what is known in the business as a novelty song.[2] It was his one and only hit, but it made a splash. That year, it hit number 6 on the country charts and number 63 on the Hot 100 charts. The title was "Welfare Cadilac" [*sic*].

Second only to the welfare queen, the welfare Cadillac perseveres as one of the most pervasive symbols of welfare in the United States today. It was a Cadillac in 1976 that made headlines when Linda Taylor, Reagan's welfare queen from Chicago, had her car confiscated by the government (*New York Times* 1976b). It was "a silver-toned Cadillac" in 1978 that Barbara Jean Williams—dubbed "the Queen of Welfare" by the *New York Times* (1978)—drove to her trial for welfare fraud.[3] It was a Cadillac when the *Washington Post* wrote a mocking tribute to Dorothy Woods on her conviction of welfare fraud by noting, "Mrs. Woods is reported to have driven a Rolls Royce. That may confuse some people who have reported sighting her at supermarkets (buying premium grade steak, packaged lobster Newburg and vodka with her food stamps, we guess) driving a Cadillac. Well, Mrs. Woods had a Cadillac too. Also a Mercedes-Benz" (1983). And it was a Cadillac in 1992 when Gary Alan Fine became the first folklorist to mention welfare legends (1992, 8).

Yet in 2013, Silas Matthews describes his version of the welfare queen riding off in an Escalade, as did Janet Haley a few years earlier on that fateful evening that set this project in motion. But the adage holds: the more things change, the more they stay the same. The Escalade is made by Cadillac.

Most obviously, the Cadillac represents luxury and wealth and in doing so captures the central complaint of so many narratives told about aid recipients: that the creature comforts unattainable through hard work can be enjoyed by people who do not work at all. As with so many of the symbols, images, and stereotypes surrounding public assistance in the United States, however, the Cadillac is also racially coded as black. It wasn't always this way.

When the Cadillac was introduced in 1902, it was designed as a luxury car for wealthy whites. To ensure this image, the company had a policy of not selling the car to African Americans. That did not deter wealthy African Americans who were willing to pay a significant charge to white men to purchase the vehicle for them. By the 1930s, the Cadillac employee Nicholas Dreystadt discovered that "a Cadillac was the only success symbol the affluent black could buy; he had no access to good housing, to luxury resorts, or to any other of the outward signs of worldly success" (Cray 1980, 279). Sales in the African American community really took off, however, only after the company reversed its policy and began marketing the car specifically to wealthy African Americans. The strategy was the brainchild of Dreystadt who increased sales tenfold in less than ten years (ibid.).[4] By 1970, the image had been reversed. When Johnny Cash refused to play Guy Drake's "Welfare Cadilac" at the White House that year, he noted in his autobiography that the song was a lightning rod for antiblack sentiment.[5] Both welfare and the Cadillac had become irrevocably associated with the black community.

The vernacular oral tradition among nonrecipients provides clear evidence of this connection as well. A derogatory term for a black man in 1964 in Ithaca, New York, was a "Cadillac cowboy." A joke told by a black man to his white coworker in 1965 in Nevada describes two black men discussing what they would buy with a million dollars; both name first and foremost a Cadillac. A year later, a college student in California recounted a joke his uncle told him about three black kids walking through Harlem, a traditionally African American neighborhood in New York City, who are granted three wishes by a genie. Each boy devises a wish that will get him more Cadillacs than the boy before him. A joke recorded in 1968 and again in 1971 defined black power in relation to a Cadillac, while another suggested that predominantly black neighborhoods could be identified by the existence of a Cadillac dealership on every corner. A joke told in 1987 in California describes a Harlem High School cheer that includes a reference to a Cadillac. As if the Harlem reference was not enough to make the connection, the joke teller later explained that the Cadillac is "driven by black pimps." In 1996, "Pontiac" was said to be an acronym for "Poor old n——thinks it's a Cadillac." There are dozens more jokes built around the same assumption that Cadillacs are desired by and driven by African Americans. One joke told in 1969 among liquor store employees combined African Americans, Cadillacs, and welfare checks into a single punch line.[6]

The Cadillac has continued to be connected to the black community, with one African American journalist crediting black music moguls and rappers with popularizing the Escalade by showcasing it in a number of music videos (Shopshire 2013). While car sales make it clear that Cadillacs remain firmly within the luxury market, out of reach for most Americans black or white, it has remained desirable within the African American community and was ranked fourth in showing the most growth within the African American market between 2009 and 2011 (Auto Remarketing Staff 2011). That said, the meaning of the symbol of the Cadillac is context specific. Seen in a wealthy community, the Cadillac may be read as white or, at the least, nonracial. Shift that context to an impoverished one, however, and the driver is assumed to be black.

STOCK CHARACTERS

Racially coded symbols like the Cadillac are part of a larger system of racism tied to perceptions of welfare in the United States that is not always so subtle or implicit. Declarations are no bolder than in an example of decades-old Xerox lore that now circulates via the internet purporting to be a job application form for black men (see fig. 7.1). Daryl Cumber Dance includes a version of this application in her book *Honey, Hush*, including it in the chapter titled "Self-Denigrating Tales,"

Date: Sat, 27 Apr 1996 15:24:39 +0000
From: Bob Collins <rcollin1@IX.NETCOM.COM>
Subject: Employment Application (Off to blacks)

             APPLICATION FOR EMPLOYMENT TO JESSE JACKSON'S STAFF

Name:_____
Address: (If Living in Auto, Give name, make and License #)
_____
_____

Yo' Momma's Name:_____

Yo' Daddies Name: (if known)_____

Yo' Auto:
Cadillac_____   Lincoln_____
Financed_____   Stolen_____

If financed, date of repossession_____

Yo' Martial Status: Common Law_____   Shacked up_____

Yo' Sources of Income:
Theft_____   Relief_____   Welfare_____   Unemployment_____
          All of the Above_____

Length of last Jail Term:_____

Why Out?: Escape_____   Probation_____   Other_____

How fast can Yo' steal and strip a car?_____

Yo' Place of Birth
      Free Clinic_____   Alley_____
Colonel Saunders_____   Church's Fried Chicken_____
            Zoo_____   Unknown_____

How many words can Yo' Jive per minute?_____

Machines Yo' can operate
Pinball_____   Crowbar_____   Switchblade_____
   Trojan Dispenser_____

Yo' Favorite Foods:
Bar-B-Q Chicken_____   Fried Chicken_____   Carp_____
    Watermelon_____   Chitlins_____

Yo' prior experience:
Gov't Worker_____   Black Panther_____   Evangelist_____
        Pimp_____   Dope Dealer_____   Postmaster_____

How many Kids do you have by:
1st Wife_____   2nd Wife_____   Neighbor's Wife_____
   Sister_____   Others_____   Yo' Momma_____

In 50 words or less, state your greatest desire in life,
(Other than a white woman)_____
_____

Note: No Photo is necessary, since you all look alike anyway.

Figure 7.1. Example of racist Xerox lore and internet lore
that parody job applications for black men.

suggesting it either began or at one time circulated within the African American community (1998, 453). The internet version included here was added with another joke about "Polacks" and "Wops," situating it firmly within a racist discourse that is anything but self-denigrating. If the racial dimension of the welfare queen was up for discussion in Reagan's stories or lying just below the surface in his young buck stories, it is on full display here, portraying all black men not only according to the prevailing stereotypes about all black people—watermelon, fried chicken, poverty—but with those about welfare as well: use of public assistance, involvement in crime, use of drugs, and fathering multiple children with multiple partners.[7]

Reagan's welfare queen also had a younger counterpart that has similarly survived into the twenty-first century. Growing up in Boston in the 1980s and 1990s, Daniel Palmisano remembers the talk radio host Howie Carr talking about "gimme girls," "who were just pumping out kids, who were there to collect. . . . If you listened to what they were saying, listened to what the callers were saying, they were basically saying there's a number of African-American women who were poor and single moms who were taking our money month after month after month, and we keep giving them more, and what the hell was wrong with this world."[8]

Parthenia Ingram, who, in her fifties, found herself disabled and in need of aid before finding a stable job "on the other side of the desk" as an aid provider, remembers her view of aid recipients was similarly shortsighted, targeting young, single black women as the undeserving recipients of a system biased against women her age. "The general perception, which was mine before I got in this predicament myself, so I can tell you what I thought . . . I thought they was all young, long-finger-nailed, wig-wearing, short dresses, five kids, hoochie mamas."[9] Parthenia doesn't mince her words; nor does she shy away from admitting that even as an African American woman herself, she initially thought the welfare system was mostly black and Latina.[10] That view has changed now that she is working within the system and sees the clients who come to her for help with their utility bills, but that perception took extensive firsthand experience to displace. Gimme girls and hoochie mamas place a younger face on the welfare queen, but as the oral tradition makes clear, the matriarch Reagan described who had created a full and extravagant life on welfare remains as well.

Like the Cadillac, many of the details included in describing these negative stereotypes of young women receiving public assistance are racially coded, some more explicitly than others. Take the letter to the editor written by Dr. John Starner and published in Jackson Mississippi's *Clarion Ledger* newspaper that was shared on the internet, splintering into multiple variants that tended to exaggerate the rhetoric of the original. Under the headline "Why Pay for the Care of the

Careless," he begins, "During my last night's shift in the ER, I had the pleasure of evaluating a patient with a shiny new gold tooth, multiple elaborate tattoos, a very expensive brand of tennis shoes and a new cellular telephone equipped with her favorite R&B tune for a ringtone. Glancing over the chart, one could not help noticing her payer status: Medicaid. She smokes more than one costly pack of cigarettes every day and, somehow, still has money to buy beer" (Friedman 2011; D. Mikkelson 2015b). Dr. Starner never mentioned the race of the patient, but he did not have to: the gold tooth and R&B music make it abundantly clear (see Baxter and Marina 2008).

In example after example, welfare recipients are imagined as African American. In a joke recorded in Indiana in 1984, California in 2001, and sent on email around the country in 2017, race is once again signaled through symbols, in this case, symbolic language.

LEROY

A woman walks into the downtown welfare office, trailed by 15 kids.

"WOW," the social worker exclaims, "are they all yours?"

"Yep, they are all mine," the flustered momma sighs, having heard that question a thousand times before.

She says, "Sit down Leroy." All the children rush to find seats.

"Well," says the social worker, "then you must be here to sign up. I'll need all your children's names."

"Well, to keep it simple, the boys are all named Leroy and the girls are all named Leighroy."

In disbelief, the case worker says, "Are you serious? They're ALL named Leroy?"

Their momma replied, "Well, yes—it makes it easier. When it's time to get them out of bed and ready for school, I yell, 'Leroy!' An' when it's time for dinner, I just yell 'Leroy!' An' they all comes a runnin. An' if I need to stop the kid who's running into the street, I just yell 'Leroy' and all of them stop. It's the smartest idea I ever had, namin' them all Leroy."

The social worker thinks this over for a bit, then wrinkles her forehead and says tentatively, "But what if you just want ONE kid to come, and not the whole bunch?"

"Then I call them by their last name."

Like the Cadillac, gold tooth, and R&B, "Leroy" signals an African American identity, part of a common naming tradition among many African American families that confers the status of royalty. (The name Leroy is derived from the French le roi, "the king.") As if that were not enough, the joke teller uses African American vernacular English to signal the race of the applicant—dropping the final consonant on *and* and *-ing* verbs and using such phrases as "they all comes a runnin'"—while the caseworker speaks in Standard American English dialect. Finally, the alternate spelling of "Leighroy" for the girls echoes a well-documented history of altering the typical spelling of names within the African American community. In the version from California, the name is Bobby rather than Leroy, but the storyteller fills in the gaps, explaining that "a lot of people who receive welfare are from the ghetto." Official denotative definitions of the term *ghetto* describe "a part of a city, especially a slum area, occupied by a minority group or groups." For many in the United States, however, ghettos describe communities of low-income people of color, most often black.[11]

These racial codes provide a degree of plausible deniability, albeit small, to joke tellers who want to avoid accusations of racism. But not all joke tellers do, as with the white male college student who began his version in 1984 with "A colored woman was filling out forms in the Welfare office . . ." When asked if there was anyone he would not tell the joke to, "he said he wouldn't tell it to one of his black friends."[12]

The folk tradition, performed most often among small groups of friends and family, assumes a level of trust and shared perspective that makes such linguistic sleight of hand either perfunctory or unnecessary. More public performances require subtler racial markers. But as researchers have shown, even less obvious symbols can be incredibly effective. "Urban," "underclass," and "welfare" have signaled African American since at least the 1970s and continue to be used in political speech today. Such dog whistling attempts to thread the needle, avoiding accusations of racism but effectively evoking racist stereotypes all the same.[13]

A FEW BAD MEN

In 1995, NBC News asked people the following question: "When you hear about someone on 'welfare', do you think of a white man, a white woman, a black man or a black woman?" (chart 7.1). People thought of a man 4 percent or less of the time. A year earlier, a joint Kaiser/Harvard poll showed that people believed that 90 percent of recipients were women and children and 5 percent were male. Broadly speaking, the answers parallel the legend tradition that portrays welfare as predominantly black and female. But on closer examination, the two diverge.[14] Polls suggest that gender is more important than race: 62 percent of white respondents and 70 percent of black respondents pictured a woman when asked about someone on welfare, while only 6 percent of white respondents and 2 percent of black respondents said a man. Those numbers were slightly but significantly smaller for race: 46 percent of white respondents and 58 percent of black respondents said black, while 21 percent and 14 percent said white, respectively.

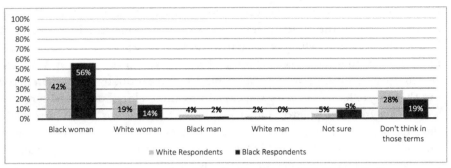

Chart 7.1. Perceptions of race and gender of aid recipients (NBC News Poll, June 1995).

The nonrecipient narrative tradition, on the other hand, sees race as more important. Welfare legends and jokes are consistently coded racially as black, while providing ample room to target men as well as women. For example, of the 123 examples of welfare lore shared in contemporary social media, 30 percent specifically targeted women, but 20 percent targeted men (chap. 9). This is not a new trend. In the 1940s and 1950s, the mass media shared stories of welfare kings, who gamed the system like the welfare queens of the following decades. In the 1960s and 1970s, Reagan introduced the country to "young bucks" who gamed the system by getting change back from the purchase of a small item that could then be used to buy taboo items, such as alcohol, cigarettes, and lottery tickets (chap. 2). Of course, even before the EBT card was introduced, which stopped the return of cash as change, such a practice was hardly viable, as the most change one could receive was ninety-nine cents. All the same, the story marked the male recipient as a cheat and likely addicted to alcohol, cigarettes, gambling, or drugs.

Today these stories are some of the most commonly told about aid recipients, though rather than using change from their food stamps—which is no longer possible with the EBT card—recipients are described as using their EBT card for approved food purchases and then pulling out a wad of cash for luxuries and vices. Such stories still skew toward men. Although women are accused of engaging in similar financial gymnastics, their crime is more often purchasing luxury food items, such as steak and birthday cakes, with their EBT cards, which are allowable but in the minds of some shoppers should not be.

The lore shared by nonrecipients focuses on criminal and immoral behavior. The men using welfare are portrayed as supporting bad habits rather than supporting their children. However, stories shared by some aid recipients and providers describe a slightly more sympathetic stock character that is predominantly male but not racialized: the shelter hopper.

After sharing the story of her favorite shelter guest who took advantage of every opportunity to get back on his feet, a volunteer at the local homeless shelter described another type of shelter guest: "Then we have people we call 'shelter hoppers' that are never going to use the resources, that have spent over ten years going shelter to shelter to shelter. So there are those people, too." Typically single, with no children or spouses to tie them down, these men move from shelter to shelter as a form of nomadic housing. Shelter residents often share stories about the shelter hoppers they meet. "I was talking to a guy last night," begins James Bryant, a temporary shelter resident at the time.

> A guy, he was coming out of Greensboro shelter. He told me, "Well, we got it made here."
> And I was like, "Why you say that?"
> And he said, "In Greensboro you got sixty days; here you got ninety days."
> He said five thirty in the morning you up. It's entirely different.
> Shelters are different. Had a lot of people come here before and don't like it. Take off here and go to Greensboro. A couple days they back. A couple days they back.

Another shelter resident, Chad Buckley shares a similar story on a much larger scale.

> I've met one guy; he travels like across the country going from shelter to shelter, and he gets like a government check I think for disability. Some people just like it. It seems like they don't want to come out of this situation. I don't know.
> I mean he's a really nice guy, but he said he started in California. He's worked through Utah, Texas. He's come all the way through the South, and now he's in North Carolina. And he just goes from shelter to shelter, and he actually likes it. He'll talk about how some shelters vary from one another, and some of them are rough and whatever, and then some of them, he said, it's actually like a home atmosphere. And he just says that he gets his, I think, SSI or something like that.
> He doesn't do drugs or anything. He just said the lifestyle suits him.
> I don't know; I don't think I could do that.

The stories stand out in the minds of fellow homeless men and women and the aid providers who see them come through their doors. Most register confusion, perplexed that such a lifestyle would be as satisfying as the shelter hoppers—or "transits," as Parthenia Ingram calls them—claim.

SYMBOLS OF LUXURY

One of the great powers of symbols is their ability to evoke multiple meanings at once. The Cadillac, for example, evokes luxury as well as race. "We know the old myth that they come in with food stamps and go out and get in a big SUV or

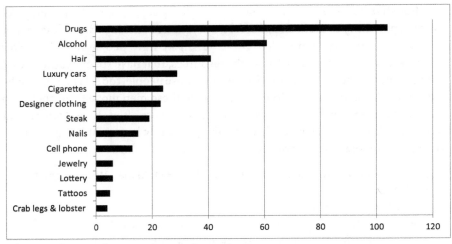

Chart 7.2. "Luxury" items mentioned in oral narratives.

Cadillac," Alamance County commissioner Tim Sutton explains. Derick Stark says that even his southern Democrat-leaning grandfather who works at the food pantry is incredulous when he sees the luxury sedans pull up: "He will sit there and say, 'I don't understand it. I work at the food pantry and people pull up in a Cadillac and then just fill up their Cadillacs with all these boxes of free food. It's not right. It's not right.'" Witt Hicks reaches further back in time for his story, back to the early 1980s, when food stamps were coupon books, not money on an EBT card.

> I had just come home from [military] service. I just got the plant started up, working fifteen, sixteen hours a day. Wouldn't take in but five dollars a week for salary. Wife working full time.
> She says, "I'm out of sugar. Would you get a bag of sugar at Food Lion or something?"
> I said "Yeah, sure."
> Gave me three or four bucks. Went up there and got it.
> Stood behind somebody that filled up a brand-new Cadillac and paid for it with food stamps. And I was livid. The store manager happened to come by, and I said, "What in the hell is going on here?"
> He said, "Sir, it happens every day."
> "Well, it beats anything I've ever seen."

While the Cadillac remains a preeminent symbol of the unearned luxury of aid recipients in the popular imagination, the oral tradition makes clear that we should expect to find less extravagant examples on a daily basis in our grocery stores. In fact, it is these smaller, more mundane examples that dominate the personal experience, secondhand, and legend narratives shared among friends and family (chart 7.2).

On the one hand, the list of luxury items mentioned in these stories may accurately represent the kinds of items recipients splurge on from time to time. Yet if that were solely the case, one would expect to see other items on the list as well, such as brand-name cereal or marshmallows, items that hardly make the "basic necessities" list aid recipients are expected to adhere to. Additional interpretations are needed. Chapter 8 considers how narrators position the people in their stories in opposition to one another, which suggests the image of aid recipients has far less to do with who the poor are than with who the general public are *not*.

NOTES

1. Teun Van Dijk notes that the specific encounter can sidestep accusations of racism that the generalized comment cannot (1993).

2. For a video clip of the performance, see Drake (1970); for lyrics, see Genius (n.d.).

3. The *Washington Post* article describing Williams and her trial opened with "A 33-year-old woman who drove to her trial in her silver-toned Cadillac has been convicted of welfare fraud and perjury in what is believed to be the biggest such case ever" (1978). The *New York Times* article also mentioned a "silver-gray Cadillac" in the second sentence of its coverage, under the headline, "'Queen of Welfare' Ordered Jailed in $239,500 Fraud" (1978).

4. In his June 20, 2014, conversation with Ta-Nehisi Coates, television host Bill Maher seemed to reference the Dreystadt origin story when he argued, "Trust me, the white people know what I'm talking about. Yeah, that black people love their Cadillacs because that was, for so many years, the biggest thing they could buy, when you're not allowed to buy a house, or a house in a good neighborhood, when you can't get a mortgage, you know, the biggest thing you can take pride in is your car" (Maher 2014). See also Steele (2009).

5. Cash does not try to claim the moral high ground in hindsight, however. The reason he did not play Drake's song or Merle Haggard's "Okie from Muskogee" "wasn't the songs' messages, which at the time were lightning rods for antihippie and antiblack sentiment, but the fact that I didn't know them and couldn't learn them or rehearse them with the band before we had to leave for Washington. The request had come in too late. If it hadn't, then the issue might have become the messages, but fortunately I didn't have to deal with that" (Cash and Carr 1997, 286).

6. All of these jokes can be found in the University of California, Berkeley (UCB), Folklore Archives under Blaison Populaire, American, A4 Anti-African American: M6 Money Status, M6 C3 Big Cars, R45 Reverse Discrimination, and S5 Similes and derogatory puns.

7. The version presented by Dance includes a section on illnesses that includes "VD" and "Food Stamp Poisoning."

8. Howie Carr has continued to make these claims. For example, in an online column on the website for his radio show, he ridicules Rep. Ruth Balser of Newton, Massachusetts, for suggesting poor women aren't able to buy lipstick for their job interviews: "Lipstick? As if a lot of gimme girls are going out on job interviews. And should they also be allowed to use their EBT cards for, say, tattoos?" (Carr 2018).

9. The online *Urban Dictionary* provided two definitions for *hoochie mama* in January, 2018 when I accessed the site. The first is simply "a ghetto version of a 'Gold Digger.'" The second is more elaborate: "A female who dresses ghetto ho fabulous. Lots of gold, lots of weave—typically Pattie LaBelle style with red, purple, gold, or orange streaks, and long nails with lots of airbrush glitter, and color. This female's goal in life is to use her female attributes to obtain a male with lots of money or any money to spend on her. Weaves, rent, & diapers for her baby from another daddy included" (Urban Dictionary n.d.).

10. Parthenia is hardly alone. In 2003, Melissa Harris-Perry held focus groups with forty-three African American women in cities across the United States, asking them to reflect on the stereotypes and myths of African American women. While they critiqued many of these stereotypes, several women argued that the welfare queen was real (2011, 33–34). While observed behaviors may provide a partial explanation for these views, Harris-Perry's experiments involving the impact of the stereotype of the "strong black woman" provide another, where this stereotype primes women to blame individuals rather than structural inequities (2011, 207–15).

11. For naming practices, see Black (1996), Lieberson and Mikelson (1995), and Paustian (1978). For connotative meanings of *ghetto*, see Patillo (2003) and Wacquant (1997). For the California version of the joke, see the UCB archives: American, Blason Populaire, P66 Anti-poor, recorded November 24, 2001. Originally shared among two white college-aged students, one of whom was at the US Naval Academy in Annapolis.

12. Indiana University Folklore Archives, "#17 Welfare Office Joke," collected by Malinda Mundy, Spring 1984.

13. See Edsall and Edsall (1991), Gans (1990, 1996), Gilens (1996, 1999), Hurwitz and Peffley (2005), Katz (1993), López (2014), Neubeck and Cazenave (2001), and Quadagno (1994). See also chap. 3.

14. Social desirability may partially explain the discrepancy between public polls and the narrative tradition, where it is more acceptable to feminize welfare than racialize it, but more likely the discrepancy can be explained by the lopsided perspective of welfare legends and jokes that demean, ridicule, and demonize aid recipients (a topic picked up in chap. 9).

EIGHT

—ᴡ—

HARD WORKERS AND THE WORTHY POOR

US VERSUS THEM: THE SHIFTING SANDS OF IDENTITY

One of the ways Western Apache men have joked with each other is by pretending to be white men and teasing their peers in ways that highlight the ridiculousness of some of the traditions of their white neighbors. As Keith Basso argues in his book *Portraits of "the Whiteman,"* the images the Apache constructed were often more accurate barometers for what Apache should *not* be than for what white people actually were. Whether from a history of antagonism between the Apache and the US government or from the observation of very real behaviors that were antithetical to Apache values, the Apache had come to see whites as their foils. With such a contrast established, the Apache began ascribing behaviors to whites that described anti-Apache behavior rather than anything white people actually did on a regular basis. For example, "Whiteman" jokes often depicted whites as stupid, sloppy, and impulsive (Basso 1979, 58), qualities that whites do not appear to have in greater measure than any other ethnic group. Simply put, "'The White-man' is a symbol of what 'the Apache' is not" (64). Basso never coined a term for this phenomenon but in lieu of the "you are what I'm not" theory, I would suggest the *theory of inverse identity.*

Examples of this tendency abound. A visitor to a college campus may initially see very little difference between one Greek organization and another. But with recruitment of new members so crucial, many fraternities and sororities have constructed identities that ignore their vast similarities and instead highlight and exaggerate their differences, real or perceived. The Betas become rowdy mad men compared to the effete Kappa Sigs. The Alpha Phis become the party girls com-pared to the settle-down-and-marry Kappa Kappa Gammas. Once the rivalries are in place, the stereotyping begins in earnest. Whatever a Beta man would do, a Kappa Sig would shy away from and vice versa. Reality begins to take a back seat to these constructed identities.

Such an inverse relationship between aid recipient and "hardworking tax-payer" has clearly existed in the political discourse, mass media, and oral traditions of public assistance for at least the past fifty years and arguably much longer. Accordingly, the image of the aid recipient may reflect those values and behaviors the narrator eschews more than the actual values and behaviors they have witnessed among aid recipients. It is likely no accident that by far the most frequently cited luxury item that suggests inappropriate use of government funds is drugs. Drugs are the only item on the list that is illegal, not just unadvisable, cast not only as an unnecessary expense but immoral at any level, clearly antithetical to the values of the narrator.

In fact, of the top five most frequently named luxuries, three are common vices: drugs, alcohol, and cigarettes (see chart 7.2). Is this because recipients are engaged in these behaviors more than buying steaks or getting their nails done or because nonrecipients are simply more outraged and morally offended by them? Consider the stories about drug use. In 73 of the 104 stories that mention drugs, no evidence of drug use is offered. Rather, people *assume* drug use. Silas Matthews makes this assumption in his story of buying food stamps at half price.

> As far as welfare goes, I knew a white dude, sorry white dude, who was friend of a friend of mine who I worked with. And this guy was getting food stamps, had like six kids.
> And I guess he wanted drug money or something. I don't know what he wanted, but he actually . . . I went to the grocery store with him, and I went grocery shopping, and I got like sixty dollars' worth of food on his card, his food stamp card, and I paid him half price. We walked out of the store, and I gave him thirty bucks.
> That's how they make money. And do I feel bad about that? Yeah. I did it one time because I thought, "Yeah, I'm going to do something cool and make out." And after I did it, I felt so guilty I never did it again. But yes, I did do it; I did it that one time. That was about seven, eight years ago.

The perception that many aid recipients are on drugs is repeated again and again by nonrecipients. Neil Bardwell assumes people are buying drugs with the cash they get from selling food stamps "because it's just extra money." Aid recipients like Chad Buckley and Parthenia Ingram also admit to having believed these stereotypes until they found themselves in need of assistance and met people like themselves just struggling to make ends meet. The DSS fraud investigator Gary Douglas hears it all the time from people who assume drug use by their aid recipient neighbors.

> I get them [calls] all the time where they say, "Well, they're trading their benefits for drugs."

And I say, "Well, do you know who they're dealing with?"

I can at least get Drug Enforcement into it and all. If Drug Enforcement busts a drug dealer and they have an EBT card, then we can assume that these clients had traded their EBT cards for drugs. And we can then charge that overissuance, whatever was on the card and all, to the client and make them pay back the money and all.

But most of the time you ask them, "Do you know who it is?"

"No, I don't really know who. I've just heard; I know he's on drugs, I think. And he's always . . . He's never got any groceries in the house."[1]

As aid recipients are ascribed the behaviors antithetical to social norms, they become the scapegoat for all the ills of society. Drug addiction is just one. Teen pregnancy, broken homes, inner-city crime, alcoholism, unemployment: all are laid at the feet of aid recipients.[2]

Even when nonrecipients shift to a binary that does not include them at all—distinguishing between the deserving and undeserving poor—many speakers continue to project the inverse of their own values onto aid recipients. The result is that the already heavily restricted category of the deserving aid recipient disappears almost completely.

Deserving and Undeserving

The distinction between the deserving versus the undeserving poor is the most well-established binary in the scholarship of welfare, cemented in academic and popular discourse alike by Michael Katz's acclaimed 1989 book *The Undeserving Poor*. It is a binary, as deceptive and destructive as it is pervasive, recapitulated through literature, the mass media, journalism, and even social science research. The deserving poor have done nothing to justify their poverty; the undeserving poor are to blame for their lot in life. In her work with stigma surrounding diabetes, Sheila Bock spoke with a young white surgeon, who admitted, "I tend to have more sympathy for the type 1 diabetics I get than the type 2." He explained, "A type 1 diabetic is just walking down the street and gets shot. A type 2 diabetic is in a gang, robs a liquor store, pulls a gun, and then gets shot" (Bock 2012, 156). Such views place the blame squarely on the shoulders of the individual, though cultural norms are often implicated as well.

Even those people most outraged by welfare fraud and misuse of funds, however, typically acknowledge the presence of the deserving poor. "I have no problem with people who need some assistance and some help to get up and get going, but this career safety net, these career welfare people, it sucks," Silas Matthews says by way of introducing his story of the woman he saw buying "rib eye after rib eye." It is a rhetorical move as likely to be used to introduce a story as to conclude it. In both, the point is simple: I am not heartless. I recognize need. But that is not what is going on here.

The categories of people that history, policy, and surveys suggest Americans care about have typically included children, widows, the elderly, and the disabled. But the antiwelfare narrative tradition is far less generous. Despite composing the majority of the population receiving public assistance, children are absent from the welfare stories told by nonrecipients unless they are cast as moneymakers for mothers or black marks against a woman's morality as their numbers soar. The widow is also absent, as are the elderly. Rather, these stories focus on one thing: able-bodied men and women. If you are able-bodied, you should work; if you work, you should be self-sufficient. Therefore, the only deserving aid recipient is one who cannot work.

But these stories are typically even more restrictive. The reason people cannot work must be no fault of their own. In a context where the poor are viewed as having made poor choices, only those people who have done everything in their power to fit the ideal, independent, moral individual demanded by the American ethos and codified by the American dream are deserving.

Silas Matthews acknowledges there are people who need assistance but never shares a single story of such a person. The deserving aid recipient seems to shimmer in the distance, without corporeal substance. As such, the category of the deserving aid recipient holds little sway over how Silas interprets the aid recipients he encounters in the grocery line. The woman he describes with all the rib eyes might in fact fit his description of a deserving recipient role perfectly—someone getting help in the short term to get back on her feet—but because her food purchases fit the stock character of the welfare queen, Silas instead casts her as one of the "career welfare people," despite no corroborating evidence.

For these narrators, the deserving aid recipient exists in the abstract as a rhetorical foil rather than a coherent figure. The move is useful for creating a sympathetic ethos for the narrator but does little to engage any real discussion of deserving recipients. In those rare instances when the deserving aid recipient does appear in the stories of narrators who share a dim view of welfare, it is in contrast to the focal point of the story: the undeserving recipient. In a conversation with friends and Elon student researcher Jessica Elizondo one morning, Frank Ellis compares his father—one of the good guys—with the stereotype of the welfare queen or young buck in the grocery store, clearly one of the bad guys:

Frank: Let me give you an example of public assistance now. My father's been dead for twelve years, and he was visually impaired for a while. So he was able to go on SSI, OK? I term that as public assistance, and it really helped the family as a benefit to help his care. So I think that's a good public assistance item.

Now when I go to Harris Teeter, and I see somebody with their—what did you call that food stamp card?

Jessica: EBT card.

Frank: Whatever you call it. And they're dividing up their groceries into alcohols on one end and items you can't use that card with, and their regular items are in the front to use the card. That sucks.

Bob: Better cut of meat than we got. [*Laughter*]

Frank: Right.

Bob: They got rib eyes, and we got hamburgers.[3] [*Laughter*]

Frank: That's abuse, and that's wrong, and that's so . . . I view that as broken.

It is unclear what story would be told if someone were to have seen Frank's father at the grocery buying steak with an EBT card or paying cash separately for a bottle of wine or six-pack of beer. Presumably Frank believes his father has a right to relax with a beer at night or treat himself to a steak from time to time. And yet when these luxury items signal fraud and a broken system, as they so clearly do for Frank's audience and so many others in the United States today, there is a good chance that Frank's father's actions could spawn similar outrage among fellow shoppers not aware of his disability.

The bulk of the narratives shared by nonrecipients suggest narrators have virtually no capacity to grant deserving status to someone they see but do not know. Rarely do people look for the story behind the story or ponder whether the exceptions they grant their relatives and friends whose stories they know might also apply to the people they do not (chap. 10). The result is that positive examples remain exceptions, and all other examples become confirmations of a stereotype that requires no evidence for proof. By restricting the category even further to family and friends, the deserving aid recipient virtually disappears. In its place is a figure that brings the us-versus-them dichotomy to a new level: the deserving nonrecipient.

The Only Good Recipient Is a Nonrecipient

"My daddy-in-law, he was unable to work," explains Eddie Wade.

He was blind in one eye, and he lost use of his left arm. And he went to the welfare people, and they sent him out on a job. When he went out on the job, "Man, what are you doing here?"

He said, "I come, they sent me out on this."

"I don't need you! You can't work!"

And went back to welfare, and they told him, they said, "You can work. We've seen you out on another job."

And he kept on, kept on, and said, "Well, I want to tell you something. If I paint myself black, I can get welfare, can't I? Probably can.'

And he drew one check, and we had to send the other one back because he died.

In keeping with the assumptions of many white nonrecipients, Eddie Wade's father blames reverse racism on his inability to receive aid. Others, like Ricky Thorne, point the finger at a more generic, bureaucratic system that allows fraud to run rampant.

> And then there's another case. I know this lady that she's been disabled since ninety-three. She had a pacemaker put in, in ninety-three. She had two surgeries then. Then last year, she had four surgeries, including an open-heart surgery, and she gets a measly five hundred dollars a month to live off of.
>
> See, that's why it is so easy for families to get welfare or whatever and abuse the system. But people that really need it? They're just pushed to the side. They can't get nothing hardly. That's why the government needs to really buckle down and check these people out before they just freely give out money and food stamps and all that stuff.

The mirage of the deserving recipient is so strong that even when a deserving person does receive assistance, the benefits are not enough, paling in comparison to recipients whose stories are imagined rather than known. Ricky's friend with the pacemaker is deserving but underserved, victimized by a system that supports the wrong people. In the context of a narrative tradition that racializes recipients so heavily as black, such narratives operate for many as coded language that deserving white people are unfairly ignored while undeserving black people are unfairly rewarded. Ricky Thorne may not believe the welfare system favors black people, but his narrative provides ammunition for those who do.

Catch-22

While the deserving *poor* are assumed to exist widely but abstractly, the deserving *aid recipient* is virtually nonexistent, confined only to friends and family. But there is yet another restriction placed on deserving aid recipients, insidious in its brilliantly circular logic. To be deserving is to value self-sufficiency. To show evidence of valuing self-sufficiency is to not accept government aid. Accordingly, a person who receives aid is a priori not deserving.

Stigma helps accomplish this feat. The truly deserving person is expected to be too embarrassed to accept aid, recognizing the socially symbolic damage of accepting even temporary assistance. Tim Sutton regularly tells the story of being offered reduced school lunch for his children but refusing the aid (chap. 10). Bill Steeple points to his parents:

> Like Social Security. A lot of this stuff started after the Great Depression.
>   I was thinking last night that all of us are sons of what they call "the greatest generation." These guys worked their butts off. Some are still alive, some aren't. They didn't even think about . . .

My dad grew up the son of an alcoholic. He never thought about anything being handed to him from the system. My mom is ninety-three years old. You try to give her something, for God's sake. We will all sit here, and she'd want to pay for breakfast.

Cindy Powell explains that while she believes she is eligible for aid, she will not apply.

Mine is too much pride. I don't want other people to look at me and say, "Oh, she's on welfare." Because they don't know that I work two jobs; I have businesses and work really hard. And they're just going to see me with the EBT card at the grocery checkout with my fake nails and be like, "Oh, uh-uh." [shaking her head disapprovingly]

So it's very difficult because you tend to judge people, but we as humans do that.

She recognizes that the moment she is on welfare, she will join the ranks of the undeserving, the stigmatized, the outcast. She knows because she admits to holding those views herself. These are the same narratives once told by people like Elliot Dunn and Leslie Forester, who finally swallowed their pride and "crossed over" (chap. 3). Such stories create foils: one idealized, the other demonized. If the ideal aid recipient commits to the rugged individualistic values seen as a mark of moral strength in the United States and therefore feels embarrassed to seek aid, the undeserving aid recipient feels entitled to aid and seeks it the moment things get tough. This inverted identity has spawned a recognizable subtype of the welfare queen: the entitled recipient.

"Any job is better than no job at all," avers Bethany Chance, complaining that unemployment should not be an excuse to sit around all day.

But some people don't see it like that. And I'm not going to lie. My brother-in-law was like that.

He was in the National Guard, and they sent them out to active duty, and he did a tour over in Iraq. And when he came back from Iraq, he was no longer active duty, so he wasn't getting that military pay. And he found out he was able to draw unemployment based on his active duty status in the military.

So, for two and a half, almost three years, he sat on his tail and collected unemployment. OK, he's sitting at home on, I think, three hundred and sixty-seven dollars a week or three hundred and forty-seven a week, and he's like, "I'm making more money sitting on my butt than I would be at work."

And my husband had to start working at his previous company and was making twelve dollars an hour working fifty, maybe sixty hours a week. And he was bringing home seven hundred or maybe eight hundred dollars a week.

And we tried to get him to go over there and apply for a job because at that time they were hiring. But he goes, "No, I just want to sit on my butt and collect unemployment."

And that's what he did.

And when he ran out of all of his options, like his extensions, until finally he was forced to get a job.

We're not going to get into that history. But it's people like that, that kind of an example . . . But there was nothing wrong with him! He could've worked. He just felt entitled, because he did a service . . . you know, he did a stint in the military.

Bethany's brother-in-law feels entitled to unemployment because he served in the military. More common are assumptions that people feel entitled to benefits by virtue of living in the United States. This is the assumption driving the stories of immigrants who supposedly flood across the border to take advantage of welfare and the "anchor babies" of poor immigrants who supposedly come to the United States to have children in order for them to get US citizenship, thereby providing legal grounds to remain in the country (chap. 9).

Often, however, this entitlement is portrayed less as a legal right than an ungrateful tone that runs counter to the shame, humiliation, and embarrassment aid recipients are expected to feel. There are aid recipients who know the rules, who understand the benefits they qualify for, and who therefore advocate for themselves if they are denied eligible aid. Such advocacy can appear "entitled," particularly if one expects government assistance to be reserved for the thankful rather than the needy.

Not surprisingly, such expectations for aid recipients can be a heavy burden to bear, impossible to win no matter how hard one works. "When we somehow managed to buy our children a decent pair of shoes, sewed a blouse, or saved our food stamps to buy our children a birthday cake, we were accused of being cheats or living 'too high.' If our children suffered, it was proof of our inferiority and bad mothering; when they succeeded we were suspect for being too pushy, for taking more than our share of free services, or for having too much idle time to devote to them" (Adair 2000, xvii). In other words, no amount of evidence is sufficient to salvage the image of the aid recipient. To fail is to confirm one's unworthiness; to succeed is to confirm fraud.

Better Than Me

The theory of inverse identity helps explain the sharp contrasts in these stories and the high prevalence of such vices as drugs, alcohol, and cigarettes ascribed to aid recipients. But other luxury items so often used to stereotype aid recipients need other explanations. Some clearly operate as racial signifiers, like hair weaves and elaborately manicured fingernails, both associated with African American women. But others such as steak and crab legs, cell phones, nice clothes, and jewelry suggest similarity rather than difference. Paul Johnson is a college student who works as a grocery store cashier to help pay his bills.

A personal story for me is when the conveyor belt is full, and there's all this food, and you can't help but think, "So we're paying for this," you know?

And I know this is the wrong attitude, and it's like completely negative, but I'm not eating steak even once a month. I mean, I'm in college trying to make a better life for myself, and still you have all these steaks and all this stuff that I don't have at home?

And so that's been my fault many times, and I know that's completely negative.

Paul feels guilty for begrudging people their food stamps and their occasional steak, but it is a common reaction. Derick Stark, who works as a caseworker for DSS, also feels the twinge of envy.

When I did food stamps in Memphis, if there was ever a power outage for a really long time, we would get phone calls from clients saying they lost food in their fridge, and we were able to supplement them for that month up to half of what they got a month, but we would have to go through a verifying process to make sure that their power was out, how long it was out, and all that stuff like that unless they considered it a statewide emergency for whatever reason, like up in New Jersey and New York and stuff.

And it was a little tough when people would say, "I lost all six hundred dollars' worth of my food"—they got six hundred dollars in food stamps. "I lost all six hundred dollars' worth of my food this weekend."

"What did you have?"

And they'd say, "Well, I lost all my pork chops; I lost all my steaks, all my chicken and this and that." And I'm just thinking, "We don't get paid a lot in this job. That's all there is to it."

This is not a job that . . . This is almost like getting into a pastoral church job. My job is a pastor, and you get in to want to help people and not to make money because this is not a job to make money.

And you hear that stuff, and you're just like, "Oh, I wish I had a freezer full of steaks at home."

These stories continue to maintain a clear divide between storyteller and aid recipient, where one values fiscal responsibility and the other does not. However, these stories also suggest points of similarity: we are in the same boat, sharing the same challenges, expressing the same desires. It is this recognition of similarity that sits at the root of the intense frustration and anger conveyed through so many stories about aid recipients.

For some, such shared experiences are legitimate. When working-class men and women like Ricky Thorne and Silas Matthews describe their struggle making ends meet without public assistance, their frustration watching people use their EBT cards for food items they feel they cannot afford is understandable. It can feel as if they are working hard and living a meager existence in order to subsidize people who are not working at all and living in luxury.

But for many of the people sharing stories of watching aid recipients buy steaks, the suggestion of shared challenges suggests a deep myopia of their own privilege and the extent and degree of the trials faced by people living at or near the poverty line. Cindy Powell complains about not being able to qualify for assistance when her clients can, despite making close to $100,000 a year in good years, with one bad year that took her as low as $32,000, still more than three times the poverty level for a family of one and more than double for a family of two.[4] When Frank Ellis, a successful businessman and financial analyst, describes what he views as a common practice of dividing up acceptable food items and unacceptable luxury items, many of his fellow breakfast companions, all successful businessmen, are offended by the idea that someone dependent on the government can afford luxuries they cannot. "Better cut of meat than we got," Bob Dartmouth says to the laughter of the others. "Right," Frank agrees. "They got rib eyes, and we got hamburgers," Bob continues to more laughter. "That's abuse," Frank concludes, "and that's wrong." Bob can afford steaks; the suggestion otherwise is disingenuous, a point perhaps underscored by the shared laughter. But for all the laughter, the indignation is real; the response, common.

POINT, COUNTERPOINT

Not all the stories told about welfare are so negative. As we know from chapters 3 and 4, aid recipients, as well as aid providers, tell very different stories about life on public assistance. Aid recipients have not eliminated the deserving aid recipient. Their stories of applying for and receiving aid are cast as necessary codas to facing difficult challenges and trials, not as a capitulation of self-sufficiency or self-worth. Further, stories of entitled aid recipients are countered by stories aid providers tell of people who worry they do not need food stamps as badly as someone else or who drop their benefits as soon as they can.

"The majority of the people I deal with don't want to be there, don't want that handout," explains aid provider Parthenia Ingram. "I have more than one ask me, 'Where can I send this money back?'" Kate Garnett at DSS has seen the same.

> I've had more than one person that's called me up after I've done their intake, and three months later, "I don't need food stamps anymore."
> "Oh, OK." And I always say, "Well, I'm not your caseworker," but I say, "How come?"
> "I got a job."
> I said, "Well, you might still be eligible."
> "No, no, I don't need them anymore. I got a job. I'm good." And even though they might still be eligible, they will say, "Nope, I don't want them anymore. I got a job. I'm good." And they always say, "What if I need them again? I want them to be there," as though it's a bank account that you can only take so much out.

Especially older people, again, demographic I'd be looking at fifty plus, maybe forty-five plus, and they see it that if they get food stamps that they're not entitled to, maybe someone else will go without, like there's only a certain amount.

Luxury Stories Revisited

When Susan Phillips describes her childhood growing up in Greensboro, North Carolina, with six siblings, it was full of play: fishing with her dad, climbing trees with her brothers, playing football in the yard. Money was tight, and her family moved from rental home to rental home, but her parents were always able to create a sense of stability and ensure she and her siblings found joy in life even in a family on a budget stretched to breaking. She has tried to do this same in raising her five-year-old son, but finding such balance was not easy then and is not easy now.

> I remember one time [growing up], it came down to paying the rent and us having Christmas. And he [my father] said, "Well, I'll deal with the rent, but y'all can have Christmas."
>
> I do remember that.
>
> And so, I took that, and I apply it now to my life, my situation. With my son, when it comes down to him having his Christmas, you know, being like normal kids, waking up Christmas . . . I don't care if it's just one toy under the tree or me struggling and worrying about paying a bill.
>
> Now, food is a different matter. If it comes down to the food, the toy and the food, food first. But like I said, my dad taught me how to juggle things around where I can still keep my place, still have his Christmas, and then deal with it like that. So, my parents taught me a lot with this.

The stories of many nonrecipients provide little room for such luxury, even a toy or two under the tree. Nor does welfare policy. DSS employee Latawnya Hall recounts a secondhand story that could apply to Susan and many like her.

> Now, I can recall in the past where an employee has told me that a customer came in for help with some kind of utility bill, and she informed the employee that the reason she couldn't pay her bill was that she bought Christmas gifts for her children.
>
> Of course, that's unfortunately not a valid reason. That's not considered a crisis so to speak. Although we firmly believe that Christmas is something . . . buying gifts for your children is something that you have to do. It's not something that aids them being healthy or keeping them safe. It's not a necessity; that's really what I should say.
>
> So I've heard of that before. Now, I didn't see the customer, but I had an employee run it by me to make sure that it was OK not to assist this customer because she decided to buy Christmas gifts.

Latawnya sympathizes with the woman. "Buying gifts for your children is something you have to do," she says, perhaps thinking about her own children on

Christmas morning. Not all aid providers are so sympathetic. A fellow DSS employee recalled another case.

> We even had a case one time, the person called, and they were out of food. And their food, I think they got like six hundred or seven hundred dollars in food stamps.
>
> Well, we have a way to go in and look. I don't, but Food and Nutrition does have a way to go in and see how they're spending it.
>
> A child had had a birthday party and they had a huge cookout, so they'd spent all the money on that.
>
> And it's things like that that give it [welfare] a bad name.

Although the story raises some questions—even if the receipt included the words "Bakery item: cake," it is unclear how investigators would know the food was for a cookout for a birthday party and not an attempt to stock up on sale items, a common strategy to make ends meet—such stories make it clear that aid recipients are expected to forego even birthday parties for their children. These stories beg deeper questions about life, as well as about whether the role of government is it to ensure only the basic needs for survival or whether it should assist people in achieving a minimum level of quality of life.

"As far as buying steaks and things like that," Reggie Danell muses, "there aren't many luxuries when you're living at a certain level, in an economic class. So yeah, to have a good meal is one of the simplest luxuries I think people can have." Aware of the stigma of purchasing luxury items, many aid recipients nonetheless refuse to accept a life of mere existence, sharing stories of the small luxuries that make life worth living. A few mention getting their nails or hair done, but these stories suggest a very different interpretation from the stories heard so often in the media and the narrative tradition among nonrecipients. Rather than fraud or unethical use of funds, these luxuries are traded among each other—a ride for a haircut, childcare for a manicure (chap. 5).

Further, as many have pointed out, such luxury items may do far more than provide temporary pleasure. The former aid recipient Tressie McMillan Cottom points out that when poor black women buy nice things, part of the rationale is psychological. The pressure to fit in is no less and typically much more acute for marginalized people such as the poor, women, and African Americans. The same is true when buying a nice pair of tennis shoes for their children, where the stigma of poverty can be devastating for young people (Seccombe 2011, 113–15). As a black woman who grew up poor, however, Cottom also gives example after example of times when dressing up and showing she could "fit in" landed her a job or gained her access to opportunities that she otherwise would have been excluded from (2013). Accordingly, the few luxury items and status symbols poor black women may afford themselves can be a practical strategy for exactly what they are so often demonized for not wanting: employment.

The public's appetite for such stories, however, is typically thin. Only when Lorrie Carter began working at the Open Door Clinic was she able to view these small luxuries, even some as harmful as smoking, as understandable if not ideal.

When I first came, I was more of the assumption, kind of in that crowd, of not necessarily lazy people but just people that didn't work and a lot of people trying to take advantage of the system. I didn't realize how many people just were hardworking and found themselves in a difficult situation.

And I also think I've learned how to see both sides of the situation.

For example, a lot of people read an article about a family staying in a homeless shelter, that he used to actually work in a bank and he ended up in a homeless shelter in Greensboro. And he finally found a job. But one of the things that was mentioned in the article was that he smoked. And people were very negative about that.

But if you think about it, if you're going through that much stress, you've lost your home and all that, smoking is anxiety driven basically. And a lot of people smoke when they're nervous or upset. If I lost my home, I'd probably be a chain smoker. So I think that my ability to see both sides has definitely changed, and I think the ability to not be so judgmental.

Martina Morales describes the ways she scrimps and saves when her husband, whose work fluctuates with the season, brings home a particularly small paycheck.

We have to cut back on spending what we have. Let's say that we go out to eat on Sundays. We just stay in and make something here or right outside. Although the kids are always asking for everything.

For example, yesterday, they were telling me to take them to McDonald's and yesterday it was really cold. What I did instead was, I took them to a store to buy the baby something, the kid that I have, some shirts for the cold and a sweater for them to go to school in the morning. And what we did was pass through the Wendy's drive-through for a dollar something. If I take them to McDonald's, I will spend more, so what I did was just pass through the window.

And for them, it is exciting. They were eating their ice cream in the cold [laughter] because kids always want a bit of everything.

For example, last year we celebrated the birthday of the younger one who goes to Head Start, so we celebrated it. We bought him ... well, I also have my brothers here, so they bought him ... Well, let's say when we do something like that, one takes the soda, another one takes something else; we only prepare the food. Last year we celebrated it, but this year we are cutting back; we didn't celebrate it. I didn't throw him a party. What I did was buy him a small cake, and we sang happy birthday here, and he didn't say anything.

No, because they want their birthday. Now they are asking me for some tablets, but I told them no. That they don't need them. That first I need them to learn right in school. I need them to learn how to write their names and address, learn more, and then when I see that, I will make an effort in order to buy it for them.

Martina found that for just a few dollars, she could treat her children to ice cream out. When the paychecks are relatively large, she is able to throw a birthday party, but even then, she relies on relatives to buy the food while she does the cooking. When the paychecks are smaller, she settles for a small cake and a song. Of course, that small cake, bought in the local grocery, may spawn stories like those told by some aid providers or by nonrecipients like Sarah Reston, who vaguely remembers, "Maybe it was like on Twitter or something, but it was somebody saying like, 'Oh, I just saw a lady buy a forty-two-dollar birthday cake with food stamps.' And she was like, 'What is our government money going to?'"

Lisa Waterman describes paying the monthly rental fee on a storage unit, an expense that might initially seem extravagant for someone who is homeless. But as she describes it, it is not a luxury but a promise to herself that she is not giving up.

> I have sold mine [food stamps], but I have a storage building. I have a storage building that costs me sixty dollars a month, so I don't lose . . . I don't have much in it, but the stuff that I have in it, my pictures, stuff for my sons, and stuff that I need, I have to have.
>
> So I've sold mine to pay my storage building. It don't make it right, and I don't really consider that a luxury. I just consider it somewhere to keep my stuff.

Lisa is determined to get her home back. She is working at a restaurant and saving money to get her life back on track. Soon, she hopes she can pull those items out of storage and put them back where they belong: in her own home. From a symbolic and emotive perspective, those pictures and personal items serve as a touchstone of who she is and who she will be once again. From a purely practical standpoint, those items of necessity—furniture, tableware, and the like—are cheaper to keep in storage than to rebuy when the time comes.

Lisa's story signals a shift in welfare narratives up to this point. So far, the stories told by recipients and nonrecipients alike have typically described legal activities—using food stamps for food, and cash for cigarettes and alcohol. While many nonrecipients label these stories not just as immoral or unethical but as fraudulent, they are not in fact illegal. But Lisa's story moves from assumptions of fraud to actual fraud. It is illegal to sell food stamps. Silas Matthews and his friend were breaking the law when he bought the man's food stamps for fifty cents on the dollar. The same was true when Lisa sold her food stamps for the cash needed to store her material possessions. Chad Buckley describes selling food stamps to afford a night in a hotel instead of the shelter or a friend's couch, the only way to enjoy some intimacy with one's partner during months and months of homelessness. Andrew Currier describes eating a meal at a restaurant instead of the soup kitchen to finally eat something he likes, something he chooses, rather than whatever is being served that day. It is a small but meaningful luxury that reminds him that life is not supposed to be all drudgery, all pain, all struggle, all the time. These luxuries remain few and far between, however. Far more often, selling food stamps is a critical strategy in simply making ends meet.

Fraud Stories

"They trade their food stamps," Louise Howard says matter-of-factly.

> If somebody's in a grocery store lot, they will, because I've done this before, I have. But that was only to pay the gas bill or something. And I didn't have the money to do it with.
>
> So the person in front of me, if they would let me pay for their food and give me the money that they're going to pay, that's the way I would do that.

Lamar Reed concurs.

> Some people trade them off, so they can have pocket money because, see, sometimes you just have food stamps, and you cash them to buy items that you can't buy with food stamps, so you have to sell some in order to survive. Because women have feminine hygiene; they have to have things that they have to buy with cash money; you can't buy with food stamps, so you have to use some of your food stamps in order to survive.

Paying utility bills and buying toiletries are hardly luxuries, yet government policies and narratives about fraud ask aid recipients to view them as such. "It depends on what you consider luxury items," Etta points out. "Luxury items may be cars and other things, but to some people, luxury items may be having to sell their food stamps to get toiletry items or clothes and shoes for the kids. That's luxury to them. But yes, there are people that do sell their food stamps."

Because selling food stamps is illegal, aid recipients rarely share stories of selling their own stamps outside of close friends and family and among other recipients. The stories of selling food stamps heard and shared by the general public therefore tend to be from the perspective of nonrecipients who are asked to trade food stamps for cash. Such stories describe the crime but not the cause. The result is that people fill in the blanks, often assuming the worst. Situated in between the general public and aid recipients, however, aid providers provide a particularly useful vantage point for interpreting stories of fraud.

Gary Douglas is the fraud investigator for the Department of Social Services in Alamance County, North Carolina. An inveterate storyteller, Gary shared fifty-five stories in the span of two hours (charts 8.1–8.3). The vast majority were eyewitness narratives, primarily of cases he has investigated for fraud. Of those fifty-five stories, seventeen either were not about fraud at all, described his

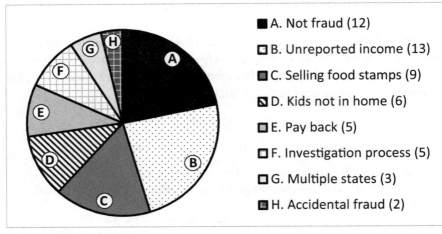

Chart 8.1. Types of fraud.

- A. Not fraud (12)
- B. Unreported income (13)
- C. Selling food stamps (9)
- D. Kids not in home (6)
- E. Pay back (5)
- F. Investigation process (5)
- G. Multiple states (3)
- H. Accidental fraud (2)

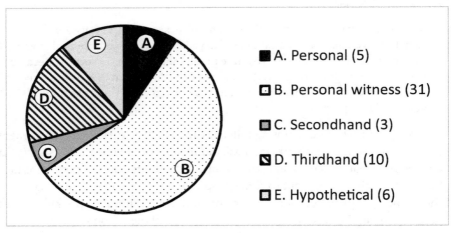

Chart 8.2. Narrative distance.

- A. Personal (5)
- B. Personal witness (31)
- C. Secondhand (3)
- D. Thirdhand (10)
- E. Hypothetical (6)

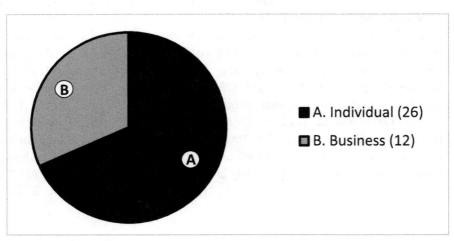

Chart 8.3. Fraud perpetrator.

- A. Individual (26)
- B. Business (12)

practices of investigating fraud, or were cases that ended up not being fraud. Of the thirty-eight stories of fraud, the most common type was unreported income (thirteen)—whether from having someone living in the home (six), from not reporting income from a job (four), or from not reporting assets that would affect their benefits (three). Only one of the stories about not reporting income from a job focused on the client; the other three focused on employers who would not provide the state with the information needed to confirm or refute a claim of fraud. In fact, almost a third of the fraud stories focused on business owners rather than aid recipients.

Gary's stories provide a glimpse into a narrative tradition shaped by experience that reveals clear divergences from fraud narratives shared among the general public. For example, only aid providers and recipients tell stories about stores that buy food stamps or fraud perpetrated by insurance agencies, hospitals, and doctors, where the vast majority of fraud occurs (chap. 1). The same is true of stories of unreported income and unreported people living in the home. One reason for these omissions can be found in how such abuses are witnessed and reported: from family members and neighbors, typically unseen by a wider public. The other is that such fraud violates policy but not social and moral norms against laziness or unearned luxuries. In fact, they hint at values that could be interpreted as positive. Pooling one's resources by sharing a roof to make ends meet can be a good thing. The same is true of working hard to bring in additional income to make ends meet. Stories of being paid under the table undercut the lazy welfare queen stereotype and therefore may not be eagerly shared by people who are convinced that hard work and welfare are mutually exclusive.

THE UNEASY RELATIONSHIP BETWEEN AID RECIPIENTS AND THE WELFARE QUEEN

Politicians, the mass media, and the general public are not the only people who tell stories about welfare fraud that perpetuate the stereotype of the welfare queen. So do many of the people who are most damaged by such stories: aid recipients themselves.[5] The simplest, knee-jerk explanation is because some of the stories are true. Adopting the same distrust of the system where those who need help do not get it and those who do get help do not need it, the aid recipient Martha Sadler distinguishes between deserving and undeserving aid recipients. "I've seen plenty cheat the system, and I've seen some that need to be on the system that the system cheats them. I've got friends that can't work; they can't get assistance. I've got friends that can work that are on the system." Like stories told by low-wage earners who complain of not being eligible at all while undeserving people get aid they do not need, so, too, do some recipients see eligibility determined in ways that do not seem fair. "It's a messed-up system," concludes Martha. Yet while

Martha blames the system, others blame their fellow recipients. Michael Caster served in the army, worked for years in various industries (including factory work, telemarketing, and fast food), and paid his taxes. So after an accident in 2004 left him with a severe limp and the inability to stand for long periods, he applied for Social Security Disability Insurance. He has been rejected twice already and has been told he will never be approved without a lawyer.

> You might go years trying to get Social Security. Some of these people I know, ten or fifteen people floating all the time. They're getting checks for no visible reason. There's nothing wrong with them. I don't understand what the thing is but they're getting . . .
>
> There's one guy, perfectly sane. I've talked to him many a times. He just wears two different kinds of tennis . . . one different tennis shoe on each foot from different sets, and just does stupid things when he's around any kind of a like a social worker or something like that. Other than that, if you talk to him off to the side and he's perfectly sane. He's probably smarter than I am.
>
> But I just . . . I don't know. In my situation, I think at least put me through Medicaid for a little while, you know?

The frustration is real, especially for those who believe in a world of limited good.[6] Consider the post by "Kylie" on the online forum My Biggest Complaint:

> Just received a cut to my unemployment and I am very angry about it. I know 5 different people on welfare, food stamps and cash assistance. 3 of the 5 drive extremely expensive cars, mercedes, range rover and audi. I know they are on welfare because I have been told by them. I believe hard times can come to anyone and assistance should be available for them but that is not the norm. The people I know are quite proud of how they can live the high life on other peoples money. The cars are simply put under another family members name, not saying they bought the cars with that money but if my daughter was on assistance and I could afford to buy her a range rover you best believe I would rather get her out of a section 8 housing situation, off food stamps etc and have a drive a reliable reasonable car. I too have seen people in the market with food stamps dripping in gold and found them getting into an expensive car. Big screen tvs mani's pedi's are always present and like it or not that is a fact and it is disgusting! I at 54 years old have worked steady for 35 years and now for the first time am on unemployment. I have just received a cut to my unemployment and I am very angry about it. I also know of one particular mother who uses her money that should be for her daughter for weed, new sneakers 2x a month and constantly gives the kid rice for her dinner. Open your eyes these are facts! (kylie on April 24th, 2013 at 9:49 am)

All of the major public assistance programs are funded according to eligibility. Having additional applicants does not mean a reduction to someone else's benefits. Guidelines for payment are fixed. Yet the fear that one person's gain is another person's loss is fueled by public claims by officials who are in a position to know better. "We have a long waiting list of people who need to be on this program who can't be on this program," declared one local DSS official during a television interview, followed by another who explained, "You've got families out there that live together but claim they're single that have the same kids, and they're claiming food stamps."[7] Some of the smaller aid programs do run the risk of running out of spots or funding. Childcare vouchers, for example, are limited by both funding and the open spaces available. Emergency funds for heating and cooling bills through such programs as LIHEAP (Low Income Home Energy Assistance Program) can also run out. So the concern—whether of taking from someone who needs it more or having it taken by someone who needs it less—is justified enough to perpetuate the anxiety and frustration over recipients who milk the system or fudge the rules.

Buying In

Frustration with the system and anxiety over their own precarious financial situation can explain why aid recipients might be prone to sharing stories of fraud among their fellow recipients. And some of these stories are, no doubt, accurate reflections of unethical or even illegal behavior. But like the stories told by non-aid recipients, the vast majority of stories aid recipients tell are either secondhand or built on cursory observations that employ the same assumptions and stereotypes to fill in the blanks that people without the benefit of lived experience use. Michael Caster is annoyed by the man who appears sane in private and mentally ill in public, but mental health is hardly so easily assessed. Martha Sadler says she knows many people who get aid but do not need it, but when asked about her stories, she was unable to provide a single specific instance. Ayanna Spencer also believes that abuse is widespread, but when asked about specific stories, she shared only the generalized experience narratives told by others. Such responses were common. While Michael's assessment may have been accurate, and Martha and Ayanna's claims supportable, the lack of concrete examples suggests that their interpretations may be colored by the same widespread stereotypes that lead nonrecipients to fail to consider the story behind the story that gets far closer to the truth (chap. 11). Stepping back to consider the performance context of these stories, conversational and narrative structures, and cultural assumptions suggests additional reasons fraud stories may be told with such frequency among aid recipients.

Avoiding Stigma

Although aid providers and the general public tell more fraud stories than recipients (53 percent, 26 percent, and 20 percent of the stories told, respectively), the vast majority of aid recipients (71 percent) tell at least one story of fraud, more than the general public of whom only 66 percent tell such a story. Conversational contexts for these stories make it clear that one of the reasons aid recipients tell these stories is to avoid the label for themselves.

Susan Phillips shares the story of her partner, who faces mental and physical illnesses that make it difficult to find a job. "He wants to work. He's not one of the ones that wants to just sit around." Etta Washington makes a similar point when narrating her future, beginning by explaining, "I'm the type of person, I like to work for what I want. And right now, what I want, I want to move up in life. Me moving up, meaning getting my own house, one day opening up my own salon. So I don't plan on being in public housing or being on public assistance the rest of my life." The specter of the welfare queen lurks just below the surface of her comments. First, if she is the type of person who likes to work for what she wants, there must be others who do not. Second, she does *not* plan on receiving welfare the rest of her life, suggesting that her audience might think otherwise because there are people who plan to do exactly this. Third, and most explicitly, she positions herself in direct contrast with this other group: those who sit around waiting for a handout.

The aid recipient "Lisa," posting online, makes one of the most common moves of all: admitting there are instances of fraud but distinguishing herself clearly from such people and activities.

> Hey everyone, I understand the feelings about people abusing the system. I have seen a FEW people that do that however, I am on section 8 housing, I work 40 hours a week sometimes more because I also own my own business, I'm a single mom and receive no child support. Yes I do own a computer that I bought with my own EARNED money, and I use it to better myself through online schooling so that I don't have to be on welfare the rest of my life. I sometimes wear nice clothes because I find good deals on brand name clothes at garage sales and thrift stores because rich people dispose of clothes after wearing them a few times . . . I am not lazy. (Lisa on November 9th, 2012 at 2:21 am)

Non-aid recipients typically tell a fraud story and then close by noting how such behavior compares to them: how they cannot afford steak, the latest iPhone, or a flat-screen TV. In contrast, aid recipients typically start with the comparison to distinguish themselves from the stereotypes and then follow with their own story of working hard.

In these cases, the stories aid recipients tell are best understood as counter-narratives highlighting the struggles that justify their need. But they are framed within an expectation that welfare conjures images of lazy recipients who commit fraud. Whether *they* believe this is common or whether they simply understand that their audience believes it to be true is debatable. What is clear is that the stereotype of the lazy aid recipient is so widespread that aid recipients assume they must address it, specifically by distinguishing themselves from it. To ignore the stereotype is to risk having it applied to them.[8] In this way, fraud stories become required stories for aid recipients. This is in sharp contrast to the untellable tale where trauma, stigma, and social norms stifle rather than prompt.[9]

The welfare queen legend operates as a hegemonic narrative where hierarchies, biases, and social norms get internalized and recast by the very people who are harmed most by them. In this context, legitimation theory and fundamental attribution error help complete the interpretation. Legitimation theory suggests we accept dominant beliefs as inherently true and legitimate them, a process fundamental to the concept of hegemony. Fundamental attribution error suggests that we overestimate the degree to which other people's behavior can be attributed to individual traits within their control and underestimate the impact of structural and environmental factors (see Ross 1977). At the same time, we reverse the rules for ourselves, attributing our own shortcomings to structural and environmental factors beyond our control rather than personal shortcomings (Jones and Nisbett 1972). Despite intimate knowledge of all the obstacles and challenges of poverty, many aid recipients allow hegemonic narratives and stereotypes to trump personal experience when evaluating the lives of fellow recipients. The result is that aid recipients are likely to see themselves as exceptions rather than the rule.

Fraud stories shared among aid recipients can also be explained by the proverb that a few bad apples spoil the barrel. "It's the ones who milk the system, and who chose to just basically live off of welfare that give everybody else a bad name," complains Bethany Chance. "And then that makes the rest of the population think that we're lazy." Recipients recognize that stigma operates as a paint roller not a fine-pointed brush. At least one aid recipient worries about more structural impacts as well.

> It's kind of like cancer. It starts off small and gets bigger and bigger and bigger and bigger and bigger, until one day, somebody's going to say, "Hey, enough. We need to get rid of this. We don't need these systems, these services, anymore because they're being taken advantage of." You know?
> "You're taking advantage of somebody that could actually use it, that needs it."
> And then, one day, that's what's going to happen. It's going to be all cut out. And then nobody's going to have anything. No food stamps or nothing. And if you really need it, you're going to be on the street, starving. Or worse, you're going to need medical care and you're going to die.

Bradley Jewell's worry is exaggerated but not unfounded. As discussed in chapter 2, welfare stories shape public policy and funding decisions. Funding for social programs are regularly put on the chopping block, and while entire programs are rarely cut, their funding certainly has been, often justified by stories of fraud and waste. So what may initially appear as either confirmation of the welfare queen legends or a shocking lack of sympathy for one's peers in poverty can be at least partially understood as a defense mechanism against stigma and a very real concern of losing access to much needed funds. Ironically, the social pressures that encourage stories of fraud to be narrated disproportionately can exacerbate rather than mitigate these concerns, fueling perceptions that fraud outweighs need and the undeserving outweigh the deserving.

This stigma is perpetuated not only by stories shared face-to-face among friends, family, coworkers, and neighbors. Online forums provide additional avenues for storytelling, just as digital formats provide the mode and means for additional forms of folklore to be shared widely. Chapter 9 considers these additional forms that spread particularly powerfully through social media.

NOTES

1. Unfortunately, aid providers are not immune to these interpretive leaps. When Greg Williams, Guilford County's fraud investigator, was interviewed by a local television station about their fraud hotline, he initially suggested that people might sell their food stamps for greed—insinuating that people receiving aid do not really need the help—but quickly followed with the possibility of drugs (WFMY News 2013).

2. One might consider this an ironic example of the Goliath effect, when the biggest or most well-known figure becomes a magnet for all the legends, rumors, and negative stereotypes associated with that topic (see Fine 1985).

3. This comparison echoes Ronald Reagan's critique on the campaign trail, where he described "a strapping young buck" or "some young fellow ahead of you to buy a T-bone steak" while "you were waiting in line to buy hamburger" (López 2014).

4. These numbers are for 2011 (US Department of Health and Human Services, Office of the Assistant Secretary for Planning and Evaluation 2011). Over the years, Cindy has lived alone and as the guardian of her daughter.

5. This appears again and again in welfare research, with researchers endlessly disturbed and surprised by the tendency for aid recipients to blame each other.

> As Mun's interviews with women on welfare proceeded, he always hoped
> that they would be perfect critics, able to pierce the veil of structured
> and state hypocrisy. It is interesting to note how so many hegemonic and
> victim-blaming positions were narrated by these profoundly oppressed
> men and women; judgments about "others" often resonated with a broad
> cultural discourse of holding victims of poverty, racism, and sexual violence

accountable for their woes. In many of our interviews, poor women on welfare blamed other women, labeling them "welfare queens," "neglectful mothers," and "insensitive bureaucrats." Our own romanticized images of the resistor—one who desires to speak out against injustice and to act with a collective—turned on us. (Fine et al. 2003, 185; see also Gustafson 2011)

6. Although the initial articulation of limited good by George Foster in 1965 has been critiqued in its specific application to Mexican peasant society and the interpretations he draws, current, pared-down definitions that focus on finite resources in which one person's gain necessitates loss for another provide a useful model for understanding common tensions within groups and communities.

7. It is possible that the misleading information was due to editing by the television station. The first official may have been talking about emergency assistance funds, which can be limited in times of high need. Unfortunately, the caption underneath him named food stamps, as did the official who followed with his story about unreported people living in the home, leading viewers to think needy families cannot get food because undeserving families are cheating the system (WFMY News 2017).

8. Substituting class for race, this social onus reveals the kind of double consciousness that W. E. B. Dubois wrote about: of always seeing oneself through someone else's eyes and of believing one thing about yourself while recognizing that others believe something very different (1903). In terms of the position narrators find themselves in, Goldstein and Shuman point out, "Narrators align themselves, the characters in the taleworld, and the storyrealm . . . in order to produce a particular stance. Along these lines, Bamberg's three elements of positioning (how characters are positioned in relation to events, in relation to the audience, and in relation to themselves) could be applied to stigma—for example, to consider how particular practices or events are stigmatized, how narrative is used to persuade listeners to accept or reject particular characters and their practices, and how people describe themselves and others—whether as protagonist or antagonist, blameworthy or innocent, or credible or disbelieved" (2012, 120).

9. See Goldstein and Shuman (2012). For additional reasons a story may be untellable, see Shuman (2005, 12–22).

NINE

———ɱ———

WELFARE LORE IN SOCIAL MEDIA

I RECENTLY ASKED MY FRIENDS' little girl what she wanted to be when she grows up. She said she wanted to be president of the United States. Both of her parents, liberal Democrats, were standing there. So I asked her, "If you were president, what would be the first thing you would do?" She replied, "I'd give food and houses to all the homeless people." Her parents beamed.

"Wow, what a worthy goal," I told her. "But you don't have to wait until you're president to do that. You can come over to my house and mow the lawn, pull weeds, and sweep my driveway, and I'll pay you fifty dollars. Then I'll take you over to the grocery store where the homeless guy hangs out, and you can give him the fifty dollars to use toward food and a new house."

She thought that over for a few seconds; then she looked me straight in the eye and asked, "Why doesn't the homeless guy come over and do the work, and you can just pay him the fifty dollars?"

I said, "Welcome to the Republican Party."

Her parents still aren't speaking to me.

That is the end of the story. But whose story is it? Is it mine? Is it a true story? Is it just a joke? The first question is easy: no, it's not mine. The second is a little trickier but probably still no. The third is harder and not agreed upon. Many readers will say, yes, it's a joke (thus making the first two questions moot). But as this story made its rounds through social media, at least one man believed it was intended as true, even if he did not believe it was, commenting, "I don't believe this happened."[1]

If genres are assumed distinct, requiring different structures, formulas, styles, and even content, how could they bleed, blend, and blur so much? How could the same story be a personal experience narrative, a legend, and a joke all without changing a single word?

182

In the case of "The $50 Lesson," the title by which the story above is known online, the problem has an easy answer. Jokes come in many forms, narrative being one of the most common. So a joke told as a story, even a personal one, is not only possible but common, particularly as a way to heighten the surprise of the punch line. Doing so reverses the expectations not only of content but of genre. The common exclamation "You got me," at the end of the joke, is high praise for the joke teller who managed to make you believe you were hearing a true story when you were not. The equally common "You're pulling my leg," questioned during the telling of the joke, suggests the subterfuge was somewhat less successful. Blurring of first-, second-, and thirdhand stories is also common, where a true personal experience narrative may be confused with a legend and vice versa. Yet in these cases, once labeled, genres can perform different functions and lead to different interpretations, even without changing the text.

Such blurring and borrowing does not happen willy-nilly, however. While jokes are not particularly picky in the genres they draw on for misdirection, other verbal genres are more rigid. Proverbs, fairy tales, and riddles, for example, have clear structures and formulas that make generic borrowing more difficult. The power of the generic form comes in part from providing expectations that both performer and audience have agreed on, greasing the wheels of interpretation. The storyteller who begins her personal narrative of the aid recipient at the grocery store with "Once upon a time" is doomed to be disbelieved.

Welfare in the folk tradition is not confined to narrative. Jokes, memes, cartoons, Xerox lore, news parodies, adages, and a host of other forms have provided the structures to think about, discuss, critique, and defend welfare programs and their recipients. Some of these genres blur and bleed into one another, but others provide new avenues for creative expression. Social media provides a particularly fruitful arena for exploring these genres, having emerged in the past few decades as vibrant, eclectic, and flexible avenues for the dissemination of a wide range of folklore genres. Even by focusing just on email and Facebook, it is possible not only to consider the dominant patterns of thought that underlie the folk tradition but also to take up a question that has often been claimed but less often supported: namely, that genres favor not only certain topics but certain ideologies as well.[2]

LANDSCAPE AND METHODOLOGY

On Friday, April 6, 2011, at 7:33 in the morning, Ben Nowak forwarded an email he received titled "West Coast Bumper Stickers" to four friends, including Ahmed Abadi, adding "Pretty Good" and signing his initials to the message before hitting send. The email followed with a pair of clapping hands that introduced sixteen bumper stickers with the opening title and caveat.

WEST COAST BUMPER STICKERS

> In California you measure highway distance not by miles, but by travel time.
> Sometimes it can take forever to go a couple of miles, which gives you a lot of
> time to read people's bumpers. Obama wanted change and he is getting it from
> the bumper messages; they are a changing.

None of the bumper stickers is pictured on a car; rather, they appear to be cut
and pasted from the various websites that created them, such as PatriotDepot
.com and DirtyLiberal.com. The email ends with a cartoon deriding all politicians as liars, despite the clear support for Republicans in the bumper stickers.

By that evening, Ahmed had read the message and forwarded it to eleven of
his friends, including a friend of mine. The following afternoon, aware of my
research into folklore about the welfare system, my friend forwarded the message to me.[3] Over the next few years, I would receive a dozen emails from this
friend, as well as others from a dozen more friends, family members, students,
and colleagues. Most were forwarded emails, but about a third were Facebook
posts of material they had seen shared around the internet through social media.
In the end, I received 130 examples, including 35 from snopes.com that came from
examples that readers had sent in from their own email inbox for verification.
They include

- personal narratives: 26
- secondhand stories: 4
- legends: 4
- jokes: 23
- memes: 18
- adages: 10
- official documents: 15
- treatises: 38
- news: 6
- lists: 13
- cartoons: 4

There were also two folktales, one song, one poem, and one photoshopped
image that I included in my general analysis but did not attempt to break out
for genre-specific analysis since there were so few examples. The categories are
not mutually exclusive. Lists can appear embedded within treatises, jokes, and
official documents. Official documents operate exclusively as parodies and parallel jokes in many ways, as do cartoons. Treatises occasionally subsume other
genres as when people use stories to make their point. Yet despite these overlaps
and parallels, clear distinctions emerge.

GENRE EXAMPLES

Personal Narratives, Secondhand Stories, and Legends

The example below appeared so often in people's emails that no fewer than three online sources fact-checked the story, including the *Florida Times-Union*, with spokespeople from Publix grocery store weighing in to help resolve the matter by distinguishing between EBT cards, where such cash back schemes are not possible, and prepaid ATM cards handed out by blood banks.[4]

YOU ARE NOT GOING TO BELIEVE THIS

At approximately 2:30 pm, September 6, 2012, I entered the Publix store on Main St. in Gainesville, FL to pick up a few items. I gathered my items and went to the 14 and under register to check-out. The person in front of me (a White female, approximate age 35–43, fake nails, big braided hair do, clean clothes, carrying a purse and a plastic drinking cup) put her purchase on the check out surface ONE GRAPE.

Yes, that is correct ONE GRAPE. The cashier asked if that was all, she replied yes. The cashier then weighted the GRAPE and told the women the cost was $.02 (TWO CENTS), the women then pulled out her Food Stamp EBT card and swiped it through the credit card machine, requesting $24.00 in cash back. The cashier asked if she wanted the GRAPE, the woman replied no and the GRAPE was put in the garbage can. The register recorded the sale as .02, cash back $24.00. The cashier then asked if two fives would be okay because was out of tens, the woman agreed and took the $24.00 folded it up and put it in her pocket and left the store.

As the next person in line I asked the cashier as a tax payer what in the hell just happened here she said she was on the clock and could not comment. I then asked if I had actually seen this person purchase and discard a GRAPE, then get cash back on her Food Stamp EBT card. The cashier responded that it happens all day every day in their store. She also said that if the person buying the GRAPE has it ring up over .02 they get mad and make her reweigh it.

My next comment was to ask the cashier if she planned to vote in November and she said she could hardly wait for 11/6/12 to get here as one tax payer to another. I paid for my groceries, in cash, and left the store madder than 10 wet hens.

Unbelievable—this is true!!!

Recipients with cash benefits can use their EBT Card like cash for purchases and cash-back with purchases at grocery stores and at most ATMs (automated teller machines).

The narrative mirrors the kinds of stories frequently told in the oral tradition, where nonrecipient narrators witness fraud or manipulation of the welfare system.

Jokes and Official Documents

The "Black Employment Application" discussed in chapter 7 is an example of a mock official document parodying the agency, people, or both that it references. Satirical applications for public housing, a mock math test skewering urban students, and a fake schedule of events for the Democratic National Convention are other examples. All are fictional, all intended to be humorous. Far more common are jokes that ridicule the welfare system, its recipients, and the government that created it. Short but packed with memorable details, this joke was forwarded on Monday, April 18, 2016, with no commentary and received no comment among the family members it was sent to.

> The IRS has returned the Tax Return to a man in New Jersey after he apparently answered one of the questions incorrectly.
> In response to the question, "Do you have anyone dependent on you?"
> The man wrote: "9.5 million illegal immigrants, 1.1 million crack heads, 3.4 million unemployable scroungers, 80,000 criminals in over 85 prisons plus 650 idiots in Washington."
> The IRS stated that the answer he gave was unacceptable!
> The man responded back, "Who did I leave out?"

News

Like parodies of official documents, news stories have been similarly borrowed for satire. In the example below, the structure, language, and use of quotes maintain the illusion, while the content of the quotes stretches credibility. Introductory and concluding remarks frame the story, expressing dismay and then echoing the political rhetoric of ad campaigns by suggesting the story was endorsed by some of the Right's favorite liberal targets.

TODAY'S NEW WASHINGTON ACT? REALLY?

The Americans With No Abilities Act (ANAA)

The Democratic Senate is considering sweeping legislation that will provide new benefits for many more Americans. The Americans With No Abilities Act is being hailed as a major legislative goal by advocates of the millions of Americans who lack any real skills and ambition.

"Roughly 50 percent of Americans do not possess the competence and drive necessary to carve out a meaningful role for themselves in society," said California Sen. Barbara Boxer. "We can no longer stand by and allow People of Inability (POI) to be ridiculed and passed over. With this legislation, employers will no longer be able to grant special favors to a small group of workers, simply because they have some idea of what they are doing."

In a Capitol Hill press conference Nancy Pelosi pointed to the success of the U.S. Postal Service, which has a long-standing policy of providing opportunity without regard to performance. At the state government level, the Department of Motor Vehicles also has an excellent record of hiring Persons with No Ability (63 percent). Under the Americans With No Abilities Act, more than 25 million mid-level positions will be created, with important-sounding titles but little real responsibility, thus providing an illusory sense of purpose and performance.

Mandatory non-performance-based raises and promotions will be given to guarantee upward mobility for even the most unremarkable employees. The legislation provides substantial tax breaks to corporations that promote a significant number of Persons of Inability (POI) into middle-management positions, and give a tax credit to small and medium-sized businesses that agree to hire one clueless worker for every two talented hires.

Finally, the Americans With No Abilities Act contains tough new measures to make it more difficult to discriminate against the non-abled, banning, for example, discriminatory interview questions such as, "Do you have any skills or experience that relate to this job?"

"As a non-abled person, I can't be expected to keep up with people who have something going for them," said Mary Lou Gertz, who lost her position as a lug-nut twister at the GM plant in Flint, Mich., due to her inability to remember "righty tighty, lefty loosey." "This new law should be real good for people like me. I'll finally have job security." With the passage of this bill, Gertz and millions of other untalented citizens will finally see a light at the end of the tunnel.

Said Sen. Dick Durbin, IL: "As a senator with no abilities, I believe the same privileges that elected officials enjoy ought to be extended to every American with no abilities. It is our duty as lawmakers to provide each and every American citizen, regardless of his or her inadequacy, with some sort of space to take up in this great nation and a good salary for doing so."

And, oh yes, incidentally. . . .

This message was approved by Jesse Jackson, Al Sharpton, Diane Feinstein, Barbara Boxer & Nancy Pelosi

Memes

As a small unit of cultural information shared from one person to another through imitation and replication, memes encompass many of the jokes, cartoons, legends, and bumper stickers included in this analysis.[5] In terms of form, however, one can usefully distinguish a particular type of internet meme that combines image and text for a brief, often humorous commentary shared widely on the internet in multiple variations. It is a particularly democratic form of online discourse, with meme generators that make combining an image with text particularly easy.

Figure 9.1. Cosby meme.

One of the most common forms combines an image from popular culture with brief text to comment on a particular issue. The Cosby meme (fig. 9.1) is a classic example, with initial text on top, the "punch line" below, and a recognizable image from pop culture. The text is written with the sans serif Impact font in white with black outline, which has become the unofficial font of internet memes. As the meme circulates around the web, viewers shift from audience to creator, reusing the image with new text to suggest an endless range of commentary—in Cosby's case, on such topics as welfare, celebrity news, college drinking, corporate profits, Facebook etiquette, and the accusations of the comic's numerous cases of sexual assault. The "Welfare Chex" cereal box meme (fig. 9.2) might also be categorized as a "photoshop" (Frank 2011), referencing the software used to alter the original cereal box. The Cosby example appeared on personal Facebook pages as well as a more public Facebook site titled Pop Culture's Conscience. The cereal box was part of a series of memes about Obama shared via email.

Bumper Sticker Adages

Pithy and shared as a copied image, bumper stickers circulate electronically as a type of meme, capturing a single idea but often modified visually and occasionally textually as it is shared. Most can be found for sale, often leaping from bumper to

Figure 9.2. "Welfare Chex" meme.

Figure 9.3. Bumper sticker.

mug or T-shirt. Their lives online appear to be more robust than on car bumpers, though colleagues and I have seen "Work Hard. Millions on Welfare Depend on You" on at least one car in town, as well as on the sign outside a church in Buffalo, South Carolina (*USA Today* 2017). (The pastor later apologized, apparently surprised that it might offend people.) The bumper sticker shown here (fig. 9.3) was shared via email, as they often are (in collections rather than solo), in the batch of sixteen that started my electronic collection.

Treatises

Treatises that construct arguments around hot-button issues abound in discussions about welfare, often showing up in letters to the editor and op-ed pages. These are typically not part of the folk tradition. But when they are picked up and shared widely, they can become part of an informal tradition that reflects the views not of a single author but a larger group. One of the most popular was the "lesson" in figure 9.4, showing up in the email boxes and Facebook accounts of a number of my colleagues, as well as in two well-publicized examples of Republican politicians posting the message, first in 2013 by the South Dakota GOP candidate Annette Bosworth on her Facebook account (she lost in the primaries) and then two years later on the Oklahoma Republican Party's official Facebook page (Whitaker 2014; CBS Houston 2015).

Lists

The list genre is immediately recognizable though it as often appears embedded within other genres as it does as a stand-alone example.[6] The form and scope of top-ten lists popularized by David Letterman are borrowed on the internet (Frank 2009, 106), but as Elliott Oring points out, lists lend themselves to addition and subtraction as they are shared (2012, 111). The "Welfare Letters" Xerox lore reproduced here in figure 9.5, has been recorded fairly consistently since 1934, including the "original" Xerox deposited in the Memorial University Archives in Newfoundland, Canada (McKinnon 1988).[7]

TODAY'S LESSON IN IRONY

THE FOOD STAMP PROGRAM IS ADMINISTERED BY THE
U. S. DEPARTMENT OF AGRICULTURE. THEY PROUDLY
REPORT THAT THEY DISTRIBUTE FREE MEALS AND
FOOD STAMPS TO OVER 46 MILLION PEOPLE ON AN
ANNUAL BASIS.

MEANWHILE, THE NATIONAL PARK SERVICE, RUN
BY THE U. S. DEPARTMENT OF THE INTERIOR, ASKS
US, "PLEASE DO NOT FEED THE ANIMALS". THEIR
STATED REASON FOR THIS POLICY BEING THAT..

"THE ANIMALS WILL GROW DEPENDENT ON THE
HANDOUTS, AND THEN THEY WILL NEVER LEARN
TO TAKE CARE OF THEMSELVES".

THIS CONCLUDES TODAY'S LESSON ANY QUESTIONS?

Figure 9.4. Treatise: "Today's Lesson in Irony."

Cartoons

As with bumper stickers, cartoons may start as professional products, but once adopted, adapted, and disseminated through informal networks on social media, they can become part of a folk tradition. The trick-or-treating cartoon in figure 9.6 was drawn by the professional political cartoonist Gary McCoy and typically circulates as is, with additions of support and commentary as the only alterations. In the version included here, "OBUMMER" is a common phrase intended to negatively comment on President Barack Obama's policies; "ROFL" stands for "rolling on floor, laughing." (For a liberal response to this cartoon, see chap. 12.)

In what appears to be a classic case of ostension, where people enact the folklore they encounter, Donald Trump Jr. tweeted the following: "I'm going to take

THE FOLLOWING ARE EXAMPLES OF UNCLEAR WRITING - SENTENCES TAKEN FROM ACTUAL LETTERS RECEIVED BY THE WELFARE DEPARTMENT IN APPLICATION FOR SUPPORT.

I am forwarding my marriage certificate and six children. I have seven, but one died which was baptized on a half sheet of paper.

I am writing the welfare department to say that my baby was born two years old. Where do I get my money?

Mrs. Jones has not had any clothes for a year and has been visited regularly by the clergy.

I cannot get sick pay. I have six children. Can you tell me why?

I am glad to report that my husband who is missing is dead.

This is my eighth child. What are you going to do about it?

Please find for certain if my husband is dead. The man I am living with cannot eat or do anything until he knows.

In answer to your letter I have given birth to a boy weighing 10 lbs. I hope this is satisfactory.

I am very much annoyed to find that you have branded my boy illiterate. This is a dirty lie as I was married a week before he was born.

I am forwarding my marriage certificate and my three children, one of which is a mistake as you can see.

Unless I get my husband's money soon, I will be forced to lead an immoral life.

You have changed my boy to a girl. Will this make any difference?

In accordance with your instructions, I have given birth to twins in the enclosed envelope.

I have no children as yet, as my husband is a truck driver and works day and night.

I want money as quick as I can get it. I have been in bed with the doctor for two weeks and he does't do me any good. If things don't improve, I will have to send for another doctor.

My husband got his project cut off two weeks ago and I haven't had any relief since.

Moral . . . . Be careful how you compose your letters. . . .

Figure 9.5. List: welfare letters (MacKinnon 1988).

Figure 9.6. Cartoon: trick-or-treating.

half of Chloe's candy tonight & give it to some kid who sat at home. It's never to [*sic*] early to teach her about socialism" (fig. 9.7).[8]

DIFFERENT GENRES, DIFFERENT WORK

Function

Each genre can be grouped according to primary, stated, assumed, or intended function:

- describing an event: news, personal experience narrative, secondhand, legend
- evoking a laugh: joke, official doc, cartoon, lists
- making a point: treatise, meme, adage

However, these categories are not mutually exclusive; all examples achieve at least two of these functions, and most, all three. Performance often dictates which function is foregrounded. Memes are often shared for a laugh as much as for the point they make, while narratives shared on social media are almost always intended to make a point as they describe a past event. Folk lists are particularly flexible, able to stand alone as parody or be folded into a treatise with no hint of humor at all. More importantly, *all* of the examples in this collection make a point,

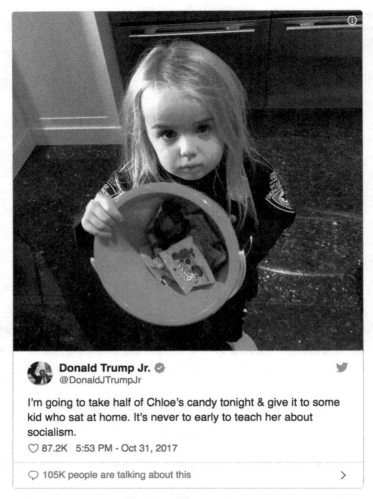

Figure 9.7. Tweet variant.

whether social, rhetorical, political, economic, or ideological, shared as part of a larger conversation about public assistance in the United States. These functions become clearer through thematic, rhetorical, and contextual analyses.

Themes

On the surface, the general content of the collection appears fairly uniform. It would have to be; after all, the data set is constructed topically around the issue of public assistance and the poor. However, the nature and focus of the commentary that emerges vary across genres. Overall, the scapegoats in email and

Target	Percentage of Total
Aid Recipients	69%
Government	44%
• General	25%
• Democrats	28%
• Obama	15%
Blacks	41%
Immigrants	21%
Hispanics	14%
Muslims	6%

Table 9.1. Targets of lore on social media.

on Facebook mirror political rhetoric that extends far beyond welfare and into such hot-button issues as immigration, Islam, terrorism, and partisan politics. In keeping with the dominant ideology that aid recipients are de facto undeserving, they are scapegoated explicitly in 69 percent of all the examples (table 9.1). The government trails as a distant but significant second-favorite punching bag. African Americans continue to be singled out as the racial minority most commonly associated with welfare, with virulent racist stereotypes driving many of these examples. Immigrants are a large part of the *economic* arguments made about welfare. Although Mexican immigrants specifically and Hispanic immigrants more generally are sometimes singled out by name, more often racial identity is either assumed or the net is cast more broadly.

Not all genres point the finger at the same targets for the same reasons, however. In personal narratives, almost 70 percent of all narrators operate according to the assumption that the only obstacles to success are those of one's own making. Both blame and narrative focus are centered on the individual. One significant reason why is that these stories are predominantly eyewitness stories in which the aid recipient serves as focal point and antagonist while the nonrecipient narrator serves as protagonist, judge, and jury. The structure of these interactions inherently perpetuates an us-versus-them ideology at the level of the individual, initially erasing structural, material, racial, geographical, or physical obstacles.

Yet narrators often imply or explicitly generalize from the individual to the group in the coda to their stories. In doing so, narrators get to have their cake and eat it too. The injustice they perceive is a personal affront, but the significance of the interaction has implications for all aid recipients and, in the case of African Americans, whole groups. In 79 percent of the personal narratives that implicate African Americans, coded language is used to signal race, providing the crucial element of plausible deniability against claims of racism.[9] The Cadillac has already been noted for this ability; hair extensions, elaborate fingernails, sagging pants, and gold teeth also signal race, as do nouns recast as adjectives, such as *ghetto* in *ghetto family* and *pimp* as in *pimp car*. Other seemingly more ambiguous terms, such as *urban* and *inner city* do the same (see López 2014; and chap. 7). As for the other 21 percent, all were fabricated or skewed narratives about Hurricane Katrina evacuees. The stories referenced a nationally televised event that already made race a centerpiece of coverage and analysis, unlike an encounter in a grocery on any given Tuesday. Naming African Americans in the context of New Orleans and Hurricane Katrina, then, was socially acceptable, even expected, with built-in plausible deniability that could substitute a bullhorn for a dog whistle.

In all other genres except one, race and immigration status is explicitly referenced, and frequently (table 9.2, column 2). As with personal narratives, examination of the examples within each genre helps provide reasons why. While some of the highest percentages appear in genres that regularly employ humor and parody (table 9.2, column 3), these numbers are not predictive. Closer study suggests that it is not the humor involved in jokes and parodies that best explains these patterns, but plausible deniability. "It's just a joke" is a common refrain, indicating how often joke tellers try to distance themselves from the message. Deniability is presumed to be inherent in the genre. Accordingly, jokes not only address sensitive topics but do so in some of the most insensitive ways. Jokes and official document parodies about welfare shared on social media and via email, for example, do not shy away from racist and xenophobic attacks against African Americans, Hispanics, Muslims, and immigrants.

Jokes and parodies have hardly cornered the market on such attacks, but they attack with a degree of consistency and vitriol not seen in other genres. Considering that the primary goal of parody is to subvert and challenge existing paradigms or ideologies, it should not be surprising that the other side of the coin is represented here as well. Parodies are the sole genre where pro-poor and pro-welfare messages emerge (chap. 12).

Where parody fails to explain the mention of race, the use of statistics and quotes from authorities does. The genre of treatise includes very little parody: only three of the forty examples, or 8 percent (table 9.2, column 3). Two of those three examples of parody (67 percent) address race. More significant, however, are the nineteen examples that reference race, fifteen (75 percent; column 5) of which use statistics and authoritative quotes. Between the two, 94 percent of the examples that address race include either humor or statistics and quotes. Similarly, six out of nine of the folk lists that mention race are parodies, while the other three use statistics to create plausible deniability. Statements such as "You

Genre	% of Texts: Race	% of Genre: Parody	% of Texts: Race and Parody	% of Texts: Race and Stats	% of Texts: Race and Parody or Stats
Treatises	50%	8%	10%	75%	94%
PENs	58%	0%	0%	67%	67%
Jokes	75%	100%	100%	11%	100%
Memes	42%	100%	100%	38%	100%
Official Docs	80%	100%	100%	0%	100%
Folk Lists	69%	62%	67%	33%	100%
Adages	0%	0%	0%	0%	N/A
News	83%	83%	100%	0%	100%

Table 9.2. Correlations between race and parody, and race and statistics.

can't argue with the facts" and "The numbers don't lie" provide the folk wisdom to explain that the inclusion of race is not the choice of the narrator but of the objective factual record. The result is that 100 percent of the folk lists that mention race include either parody or statistics.

One genre, however, stands out for making no explicit mention of race or immigrant status: adages. While personal narratives focus on the individual and jokes on the stereotypical, adages focus on the political. All but one of them take up a political stance, often a clearly partisan one, without a single mention of ethnic or religious minority groups. Performance context provides a clue as to why. The adages about welfare shared in email and on Facebook are all created as bumper stickers, even if they are not confined to the back of a car. While front yards may dominate personal yet public political expression during election seasons, car bumpers win the rest of the year—with more permanent, diverse, and creative messages. Again, plausible deniability appears as a crucial factor to explain this omission. In being connected directly to an individual in a visible, public, and personal way, more sensitive topics are typically avoided on bumper stickers in favor of sentiments with wide popular support. Accordingly, the intersection of form (small space), function (express political and personal views), and context (publicly associated with an individual) shapes the acceptable ideology. Even when the context shifts from public displays on cars to far more private displays on social media and via email, the form and its related ideologies remain fairly stable. As these bumper sticker adages are forwarded around the internet, some users tweak the format or the language, but all hold to generic expectations of the bumper sticker. Particularly telling, however, is who these bumper stickers do target: aid recipients. While overtly racist, Islamophobic sentiments remain mostly taboo on bumper stickers, aid recipients receive no such protection. One hundred percent of the adages take direct aim at aid recipients; 70 percent label them lazy, suggesting that such a view is perceived by many as acceptable public commentary.

While bumper sticker adages may be politically oriented, they have little space to articulate an argument beyond the sound bite. The same is true of cartoons, at least three-quarters of which were drawn by professional political cartoonists before gaining new life on social media to continue their political critiques. Treatises (60 percent) and personal narratives (42 percent) also tackle politics: treatises typically by focusing on policy, personal narratives by linking bad behavior by aid recipients to lax government regulation. In all cases, the critique is clear: government is uninformed, ineffective, and wasteful at best, incompetent, counterproductive, and destructive at worst. The message is not a novel one, reflecting a deep tradition of antigovernment sentiment that runs through political, popular, and folk discourse in the United States.

As in the oral tradition, drugs (24 percent) and alcohol (15 percent) are some of the most frequently mentioned "luxuries" in the lore on social media. In many cases, the example serves primarily as a way of discrediting recipients as undeserving of help due to personal immorality, but as often, the implication is that if they can afford drugs, they do not need public assistance. It is a simple economic argument: use the money spent on drugs for rent, food, and utilities, and there is no need for government help. It is the same argument that extends to other luxury items mentioned: high-end food (steak and crab legs are named most often, 11 percent), iPhones and jewelry (each 11 percent), cigarettes (7 percent), high-end electronics (6 percent), salon-styled hair and nails (5 percent), designer clothing and expensive cars (each 4 percent), and gambling (primarily lottery tickets, 3 percent).[10]

In terms of genre, two take up the critique of luxury items most aggressively and consistently, accounting for 78 percent of all instances: narratives and treatises. Personal narratives, secondhand stories, and legends mention drugs, alcohol, and cigarettes more than any other genre but also frequently mention phones, food, and jewelry. Treatises are more ecumenical, mentioning all the luxury items in relatively large numbers, including flat-screen TVs and cars, likely because treatises do not rely on eyewitness accounts.

Persona

There is an old playground saying that when you point your finger at someone else, three fingers are pointing back at you. The scapegoating that appears so often in the lore on social media is intimately tied to the persona of the speaker, author, or protagonist.

All genres provide a glimpse into the persona of the performer, even the short-est adage or meme. The bumper sticker that reads "Actually ... No one owes you CRAP!" conveys a clear sense of the person's stance, personality, and emotion. In terms of creating a *credible* persona, however, not all genres are created equal. Personal narratives provide the most latitude for establishing a credible ethos, followed by treatises, both of which are typically told in the first person. In these stories and treatises, most people attempt to establish authority situationally, the most common being an eyewitness to the events. Others reference more generic but stable authorizing characteristics, such as education level or employment status. Far more common, however, is establishing an ethos of equality rather than superiority. "Listen to me because I'm like you" rather than "Listen to me because I know more than you." The common denominator that links author with audience is assumed to be shared political ideology. Treatises, for example, often evoke these values by referencing well-worn bogeymen, such as "the liberal media": "Some VERY interesting #'s that the SLANTED Liberal Media won't share with us !!!" warns one. "Pass this on because we'll NEVER see these facts ... in the main stream media!!!" warns another. More often even than claiming to be a hardworking taxpayer, people express conservative values and beliefs as a way to speak to their audience. Arguments built on what is conveyed as common sense follow as being some of the most frequent forms of reasoning. This appeal to the "everyman" is the foundation for two of the three most common personas created in these electronic examples.

First, there is the sincere, well-meaning, honest everyman who is surprised and shocked by the abuses of welfare they perceive in the grocery store line. Many attempt to establish a baseline of sympathy for the poor to avoid being written off as an insensitive boor. "Don't get me wrong," protests one woman after sharing her story. "I understand unemployment, and actually was on it for a short period of time. My gripe is more the food stamps and WIC checks people use, then spend their cash on chocolate lottery and garbage."

The second most common persona is an angrier, more emotional version of the sincere everyman whose outrage sits right on the surface and makes no attempt to sympathize. "'Fairness' isn't giving my money to lazy people," declares one bumper sticker; "I'm NOT sorry if this offends anyone because this is MY COUNTRY," shouts the author of a photoshopped image railing on Mexican immigrants. Frustrated, overworked, tired, and angry, this persona draws on both the conservative values of the sympathetic everyman and the hardworking taxpayer so prevalent in the narratives told in the oral tradition.

The third most common persona diverges from the frustrated or outraged everyman to create the more entertaining but snide and cynical critic. Most use humor as a way to blunt or mask their outrage. "Honk if I'm paying your mortgage," declares one bumper sticker in mock gaiety, while a meme shows a 1960s woman in the grocery store daydreaming: "Someday, I hope to be able to afford a new iPhone ... like the girl in front of me with the food stamps." There is also the mock letter that begins, "Dear President Obama, Hillary, the Senate and Congress: I'm planning to move my family and extended family into Mexico for my health, and I would like to ask you to assist me." The list of requests includes "a local Mexican driver's license so I can get easy access to government services," "a nice job without paying any taxes, or have any labor or tax laws enforced on any business I may start," and no "complaints or negative comments from the locals," when I "fly the U.S. flag from my housetop, put U.S. flag decals on my car, and have a gigantic celebration on July 4th." In case the irony is lost on the reader, the letter writer ends, "I know this is an easy request because you already do all these things for all of his people who walk over to the U.S. from Mexico. I am sure that the President of Mexico won't mind returning the favor if you ask him nicely." Lest the playful critique appear to be a harmless joke, the email sender added the final line in a larger, bright red font to distinguish his or her voice from that of the letter writer: "See how stupid this actually looks when it's put in writing?"

Although common in unattributed memes, cartoons, jokes, and adages, this third persona is never used in personal narratives. Sarcasm risks alienating the "I'm like you" everyman connection that personal narratives strive to achieve. Audiences can enjoy sarcasm vicariously but may be less likely to see themselves in the role of the snide, rather than sincere, critic. Official document parodies, on the other hand, play with this third persona by substituting the bland, clueless, possibly ignorant bureaucrat whose professed objectivity is anything but. For the "Democrat Convention Schedule," the entries are listed matter-of-factly, as the below sample suggests:

MONDAY, JULY 25, 2016

11:15 AM: Free lunch, medical marijuana, and bus ride to the Convention
1:30 PM: Forms distributed for Food Stamp enrollment
3:15 PM: Group Voter Registration for Illegal Immigrants
5:00 PM: "How to have a successful career without ever having a job, and still avoid paying taxes!" A Seminar moderated by Al Sharpton and Jesse Jackson

The formal structures, language, and tone of these parodies suggests neutrality while the sarcasm of the unseen author is conveyed by the pointed examples offered. Cartoons, on the other hand, convey no language of objectivity. As political cartoons, they are expected to offer subjective critiques and commentaries that play heavily on partisan political ideals.

Conspicuously missing is an aid recipient as narrator or protagonist. The only exceptions are cartoons and memes that parody aid recipients by placing them front and center to confirm the stereotypes levied against them. There is the cartoon of two hippies talking about all the benefits they need to go out and apply for, ensuring they still have time to get to the statehouse to protest the greedy Republicans. There is also the meme of the woman screaming in horror that "Trump is gonna make me work for my benefits." But the sympathetic aid recipient is nowhere in sight.

Truth and Reasoning

Not all genres claim to be true. Jokes and parodies are explicitly fictional, though all purport to illuminate deeper truths. Treatises and adages claim truth but primarily the rhetorical truth of values, beliefs, and opinions. Only personal narratives and their second- and thirdhand counterparts claim historical truth, describing events that are supposed to have taken place when, where, and how the speaker recounts them.

All of the genres are capable of providing factual and false information, however, and occasionally in equal measure. Treatises and eyewitness narratives for example may build an argument with both true and false information, as with the email that circulated about the so-called Obama phone to ensure that low-income families had a way to reach and be reached by employers, doctors, family, and 911. The program was created by Ronald Reagan in 1984 for landlines, expanded by Bill Clinton in 1996, and then expanded again to include cellular service under George W. Bush in 2008. The email is correct that the basic parameters of such a plan exist, but attributing it to Barack Obama is misleading—especially when the phones are used as evidence that Obama bought the votes of poor minorities by promising handouts—as are the claims that phones are free, only for welfare recipients, and paid for by taxpayers (D. Mikkelson 2012). The accuracy of the eyewitness narratives of people talking about the phones in the grocery line are more difficult to determine. While claims about the Lifeline phones are verifiable, personal stories rarely are. They may be accurate, embellished, adapted from someone else, or made up out of whole cloth.

In the end, the vast majority of the lore either does not purport to be factual or cannot be verified (table 9.3). Almost half of the examples were either jokes or opinion where factual truth was moot (49 percent). Of the rest, the vast majority of the examples are either false (19 percent), likely or mostly false (22 percent), or have a mix of true and false information (16 percent). Of all 130 examples, only 1 is verifiably true: the celebratory treatise about drug testing that cites the recent news that aid recipients in Florida will be drug tested.

Genre	NA	True	True?	False	False?	Mostly False	Mixed
Treatise	65%	3%	0%	8%	5%	8%	13%
PEN	4%	0%	19%	46%	19%	4%	8%
Joke	79%	0%	0%	13%	8%	0%	0%
Meme	67%	0%	11%	11%	6%	0%	6%
Official Doc	40%	0%	0%	7%	53%	0%	0%
Folk List	0%	0%	0%	8%	62%	8%	23%
Adage	100%	0%	0%	0%	0%	0%	0%
News	50%	0%	0%	17%	0%	0%	33%
Legend	0%	0%	0%	75%	0%	25%	0%
Cartoon	100%	0%	0%	0%	0%	0%	0%
Secondhand	0%	0%	0%	25%	50%	0%	25%
Total	49%	0.6%	4%	17%	17%	4%	8%

Table 9.3. Factual truth of examples from social media. Numbers for each genre indicate percent of that genre rather than of the entire corpus. Percentage totals in the final row indicate percent of all examples.

A variant situated in Kentucky, however, is false, and in the case of the Florida story, the law was quickly struck down as unconstitutional.

In terms of evidence or logical reasoning, the most common strategy of bolstering one's argument is to quote statistics and facts, a strategy most common in treatises but also common in memes, where a single statistic or fact forms the basis for the entire claim. "Obama Fun Fact #301" headlines one misleading meme: "For every one job created under the Obama Administration 75 people went on food stamps."[11] Two frequently shared personal stories relating to Hurricane Katrina used statistics, but most did not, relying instead on the one piece of evidence they all shared: eyewitness testimony. Quoting authorities was also common in treatise and news stories but rare elsewhere.

Overall, however, there was little evidence proffered among the examples. Structure explains much of this, as with relatively brief genres such as adages, memes, and cartoons that rely on commonsense claims, opinions, and analogies to make their point. Analogies provide some of the most compelling arguments, particularly in examples where humor is employed. Humor is often achieved through a process of what Elliott Oring has called "appropriate incongruity" (1992, 2). A scenario is presented that initially seems incongruous but, upon further reflection (usually at the point of the punch line), is deemed appropriate. The sudden recognition inspires laughter; extended recognition makes us think. A bumper sticker declares, "A taxpayer voting for Obama is like a chicken voting for Colonel Sanders." Analogies are incredibly powerful in creating aha moments that confirm a particular view. The problem is that false analogies are a common logical fallacy in these examples. The analogy in "The $50 Lesson," which opened this chapter, seems apt if one believes the homeless are perfectly fit both physically and mentally and jobs are easily accessible. If not, comparing one day's worth of yard work by a young, able-bodied youth to securing a living wage job by a homeless man becomes more problematic. The uproar that ensued after Republicans posted the "Please Don't Feed the Animals" treatise suggests that at least some audiences felt that the comparison between feeding wild animals and feeding the country's poor was a false analogy, inappropriate as well as offensive.

While false analogies are one of the logical fallacies that appear regularly in these examples, they are hardly the only. As thematic analysis made clear, scapegoating is also common across all genres. As with most arguments crafted with tight space limitations by a single author, hasty generalizations and card stacking are also easy accusations. The use of fabricated information and the false use of evidence also occur frequently, such as the false claim that eleven states have more people on welfare than they have employed or the true information that some government aid information in Michigan is provided in Arabic but the erroneous assumption that this is evidence that Muslim men can claim benefits for four wives.[12]

Underlying most online lore are claims based on contested or faulty assumptions. As with "The $50 Lesson," depending on the initial assumption, the logic of the argument or claim that follows may appear rational and logical. If a person starts with the belief that poverty is caused by laziness, then punitive and severe policies appear reasoned. If a person starts with the belief that benefits are incredibly generous, then regulating purchases or slashing funding similarly appear reasoned. Seeing someone paying for their groceries with food stamps but wearing nice clothes or driving a nice car reinforces the validity of these assumptions. Exceptions are granted, of course: the disabled veteran, the widowed mother, the child. But these are exceptions rather than the rule. In the absence of a back story, the assumption reigns supreme.

Aesthetics

Laughter is said to be the best medicine. According to the lore on social media, it is also assumed to be an effective persuader. Second only to anger and frustration, humor sets the tone for many of these examples. In most cases, that laughter is derisive, as with the meme of the woman wailing, "Trump is gonna make me work for my benefits," or the Los Angeles math proficiency test and "Black Application for Employment" form that play on virtually every race- and class-based stereotype of urban youth and black men. Others are less pointed but similarly keep aid recipients clearly in their sights as the butt of the joke, as with lists of humorously naive or ignorant quotes from purported real letters written by aid recipients to welfare offices and the Leroy joke that suggests female aid recipients have numerous children with different husbands. While these examples lead with humor, outrage is never far behind. Laugh first, get mad second.

Memetics provides one explanation for why outrage and laughter rise to the forefront of the affective responses to these examples. In 1976, Richard Dawkins argued that ideas can operate like genes, competing to "live" the longest through widespread dissemination. The most successful ideas are those that have accrued characteristics that help ensure their replication and dissemination. While Dawkins's theory has come under fire for a lack of clear definitional rigor and sufficient evidence to support it, memetics has spawned a host of studies taking seriously the issue of transmission. One of the most relevant is the experiment conducted by Chip Heath, Chris Bell, and Emily Sternberg, who tested which contemporary legends were more likely to be passed along. What they found in three separate experiments was that the more the legend evoked a feeling of disgust, the more likely people were to share it. But the significance of their research did not stop there. The researchers discovered that when people shared the stories that evoked the most disgust, "they were also passing along stories that produced higher mean levels of other negative emotions (i.e., anger and sadness) and were passing along stories that they admitted were less plausible" (2001, 1037). The result was that emotional response trumped the veracity of the content when people were deciding whether to share or not. Similar results were found by Vasoughi, Roy, and Aral, who found that stories that inspired fear, disgust, and surprise were shared faster, farther, and more often on social media than stories that inspired truth, sadness, joy, or trust (2018).

These results parallel those found by Guerin and Miyazaki (2006), who argue that contemporary legends are often shared as entertainment rather than as part of a rhetorical argument, supporting what folklorists had been saying for years: that belief in a legend may have no bearing on a person's decision to share a legend. Stories have to be plausible, but they do not have to be believed, and sometimes it is those stories that are *not* believed that are shared most often. People share lore as entertainment, and humor is incredibly entertaining. Accordingly, people are more likely to select the most negative and humorous examples as worthy of sharing with one's friends and family.

People who create and disseminate digital folklore often work to ensure their meme, story, treatise, or joke gets read fully and shared as widely as possible. "Please inform every red-blooded American you know that this is happening. It is outrageous"; "Please pass this on; this is worth the short time it takes!"; "Re-post this if you'd like to see this done in all 50 states." Before email, chain letters carried the same requests, often with warnings of dire consequences for not sharing, including, "One person did not pass this letter along and died a week later."[13] In the fast-paced world of social media and email, however, more common are requests simply to read the email in the first place rather than hitting the delete button. Efforts range from the subtle (comments like "Love the last thing she would do—the best," which introduces a list of welfare reforms) to the explicit: "Here are some amazing stats: Make sure you read to the bottom. An eye opener!"[14]

Overall, commands to share, warn, or act appear almost a third of the time (31 percent). While requests to share the message are the most common (15 percent), warnings that Muslims or immigrants will take over the country or spending on social services will bankrupt the United States financially and morally appear 9 percent of the time, followed by calls for a specific action, such as "Click 'like' if you think welfare recipients should be drug tested before they take my money for doing nothing!" (7 percent). Often, warnings and requests to share and act go hand in hand: "If you are in favor of this, then by all means, delete this message. If you are not, then pass this along to help everyone realize just how much is at stake, knowing that apathy is the greatest danger to our Freedom." Of all the genres, the treatise is by far the most rhetorically charged, with 60 percent of all calls to share, warn, or take action, making it the most explicitly focused on persuasion of any of the genres.

The aesthetics of emotional response are often paired with visual and linguistic elements. Outrage is conveyed through visual "shouting": the use of all caps, underlining, bright colors, and exclamation points. Such shouting is most common in treatises and personal narratives, where first person dominates. More nuanced aesthetics are employed in jokes, memes, and adages, where communication must pack a punch in a small space. Adages rely on quick punch lines, as in the bumper sticker that says, "Work Hard. Millions on Welfare Depend on You," or the word play in "You Think Health Care is Expensive Now? Just Wait Till Its FREE!!" In the mock news story of an interview with a Mexican immigrant, "Juan" confuses the *unalienable* rights of the Constitution with *alien* rights he believes extend to him, while a joke opens mildly with three examples of word play—for example, "Did you know that 'listen' and 'silent' use the same letters?"—and then suggests that rearranging the letters in "illegal immigrants" results in a lengthy, profanity-riddled tirade against Arab and other non-English speaking immigrants.[15]

Along with visual shouting, digital folklore has a storehouse of stock images and animations often referred to as GIFs, for the graphic interchange format that produces them, that can be dropped into an email to make it more visually or emotionally compelling or to add or augment a particular theme. In an email treatise that denigrates immigrants while praising American troops, pro-US images abound. There are fireworks exploding, American flags waving, sparkling American flag butterflies flapping, and a pair of military dog tags inscribed "Remember Our Soldiers, Bless Them All." Such GIF dumping parallels the tendency of some people to add dozens of emoticons to each of their texts. Although these images were consistent to the pro-US theme, more common are such generic GIFs as the clapping hands added to a list of bumper stickers that the sender thought was particularly praiseworthy.

Repetition, parallelism, figurative language, and genre borrowing are also used to heighten aesthetic appeal. "Don't spread my wealth . . . Spread my work ethic!!!" employs repetition, parallelism, and alliteration. The treatise "Put me in charge" repeats the phrase again and again, often ending each paragraph with the refrain "then get a job." Other times, people borrow recognizable cultural forms to make their point, such as the cartoon that models itself on the children's "spot the difference" games, where two images are presented, one slightly altered from the other, or the trope of opening with "Today's lesson in" and closing with "This concludes today's lesson. Any questions?" as the "Don't feed the animals" examples do. Such obvious artistic efforts are most common in such genres as jokes, parodies, and memes that do not pretend to be either historically factual or the authentic expression of "an average joe," the everyman persona seen in so many personal experience narratives. What is artistic in a joke can seem like artifice in a personal narrative.

Personal narratives are not void of artistic qualities, however. Evocative description, dramatic tension, measured use of profanity, and folk speech all create a compelling narrative without undermining credibility. The woman at the grocery store furious at a woman she believes got cash back from her EBT card describes leaving the store "madder than ten wet hens." The man in North Dakota who recounts his story of fortitude in the face of a blizzard compared to his southern neighbors in Louisiana who crumbled under Hurricane Katrina wraps up his story with a folksy moral replete with colorful folk terms: "We did not wait for some affirmative action government to get us out of a mess created by being immobilized by a welfare program that trades votes for 'sittin at home' checks." Personal narratives, as well as treatises, jokes, and memes, also use rhetorical questions to build an ethos of equality to connect with the audience. "Doesn't it seem strange that so many are willing to lavish all kinds of social benefits on illegals, but don't support our troops?" "You wonder why SSI is going down the toilet?" The nurse who administered to Hurricane Katrina evacuees asks one rhetorical question after another, eleven in all, that compose her entire story, adroitly conveying her experiences through the questions she asks, such as "Does it seem wrong that one would remember their cell phone, charger, cigarettes and lighter but forget their child's insulin?" and "Am I less than compassionate when it frustrates me to scrub emesis from the floor near a nauseated child while his mother lies nearby, watching me work 26 hours straight, not even raising her head from the pillow to comfort her own son?"

REVISITING GENRE

Using welfare lore as a case study provides a glimpse at how different genres do different work. Much of the differences across genres has less to do with the formal structures of the genre, however, than with situational context and narrative distance, both of which implicate the construction of persona and the room for plausible deniability. Consider the adage on the bumper sticker. Located in public, directly tied to the individual, it provides no plausible deniability. The messages, therefore, are more tempered in their attacks on minorities, more aggressive in their declaration of political party affiliation. Jokes, on the other hand, as well as humorous parodies of official documents, news reports, and memes, all provide generous coverage of plausible deniability, providing people the comfort of believing they have get-out-of-jail-free cards from claims of racism, sexism, xenophobia, and the like. Situational context and narrative distance also contribute to two major developments in the creation and transmission of folklore on the internet: the promise of an eternal personal narrative and the treatise as folklore.

Personal Narrative Reboot

New technology often provides new ways to create. With the advent of the copier, for example, Xerox lore was born, allowing people to share exact copies of cartoons, jokes, sayings, and other lore. Yet that is not always what people did. Instead, folks used Wite-Out to change parts, adding the name of their company, boss, or colleague into the lore to localize it in much the same way people do verbally with stories.

Electronic media allow the same choices: to forward a joke or story verbatim or to edit it to make it more local or relevant. We see both in the welfare examples. The fire chief story about a fire that decimates an apartment building, killing all the minority families but sparing the white family because all the members of the household were at work, has emerged in multiple variants, including abroad, where the stereotyped minority groups shift to meet local norms. African Americans and Hispanics appear most often in US versions, Nigerians and Albanians in British versions.

None of this is particularly surprising; we expect changes and adaptations in the course of transmission. What is more noteworthy is the potential to believably argue that no change has occurred. The concept of a friend of a friend relies on the idea that when we hear a story from our neighbor about his sister-in-law's coworker, we are apt to retell the story as our neighbor's sister-in-law or his coworker or perhaps even our own neighbor. Rarely do we provide attributions beyond three people. We either reduce the narrative distance by shifting the story closer or forego attribution altogether and dive in: "Did you hear about the guy who . . ." or "This lady in Greensboro . . ."

Even when we do not adjust narrative distance, the possibility that any story not told firsthand has been altered in transmission is a fact of life. We are not parrots. Each retelling of a story is a new creation. But with computers, a personal narrative can be shared as a verbatim firsthand account ad infinitum. Rhetorically, this is incredibly powerful, providing a reach and credibility to a single personal narrative unheard of outside the publishing world. And unlike published narratives in books, these "eternal personal narratives" can be altered. This helps explain why the digital tradition is rampant with firsthand narratives and almost completely devoid of second- and thirdhand iterations.

A Genre Is Born

Just as the internet has brought great power to the personal narrative, it has virtually created a new genre—the folk treatise—challenging key assumptions about the difference between narrative and argument. Narrative is particularly powerful because its recognizable structure and concrete details make it memorable and transportable to new contexts. But with email and social media, carefully constructed arguments can be captured as memes, screeds, and letters from celebrities shared easily among family and friends. Complex arguments and statistical data do not need to be remembered to be shared; with the internet, they can be disseminated with a simple push of a button.

Bypassing the individual as performer and substituting the individual as passive disseminator, however, begs the question of whether these treatises are as powerful as they appear. The time stamps of each forward make it clear that if someone was going to forward a message, they were going to do it right after reading. Not one of the email chains had longer than a few hours between forwards, raising the question of whether this lore is remembered, digested, and shared again after that initial forward. In a few cases, people forwarded the same email again months or years later as the email continued its circulation and cycled back to them. In none of the cases did they indicate that they were sharing the message a second time. One result, however, may be that a single email, cycling back around, could suggest a scale and scope much larger than is warranted. Another is that while the specific example may not be remembered, the underlying message may be. The folk treatise, as well as the rest of the forwarded genres of folklore, need not be remembered well enough to perform offline or without the aid of the original text to confirm and cement existing ideologies.

Genre and Ideology

Finally, not only is it clear that different genres do different work but also that genres can be oriented ideologically. Eyewitness narratives, for example, set up a binary of witness and recipient that highlights difference and fosters antagonistic and unsympathetic views. Empathetic nonrecipients theoretically could tell stories of seeing an aid recipient in the grocery store and narrating an encounter that affirms their similarities rather than their differences, but no one did.

The point is not that genres can never be used for a particular ideology but rather that a particular genre (1) may be constructed to convey some ideas more effectively and efficiently than others, (2) may be adopted more readily by people with those ideas, and (3) may encourage audiences to interpret a performance as evidence of those ideas. In other words, genres are not determinative as much as predispositional.

Beyond the eyewitness narrative, one might ask whether all welfare lore shared through social media is ideologically biased toward conservative politics. Out of 130 examples, only 9 defended welfare and its recipients. This does not appear to be a sampling error. All but one of the people who shared examples from their social media identify as liberal; the majority of the examples they saw, however, were shared by more conservative family and friends. One possible explanation for this imbalance lies in the tone of many of these genres. Analysis of generic form, mimetics, context, and transmission all help explain why negative messages have spread so far so fast.[16] The dominance of parody, for example, ensures the messages are framed as critique rather than accolade by pointing out faults, hypocrisies, ironies, and shortcomings. Positive attributes often lie just below the surface, but they are by-products rather than focal points. For example, the critiques of Democrats in "The $50 Lesson" and the trick-or-treating cartoon suggest a positive valence for the Republican platform but only by more explicitly attacking Democrats. Yet while there is evidence that many of these genres cannot accommodate a positively oriented message, there is little evidence to suggest that they cannot accommodate a countermessage against the demonization of public assistance and its recipients. Of the 9 examples that defend welfare and its recipients, 6 do so by attacking or ridiculing corporations and the wealthy (see chap. 12). But this move requires finding a new bogeyman. Whether the interest among liberals in defending welfare and the poor on social media is too weak or the challenge of finding a new bogeyman too strong, the lore on social media from the Left is conspicuously absent.

These questions about genre raise more general questions about folklore, form, and narrative. Section 4 picks up these questions in earnest, considering context, performance, and legend, ultimately concluding by synthesizing what we know about how legends and rumors are shared and how this understanding can help overthrow the image of the welfare queen in favor of a more accurate image of welfare in the United States today.

NOTES

1. The story has been circulating at least since 2009 but appeared online, on public Facebook sites, and in the social media of friends and family particularly frequently in 2012. The person who believed the story was told as fact was responding to a post on the Positively Republican! Facebook site on June 26, 2012. When I checked on October 2, 2017, 370 people had commented, with the last on May 31, 2017. The vast majority of comments discussed the implications of the story, deciding whether it was true or not to be irrelevant. The comment above questioning the truth of the story was posted near the end of this chain on March 14, 2016, the 344th comment (Positively Republican! 2012).

2. In the study of rhetorical genres, genre is often defined by its pragmatic functions, which operate at a level of specificity where norms, structures, and ideologies are embedded and expected (e.g., Miller 2015). Taking the broader folkloristic approach to genre that is composed of a range of communicative forms that include the material, customary, and embodied as well as the verbal and written, however, such expectations of predetermined ideology is less clear, particularly when working with both emic and etic genres at the macro level. It is one thing to argue that corporate letters responding to consumer complaints carry with them particular ideologies; it is quite another to say that proverbs, jokes, oral narratives, rituals, or memes are ideologically predetermined as well.

3. For additional discussion of the transmission of email lore addressing aspects of the messages, the types of people who engage in the activity, and the ways in which they assess, interpret, and engage with the material, see Kibby (2005) and Frank (2011).

4. See TruthorFiction.com (2015) and Fader (2012).

5. For an efficient summary of many of the definitions of *meme* as used in the study of folklore, see McNeill (2009).

6. In his book chapter "Jokes on the Internet: Listing toward Lists," Elliott Oring provides evidence of jokes that employ lists and lists that serve as the humorous genre itself (2012). See also Fine and O'Neill (2010).

7. For examples, see Dundes and Pagter ([1975] 1992, 141–43), Jaffe (1975), MacDougall ([1940] 1958), and B. Mikkelson (2007).

8. For a discussion of Donald Trump Jr.'s tweet, see Couch (2017). Coincidentally, one of the most well-known cases of ostension also relates to Halloween, with the case of Ronald Clark O'Bryan, who poisoned his stepson on Halloween, assuming that the legends were real and that he could hide his crime

behind the widespread candy tampering of the legends. Technically, this would be a case of "pseudo-ostension" since the story was a hoax. Unfortunately, the act was all too real and the boy died (Ellis 2003, 162).

9. Of the twenty-six personal experience narratives, fourteen referenced African Americans: eleven implicitly, three explicitly.

10. Cf. chart 7.2, which examines the luxury items listed in the oral narrative tradition. While drugs and alcohol dominate both traditions, and most of the luxuries are present in both, the oral tradition includes tattoos, which get little mention in social media and email.

11. The statistics came from a press release by the Republican staff of the Senate Budget Committee and have been fact-checked by a number of online sites noting that the statistics use a single snapshot in time rather than the standard seasonal adjustment method that provides more accurate data. More accurate statistics would be 1.5 to 1 or 3.1 to 1 rather than 75 to 1 (Jacobson 2014).

12. For fact-checking of these claims, see D. Mikkelson (2013, 2014).

13. For hundreds of examples, see VanArsdale (2015).

14. The strategy of spotlighting the ending as particularly worthy of attention has become so common that people have begun to use it as a way to craft punch lines for jokes. In an email unrelated to welfare titled "Italian Auction," the message briefly describes a hyperlinked video that "YOU REALLY DO HAVE TO WATCH" by describing the bidding process and the exorbitant price the auctioned vase fetched and ending with "Please note the excitement on the auctioneer's face after the final bid." The viewer expects to see joy, but the auctioneer accidentally smashes the vase with his gavel. It turns out to be an ad for aspirin, but the video linked in the email ends before you see the full ad (cotletdude 2010).

15. As for the "unalienable rights" of the Constitution, some will wonder if this is a typo and that it should read "inalienable." An article in the *Washington Post* clarifies that while early drafts used "inalienable," the final draft has "unalienable." Confusion has continued to this day, with "inalienable" being inscribed on the Jefferson Memorial and many high-ranking officials, including President Barack Obama, using both (Strauss 2015).

16. The power of the negative in welfare lore is also discussed in chap. 6, with respect to the negative valence ascribed to public housing in the narrative tradition due at least in part to the performance contexts for these stories, and in chap. 10, in a broader discussion of narrative performance. The power of the negative to be remembered and shared appears again and again, not only in this case study but in case studies throughout the psychology literature (for a survey of this literature, see Baumeister et al. (2001). See also Nass and Yen (2010) for current research on brain processing and negative information, experiences, and emotion.

SECTION 4

REENVISIONING LEGENDS

TEN

—∭—

CONTEXT AS CREATOR OF TRADITION

TRACY SALISBURY HAS LIVED IN Alamance County all her life. She is now married with two kids, living in a comfortable home in a suburban neighborhood. As the director of the Open Door Clinic, she works daily with administrative staff, nurses and doctors, and county residents who cannot afford health insurance but do not qualify for Medicaid. Her role is constant even if her interactions vary considerably. But it did not always use to be that way, and old roles bleed through. "It seems crazy," she said one day while we were taking about the stigma many of her clients feel when asking for help. "We've been doing this project for how long? And I've been embarrassed to share my story. But my son received state health care." She took a deep breath and, like the majority of aid recipients we talked to, began with an explanation of how she came to need help.

> My ex-husband and I owned a restaurant, and the restaurant . . . It started not going very well. And so, he actually started having a drinking problem. So at that point, I decided to move out.
> So my son, who was three or four at the time, we moved into an apartment, and of course, trying to maintain two households . . . So at any rate, I had worked at the restaurant before, but then I decided to go back to work and started working for a chiropractor and started out in claims, not a lot of hours, and then ended up being the office manager.
> So we had family coverage. But as time went on and the restaurant continued to fail, the insurance was dropped. So I got health insurance through my employer at that time, once I became the officer manager. But to get family coverage, it was very expensive, so I was trying to keep up paying my rent—utilities, food, all of this, and . . . I'm trying to think—my son was not in day care at the time; he was with a family member, so I didn't have the day care expenses. But I didn't use public assistance at all.

And so we had a patient that came in that was an RN, had three or four kids. Her husband had been in the military and had some mental issues, so he was on disability. And she brought one of her sons in there, and he had NC Health Choice. It's insurance for children. It's almost like, you make too much for Medicaid, but it's still an option so that your children are covered. So anyway, she—just being honest—she drove a 4-Runner and she was a nurse. And in my mind, I'm going, "How in the world does she have her kids on this NC Health Choice?"

And so I just got to looking into it and found out that I might be eligible for it to get my son coverage.

I was just brought up . . . My dad was a firefighter. He brought us up with a lot of morals and work ethic, and he would always say insurance is important. And I knew it was.

So anyway, I checked into it, and I thought, "Well, I'm just going to see if I can get my son on this NC Health Choice." So at first, it was hard for me to walk over to DSS because at that point, they didn't have things online that you could get the application. And I didn't even know really where DSS was. So I got over to DSS, didn't know where to go, and I mean, I was looking around going, "I should not be here. I don't belong here," you know?

So anyway, I went through the process, and a social worker called and said, "Well, he's been approved." And I was actually shocked because, I thought, at that time I was making fifteen dollars an hour. This was thirteen, fourteen years ago. I really did not think that he would be entitled to it. So I was really shocked that they did it. At any rate, it helped me through a tough time.

So he stayed on it a year, and then I was more able, after his dad and I divorced, with settlement and all that and then working more hours and that kind of thing, that I was able to put him on my insurance. So he had it for a year, and even though I was ashamed at first to do it, I got to thinking, "I have worked all my life. I have worked since I was fifteen years old, and I have paid taxes. And if they say he's entitled to it, then I might as well use it so that he can." Because at that age, they go to the doctor more on a regular basis when they're small.

Because actually, during that time, my son was a carrier of strep throat, and so we were going back and forth. They would put him on an antibiotic, he would be fine for a month, and then bam, he'd have it again.

Plus it covered dental, so I made sure he went and got his teeth cleaned twice a year. And it also covered eye, and at that time he actually was in glasses. So it covered that, so that was important to me to make sure that he got the care.

And I mean, I had family that would not have let him go without, but I don't like asking people for things.

I know a friend of my husband, and she was in a similar situation, and I told her that she could probably get her kids on NC Health Choice. And her dad is an attorney, and she was actually interested in checking into it, but her mother is a wife of an attorney, and they pitched a fit. They said, "You are not putting those kids on welfare. My grandkids will not be on welfare."

Not only did the situational context provide her the space for sharing her story—one on one with someone she had grown to trust—but the conversational context made it clear that her story was far less about the factors that led her to seek aid than the stigma that plagued her decision. As important is biographical context. Her past shapes how she views her work and her clients today. As an aid recipient, she tells stories about the stigma of getting help. As an aid provider, she tells stories not only of helping clients but, as often, of her clients' stigmatizing experiences. And old stories die hard. When she remembers her work as a cashier at a grocery store before her experiences receiving and providing aid, her stories echo long-standing legend traditions.[1]

Tracy is not as unusual as one might think. Many aid providers once sat on the other side of the desk as recipients. This perspective allows them to share stories with clients empathetically rather than just sympathetically. Further, whether they have been recipients or not, all aid providers have the potential to narrate stories either as providers ("A client came in") or as community members ("I was in the grocery"). Code switching among these roles is common, but our identities can follow us across socially constructed boundaries, particularly identities tied to gender, race, ethnicity, class, and region. Accordingly, it makes sense to be flexible in analysis, considering the specific performance context as a starting point and then considering the roles people inhabit during those performances. Chapters 3 and 4 considered text and context together for the stories aid recipients share. This chapter will consider performance contexts for the stories told by those who currently do not receive aid but whose stories dominate the public welfare narrative tradition. By doing so, we can begin to understand how stories about welfare continue to be created, shared, and imbued with meanings that may not always reflect the balance of lived experiences.

THE DIGITAL LANDSCAPE

Mainstream Media and Letters to the Editor

Stories about welfare are not hard to find. But presence does not equal impact, and the views of one may not reflect the views of many. A news story crafted by a small handful of journalists broadcast to millions may have little impact if no one repeats it; the story shared and reshared among a group, however, can more confidently be used as a reflection, if not an exact one, of what people think and believe.[2] So the tree that falls in the woods that no one hears pales in importance to the tree we chop down and use to build a home. This is the power of folklore.

Of course, stories in the mass media often *are* heard, especially as media outlets have narrowed their niches, catering to more and more homogenous audiences. The analysis of the stories, articles, and images of welfare in the mass media has been taken up by other scholars and must continue to be studied.[3] This book, however, is focused on the folk traditions created and perpetuated not by one but by many. The bulk of those traditions continue to thrive in face-to-face interactions. However, thanks to web 2.0 technologies that allow for users to participate in the dialogue, there are a growing number of online spaces for vernacular commentary and storytelling.

In the mass media, that folk tradition emerges most clearly in the comments sections of op-eds and stories dealing with public assistance. Firsthand accounts of living with the help of public assistance appear both in print and online, and they often spawn vibrant debate. When Darlena Cunha shared her story of going from successful television producer to a new mother of twins in need of public assistance when the economic downturn hit and her husband lost his job, the response was overwhelming: over five thousand comments in fourteen days (2014). In fact, the response became the next story, with media outlets seizing on the backlash she received. An educated, professional woman, Cunha wrote her own story. The same is true of Travis Reginal, Kaitlyn Greenidge, Duane Tollison, and scores of others who rose out of poverty to reflect on and share their experiences with public assistance.[4] More often, the stories of the poor are told by journalists who have interviewed aid recipients as part of their story. The comments to these stories are not appreciably different from those posted on ideologically neutral discussion groups and blogs that draw an audience that spans the political spectrum. Analysis of one of these sites provides a view into this online narrative tradition.

ONLINE DISCUSSION GROUPS AND BLOGS

There are a lot of things that tick me off. But my biggest complaint for today is about people on welfare and other government assistance having luxuries that regular working people can't afford.

So begins the unsigned post on a site aptly titled My Biggest Complaint, where people post their complaints publicly, presumably as a way to vent their frustration. The post continues:

Every time I see someone on welfare smoking, while talking on an expensive cell phone, wearing the latest fashions and gold jewelry, with their hair and nails done, and drinking store-bought coffee from a container, I just want to go nuts! Why am I so angry? Lets break it down:

Cigarettes . . . $7.00 per pack (times 30 packs per month $210.00)
High Tech Cell Phone . . . $200.00 Phone, $400.00 2 Year Contract, $100.00
Monthly Bill, $50.00 Extra Minutes Charges

Hair[5]

Perhaps the original author tired of trying to compute costs for the various luxuries he or she wanted to catalog. Or perhaps the author simply hit "submit" before finishing. Whatever the reason, the complaint appears to have been cut short by the author rather than by a maximum word or character limit imposed by the site since other complaints on the site are significantly longer. There is no date for the original post, but the first response appears on December 12, 2009.

One might assume that this anonymous complaint would spawn similar complaints so that a sort of nihilistic *communitas* was reached. That does not, however, appear to be the case. Rather, in line with previous scholarship, posts on the site turned antagonistic quickly, with virulent insults, baiting, and blanket ad hominem attacks dominating the discourse.[6] Although loose alliances were formed among people with shared viewpoints, attacking those who disagreed was more important than securing allies. The nature and structure of the online group helps explain why.

The folk group formed by this site could be described as *low context*, meaning participants shared little in common and therefore could not draw on shared contexts, assumptions, and prior knowledge to communicate. The result is that the majority of the data required to interpret the text must be embedded in the message itself. High reliance on text, low reliance on context.[7] Contributors represented a broad swath of views, with the most extreme, dogmatic, and polarizing perspectives claiming the most space. Less like a group of friends and more like a public hearing, the voices and motivations are widely divergent but seem to share the goal of proclaiming one's point of view and defending it against attack from others.

The collection of contributors responding to this complaint about welfare and luxury goods was a transitory group, though it lasted longer than one might expect. The first post was on December 12, 2009; the last, on July 6, 2013. Posting was hardly consistent, however. There were 7 posts in December 2009, all within a few days of each other; just 2 posts in 2010 and 2011; and then, with a few posts in the first few months of 2012, the topic finally caught on in August, with 104 posts between August 2 and September 4. In other words, while the thread was active between 2009 and 2013, almost 60 percent of the activity occurred in a single month.

Participation in the conversation was also lopsided. A total of fifty-one different people posted to the site, but thirty-eight of them only posted once. That number rises to forty-three if one considers as a single post those entries from a single contributor with no one posting in between and all within minutes of each other. In other words, 83 percent of the participants chimed in once and then never came back. Further, the bulk of the conversation was held between just three people (61 percent of all posts), with one person, knight4444, dominating the conversation, responding sixty-eight times (38 percent of all posts). Once knight4444 showed up, no one escaped his attention, and vice versa until he finally signed off nearly a year later. Knight4444 was ever present; it was rare for a person to post something without his immediate retort. He and Disabled Mom conversed in near full agreement throughout the middle of August until Joseph T. showed up and sparred with him until the first week of September.

Not surprisingly, online discourse is dramatically different from discourse in face-to-face interactions, where speakers know each other and can gauge responses in real time. Posts were often rude, disrespectful, and juvenile, with contributors resorting to name-calling. It was extremely rare to find any effort to come to consensus. Instead of resolution, one finds entrenched views with applause and backslapping for those who agree, harsh criticism and personal attacks for those who do not. As with road rage, when we cannot see each other and assume no chance of facing one another at some later point in time, we are far more apt to become unreasonably angry and aggressive, particularly with the anonymity of this low-context group (see Santana 2014; Ellison-Potter et al. 2001).

The discussion was dominated by argumentative claims made with little if any evidence. Declarative statements were typically unqualified, presented as fact, and involving stereotypical claims with the anonymous, all-encompassing pronoun "they," particularly in reference to aid recipients and Republicans. When evidence was provided, it was most often from personal experience, though a few contributors cited statistics about the scope and use of public assistance. Considering the primary function of the site, it is not surprising that stories emerged primarily as illustrative examples whether as legends, kernel narratives, personal experience narratives, or generalized experience narratives.

In terms of discursive genres, the original author of the complaint makes an argument about why welfare recipients make them so angry. In order to justify that anger, the author provides numerical evidence to suggest just how inappropriate, infuriating, and (implicitly) immoral such luxuries are for someone receiving public assistance. In terms of narrative, this anger is prompted by the recurring experience of seeing aid recipients with luxury items like nice fingernails, hairdos, and designer clothing, though how the author knows the people are receiving public assistance is not explained, a point made by one of the contributors about another contributor's post later on the site. The initial complaint serves as a prototype for much of the discourse that follows: personal experience narratives shared either as single events or as generalized experience narratives, the vast majority of which echo the legend tradition.

> at the food store a man and woman togather had 2 large buggys the womans full
> of the best meats cleaned the meat cooler out. the mans buggy full of all outher
> kinds of food. at the checkout paid for food with gov. food card == then got 2

cartons of smokes and a case of beer and 2 six packs and paid for them with cash
then i watched them drive away in a brand new fancy white buick a high price'ed
one === and i work every day at a plant for 38 years and i can't do that kind of
makes you wonder if its realy worth it to work anymore. (loyd on August 2, 2012,
at 1:47 p.m.)

Loyd's story includes some of the most pervasive motifs in the welfare legend
tradition: expensive steaks, alcohol and cigarettes, and expensive new car (not a
Cadillac but a high-priced Buick, also made by General Motors). But like many
welfare narratives, Loyd shares his story as a personal narrative, not an unattributed legend, individual if not necessarily generalizable. In virtually all of the
stories shared on the site, narrative distance is minimal. Most describe events
personally experienced, personally witnessed, or involving people personally
known to the narrator.

Considering the combative nature of the posts on this website, it is not surprising that contributors regularly responded to each other with competing or
counternarratives. The initial post serves well as the referential narrative against
which counternarratives are constructed, not only because it is hegemonic but
because it is positioned as the prompt to which all other contributors are encouraged to respond.

People who complain about people on welfare are so damn stupid they have no
idea. First of all I went to school graduated got a trade worked for 11years with
no assistance, I got layed off of work and I don't do drugs I'm not trying to abuse
the system, I've been looking for work went to interviews and still no job and
now here in California you can't sit on your butt and receive cash aid you have
to volunteer somewhere SO STOP COMPLAINING ABOUT YOUR DAMN
TAX MONEY GOING TO PEOPLE ON WELFARE I've worked and paid my
dues! You people are so fuking stupid just because you have a job doesn't make
you any better I've worked for people who have money and are on drugs it just
easier for you people to cover up you fkd up life just because you work doesn't
make you any better. There is a teacher where I volunteer so no one is exempt
from being layed off. (Ang on June 13, 2012, at 1:08 p.m.)

At least one contributor—knight4444, the most prolific contributor on the
site—aimed his counternarrative directly at the welfare legends evoked by other
contributors, whether explicitly or implicitly.

Question how the F*CK do any of you actually know who is or isn't on welfare?
when you see someone with a luxury car do you ask them hey are you on
welfare? or do you actually personally know many not a couple MANY people
really abusing the system? because many people on welfare either don't have a
car or are dependant on family or friends for transportation. I own a 1991 Acura

NSX valued around 37,000 dollars and my former girlfriend who was on welfare drove my car on occasion and I drove her on occasion to the welfare office so when you idiots see a decent vehicle at DHS maybe it's not a clients car! now did you rocket scientist ever consider that?? HELL NO! About the iphones deal! boy you idiots are lost! anybody with a functioning brain knows that you can go to most cell phone stores and usually get a iphone with a contract very cheaply! HELL I could have gotten a iphone for free at my cell phone provider! with no contract at Metro pcs and their month to month! Boy you people are so incredibly ignorant! (knight4444 on August 2, 2012, at 11:49 a.m.)

He began by referencing the common legend motif that aid recipients drive luxury cars, such as Cadillacs, followed with his counternarrative about his own car, and then ended with reference to yet another common motif of many welfare legends: owning expensive technology, such as iPhones. Later, he was even more explicit in his attacks on these stereotypes: "see your boy Reagan started this BULLSH*T almost 30 yrs ago talking crap calling people welfare queens!!"

As discussion on the site continued, counter-counternarratives began to emerge. Just as aid recipients shared stories of their hard work and unavoidable hardship to respond to accusations of fraud among all recipients, critics of aid recipients responded with their own stories of hardship. Joseph T., for example, positioned himself as also having financial struggles: "I have a student loan as a result of my education. I pay for my education. To help me end my debt I go without cable . . . Welfare recipients if they are as poor as they claim, need to give up the gadgets and other services that do not provide the food and clothing they claim they need. End of story." Suz Marie is even more direct in her criticism, specifically targeting the counternarrative of Ang, who shared her experience of working eleven years but getting laid off and needing some help.

For the person that worked 11 years; whoop dee do. Try 30 years +10 + 9 years. I bet you can't add that up. When I was getting my undergraduate degree there was a woman I came to know who was on welfare. I was working full time 3p.m. - 11 pm while going to school full time. I never missed a class; she was always absent. The state was paying for her education. As the end of the year approached and we were both graduating I asked her what she would be doing. She stated she was going to take a break for a while before looking for work. OMG. She really needed a break poor thing. Additionally, she stated she was going to buy a class ring. Myself, the full time worker, could not afford a class ring. . . . If you are poor and need government assistance you would think you would use any extra cash for necessities not jewelry. Welfare recipients are allowed to receive welfare from 2-5 years. I was just laid off and after a year and a few months my unemployment ran out. Why does the laid off worker who never chose to be unemployed get less time than the welfare recipient who is usually able bodied and capable of working. People who work and lose their jobs due to lay offs should not be cut off after a year. What makes people on welfare so unique? (Suz Marie on August 18, 2012, at 11:49 p.m.)

Stories on My Biggest Complaint were shared much more conclusively, with fixed interpretations meant to support a clear point, than in face-to-face conversations in which interpretation was open for audience members to discuss. While experiences shared through story were positioned as the source for many of these frustrations, the narratives operated primarily as evidence in a polarizing debate, sandwiched between claims as exemplars and, in many cases, providing the only support for what was otherwise a series of unsubstantiated claims. The power of stories as evidence was recognized explicitly by at least one contributor, who argued, "In my posts, I have cited real life examples of welfare abuse. I have fifty or more other documented interviews with welfare abusers. You have not provided one ounce of documentation."

FACE-TO-FACE

Among Friends

Two days before Thanksgiving 2011, school break had officially begun. To celebrate, we joined some work colleagues and their families for dinner at a Mexican restaurant. Eventually, conversation turned to current research, and I mentioned my new project. Steve was the first to chime in. "Those stories are awful," he said, referring to the welfare queen narrative I had shared. "I'll tell you, though, I used to work in a Mexican restaurant and these guys would work for a while and then look for ways to be fired. They'd pick fights with the boss, come in late, slack off, be disrespectful, anything to get fired. They knew exactly how long they had to work before they could be fired and go back on unemployment and welfare. They'd work for just long enough." Around the table, we expressed general surprise that people would so boldly admit to such behavior and raised halfhearted righteous indignation. He continued, "I'd be like, 'Why don't y'all work and move up and get better jobs, better-paying jobs?' And they were like, 'Why, man? I'm done with this bullshit.'" It was a conversational move I was becoming familiar with: the initial agreement that welfare queen stories were harmful and pervasive, followed by a person's own story that suggested that there was, however, some truth to them. Earlier that October, I was in Bloomington, Indiana, for a conference and was having lunch with some old work friends. One of our friends had become a lawyer for the Department of Social Services and pounced on the idea of welfare fraud: "Oh yeah, there are loads of welfare queens. Many of them live nicer than we do." When I returned to North Carolina, I shared the story

with a colleague who was helping supervise an after-school program in one of
the public housing communities.

> I sympathize with her. When our foster daughter came to live with us, she
> complained about our car and our TV.
> "My grandmother has a nicer car than you."
> And she does. She has an Escalade with a TV in it. And she receives food stamps.
> So you hear that, and you do wonder. But then you see her house, and there's barely
> any furniture. And barely a TV. I mean, they really don't have much. So she's just
> choosing to spend her money on a really nice car. It's not a decision I would make, but . . .

Many of us have a story that fits the legend. Opening caveats that temper the story
and argue for a perspective that recognizes the poor are unfairly stereotyped
appear to be no match for the power of that single story that keeps us from truly
believing these are the exceptions rather than the rule. This rhetorical move is
similar to the all-too-common claim "I'm not racist, but . . ."

Two days after our dinner at the Mexican restaurant, we were finishing up
Thanksgiving dinner. Most of our guests had gone home except for two of our
friends, Aiya and her sister Noelle, who stayed for a late dessert and drinks. Our
conversation turned to work, and I mentioned my research, air quoting "welfare
queen" in my description. Noelle picked up on the term. "But 'welfare queen'
suggests the person is rich, right? A queen?"

"Yeah, that's the idea," I explained. "People claim that these women—and it's
almost always women. Welfare has been both gendered as well as racialized, so it's
not just a woman but a black woman with a whole bunch of kids—are committing
fraud, that they're cheating the government out of this money."

"Oh, we have family like that," Noelle replied. "We learned not to accept gifts
from my cousin."

"Why?" I ask.

"Because she stole them! We'd get these packages at Christmas with designer
clothes and just be like, 'Thanks but no thanks.'"

The story Noelle tells about her cousin is evoked by the description of the
welfare queen: African American, female, cheating the government to buy luxury
items. The description reminds Noelle of their cousin except for one very important detail: their cousin is not receiving public assistance. She is a thief but not a
thief on welfare.

The move is similar to what Ronald Reagan did with Linda Taylor (chap. 2).
Taylor was a thief, forger, kidnapper, and may have committed murder. She was a
criminal with welfare fraud as just one small part of her rap sheet. It was enough,
however, for Reagan to paint her first and foremost as a welfare "chiseler" and
suggest she represented many others. The conflation of welfare with fraud in the

image of the welfare queen is so strong that criminal activity by a black woman led Noelle to make a connection to her cousin. The result is that a story that has nothing to do with welfare could be interpreted as one more story confirming the truth of the welfare queen stereotype.

The pattern among self-identified progressives and liberals is often to aver the political perspective that the poor are unfairly maligned but then share the one or two stories that support the canonical welfare queen story. Among more conservative groups, the initial caveat is not needed: ideology and narrative align, at least until the personal dimension is added and aid recipients move from being an observed bogeyman to a personal acquaintance. This dynamic is on full display among a group of men who gather as part of a "breakfast club."

In towns and cities across the country, small groups of friends gather in conversation and fellowship for coffee, a meal, or drinks. In Alamance County, they are colloquially known as "breakfast clubs," although not all groups meet for breakfast. There are breakfast clubs of retired firefighters, golfing buddies, community leaders, stay-at-home moms, and residents of local retirement homes. Age and gender as well as occupation and recreation tend to be particularly relevant in the formation of these groups. The morning that Elon University student Jessica Elizondo arranged to join the breakfast club of local businessmen, there were six men in attendance, slightly fewer than their typical number. They knew she was interested in the topic of public assistance, and while she opened the conversation with a question and prodded the conversation along a few times with the questions we had developed for our project, the conversation developed primarily as natural turn taking among the participants.

The tone of the conversation was collegial and friendly with the men occasionally talking over one another in agreement as they built consensus across a fairly narrow but not homogenous group, members of which included both Democrats and Republicans. As a narrative event, there was a clear arc to the conversation. Although the men knew each other well, the conversation began with more tentative claims and examples, as when Dan Vertis shared a story and ended, "So, I mean, I don't have an answer for it, but I was just really, I don't know." The "I don't know" served as an open invitation to the other men in the group to confirm or challenge his perception without having to position themselves in obvious contradiction. Consensus built as the conversation continued and group members got a better sense of each other's views. Their statements and stories become more declarative and definitive as they found or established common ground. The one time there was disagreement among the men, the conversation remained respectful, with some friendly laughter to defray any possible tension. Most significantly, however, after "winning" his point, the speaker moved the conversation back toward a place of consensus.

The conversation that morning began with a question: "What are your percep-tions of welfare?" The immediate response was a reference to a rumor that had been circulating since the beginning of Barack Obama's first term as president of the United States: "Cell phones."

> Do you see the little tax on your cell phone bill? I think mine was like fourteen dollars this month. You know why? Everybody gets . . . certain ones get free cell phones. It's not just the old and elderly anymore. It's kind of widespread, so I mean, that's part of the welfare system now, you know, is the cell phones.

When he returned to the topic later in the conversation, he clarified, "They call them Obama phones." Calling it the "Obama phone" situates the program within a larger discourse of rumors and legends that Obama won his elections by brib-ing the poor with handouts, a claim made frequently on conservative talk shows following the 2012 election (see chap. 9).

The other men responded to the question in turn: "Handouts," replied Matt Strogue. "The credit cards," said Dan Vertis, by which he means the Electronic Benefits, or EBT, card. He explained with a story.

> You can't blame this on any one group. I was in Arkansas last year, was at a Walmart, and that was the first time I ever noticed that they gave a plastic card for food stamps, like the credit cards.
>
> And the guy had all this stuff going through the register. And then right behind it, he had like Crown Royal. I didn't know Walmart sold liquor, but they do out there. Buying liquor. It's like an ABC store the size of Walmart. Buying Crown Royal and all this stuff. Checked out his credit card, or EBT card, and then the liquor went right by. It was just amazing. I had never seen that before. It wasn't here, but I was just surprised; it is a credit card now.
>
> Being in line over here, I've seen them pull out two or three different cards where one's used up, and they'll go to the next one. And then, you know, buy certain things with it. Certain things you can't buy with it. I was surprised to see that.
>
> And it is abused. And I don't think anybody's got an answer on how they can fix it. But it's widely abused. Everybody knows that. And I could name you probably six or seven households that have got help, that come and work one or two days a week cleaning their house for cash. And these aren't illegals; these are people that are getting the same thing, but they work for cash, and it's all under the radar. That's really why it's spread. So, I mean, I don't have an answer for it, but it's just really . . . I don't know.

Among the group of friends at breakfast that morning, no one questioned Dan's story. They know him and trust him, and the story was both plausible and cred-ible. For the external observer, however, the parallels between his experience in Arkansas and stories that have been circulating for half a century may raise doubts. Perhaps the most famous version of the story Dan tells comes from Ronald Reagan in his story of the man who bought an orange with food stamps and took the change to buy a bottle of vodka (chap. 2). The scenario Reagan described was implausible if not impossible with enough trips through the grocery line. The scenario described by Dan Vertis, on the other hand, is plausible and is repeated in dozens of stories from other Alamance County residents who describe having witnessed similar transactions.[8]

Dan's story also reinforces stereotypes about male aid recipients as abusers of alcohol and, by extension, drugs, which explains Matt Strogue's immediate response to Dan' story: "Anybody on welfare should be drug tested." The concern that welfare recipients are using taxpayer dollars to fund drug habits was echoed in Frank Ellis's half-joking reference to legends about selling food stamps for cash to buy drugs when asked if he knew anyone receiving public assistance:

> **Frank:** So, for example, there are twelve thousand people in the county on food
>   stamps, here in Alamance County.
> **James:** And you've got a county of a hundred [thousand].
> **Frank:** So have I interacted with any of those?
> **James:** Oh yeah.
> **Frank:** Probably at Walmart. Has somebody tried to get me to buy their
>   groceries for them or some drug deal? No. But I read that in the paper.
>   [*Laughs*] No, I haven't interacted with anybody like that on food stamps.

Other dominant perceptions, stereotypes, and legends about welfare recipients emerged in the conversation. Frank raised concerns about cycles of dependency and evoked legends, rumors, and pervasive beliefs about women choosing to have more children for increased benefits by recounting stories from a relative who worked as a social worker for over a decade, a theme picked up by Dan, who blamed Lyndon B. Johnson for his War on Poverty, which Dan interpreted as paying women to have more children. These kernel stories operate as metonyms, shorthand references to larger stories assumed to be known by the audience. They are powerful not only because they are so efficient—a few words evoke a whole story or corpus of stories—but because they often go unchecked in conversation because their brevity does not invite follow-up or critique.

The dominant theme that emerged again and again in the stories the men shared about public assistance was a concern about fraud. Much of the concern was focused not on fraud at the grocery store or in terms of drugs and alcohol, however, but fraud in reporting income. The men shared story after story of experiences with people being paid under the table so that workers would not have to pay taxes on it or report the income to the state, an act that would almost certainly reduce their benefits. They blamed moral or unethical behavior by these aid recipients in part but also noted deficiencies in policies that allowed, even encouraged, such behavior. Such stories, like those of buying Crown Royal and having children to increase benefits, mirror the larger narrative tradition about public assistance and aid recipients by pointing out those areas of fraud, whether justifiable or not, believed to be pervasive in the system.

In terms of narrative distance, they shared stories of events they had personally witnessed—such as Dan's story of watching a person use an EBT card to buy groceries and a separate source of money to buy expensive whiskey—or of people they personally knew: stories about people they had employed who either needed assistance and could not get it or received assistance but did not deserve it. They also shared secondhand stories, narrated multiple experiences as a single generalized experience, and imagined hypothetical scenarios that captured in story what they believed to be true ideologically (chap. 11).

Similar to the narrative tradition online, many of the stories shared among members of the breakfast club served to make a particular point, exemplars of a belief system fairly well established. Such exemplars were often constructed comparatively to highlight differences between deserving and undeserving aid recipients as when Frank distinguishes between his father who received aid when his eyesight failed and the shoppers who divide up the items in their cart between the groceries that can be bought with their EBT cards and the alcohol that cannot (chap. 8). Bob followed Frank's story with another binary common in discourse about public assistance when he distinguished between the hamburger that hard-working, tax-paying Americans were buying and the steaks that filled the carts of aid recipients.

These binaries depend on the ability to stereotype, drawing conclusions based on little evidence. For this reason, observational stories and unattributed legends can convey a uniformly negative portrayal of aid recipients. Stories about family, friends, and acquaintances, however, are more nuanced and often more positive and sympathetic. Frank Ellis's father is justified in his use of aid while the unnamed, unknown, unindividuated recipients using food stamps are not. The same is true for people they knew who were working for cash paid under the table. The desire to protect the identities of the people they knew struggling to make ends meet prompted the men to ask that these more personal stories not be included in our research. What became clear, however, was that when the men knew the back story of an individual and saw how their hard work was not enough to survive, they justified the fraud. Yet these stories were insufficient in shifting their assumptions of widespread fraud and laziness among the poor more generally. In terms of the persuasive capabilities of narrative, then, the question arises: How many people must we know who defy the stereotype before we are willing to question the validity of the stereotype?

OCCUPATIONAL LORE

The views of welfare held by the men in the breakfast club are colored heavily by their experiences at work, where their primary interaction with people receiving public assistance is through the employment process. Grocery story cashiers are also positioned in a distinct way to observe aid recipients' behaviors that the general public are also positioned to see but on a more limited scale. For the average shopper, their encounter with someone using food stamps is part of life; for the cashier, it is part of their job.

Not surprisingly, the stories cashiers tell about welfare can best be categorized as occupational annoyances, having less to do with critiques of the poor than of frustrations with the process of having to distinguish allowable items from those that are not. Cashiers tell stories of having to put food back, ring items in multiple times, and divide up purchases into multiple orders. Some of their stories parallel classic legends in focusing on the appearance and attitude of the person using their EBT card, but the stories tend to express work frustration rather than political critique. Shannon Wilmer remembers one woman whom all the cashiers tried to avoid.

> There was this one woman. And she was a regular at our grocery store. And she always would go through my line. And no one would want to take her because she would always have more items than she could have with food stamps. And we'd have to take stuff back because she couldn't buy that stuff.
>
> We'd see her, and they'd say, "I don't want her in my line," and, "She's not going to be able to get everything, and we're going to have to go back."

While grocery store cashiers have a handful of customers who use food stamps and give rise to narratives about welfare, *all* of the clients of aid providers furnish potential narrative fodder. As with anyone who works outside the home, aid providers come home and share their joys and frustrations with their families. The out-of-the-ordinary experiences rise to the fore, particularly those that are funny or shocking since they make for entertaining stories outside of work as well as within. Describing those stories she "takes home," Sophie Griffin admits, "I've had some stories to tell."

> I had one lady come in here and she came in and she sat down—well, funny stories I think—but she came in and she sat down and she said, "Whoop," and started breastfeeding in my office, but no cover-up.
>
> Yeah. That was a little . . . It was like, "Whoa, OK."
>
> I'm all for breastfeeding, but it just caught me off guard.
>
> Stuff like that, yeah. But for the most part, I just try to keep work at work and not take it home and outside of here, but stuff like that? Yeah.

Sophie laughs, still amused by the memory. The story sticks with her, like the "eye-opener" that Serena Borden took home and shared.

> I think that that couple that got fired from the bank that came in here was a shock to me. I think that I did go home and was like telling my boyfriend. Of course, I didn't use any names, but, "Did you know that two people came in for assistance today, and they had this for their car payment and housing, and all of the sudden they need to come in here?"
>
> And I said, "If anything's an eye-opener, then that is."

She told the story earlier while talking about her general perceptions about welfare, noting that every case is different. "You can be married, both of you working, have two or three kids, everything is going fine, and then all of the sudden somebody loses their job."

> I mean, I had a—the weirdest one to me was—I had a couple come in and wanted to apply for Work First.
>
> Now, Work First is a program where you have to be under a certain income level for the whole family to get this type of assistance. So if you're a family of five and you make less than six hundred and forty-eight dollars a month—that's a low income.
>
> Well, he come in here and I had got . . . The front desk had already said, "Serena, he's here in a three-piece suit. I don't think he should be in here!"
>
> And I'm like, "OK." He comes in and he has . . . You thought he was working for Wall Street or something. He had on a suit. He had on that long trench coat type thing, and he had a briefcase in his hand. And I'm like, "Are you here to . . . undercover boss thing?"
>
> I mean, of course I didn't say anything, but the kind of things are going through your head. You are out of place!
>
> So he comes in here, and he and his wife work for banks. He was actually—I don't think he was the president, but he was up there. She worked for another big bank, and both banks went out of business. And they were—because it had been a while since they had gone out of business because he had tried to do some self-employment before. And for some reason he couldn't get unemployment, so there he was. Him and his family. And they were in here asking us . . . not sure of what he was here for, what he could get, what kind of assistance was he eligible for.
>
> And he told me, "I'm glad . . . I don't know about everybody else, but I'm glad I got you because you were nonjudgmental, and you were very helpful."
>
> But that one right there, I mean, you never know. They had like a fifteen-hundred-dollar house payment. Of course, that to me is a whole lot, but you never know. Two cars, they both worked for banks. They had a very nice income. They were set and then the banks go out of business.

Funny, shocking, and negative. As often as not, it is the negative experience that gets remembered and retold, both at home and at work. "What stands out in your mind when you've worked with families all day long are the ones that are trying to scam," says Susan Osborne, the director of DSS in Alamance County.

"Have you ever heard the saying that if you're happy with service, you tell three to five people; if you're unhappy, you tell twenty?" asks Kate Garnett, a caseworker at DSS. "I mean, think about the last time you had a bad meal, saw a bad movie. Did you not—like, Facebook—did you not tell everybody you knew, 'Do not go see this movie, it's awful'? But one that you really liked you might have told a few friends." For Latawnya Hall and Brenna Pound, it's the stories of people they were not able to help that stick with them. When those clients get angry, the stories are even harder to shake. "Now, within my life . . . I cannot share confidential information," explains Brenna, "but sometimes I may say like, if I had a really bad phone call."

> Sometimes I have really bad phone calls. People are very upset with me, and I take it personal. I shouldn't, but I do.
> "I'm working really hard trying to see what I can do for you, so please don't fuss. I try, but I can't get to everything."

Research in psychology and sociology provides one set of explanations for why we focus on the negative. Simply put, "Bad impressions and bad stereotypes are quicker to form and more resistant to disconfirmation than good ones" (Baumeister et al. 2001, 323). Serena Borden provides another.

> I really haven't heard of too many success stories. They don't really necessarily call you back or come back and say, "Hey . . ."
> You know how you go to the doctor, you're pregnant, you have a rapport with the doctor? The next thing you know the doctor, they got baby pictures on the wall.
> They don't do that with us. So it's hard to hear success stories unless somebody's really extraordinary and they've written a letter to DSS. We hear about those in the agency, but . . .

Success stories remain elusive in the narrative tradition, and fraud stories with their dramatic plot elements and emotional impact provide compelling fodder to fill the gap. This is true not only of the stories aid providers take home with them but the stories they share among each other. Conversation with a group of aid providers one day turned to the welfare queen. "Everyone has a food stamp story," one provider began, as people nodded in agreement. "One of our board members regularly tells a story about a person on welfare, with the Escalade and steaks on food stamps," added another. "Or how about the story of the Michigan man who won the lottery but continues to get food stamps?" volunteered another provider, explaining that lottery winnings are considered an asset but not income and only income is factored into eligibility for food stamps. Conversation continued in this way, with people sharing recent stories about welfare from friends, family, and the news, including an *NBC Nightly News* report about how Walmart has shaped their policies and practices based on how food stamps are distributed and a *60 Minutes* segment on homelessness in Seminole County, Florida, where teachers had no idea that some of their students were sleeping with their families in their cars.

Such conversations were common, with coworkers rehashing some of the most unusual, humorous, or disconcerting stories they had heard, not just from outside the office but from their caseloads within. Names are never mentioned or details that would be revealing, but fraud stories were common. "We've all told these stories," explains one aid provider. "And we want to share them also. There is fraud. That's part of it."

There is something cathartic and reassuring about stories that are black or white. Stories of clear and obvious fraud remove the nagging doubt providers carry about whether they are being scammed. Such clarity can be a relief when reality is so much more ambiguous and complicated.

Where familiarity and trust are high, social norms against trading in salacious stories of fraud are relaxed, each person knowing that as cathartic as such stories may be, they do not represent the majority of their clientele. Shared work and shared experiences make for a high context group where caveats and reminders that fraud stories are outliers are assumed. But when those caveats remain unvoiced and unchecked, the impact of those negative outlier stories can expand. Kate Garnett decided she needed to stop and question the stereotypes and stories she was coming to believe.

> You know how in every friend-of-a-friend story, every stereotype, there's that sliver of truth? There is truth to it, but it's not the whole truth?
>
> So I was looking at stuff where I work: Where is that sliver of truth? Is there a sliver of truth, and we just kind of expanded it to cover the whole thing?
>
> And I've been watching because I do intake. I watch people come in. I also work a lot with the ongoing workers; I see ongoing turnover, so I'm like, "OK, what am I seeing?" The mythology of particularly food stamps is single, young, black mother, too many kids, no child support, no interest in bettering her life, not interested in going to work, right?
>
> So I thought, "OK, am I seeing that?" And the truth is, yeah, I am going to see that. That is a truth. But it's not the whole truth. But it's the thing that we focus on.
>
> Where I work, we have the myth of the clients that come in in their pajamas, and we talk about it a lot. Every time we see somebody with their pajama bottoms and their—everybody calls them scuffs; to me, they're slippers—and the slippers, and we think, "Oh, my goodness. Really?" I've been trying to keep track of how many times I see that, and I was like, "Wow, this is starting to pile up. Five, six, seven . . . Wow, this is starting to pile up." And I thought, "Well, wait a minute, I'm concentrating on this data here, but I'm not counting all the times I don't see it."

How about all the people I see that come in here with polo shirts and khaki pants who are job hunting? What about all the people I see coming in here in jeans and T-shirts because they're out looking for construction work? So I sort of changed my dichotomy. I thought, OK, I'm going to track everything kind of in my head, my own little tracking system. Because that's what nerds do.

And I thought, you know, this truth of the welfare person in slippers and scuffs is a truth, but it's certainly not the whole story. In fact, for my own amateur looking, this person didn't cover twenty-five percent of who I serve. Not twenty-five percent. And I would argue probably less than ten percent of my clients fit that. Ninety percent of my clients are the people we don't talk about.

And as I've been watching intake, especially in the past month, what am I seeing? And what are people telling me regarding that FOAF [friend of a friend]? And what I get is—especially for men forty to fifty-five, this might be the first time they're on food stamps, out of work because they've been in textiles their whole life, they've been in construction—is, "I waited a long time." And I'll see that they have nothing in the bank; their unemployment has run out; everything's run out, no income.

Kate's survey was hardly scientific, but when she made a point of consciously keeping track of her clients, she realized that all those negative stories had begun to skew her view of aid recipients in ways that worried her. "I had to step back and really consider how I was doing my job," she told me later. "It changed how I do my work."

The stories shared around the office, what Kate referred to as "our own urban legends," not only shape personal views and beliefs subconsciously over time but are actively used to help enculturate people into the workplace. "Sometimes we tell the stories to newbies just as a way of initiation, bringing you into the group, sharing the history."

Staff meetings, training sessions, and the day-to-day workload serve as counterbalances to help ensure the culture is not shaped too heavily by these negative stories. Further, while success stories may be rare in the narrative tradition, they are not nonexistent. Some stories are actively used to both train and inspire, shifting from informal water cooler socializing to practical application.

Training and Inspiring

"We all share stories in the hallway," Kate continues. "We share it with each other. And it's a way of encouragement. It's a way of letting off steam. 'Let me tell you what happened.' And giving information. 'Whatever happens to you, don't make my mistake.' 'Do this.' Or, 'You know what? This worked really well for me.'"

We all share stories, not only with each other, but Sheila, Sheila shares stories with us about people that have come in.

When she first started, she had this client who everyone said, "This woman's crazy. She kicks doors. She's crazy. She gets mad. She's crazy."

And Sheila's a little bitty woman.

And she was like, "Fantastic."

So she sat there, and she was asking questions. "And do you work?"

"No, I don't work. I can't work." Blah, blah, blah.

And so Sheila put her pen down and said, "Well, what's wrong?" in that kind, motherly way.

And this woman told her about her physical ailments, her emotional ailments, what's wrong with her sons. And Sheila listened and nodded her head and said, "Well, I am so sorry to hear that. I do hope you feel better," and then continued with the interview.

And the woman was fine. In fact, the woman would only speak to Sheila from then on.

Such stories are valuable emotionally as well as practically. Susan Osborne points out how important it is to share success stories among caseworkers for morale.

> We share those because you can imagine, day in and day out, two hundred people every day, staff can get really worn out and overwhelmed with the need and all of that. So we rejuvenate ourselves by sharing mission moments. We call it a mission moment. Every other month at our all-staff meeting, we share stories we've gotten back from those we serve about what a difference services or staff or whatever made in their life.

Those success stories are shared widely, reminding caseworkers that for every one person who writes back to thank them, hundreds have been helped by their services that they will never know about.

Aid providers do not rely on the periodic pep talk, however. In addition to the stories they share informally with each other, caseworkers keep positive stories for their own use, to buoy their spirits rather than wait for someone to do it for them. Lorrie Carter and Tracy Salisbury both think of Lilly Gibbs and her power-ful story of recovery (chap. 3). Susan Osborne keeps a voice mail on her answering machine from a thankful client. Sophie Griffin regularly reflects on the case of a woman she helped get approved for aid the same day she applied. "That was a pretty good experience for me. And that was actually like close to right when I started, so it felt good to be appreciated and not looked at as evil." Functioning to boost morale, success stories shared among aid providers are far more likely to be caseworker successes ("I was able to help this person") than client successes ("This person is now self-sufficient and doing great").

One Paycheck Away

The practice of using positive stories to remind providers of the reason for their work, to keep the client's best interests at the fore, and to fight cynicism and suspicion engendered by the overrepresented negative stories of fraud is captured in a popular proverb: "But for the grace of God go I." So common is this sentiment that caseworkers have an industry-specific version: "We're all just one paycheck away from the other side of the desk."

The saying is used most often as a mantra among caseworkers to remain sympathetic to clients, but it works because it so effectively describes a common origin story of many clients, where an accident at work, an unforeseen illness, the loss of a job, or one poor choice can mean the difference between self-sufficiency and dependency. Seeing just how thin the line is between employed and unemployed, aid provider and aid recipient, financial independence and dependence, ensures this mantra is not just lip service. "I hope I will never have to be on that side of the desk," says Crystal Larson. "But you never know."

> Even adult Medicaid. If something happens, you have a stroke, you can't work.
> There's a guy that works for the company that my fiancé works for. Very athletic, always active. He's got a brain tumor, and he cannot work. They are broke.
> And this guy was making probably four hundred thousand to five hundred thousand dollars a year, and they're having to take up money for him and his family now because he spent all his money in hospital bills.
> That's what I'm saying. You never know.

Aid providers are not the only ones who recognize the unpredictability of life. "What I hear from people I talk to, that I sit right next to, with their families, and like *everybody* I talk to has something," explains Betsy Maller, who sought aid when her husband was hit by a train and medical bills left them homeless. "They have one sickness, they have one illness, one loss of job, one . . . just one. They're one paycheck away from being homeless. It's scary. And this is a lot of people."

When a woman looked down her nose at Gary Duggins when he pulled out his EBT card to pay for his groceries, he warned her: "'One day, you could be on this side swiping this card,' because I don't think nobody is to where that might not happen. Because I know some people that said they would never be in this position to receive assistance and they get it." Leslie Forrester imagines saying the same to the people who think she and her husband are "trash," that "we're the scum of the earth," when they could be in the same situation tomorrow. "There's good people that, one time, had businesses, had a house, car, and the whole nine yards, and then they sit there, and the economy goes sour or something happens, and they're in the same boat with us. We're not trash; we're just like everybody else."

While the phrase "one paycheck away from the other side of the desk" is typically understood to mean that the loss of one paycheck can lead to a need for public assistance, there is also a positive interpretation that describes the life stories of some aid providers, where the gain of one paycheck can also move someone from the client side of the desk to the provider side. Gary Duggins has seen both sides of the desk. The aid providers Serena Borden, Parthenia Ingram, Bernard Faucette, and Gail Coachman have as well. In fact, this phenomenon is so common, at least more than a few caseworkers save their stories about tough cases and trying clients for home rather than share at work because they know that some of their fellow caseworkers have been or are still on public assistance.

Success stories of moving from aid recipient to aid provider are often shared with clients to encourage them. Kate mentions watching a caseworker share her own story as a way to inspire her client: "They have been very open about it, not only because it helped them, but they'll sometimes say to a client, 'I've been where you are,' especially female to female. 'I've been where you are.'"

> When I was first training, I watched a caseworker say to a young woman, "I know what it's like to have two kids. I remember when it was just me and my son, and I was on Work First, and you know what? It felt like it was the end. And I had a really good caseworker who said this is your opportunity."
> And she said, "You know what? I took the opportunity to take some classes, and I got my GED, and I got my high school diploma, and I started to get better jobs and moved up, and now I'm sitting here, and you can. I did it and you can."

"One of the things I don't do is I do not judge," explains Serena Borden, "because I have been on that side of my desk before." Yet rather than share her own powerful story of raising three kids on her own after her husband left and relying on public assistance until she could get back on her feet, Serena tells clients the more recent, less personal story of her mother working two low-wage jobs while searching for one good one that matches her skills.

> I have used her. I told her, "Momma, I hope you don't mind I use you."
> Because sometimes you'll find yourself, especially the younger girls, I don't want to say counseling because this is professional work but giving them advice.
> A paycheck is better than nothing.
> And so I kind of like, "Well, my mom works here."
> And sometimes it hits home for them. And so I'll use that.

Formal Presentations

The narrative tradition of aid providers extends beyond friends, family, and coworkers. Both informally in life and formally as part of their jobs, providers find themselves talking with people who have little experience with public assistance. Whether receptionist, caseworker, or administrator, when people find out what they do for a living, the flood gates open, and aid providers find themselves sharing stories to counteract misinformation and stereotypes. "This is part of what you do in a community to combat things that you hear in the newspaper," explains Kate Garnett.

> "When I tell people what I do, they say, 'Wow, you must hear some stories.' And I say, 'I sure do!'
>
> "Let me tell you about the senior citizen that I was able give her a medical credit, and I boosted her food stamps, and that really made a difference.
>
> "Let me tell you about the guy that came in here, and he was so embarrassed. He had been in construction all his life."
>
> We don't have the construction here in North Carolina that we did, and I was not only able to get him some food stamps for the month, but I put him through to one of my community resource partners. They made sure he had food for the night. And it wasn't just the stereotype of three loaves of bread and a can of beans, but there was peanut butter. There were granola bars, things a kid would eat. Chef Boyardee or things I would eat. And that he went home with a Food Lion grocery bag feeling like he had some dignity.
>
> "Let me tell you about this," or, "Let me tell you about this person that I helped."
>
> Because that to me is more truthful than the once in a while people come up here acting crazy. That doesn't happen as often as it's your next-door neighbors. We don't understand that. When you say who comes up here, when you go to our lobby, look around. These are your neighbors. These are the people that live next door to you. These are the people who work with you.

People often expect Kate to share horror stories of working at DSS, of terrible clients trying to work the system. Instead, she shares the far more common stories of hardworking, well-meaning people who get the help they need to get back on their feet. Some caseworkers have grown frustrated and tired of trying to debunk the stereotypes, however. "For a long time, I always felt like I needed to let people know rather than them thinking everybody is the same that receives help," explains Wanda Ford. "And now it's like, 'OK, you're going to believe what you want to believe. So it really wasted my time to try to explain to you.'"

Public Presentations

For administrators, throwing up one's hands in frustration is rarely an option. Whether a federal or state agency or nonprofit, directors must answer to boards, politicians, and the public, whether to justify, explain, inform, raise awareness, or raise money. As with the people aid providers meet casually in the course of their daily lives, board members, Kiwanis Club members, and donors want to hear stories about clients. However, when speaking to external groups, DSS director Susan Osborne typically avoids stories altogether, preferring to deal in statistics or the occasional positive story.

> Usually, folks in the group have examples where they want to say, "You know, I was behind somebody in the line at the grocery store the other day, and this and that happened." Folks have stories that they want to talk about. Unfortunately, those stories focus on the ten percent or fifteen percent or twenty percent that aren't good stewards of what we try to do.
>
> I don't usually focus on those because I focus on the positives of what we do, the family that came here because of domestic violence and how they're able to function now and what they're doing and how successful they're being. The infant with thirty-eight rib fractures that we put in a safe place. The positives of what we do.

True to form, when our research group presented some initial findings to the board of the DSS, one board member asked, "What was the biggest number of children that you saw in your interviews?"

"At the homeless shelter, there was a family with five children, but that was unusual," I replied. "Most of the families we worked with had only one child, some two."

"The reason I ask," she continued, "is that I used to work for the Health Department, and there was a woman down there with fourteen children. I mean, she just about had a child every year. It was a full-time job just trying to get all the money and resources she needed to care for those kids."

"That is certainly unusual," I agreed. "But the average in Alamance County is one point two children per family."

I found myself doing what Susan Osborne described: responding to stories with statistics, worried about falling into a "he said, she said" stalemate where "you have your stories and I have mine" and "we can agree to disagree," arguments that move the conversation nowhere.

But stories are not impotent in these formal presentational contexts, particularly as an initial, orienting move. The executive director of the Open Door Clinic Tracy Salisbury finds that starting with a story to help humanize their work is incredibly effective. The executive director of Allied Churches Kim Crawford has also found stories indispensable in her efforts to raise awareness and funds, sharing them in newsletters, brochures, and public presentations. While summarized stories are good, personal experience narratives from aid recipients themselves can be even more effective, which is why recipients are often asked by aid agencies to share their stories at public events (chap. 3).

As the discussion at the presentation to the DSS board makes clear, providers are not the only ones telling stories in these more public contexts. Local leaders, including elected officials, share their stories as well. Most are personal experience and eyewitness narratives, although some officials share stories heard from family, friends, and the media. Tim Sutton, an on-again-off-again Alamance County commissioner, frequently tells a three-decades-old story of getting a notice that his children were eligible for reduced lunch.

> My wife and I, we qualified for reduced lunches at our kids' schools. And I was shocked that I did. That was my first exposure that the limits are not as they should be. I had an apartment. I had a new car sitting outside. We had nice clothes. I bought records every time I wanted a record. That's back before CDs. I had my share of . . . I mean, I could always buy a beer if I wanted to drink beer, if I wanted to have a steak if we went out to eat. But we didn't take vacations to Florida.
>
> Our family was so tight that even my own janitor in the office that I worked in rode by one time and said, "Don't you ever go anywhere?" because he always saw my car there. But we were happy. We were home. We were a family. We didn't need to go anywhere but . . . We did go places, but we didn't travel much until the boys got big enough to where I wanted to have them. They were babies, and we didn't want to go to the beaches with them being babies. But when they finally got old enough, we did travel.
>
> My father used to tell me, "Tim, you need to budget. You need to budget. You need to budget." "I'm budgeting," I said. When your own janitor comes by and says don't you ever go anywhere? The janitor! I feel like I'm doing pretty well.
>
> But we qualified for reduced lunches, but I resented it. I knew that fiscally it was excess, the program was excess, and people should need it more in my opinion. Wouldn't it be a sin for me to have reduced lunches at my kids' school and a new Thunderbird sitting in the driveway? Because that's what it was. So yes, there was something wrong. That was in 1980, roughly, thirty-two years ago.
>
> But you know what I did? I called. I was a citizen. I wasn't even an elected official. I called my congressman, and I said, "I should not qualify for reduced lunches. There's something wrong here." That's how conservative I am. I live by principle there.
>
> And he said, "Well, Tim, that's the way it is."

While he was raised not to accept handouts, part of his aversion to welfare is tied to the stigma that comes with it. "I do think kids get ostracized," he says.

> When I was in high school in South Carolina, you paid your lunch, and you got a certain color meal ticket. The people on reduced lunches had the purple ticket, and when you saw them turn in that purple ticket, the kid that didn't have to have the purple ticket looked down upon them. So I didn't like that either. I saw that a lot.

Although he has had other experiences with public assistance, it is this story that he has found particularly useful and politically expedient as a public official, sharing it regularly in meetings with constituents, interviews, and during public hearings as evidence for his general critiques of a government that has grown too big and become too generous with taxpayer money.[9]

Implicated in this study of narrative performance that considers how context not only shapes *how* we tell our stories but *which* stories we tell is the issue of audience. Many of the stories people tell about welfare are heard by friends and family as gospel truth. But when stories are shared across ideological divides, doubts can be raised. Accordingly, it may make sense to shift our study of legend from a truth-oriented approach to a doubt-centered one. The following chapter explores exactly this possibility and its effectiveness for studying widespread legends.

NOTES

1. See chap. 3 for Tracy's story of working as a grocery store cashier.
2. The reflection of belief in folk traditions is often a distorted one that requires interpretation within social and cultural contexts. See Benedict (1935) and Wilson (1989).
3. See, e.g., Clawson and Trice (2000), Gilens (1996, 1999), Hancock (2004), van Doorn (2015), and West (2002).
4. These examples all come from the *New York Times*: Greenidge (2016), Reginal (2015), and Tollison (2012).
5. Parts of this analysis were previously published in the *Journal of American Folklore* (Mould 2016). Although the site has been taken down, the majority of this exchange can be found on the Internet Archive (MyBiggestComplaint.com 2009). Unfortunately, the only capture made by the web archive was on November 9, 2012, while the last post was on July 7, 2013. However, I made a full copy back in 2013 when the site was live, allowing me a complete analysis.
6. Research into online discourse confirms this space as one open to uninhibited responses that can quickly become aggressive and insulting, in no small part because of the anonymity and lack of real-world consequences (see, e.g., Kiesler, Siegel, and McGuire 1984; Lieber 2010; and Blank 2013, 106–7, citing Bargh, McKenna, and Fitzsimons 2002). Others have suggested such aggressive and profane discourse has become normative (e.g., Lea et al. 1992; Postmes, Spears, and Lea 1998). Still others note that the antagonism and quick escalation of emotions can be partially attributed to miscommunication and the inability to read important vocal and facial cues missing in online communication (e.g., Kruger et al. 2005; McKee 2002; and Thompsen 1994). For these reasons, some sites have removed their comments section altogether.
7. Edward T. Hall introduced the concepts of high and low context cultures in his 1976 book *Beyond Culture*. Since then, the terms have been employed to describe communication styles in smaller folk groups or specific performance contexts rather than entire culture groups (see, e.g., Young 1985).

8. In our fieldwork in Alamance County, we recorded forty-three stories describing someone buying food with an EBT card and alcohol or cigarettes with cash.

9. Tim Sutton shared this story once during a conversation after a county commissioner's meeting in October 2012 with me and Elon student researcher Greg Honan, again during a formal interview with Greg a month later, and yet again during a county commissioner meeting in June 2017. Only the interview was recorded, but I took detailed notes after each of the other narrations and found clear consistency in plot elements and major claims about government largess.

ELEVEN

—ᴪ—

TRUTH AND DOUBT IN
CONTEMPORARY LEGEND

I work part time at a grocery store. Just yesterday I was checking out a lady
who was talking on her phone during the transaction (how rude!) and she was
saying something about when her next unemployment check was coming in.
She was buying ridiculous things that one on unemployment should not be
getting, like a $17 steak and frosty paws—ice cream for her dog.

I have taken food stamps from a woman that had a rock on her finger the size
of a truck and sold food to someone on food stamps who then spent $40 cash on
alcohol.

My husband lost his job last year and we were ineligible for unemployment
for reasons I will never understand. Why do these fools get so much help when
there are people out there who really need it? Thank goodness he has found
work by now, but when we were living on just my income we cleared out our
entire savings.

In 2010, Wildflower12 posed the question "Do the people on unemployment really
need it?" on Yahoo Answers online and followed with these stories from her job as
a cashier at a grocery store (2012). The answers people posted covered the range of
opinions, with some arguing unemployment benefits are not needed and are too
frequently abused, others viewing benefits as necessary but problematic, and still
others robustly defending the program. In responding, many people questioned
the story and assumptions of the original question.

Btw, if the lady had "a rock the size of a truck," one, how do you know it
wasn't cz and two, it couldv'e been a gift. Another thing, studies have shown
that having a pet lowers your heart rate . . . Some people love animals more
than others . . . doesn't mean they know the best way to handle money
responsibly.

Oh, if you're Christian, doesn't Jesus say something about "judge not," "those w/o sin cast the first stone" and doesn't he bother to help some Samaritan woman at a well even though that's a no-no? My point is, just b/c you don't agree with HOW they spend their money doesn't mean they aren't in financial trouble

My b/f was laid off from work several months ago and has been on unemployment since. He buys cigarettes and I definitely don't agree with his spending money on that but in no way do I think he doesn't need the unemployment.[1]

Im_foxygirl posed similar questions, suggesting that the ring could have been a cheap knock-off from Walmart or a family heirloom, while Elophan10538's reply ran the gamut:

How do you know the lady on the cell phone wasn't running an errand for someone? Are you an expert at determining whether jewelry is real or not, without looking at it through a jeweler's loupe? How do you know the person buying alcohol wasn't given the money by somebody else? You sure do get a lot of exercise behind your little cash register, what with jumping to so many conclusions like you do.

Herb shifted the conversation away from the specific stories to what was implied in telling them:

The person you saw talking on her phone an the people who use food stamps are not indicative of all people who receive unemployment, so don't jugde them all by the relatively few.

Despite these critiques, MK reposted the stories from the grocery store by Wildflower12 under the question "Unemployment foodstamps and WIC?" She began with the preface "Question partially taken from another yahoo user," copied the stories up to the point when Wildflower12 shared the story about her husband, and then added her own take:

Dont get me wrong, I understand unemployment, and actually was on it for a short period of time. My gripe is more the food stamps and WIC checks people use, then spend their cash on chocolate lottery and garbage. I struggle with two jobs just to keep a roof over my head and am sometimes hungary, but I'm not running for government support. These people have two crying babies and one in the stomach. (Yahoo Answers 2012)

Justagrandma responded, questioning not only the assumptions of fraud and misuse and the generalizability of such stories but the story itself:

You didn't run into that lady who posted pretty much the same thing . . . thirty years ago?

These things make the rounds, the steak with food stamps, the illegal alien getting into the Escalade, the tired white woman working hard and seeing welfare leeches walk away with cigarettes and beer.

Did I leave anything out?

These aren't true stories, they are urban legends meant to make the poor look like thieves. They are meant to fan the flames and ignore reality.

Its illegal to buy alcohol with food stamps. If someone is selling beer with food stamps they are subject to arrest, and no one can buy it if no one is selling it. So the real lawbreaker is the food store owner.

You can't tell an illegal alien by looking at someone speaking Spanish. Legal Spanish speakers, even Spanish speaking citizens abound. Something like this is not healthy, its designed to encourage hatred and resentment and I wish it would stop.

MK was not willing to be called a rube, liar, or both without response:

> Update: Hey justagram i said it was takin from another user. And urban legend my tush. I tonight witnessed, a lady buy her wic approved and foodstamp items, then with her cash ring up beer, and run to customer service for lotto. Yes I understand some people need it, but as a person living in the united states I'm pissed my hard earned taxes are paying for bull.

These relatively unfiltered responses reveal the range of doubt that people can have for a story. Some doubted the interpretation of the story, Herb doubted the generalizability of the story, and justagrandma doubted the story itself. This trifecta of doubt suggests we may be looking at legends backward.

A survey of definitions for the legend suggests that more than any other criterion, the negotiation of truth is the most common and uncontested. In examining this issue of the negotiation of truth, Elliott Oring has argued that all legends make at least one truth claim, and some make two. First, all legends make an initial claim that the account occurred as described. Second, for some legends, inferences are required to fill in the gaps to connect two separate events as meaningfully related. As an example, Oring provides a story about a man who has a phone installed in his mausoleum because he believes he will come back to life and wants to be able to call his wife when he does. A year after the husband's death, the wife is found in her house, dead of a sudden heart attack, phone receiver in her hand. When they check her husband's mausoleum, they find the phone off its hook (Oring 2008, 129; citing a legend from Baker 1982, 204).

In this legend, there is the question of whether the events described are accurate and true and whether the unstated inference that the man came back to life and called his wife is true. But there is a *third* truth claim operating here as well: whether such supernatural phenomenon such as revenants and ghosts exist in the first place. In the case of supernatural legends, there are typically *three* points where truth must be established: (1) the accuracy of the events as described, (2) the accuracy of the interpretation of those events, and (3) the existence of the supernatural.

For contemporary legends situated in the *mundane* world, the question of whether something exists is irrelevant. Yet these legends, too, have three points where truth must be established. The first two are the same as those for supernatural legends. The third, however, is even more pervasive and more powerful rhetorically: the generalizability of the event. A story may be true, but the degree to which it is widespread may be questioned.

The three truths appear interrelated. For example, if the accuracy of the event is found to be false, the other two points should become moot. But that is not necessarily the case. Let us return to Ronald Reagan for a moment. The generalizability of the stories he told was crucial to his goal: to slash the welfare system because of widespread fraud and abuse. The accuracy of these stories was challenged as soon as they were voiced, but they nonetheless retained their power as a generalizable truth about welfare recipients. In other words, generalizability was more powerful than the accuracy of the individual story. No doubt many people continued to believe the stories despite the refutations, but even some who did not could still find truth in the interpretation (the second truth) and maintain the generalizability of the story (the third truth), arguing, "That may not have happened, but the point still stands."

Reagan's press secretary David Gergen was skewered by the press for suggesting that the stories the president told as true need not be, "so long as the symbolic truth is defensible" (Kelly 1993). Nonetheless, Gergen stood by the defense: "I believe that 'parables' fairly describes how Reagan's audiences received his stories. Some listeners were, of course, outraged. Most people knew there might be an embroidery here, a deletion there. . . . They accepted the idea that he was trying to get at some of the verities of life. He was telling them fundamental truths about themselves and the country, truths that might otherwise be lost" (Gergen 2001, 225). In the case of the welfare queen, however, the idea that widespread fraud was "a verity of life" confirmed the bias of many but was not supported by the facts.

A DOUBT-CENTERED APPROACH TO LEGEND

Oring spoke of the rhetoric of truth, efforts made by narrators to persuade their audiences that their story is true. But there are many genres of narrative that are told as true and require narrators to establish credibility, believability, and truth. The distinctiveness of the legend, whether as narrative or interpretive process, is the *doubt* it engenders. Accordingly, it may be equally accurate and more relevant to talk not about the three areas of truth but of doubt.

Such an approach brings academic analysis more closely in line with vernacular views. Although summarily equating legend with "false" remains problematic in many of the same ways as when myth and folklore are similarly treated, these connotations land their punches differently. Academic definitions of myth recognize that the genre includes stories that are deeply sacred and may be revered as the most true, ideologically if not historically. Academic definitions of folklore include not only stories that are verifiably true but also a vast range of expressive culture, such as music, dance, folkways, and material culture, where questions of factual truth are typically irrelevant. Academic definitions for legend, however, do not stray so far from vernacular usage. Expressing doubt is different from averring false; as folklorists have periodically discovered, stories labeled as "legend" may turn out to be factually true. But where academic definitions of myth and folklore do not hinge on issues of truth and doubt, definitions of legend do. Emic and etic definitions alike place doubt at the center of the legend. Further, the proof is in the pudding. Consider the major folklore studies on contemporary legend: vanishing hitchhikers, satanic cults, fast food restaurants run by the KKK, and alien abductions to name a few. Folklorists do not approach stories they believe to be true and study them as legends. Rather, it is the stories with traditional patterns and multiple versions that seem too good (or bad) to be true, that we disagree with and believe to be false or do not want to believe to be true that we approach as legends (Mould 2018; Oring 2008, 159).

A reorientation from truth to doubt also reorients the focus from a performer-centered approach to an audience-centered approach. One is not inherently better than the other, but audience-centered approaches have been relatively rare in folklore and could usefully be taken up with greater vigor. Listening to people express their doubts, not just argue for their truths, reminds us that people are deeply engaged in conversations about what is true and what is not, what is fair and what is not, and what is representative and what is not, explicitly and intentionally, not just defensively.

Although declarations of truth can be solitary statements, declarations of doubt are always in dialogue. The dialogic nature of legend highlights the relevance of perspective where one person's narrative may be another person's counternarrative. Consider the stories about Barack Obama's birth certificate. According to a 2016 poll, the majority of Republicans (72 percent) continued to doubt Obama's US citizenship, despite incontrovertible evidence to the contrary (Clinton and Rousch 2016). For "birthers"—people who question the validity of Obama's birth certificate—the story that Obama was born in Hawaii is the story to be doubted; the story that he is secretly a Muslim born in Kenya is the story to be believed. For many others—including most Democrats, the mainstream media, and investigative journalists—the reverse is true. A doubt-centered approach to legend recognizes how shifts in perspective can transform narrative into counternarrative and anecdote into legend, providing a more complete and robust approach to the varied constructions of meaning.

A doubt-centered approach does not, however, make truth irrelevant. Rather, it provides a more objective stance for assessing it. Taking multiple perspectives and assessing what people doubt, how they construct that doubt, and why they doubt provide insight into epistemological processes, not just products. Further, this approach demands a distinction between verifiable and unverifiable information, as well as between factual truths, social truths, and affective truths. Factual truths are verifiable. With reasonable assurance and multiple data points, we can assess the governmental documentation of birth and citizenship or the size of an inauguration crowd. Affective truths are truths that we believe to be true. They may encompass both verifiable and unverifiable claims, but we rarely interrogate our affective truths or hold them up for scrutiny. Social truths may be empirical or affective but operate at the level of the group. They are truths that members of a group agree on, with no need to defend or support.[2] When stories are shared among small groups of people with similar ideologies, stories that might raise doubt among a broader population and labeled legend might be simply accepted as true. Accordingly, echo chambers are like vacuums for the legend: without the oxygen of doubt, they cannot survive.

Finally, doubt is not always just the opposite side of the coin from truth. Few narrators explicitly evoke the "instance of a class" argument to claim credibility for their stories about welfare, but a large percentage of people question the generalizability of the stories they hear that demonize the many for the sins of the few. Similarly, few narrators go to great lengths to convince their listeners that their interpretation of the events of the story is correct; in fact, they often assume the story speaks for itself. But people often zero in on these areas to question the validity of the story. In other words, taking a doubt-centered approach is not just tricky word play. Applied to stories of welfare, a doubt-centered approach reveals those areas that people find particularly questionable.

Accordingly, a doubt-centered approach to legend more accurately describes emic definitions, more honestly describes folkloristic assumptions, encourages an audience-centered approach that too often goes overlooked in folklore analysis, highlights the dialogic nature of legend, and reveals the fluidity between narrative and counternarrative. In doing so, a doubt-centered approach reveals chinks in the defenses that narrators construct to establish credibility for their stories. Importantly, such critiques originate not with the folklorist but with the folk.

DOUBTS ABOUT THE FACTS: THE FIRST TRUTH

I have heard stories relating to the welfare queen. I have heard stories about people going in grocery stores and driving in some kind of fancy car, going into a grocery store and using public assistance to buy all kinds of extravagant things, and then they leave. I've heard people say that people on public assistance . . . It's so wonderful on public assistance that they would never even want to get a job. I've heard all of those stories out there.

And in many cases, not in all but in many cases, I would say something. "Well, do you know anybody on public assistance or 'welfare,' as you call it?"

And really for the most part, people just say they don't; they don't know anybody specifically. It was a story they heard through the grapevine, or somebody's friend or cousin, whatever, told them the story.

Eileen Collins is an Alamance County resident and professor at Elon University. Her doubts operate on the first level of truth: the accuracy of the events described. She challenges many if not all of the people sharing stories of aid recipients buying luxury items. If the narrators do not know anyone receiving assistance, she wonders, how can they be so quick to accept these stories as true? It is the same question justagrandma asks about the string of stories retold by MK online.

Questioning the truth of a second- or thirdhand story is much easier than a firsthand one, however. The difference between saying "someone else may have gotten the story wrong" and "*you* got it wrong" or, worse, "you're a liar" is miles apart interpersonally. In face-to-face interactions, especially collegial ones with people who share the same general political orientation, such disagreement is unlikely. Even online, where disagreement and personal attacks are common, it is relatively rare for someone to publicly question a firsthand narrative even if private doubts are sown. Far more often, people express doubts about the interpretation or generalizability of a story.

DOUBTS ABOUT THE INTERPRETATION:
THE SECOND TRUTH

On a warm evening in Alamance County in 2013, a group of young men drive by the local shelter but are stopped by the traffic light at the corner. Looking out their window, they see a group of men gathered outside smoking. The cigarettes annoy them; the relaxed manner of the men angers them. They lean out the window and shout at the men to get a job, punctuating their demands with obscenities. The light turns green, and they speed off, still shouting.

The young men are disrespectful and rude, and while their shouting is unusual, their response is anything but. The narrative tradition makes it clear that we regularly judge the women in the grocery line with crying babies and junk food in their carts. We shake our heads at the panhandling men who smell of cigarettes, fingers stained with nicotine. We mutter under our breath at the women with elaborate hairstyles and designer purses filing into government offices for aid. And although few hang their heads out of windows and yell their frustrations, mostly we log away our annoyance and frustration until we can share our stories with a sympathetic ear. When we do finally tell our stories, we often find our information incomplete; we are forced to fill in the gaps to narrate a coherent and compelling story. We draw on the evidence we have at hand. For those of us without extensive firsthand experience with poverty, the poor, or government assistance, that "evidence" is often composed of the assumptions, perceptions, and stereotypes we have learned from friends and family, the media, and the stories we have heard from others. Not surprisingly, such a process can lead us far from the truth. It can also cause damage often unseen or ignored, not just on the grand scale of policy but on a more personal level. Davey Cannon was the recipient of the drive-by diatribe and tells it this way.

> We were standing outside, I think it was about a week or two ago, smoking, the other night, you know at nighttime. I didn't mean the other night; it was about a week ago. And a car come up to the stop light right there at the shelter, and they leaned out the window and said, "You all ain't nothing but a bunch of sorry MF-ers. You need to get off your ass and do something instead of us—" What was it? "Flipping . . . flipping your bill" or whatever.
> They said that, and then the light turned green, and they spun off.
> We was just out there smoking and talking, and they come up or leaned out the window and said we were all a bunch of sorry, lazy MF-ers, and we need to get off our lazy asses and go to work, so we don't have to foot your bill for you.
> That's just one example of what, you know . . . [Sighs] I've heard stuff like that my whole life. I've always worked, but everybody's like, "Everybody on welfare's just lazy. They don't want to work." That's what I've heard.

It is not just what Davey has heard; it is also what he believed until he found himself unable to work or pay his bills. Now those assumptions sting, especially about being lazy. Davey would like to be able to get a job, but he is in a wheelchair and may never walk again. "I never pictured myself as being in a wheelchair or in a homeless shelter. I mean, I just never saw that as being any part of my life, but sometimes things happen, you know?"

> In 2011, I was working full time at Wendy's in Eden. My back had been hurting me for years, years. I just thought it was normal for somebody's back to hurt them. It just got worse and worse. And then in like the summer of 2011, it got so bad that I couldn't even . . . I would go to work and have to come home early, or

when I'd come home, I would sit down and have to have help to get up. And when I would get up, I'd have to stand there for a minute before I could take that first step; it was just such a bad pain. I didn't know what it was. And then it eventually got so bad that I couldn't even go into work and went to Morehead Hospital, which is the hospital in Eden, and they kept saying it was a muscle spasm, pulled muscle, or what not. And I went back like two weeks later and said—because I knew that wasn't a muscle spasm—and they were saying the same thing.

And at the time, we was staying with Chad's aunt. We had lost our apartment because I couldn't go to work and pay the rent no more, and we were staying with his aunt, and she was going to Wesley Long Hospital for some kind of tests, and I thought, "Well, while she's going, I'll just go, you know, to the emergency room there, see if I can get something different from them." And they actually took X-rays and came back and said, "Did you know that you have degenerative joint disease?" I said, "No, I didn't."

And they said, "There's also something else that we can't quite make out." And I needed to come back the next morning for a MRI, which ... That was in Greensboro, and I didn't really have a ride, so I didn't go back for that, but they said that the condition ... They said, "If you're unable to work now, you're not going to be able to because this is something that's just going to get worse, not better."

So I applied for disability about a week or two after that. So I came back to Eubanks, so I could get my mom and dad's help, and I applied for charity care for UNC, and I went and got several ... like, a few weeks, went back and forth to see them, and they'd give me pain medicine, what not, and then they did a MRI, and they said, "Well, the degenerative joint disease is the least of your problems." I said, "Wow." They said that, "Your spine is broken in two," where it had deteriorated so bad. And I went and see them all last year, all summer, once a month for the spine center, then the pain clinic, each month, and they want a new appointment, and they also did a EEG test, and it showed that I have permanent nerve damage.

But, in December, December seventh, they went in through the front and went all the way down to the spine and removed all the deteriorated and broken bones, and then December twelfth, I was in the hospital the whole time, but December twelfth, a week later, they went in the back and replaced it all, all of that with titanium, screws, rods, pins, and plates.

And just not being able to work is, you know, one thing led to another, and you lose one thing after another, and you finally lose your home, and so we're in the homeless shelter.

Davey's origin story provides the background for how he ended up sitting outside a homeless shelter that night. The error the young men in the car made in yelling out the window—beyond the obvious violations of human decency—is *not* in failing to consider the back story of the men at the shelter but rather in assigning them one based on faulty assumptions. They saw something and filled in the blanks to make sense of it. This is the second truth claim for legends and a common target for audience doubt.

The second truth claim is an interpretive one in which assumptions are made that may or may not be correct. A person receiving aid may have nice clothes or an iPhone or be sitting outside a homeless shelter smoking cigarettes, but whether such details convict them of fraud or abuse is highly debatable. Doubt about the second truth of legends is common, voiced in oral, written, and online contexts. People responding to Wildflower12's and MK's posts posit a range of possible interpretations for the woman with a large ring using food stamps. In a letter to the editor of the local *Burlington Times News*, Judy Hall recounted the following story:

WITNESS TO WASTEFUL PURCHASE WAS ASTONISHED

Recently I was in a grocery store in Mebane when I noticed a young couple with an infant checking out. They had only two items to purchase; a small bag of charcoal and a package of beef steaks. The transaction was being split into two purchases, so while waiting I noticed the charcoal was paid for with cash. After ringing up the T-bone steaks the total came to $21 for the package of two steaks, but to my absolute astonishment they whipped out an EBT (food stamp) card and paid for the steaks with it.

I was absolutely stunned at the purchase. Never in my life have I bought T-bone steaks and certainly I could have never had them paid for with food stamps. I often see people use food stamps in the grocery stores however, I have never encountered them using coupons or buying store brand products as I do. Are there some people who do use the food stamps wisely? Perhaps.

It is hard to tolerate the abuse and waste in the program. While our tax burdens grow daily and the cost of living increases that cause working people to tighten up, do without, and worry it's often the foolish and wasteful citizens of our great country are ripping it apart at the seams.

How long will we allow the government to take more from us and give to the clueless?

Nine people responded with thirteen comments, five siding with the author, eight arguing against, mostly by questioning the conclusion that buying steaks equates to fraud and abuse: "When T-Bone steaks are on sale they are often cheaper per pound than bacon and many other meats. . . . You never know another person (or their circumstances) until you walk a mile in their shoes," wrote Susan. Becky also imagined a justifiable backstory by wondering, "Did Judy give the couple a benefit of doubt that perhaps their home had just burned down the day before and the EBT card was temporary until the couple gets back on their feet," while Diana suggested somewhat more realistically, "They may have eaten beans all month to have a little celebration, a birthday, anniversary" (Hall 2013).[3]

Aid recipients, providers, and people who personally know others in need often tell stories of women doing each other's hair and nails or bartering for such services by offering free childcare. Some aid recipients describe wearing designer clothes because they can buy these brands for a fraction of the cost at the nicer thrift stores in town. Virtually all pointed to the common experience of hitting a rough patch and needing assistance for a short time to get back on one's feet. The car and clothing a person could afford when employed remain the car and clothing they own while on assistance.

YOU CAN'T JUDGE A BOOK BY ITS COVER

The caseworker Tamara North sums up the dangers of the second truth with a proverb: "Don't judge a book by its cover. Somebody may drive a new car, but it doesn't mean they're rich. Somebody may live in a nice house, but it doesn't mean that they have everything. You have to look beyond a person's exterior."

Correspondence bias, which describes "the tendency to draw inferences about a person's unique and enduring dispositions from behaviors that can be entirely explained by the situations in which they occur," can be hard to fight (Gilbert and Malone 1995, 21). One cannot render accurate judgment on a person's character from observable behavior alone, yet the urge to do so is strong. Conjuring an alternative, more generous backstory can be hard in the face of a widespread narrative of fraud that has dominated both the mass media and legend tradition. "When something seems out of place, you're like, 'Oh, you know, you're homeless on the street asking for money, but you have this like super nice leather coat,'" explains Lizzy Giles, who volunteers at a local nursing home. "I think everyone notices, but I try personally to stay very unjudgmental and just go, 'It was a donation,' because I don't like to assume that they could be doing anything wrong." Even someone with firsthand experience like Serena Borden, who is both an aid provider and an aid recipient, has to fight against jumping to conclusions.

> I mean, we see people who come in here and request assistance, and their hair looks nice, and their nails look good.
> One, it's not my place to ask them, "Well, who did your nails?"
> And two, I'm not going to say . . . I'm not going to think, "Why you need assistance from us when you have your nails done?" because I don't know if whoever's nail shop it is—did she babysit their kids in order to get their hair done? Or to get her nails done? Did she do it herself?
> I mean, I get compliments on my hair, and I do my own hair.
> Did she go and get the little press-ons [nails], because some of those look good? Some people have the creativity to do that. One of my friends white tipped my toes one time.

I'm not going to ask, and I'm not going to make that assumption, because we don't know.

And that's my thing. I don't like how so many people can make generalizations or assumptions about things when you do not know. I mean this lady could have had to go somewhere or be somewhere. "Well, I'll watch your babies while you . . ." "Thank you!" "Well, I don't have the money to pay you, but I can do your nails for you." Maybe she did that. Of course, there's the possibility of maybe not, but to me I can't make that assumption.

THE IMPACT OF CANONICAL NARRATIVES

Welfare stories are particularly susceptible to the problem of erroneous leaps from observation to interpretation due to the nature of the most commonly narrated experiences told by non-aid recipients: observations in the grocery store. The encounter is limited to the grocery store line. The observer has no idea what the person's home life is like, their obligations and responsibilities, how long they have been receiving food stamps, or whether their purchases are typical or exceptional. Accordingly, the most common welfare story told in the United States today requires crucial leaps of interpretation to make sense of what is being seen.

Without personal experiences with clients to draw on, however, reasoned speculations can become unsupported ideological leaps, relying on stereotypes and preexisting beliefs and perceptions codified in canonical narratives recognizable throughout a group or society as common and authoritative (see Polletta 2008). Whether we draw on our own lived experience or rely on available cultural narratives, distinguishing between the two can be difficult since our stories are also cultural and ideological, not just personal constructions.[4] Nonetheless, it is possible to identify those narrative elements used most often to fill in the gaps and consider how they do or do not echo, parallel, or duplicate widespread canonical narratives.

In the frequently emailed joke often titled "Had It All," for example, a man stops to ask a homeless man how he ended up living on the streets, offering him options to choose from: "Drugs? Alcohol? Divorce?" The list of suggestions is illuminating. Losing everything because of divorce plays into canonical narratives in the United States about women fleecing their ex-spouses when they separate. The other two options assume substance abuse, one of the most commonly cited vices attributed to aid recipients in the narrative tradition of the general public and one of the most common interpretive leaps in the narrative tradition (chap. 7).

Other interpretive leaps also adhere closely to canonical welfare queen narratives, such as "more children for more money" legends. Ricky Thorne, for example, tells stories of seeing women with multiple children and assuming these mothers had the children to increase their benefits. Separately, both Ashley Colton and Ellie Fitzer assumed the same when they saw a large African American family at the local soup kitchen, and Tamara North similarly assumed that when her neighbor's son's girlfriend got pregnant, it was because she was trying to game the system like her mother, who was already receiving assistance.

Canonical narratives of welfare fraud are so widespread and so recognizable that details that mirror these stories can be enough to lead people to make even more fundamental assumptions, such as that a person is receiving public assistance at all. Posting on My Biggest Complaint, "Angry taxpayer" describes becoming incensed "when I see those anchor babies supported by welfare monies, ages 4–18, wearing manicured and pedicured nails, eating their breakfast at McDonald's every school morning, and prancing around with their own personal cell phone." Boyd responded soon after: "Do you know for a fact that the people you see with expensive items are on welfare? Are these people you know? Can you tell a Latino citizen, resident or illegal alien by looking at them? You have a valid point. I just want to make sure you're not going by any preconceived notions." Canonical welfare legends and "preconceived notions" can mean that for some people, any woman of color with an iPhone can be enough to trigger the assumption that the person is receiving public assistance.

THE INSIDE OF THE BOOK

As Serena Borden points out, maybe there is a good reason for a particular purchase, maybe not, but we should not judge. Good advice, but it does not resolve the problem of interpretation. How should we interpret the steak on the EBT card or the twenty-inch rims on the Escalade, particularly if it is our own experience? It seems clear that the canonical narrative of the welfare queen should not serve as evidence, judge, and jury. But using the similarly imagined possibilities of unseen trials and tribulations seems equally problematic, as when Lizzy Giles assumes the best because she simply does not want to imagine anything else. Fortunately, there is a vast counternarrative tradition of stories told by aid recipients themselves that can provide evidence, if not case-by-case confirmation, of the prevalence of explanatory backstories.

Tracie Rutherford tells a story about buying steak with her food stamps, but only at discount butchers or when the meat goes on sale. Martina Morales tells a story of buying birthday cakes for her children when the money is there, but more recently having to forego even this small, rare treat. Mary Barker tells a story of losing her job when she checked into a treatment facility to help with her alcohol addiction. Lilly Gibbs tells a story of taking in a stray dog as emotional comfort and physical protection after escaping an abusive husband who threatened to kill her. All of these people might be seen in the grocery store buying "luxury" items—steak, birthday cake, alcohol, dog food—that feed the legend of the welfare queen. All of them have backstories that challenge that interpretation.

Aware that people do in fact judge books by their covers, many aid recipients take pains to avoid contributing to the stereotypes. The line they must walk, however, is a fine one. Dress nicely, you are labeled a welfare queen. Dress shabbily and you are an unfit mother. The critique is levied not only by the general public but among aid recipients as well. Elliott Dunn describes being in the waiting room at the Open Door Clinic, judging and being judged.

> I'm here now. Somebody else out in the waiting room, someone's probably thinking the same thing: "Look at him. He looks like he's got it on. Halfway decent clothes and all?" And, "Why is he here?"
>
> And I'm looking at the poor street bum because you can tell, obvious why he's here.
>
> Somebody comes in dressed better than I do, I think, "Whoa, they got on these name-brand stuff and jewelry and rings on every finger. Hmmm. They got money somewhere." You see the one who . . .
>
> I don't know every situation. I see people they don't go out of the house unless they are fully dressed. I mean dressed to impress, so-called, but that's their everyday thing, like women who won't stick they're face out the door without makeup on. Like I say, you don't have to go in there, take a bath and fix your hair, just to run to the convenience store. But she'll take that hour to get ready just to get a loaf of bread just to come home, never go out again that day. It's vanity.

Elliott Dunn sees vanity. But many women see dressing nicely as an effort to maintain dignity while asking for help and to avoid the stigma of poverty. It is a double-edged sword, however, and as Elliott's story makes clear, no one gets off scot free, each of us judging the other from our respective vantage points. An aid recipient herself, Tia Solomon has to resist the urge to fill in the blanks, but she also considers ways to mitigate against the stereotyping.

> Some of the cases are ridiculous, but you can't look at them and judge them if they have an iPhone and use an EBT card. Or they walk out to a Beamer or something.
>
> You're just wondering, and you're like, "But somebody else might pay. They might have it good like that, and somebody else might pay for it."
>
> But what I would do is get rid of my Beamer, get me a nineties car, a little Honda, get me from point A to point B, and let that person that's buying that Beamer for you put food on the table. Give the food stamps to somebody that needs them.

Tia's imagined scenario of a wealthy benefactor follows a line of logic people often make when evaluating the choices of the poor. But as stories from other aid recipients make clear, such logic rarely holds up. Writing in the *Washington Post*, the aid recipient Darlena Cunha shared her story of the responses she got for continuing to drive a paid-for and reliable Mercedes rather than sell it for an unreliable clunker (2014). Her choice was a thrifty and rational one, but observed from the outside, it was yet more confirmation of the legend of the welfare queen. Ayanna Spencer's story adds yet another explanation.

> My fiancé had his truck. We've had crazy things with transportation. He had a truck, but he sold his truck to get a bigger car to accommodate all of us. As soon as he got that car, my car broke down. With the job that I was working before, I had to quit my job because I didn't have transportation. My daughter was actually going to this school. I had to actually keep her out for a couple of days. I didn't have transportation to bring her here.
>
> Then my aunt and uncle had bought me a car without me asking. My grandma told them I didn't have a car. They went and bought it, but then they made me pay them back. We actually just finished paying them off like last week. We had to pay them a hundred and fifty dollars every month to pay them off. I wasn't even going to agree on it. I told them that they could keep the car.
>
> Then my fiancé said, "You need a car. Get it. I'll pay for it." So he worked until we paid for it all. Every month he paid for me. Now that car is messed up. [Laughs] It's overheating. I don't know what's going on with it.

DOUBTS ABOUT THE GENERALIZABILITY:
THE THIRD TRUTH

The concept of generalizability for any single narrative runs counter to scholars who argue that personal stories cannot be generalizable (e.g., Miller, Cho, and Bracey 2005, 119). "Stories alone do not articulate principles likely to provide consistency in generalizations to guide future action" (Minow 2008, 259). Yet concepts of cultural narratives that bridge the personal and the social (Bell 2003, 4) and intertextuality where a story may reference or evoke past performances of similar stories (see Briggs and Bauman 1992) make it clear that personal stories can make viable claims to generalizability. The same is true for legends, though folklorists have had an ambiguous relationship with the idea. On the one hand, generalizability is acknowledged in most definitions for contemporary legend and assumed in the vast majority of theoretical approaches to legend. On the other hand, many legends are so unusual or remarkable that audiences wonder whether they happened even once, much less again and again.

Consider the common claim that legends provide expression for anxieties, fears, and desires. This claim underlies the bulk of the functional analyses of contemporary legends. A major source of the power of legends, therefore, comes in the possibility that this *could* happen again and, more disconcertingly, could happen to *us*. Gillian Bennett, Paul Smith, and Carl Lindahl have referred to this as the "this could happen to you" quality of the genre (Lindahl 2011, xi). It is just this possibility that makes contemporary legends so titillating and compelling. Could my child be abducted in a large department store with a makeshift haircut, clothing change, and drugs? Might I find a fried rat in my bucket of chicken? Could my spring break fling leave me infected with HIV?

The assumption that "this could happen to you," however, conflates plot and theme. We can fear the themes of a legend, without fearing the event. Consider the classic Mexican pet legend where a woman brings a little dog back from her vacation in Mexico only to find out that it is actually a long-haired Mexican rat (Brunvand 1988). Audiences are not worried that they might bring back a dog from their vacations south of the border—such an act is easy to protect against—but they do worry about what other nasty surprises they might unwittingly return home with (such as gastrointestinal ones) or awaiting them on their arrival due to the "filthy" conditions of these "foreign" countries. More generally, as an expression of xenophobia, the story conveys anxieties and fears about any foreign import, material or human. The fears are thematic and symbolic rather than literal.

Other legends, however, evoke fears not just in theme but in plot. Stories of travelers abroad being drugged and then having their kidney stolen raise fears of traveling alone, foreign countries, and foreign people. If the drugging happens because of the promise of a sexual encounter, additional fears of violating conservative social ideals about sex outside of marriage may also be raised. Some audiences, however, may also fear the exact scenario described in the legend: that the stolen kidney did not happen to *one* tourist in *one* country at *one* point in time but happens to tourists around the world *all* the time.

In terms of generalizability, therefore, all legends are not created equal. Distinguishing between theme and plot helps identify those differences that matter most when considering generalizability. The same is true in distinguishing between the reoccurring and the representative. Even stories that suggest a plot could be repeated again do not necessarily suggest they are representative. After all, "It could happen again" is not the same as "It happens all the time." Generalizability, however, suggests that a story *is* representative, whether of a particular group or situation. And there are contemporary legends where narrators not only claim "it happens all the time" but make this claim the primary claim of their story. In these cases, the remarkable aspect of the legend may not be that the event happened but that the event happens regularly. As the third truth of contemporary legends, generalizability generates the most doubt about welfare stories.

Returning to the online discussion about welfare on the My Biggest Complaint website, the initial writer complains, "Every time I see someone on welfare smoking, while talking on an expensive cell phone, wearing the latest fashions and gold jewelry, with their hair and nails done, and drinking store-bought coffee from a container, I just want to go nuts!" (chap. 10). Her complaint is a version of the welfare queen legend, cast as a generalized experience, something the writer claims to see all the time. Following this initial complaint, people wrote in to share their stories. Some were first person, some second and third; virtually all were about welfare fraud in the United States today. The message was clear: these stories of fraud are true, widespread, and generalizable.

But not all the people posting to the site agreed with the last point. They may be true, and people may tell them again and again, making them widespread, but they are *not* generalizable.

> While I won't deny that welfare abuse obviously DOES happen, can anyone give me any PROOF to back up "ME's" unsourced claim that "Half of people on welfare falsely apply"? Oh, really? Where did you hear that load of crap? The Heritage Foundation? Lol—Brandon

And then a few minutes later in a continuation of his post:

> I'm just so sick of ignoramuses who pretend like, "EVERYONE on welfare (or most of them, even) just uses it to mooch off taxpayers and not work," as if that's REALLY all that possible with America's ungenerous benefits.—Brandon

Lisa is more diplomatic:

> Hey everyone, I understand the feelings about people abusing the system. I have seen a FEW people that do that. However, I am on section 8 housing, I work 40 hours a week, sometimes more because I also own my own business, I'm a single mom and receive no child support. Yes, I do own a computer that I bought with my own EARNED money, and I use it to better myself through online schooling so that I don't have to be on welfare the rest of my life. I sometimes wear nice clothes because I find good deals on brand name clothes at garage sales and thrift stores because rich people dispose of clothes after wearing them a few times . . . I am not lazy.

In terms of the first truth of accuracy, people agree that true stories of welfare fraud do exist. In terms of the second truth of interpretation, some disagree that every welfare recipient in nice clothes is defrauding the government. In terms of the third truth of generalizability, however, many more disagree, and disagree passionately, over whether the few stories of fraud should define the vast majority of aid recipients.

While many stories claim to be generalizable, some are already halfway there upon creation, as in the story Bill Steeple tells:

> **Frank:** All they have to do is go maybe once a week or three times a month and walk in a door and say, "Can I get a job?" And they say, "No." "Well, will you sign here saying that I did this?" That's it.

Bill: So sometimes I've heard real examples where people say, "Great. Here's the drug test. Fill out this application. Let me give you this chair—it's right here." "Well, no. I don't want to do that." [*Laughter*]

Bob: "They might hire me!" [*Other men laugh*] "I just want you to sign this piece of paper."

Bill: I mean, we've seen it with our own eyes. How many times have y'all seen it?

Bob: Oh yeah.

Bill describes "real examples" that describe not one single experience situated in time and space but a host of virtually identical experiences blended together, what can usefully be called generalized experience narratives.[5] Generalized experience narratives are habitual narrative scripts of what people perceive to happen regularly, combining numerous, repeated events into a single, amalgamated structure. Such stories are both generalized and generalizable, suggesting a pattern not simply of the past but of the present and future.

GENERALIZED EXPERIENCE NARRATIVES

Reagan's goal with his story of Linda Taylor was to evoke outrage, and it worked. The story was compelling because the fraud was so egregious. And yet Reagan managed to tell a story that could at one and the same time be remarkable *and* generalizable. Many of the audiences that heard his story on the campaign trail did not hear a single, outrageous, unique story but rather a compelling example of a story playing out again and again all across the country, a story that was representative of many, perhaps even most, welfare recipients. The history of welfare reform in the United States suggests that many people, including the vast majority of the legislators in Congress, thought the story was generalizable.

Other stories are inherently generalizable in plot and theme. These are the generalized experience narratives.

You see the people who really abuse the system. They're in here getting everything they can, and you know they're lying. They tell you they don't have money to pay the bills, but they come in . . . The women have all those long, fancy weaves in their hair, nice fingernails, cell phones, and you think, how? Weaves aren't cheap. Cells aren't cheap. Nails aren't cheap. And you say, "Why they got money for that? Why aren't they paying their bills?"

Elliott Dunn paints a picture of welfare fraud by describing what he believes is a habitual scene describing the past, set in the present, and projected into the future. What is unclear, however, is not only how common it is to see someone in the clinic matching this description but how representative the image is of the people in the clinic. Is this one person every now and then? Most people all the time? Left unquestioned, with no alternative narrative to provide a different scene, the generalized experience narrative suggests not *an* image but *the* image of aid recipients, representative by default. Lilly Gibbs tells a generalized experience narrative of food stamp fraud, followed by a hypothetical scenario:

> A lot of people, there was a lot of legal cases where they found that people was selling these stamps for money. They take their plastic card, and this person, they're selling them, and they take somebody who is not getting food stamps, but then again, they take this one to the grocery store and get what they want, and they're giving that person the cash that they want.
>
> Like, "I'll take Tom to the store and then . . ." So they go in and get this person to fill that house with groceries, on Susan's card, and it's buying Tom's groceries, and he's giving her X amount of dollars in cash.
>
> It's still an undercover thing, but you know, like I said, they think it's being used just for Susan, but Susan is taking her card and doing her thing.

Phrases like "a lot of people" and "a lot of legal cases," coupled with the generalized story she shares, leave the impression of massive fraud. But when asked how many people she thinks does this, she laughs. "It's hard to put them on a scale. Is it five percent? Two percent or three percent?" Even when unintended, the implicit scale of the generalized experience narrative can pack a powerful punch.

More often, narrators are explicit that the habitual script represents the majority, not the minority, as the DSS caseworker Susan Davis does when she argues against such depictions of aid recipients.

> I've had a lot of clients who maybe start out not working, receiving assistance, get a job, let us know, "Hey, I got a job; I got my own insurance; you can terminate my Medicaid." "OK, good for you." There are a lot of people who per se get off of assistance. There are a lot of people who start out on it and then don't need it.
>
> So, I mean, everyone is not getting assistance forever and ever just to milk the system. There are some that do it, but from what I've seen, the majority of them don't.

Such stories are both generalized and generalizable, where one story can serve as metonym for hundreds. The process for creating generalized experience narratives and ensuring they continue to be generalizable would appear to be a fairly simple one of de- and rehydration. Start with a large batch of stories, extract the details leaving only the essential elements, and then share the essentialized story with the assumption that audiences will imagine the story expanding back out across time and space.

Susan Phillips is working on her GED and has the unwavering support of her partner, George. But George has heart problems, diabetes, and bipolar disorder and cannot work. Susan struggles to keep his hopes up.

> He wants to work. He would rather work than get disability. He wants to work. He's not one of the ones that wants to just sit around. He always has to be doing

something. With what the doctors are saying to him, he's probably not going to go back to work ever again. And we struggle with that constantly.

I tell him all the time, I said, "I'm here. I got you."

He says, "It's not the same as doing it yourself than having someone . . ."

I said, "When we got together, we agreed that we're going to stick with each other no matter what. I'm not going anywhere."

He's struggling with that.

Every time he goes to the doctor, he says, "I come home, and something else is wrong with me."

I said, "Well, the only thing I can really say is 'that's life.' I hate it. If I could take it from you, I would, but that's just the way it is."

Like I said, he's fighting with the depression, the bipolar, the heart issues. They're saying that he's going to lose his . . . I think it's his left eye. Glaucoma.

He's struggling. I'm holding him up.

Sometimes he just gets in a mood where he just don't want to get out the bed. I tell him, "We got a baby here. We got to get up and get moving. If you don't do nothing but get up and walk outside. Walk around the block. Take him around the block, come back, maybe you might feel better."

We keep him on his toes. Especially his son.

Susan moves nimbly among generalized experience narratives that capture her lived experience far more accurately than a single moment of success or tragedy in her life. Day in and day out, these are the encounters that consume her thoughts and her time. By capturing the habitual event rather than the unusual event, the generalized experience narrative can operate as an antidote to the common criticism that people cherry-pick experiences to share as story, focusing on the unusual and thereby providing a skewed image of reality. DSS caseworker Derick Stark makes this distinction abundantly clear but, in doing so, highlights the limitations of the generalized experience narrative:

Most of the time, it's they come in, and you can see that they've had a job, but then they've just lost the job, and now it's all going to shambles and that sort of thing.

A more unique story, though, I had a client come in, and she had moved here from overseas. Her husband worked for the military, worked for it. He wasn't a military guy, but he worked, like subcontracted, for the military. And one of her babies were born over there, so it was a U.S. citizen but didn't have a Social, so we couldn't do anything for that baby until we had a Social. But the main thing was, is that even though he wasn't in the household with her here in the States, we still had to count his income because he was intending to come back to the home when he finally left.

So that's one of those things where she may not have anything right here, right now tangible; we still have to look at it as she's got access to this stuff, which technically she does but just not as easily.

That's probably the most unique story I've had so far in a long time.

> But other than that, for the most part, most of the stories are people just . . .
> Everybody can't find work. They can't find work. They just lost the job. They
> can't keep a job.

The unusual case gets told as a situated, stand-alone narrative; the typical case
gets collapsed into a generalized experience narrative. Derick makes sure that
the typical client who cannot find work frames his discussion, but the generalized experience narrative pales in comparison to the unusual, specific event story
that dominates Derick's narrative performance. The danger is clear: the specific
event narrative, shared alone, can provide a skewed view of reality that even the
generalized experience narrative may be too mundane to counter.

Derick Stark's example also highlights the importance of considering narrative genre in its performance context for understanding not only the power
and limitations of generalized experience narratives but their rhetorical function. In his example, however, generalized experience narrative and personal
experience narrative do not align. He is explicit, pointing out the disconnect.
Far more often, however, they do align, with generalized experience narratives
serving as introductions that paint a picture of the forest before that of the trees.
"I have neighbors that live beside me," the public housing resident Christie
Huston begins.

> When I came, it was more of like, "OK. This is our building." Even though we
> live in the community, it's four apartments in the building, but it's three of
> us that usually work together, me and my neighbor to the left and me and my
> neighbor to the right. If I need little things, like my best friend that lives next
> door to me, she'll go, "Do the kids need clothes?"
> She bought Eric two pair of shorts a couple of weeks ago. She goes yard-sale-
> ing a lot, so she looked for Eric some sneakers because he needs some sneakers.
> We weren't able to find any, but you have to just not give up.

The generalized experiences of generosity and reciprocity remind Christie of a
specific event just a couple of weeks ago. Christie then shifts gears from talking
about caring for her kids to caring for her grandmother who helped raise her.

> She doesn't know anything that you don't teach her. I was the one that went to
> the grocery store and, "Nana, you have a hundred dollars. This is two twenty-
> nine, or this is two dollars, Nana, so we're going to get the two-dollar one so
> that we can save twenty-nine cents."
> I taught Nana how to shop. She can go in a grocery store by herself and get her
> groceries, but now it's to the point where when she counts her money out, she's
> counting it too fast; she's not paying attention to what's coming out of her hand.
> Teresa had said something about a hundred-dollar bill went missing, and she
> thinks Nana paid it out by accident, and they didn't give it back to my grandma.

Narratives often open with an orientation: information that sets the stage for the story that follows. In the case of the generalized experience narrative, an entire narrative serves this role. This can be a powerful rhetorical move: a story suggests what happens all the time, followed by a specific example as proof. The regularity with which people open with a generalized experience narrative and then shift to a specific event narrative also suggests that generalized experience narratives may operate as mnemonic devices that prime the pump of memory.

Often, this performance structure mirrors the chronology of the events themselves. The generalized experience narrative captures a series of long past experiences, while the personal experience narrative captures the recent. "Like, just the other day," "Last week," and "When I saw her last" all signal recent, often the *most* recent, of all the events drawn together into the generalized experience narrative. The result is that the generalized past remains a generalized present.

Used together, the personal experience narrative and the generalized experience narrative exponentially multiply the persuasive power of narrative. The personal experience narrative provides credibility; the generalized experience narrative, generalizability. Anonymity can do similar work, helping to untether a story to allow it to go forth and multiply. This was the brilliance of Reagan's welfare queen story. The media named Linda Taylor as the welfare queen, not Reagan. Instead, he told a story about "a woman in Chicago," giving the public an individual but generalizing her by removing her name. He was exploiting the power of generalizability by employing the power of the concrete detail, with the vague anonymity of the widespread "everyman," or in this case "everywoman."

When the generalized experience narrative does *not* lead to a personal experience narrative, however, doubts can arise about the accuracy and authenticity of the generalized experience. Rather than there being too many stories to share just one, audiences may wonder whether there is any story there at all. Ricky Thorne, for example, repeats the common claim that women have more babies in order to increase their welfare check: "You see that all the time . . . I've heard of it happening . . . a lot of families just having more kids when they get on welfare, so they get more money because they get a certain amount per child." But when Jessica Elizondo, the Elon University student interviewing him, asked whether he knew anyone who had done that, his response was illuminating: "You know, not personally I don't. But I'm sure that there is people out there that do that to abuse the system. I'm sure there is, but don't know none personally, no."

In the same way that legends may rely on a FOAF (friend of a friend) to substitute for an actual person, the generalized experience narrative may substitute for an actual event. In this way, the generalized experience operates as a mask rather than a mirror. While FOAF attributions attempt to anchor the story in time and space as a specific event, the generalized experience narrative does the opposite: unmooring the story so that it can be applied widely.

Such a possibility requires a reconsideration of the origin of generalized experience narratives. While they may be constructed from numerous examples and supported through recent personal experience narratives, generalized experience narratives may also emerge from personal beliefs and unsubstantiated legends. Rather than *reflect* and *represent* the usual, generalized experience narratives may *manufacture* it. Did the American dream become the nation's most recognizable master narrative because hundreds upon thousands of bootstrap immigrant stories of success cohered to create it? Or was it created to provide an ideal story for Americans to live up to and to provide an interpretive frame to fit our stories into, thereby shaping, even creating, the individual experience? As chapter 2 suggests, it is both. Stories shape our experiences just as our experiences shape our stories.

Recounting recent experiences to support a generalized experience narrative, therefore, is a powerful tool in establishing credibility. The lack of specific stories, however, need not indicate manufactured experience. Rather, generalized experience narratives performed with specific personal narratives can signal an additional function of this genre: a work-around to untellable narratives. Untellable narratives are those stories that are difficult to tell, whether because of social norms, stigma, or trauma (Goldstein 2009, 236). Leslie Forester, for example, has slowly grown more comfortable telling people she receives public assistance, but stigma is strong, and memories of the past remain painful. When asked about her experiences receiving public aid, the first thing she mentions is the stigma.

> It's fine, you know. It's just normal. Sometimes that's what happens to people.
> And there's some, some people out there that they'll look down on you. I know it's bad, but it's the truth.
> And I just ignore those people and pray for them because that's what Granny told me to do.
> She said, "Just pray for them, sweetheart. They can't help it, the way they are."
> Growing up, people thought it was like leprosy. You don't want to hang around or be around anybody that's like that.
> And I would talk to anybody. I would try to be nice to anybody. It didn't matter. And it's like a bad, bad thing growing up.
> And when I got on, first got on it, I know I was extremely embarrassed about it and didn't want to talk about it because I knew I didn't want people judging me or looking at me.

Leslie tells no specific stories of being treated poorly, but her conversation with her grandmother makes it clear that she sought solace and advice on how to deal with people looking down on her. She references recurring events of being treated poorly and having to "just ignore" them. These degrading experiences do not happen all the time, but they happen enough to suggest a common, habitual experience. Although not foolproof, attending to performance context, support-ing narratives, narrative distance, social stigma, and the presence of trauma can help distinguish among generalized experience narratives that operate as masks for an unsubstantiated story, as habitual scripts grounded in experience, or as alternatives to untellable stories.

HYPOTHETICAL NARRATIVES

Generalized experience narratives are rooted in the past but extend into the present. As habitual actions and experiences, there is no expiration date. Hypo-thetical narratives, however, serve as generalized experience narratives but require no such allegiance to past experience, providing wide rein to match story with belief (see Baynham 2000, 114; Linde 1986, 186; and Myers 1999). Speculative without requiring an if-then construction, hypothetical narratives are created when people speculate what might be the case, what they believe often to be the case, or what they hope or fear is the case. Hypothetical narra-tives emerge in conversation most often in one of three situations: in lieu of generalized experience narratives when describing habitual action, when sug-gesting alternative interpretations, and when imagining the future.[6]

Tired of working so hard when others seem not to, Makayla Stirling initially tells a generalized experience narrative of returning to her home in one of the handful of public housing neighborhoods in Burlington.

> I come home some nights and people sitting on their porches, and they're chilling like they hadn't done nothing all day. If I get off work at five o'clock, and I get home at six o'clock, nobody's exhausted as I am, you know? [Laughs]
>
> I mean, I've had a forty-five minute to an hour drive to work, and I come home and everybody's on the porches. Their hair is done, and they're laid back, and they're cute, and it's fine. I got to go in here find these kids something to eat. And I'm like.... [Sighs heavily]
>
> And then [knocks on table]. "Can I get some sugar?"
>
> I'm like, "No. I don't think you deserve sugar today, sweetie."

The frustration is real; the cup of sugar is not. It is a substitute for all the favors and help she gets asked for by her neighbors. As a well-known metaphor in the United States for neighborly borrowing, the cup of sugar is an evocative and efficient symbol that Makayla uses not only to complete her story but as a refrain that she returns to again and again. "If you needed some sugar, and I had sugar, I was going to give you sugar," she explains. "But if you needed sugar next week, I probably won't give you sugar because some reason, somehow, I'm keeping sugar and you're not."

Makayla uses a hypothetical example to augment her generalized experience narrative. The overlap between the two genres is common, with one regularly blurring into the other. Fraud investigator Gary Douglas, for example, regularly creates hypothetical narratives to describe what typically happens, even if there is no such thing as a typical case.

> Let's say you live next door to a family, and they're receiving food stamp benefits. Well, Mom comes over with an EBT card, says, "How would you like six hundred dollars' worth of groceries for three hundred dollars cash?"
>
> And you say, "Well, I'll do that."
>
> So then she says, "Give me the list of everything you want. We'll spend up to six hundred dollars."
>
> So they go out; they buy the six hundred dollars' worth of goods, you know, rib eye loins, crab legs, and whatever you want to put in your freezer. They buy it up; they spend six hundred dollars' worth of goods, bring it to your house; you hand them three hundred dollars cash; nobody's going to know.
>
> And we can't prove it or disprove it unless you turn around and admit you broke the law.

For Gary, the hypothetical narrative provides a solution to the ethical mandate not to name anyone in the cases he investigates. More powerful, however, is the space in hypothetical narratives for the storyteller to personalize the story and, in this case, drop the audience directly into the action. Kate Garnett does the same but in reverse, crafting the story around the audience rather than the audience around the story.

> You have to find those strategies to be a good caseworker, and the same way I'm going to model it with what I think you know and what you can really get is the same with a student.
>
> You might have to see six students; there are six students who have made an appointment to see you about a paper or about a project, and the first student will come and just wants a little bit of guidance, and you try this or this. "Great. Thanks, Mr. Mould."
>
> "Yep."
>
> "Great. Thanks."
>
> On their way, and you're like, "That's going to be a great paper. Can't wait."
>
> And the next person might come in, and they're just having trouble, and they're just going round and round in circles, not sure what they want to do, and you kind of give them a little bit more guidance, give them a bit more, and they're off, and you're like, "Well, don't know if that's going to work out, but we'll see."
>
> Third person comes in. "Sir, I just can't meet that deadline. You know, I've got this going on and that, and my fraternity brothers and I've got this that, and I'm working this."

And you're like, "You know, I'm trying to work with you." And OK, they're trying your patience a little bit, but OK, you're going to help them a little more.

And then you get to the day due, who always is late, always has an excuse though. Comes in, "Yeah . . ." And you've just . . . You're just like [takes deep breath], "Can't lose my temper. Cannot lose my temper." But this person has really tired your patience.

And it's the same with casework. I might see ten people during my intake, and the first three don't really need a lot of handholding; they've gone through their application; I'm just verifying the information, telling them what they need, you know. "Do you have any questions?" Answer their questions. "OK, well, I hope things turn around. Good luck to you, sir." Put it away, easy peasy.

Next person might be a senior citizen. Needs a little more handholding, a little gentler, little softer approach. Great.

And then the next person who comes in is a twenty-year-old who can't give me a straight answer, who looks to me like they just rolled out of bed, and everything is, "Yeah," and "Nah." Yeah. The thing about it is, I don't care if you look like you just rolled out of bed. Fine. I think that's sort of similar to grunge style. That's OK if you say, "Yeah and nah." Maybe you didn't learn any better. But if you can't give me a straight answer about things I ask you, that ticks me off.

And I just have to go through and maintain my patience. And sometimes, I have to get a little firm and say, "Really? Are you willing to sign that on this application? Because when my auditor looks at that, they're not going to believe that."

And I never call my client a liar. You never do that; that's inappropriate. I can say, "I need to verify that." But I always use my auditor or the feds as an excuse. Always. They've become the boogeyman. And I always say, "When my auditor reads that, he's not going to buy it. I need you to sign it; I need you to explain it more."

Like Gary, Kate creates hypothetical stories to explain the common, everyday experiences of casework. As they do, Gary and Kate exploit the power of hypothetical narratives to allow people to shift perspective and imagine life in another person's shoes. Betsy Maller imagines how different her life is from those who do not have to wonder where their next meal will come from. Laurie Vincent, who often works with low-income families, steps into shoes a bit closer to her own when she imagines what her fellow grocery store shoppers think about people using food stamps.

My mom worked in a grocery store when I was a kid, so she saw a lot of folks coming in. Sometimes the perception is weird when you're at the grocery store, and you see people buying things with their food stamps.

Maybe some people feel like, "Well, you shouldn't be buying expensive food because you're on government assistance. You should be buying ramen and macaroni and cheese like the rest of us."

OVERTHROWING THE QUEEN

Shifts in perspective that allow the adoption of other voices, roles, and personas can provide the same kind of plausible deniability afforded so often through jokes. Laurie Vincent avers that she does not judge her fellow shoppers, but she sympathizes with those who do. Bradley Jewell also uses hypothetical narratives to provide some distance between himself and the people in his stories when he describes his frustration with how the news media treats people like him.

> It's just a negative aspect. You know? Instead of saying something positive, they concentrate on the negative. And that's the media. Period.
>
> If, say, like if I'm on food stamps, OK? And I go out, and I buy my family dinner. News guys asks me, it's like, "Well, how'd you pay for that?"
>
> "EBT."
>
> "Oh, you're on food stamps."
>
> "Well, yeah, for right now until I can get a better job or get a job."
>
> Period.
>
> They don't concentrate on that you're trying to get work. They concentrate on the fact that you're using taxpayer money to pay for your food. That's a negative aspect, you know? Be positive. Say, "Well, good luck. I hope you find work." Be supportive. Don't show everything in a negative light. And that, that's all they do. I mean, ever since I was a little kid, that's all they ever did.

Like Laurie Vincent, who put herself in the shoes of non-aid recipients like her, Bradley Jewell put himself in the shoes of aid recipients like him. He does not suggest he has been interviewed himself, though it is possible that his hypothetical narrative references a real experience, one he finds untellable, much like the person who calls into radio shows and describes a "friend" who has an embarrassing problem. What is clear is that he has no trouble imagining how it would feel to be treated in the way he has seen the media treat others in his situation. In lieu of his own experience, he creates a narrative based on what he has seen on television that operates as a surrogate: the exact details may not be true, but the story, structure, and sentiment is. In doing so, he draws abstract ideas, beliefs, and perceptions into concrete being through story.

Hypothetical narratives also provide opportunities to raise doubts about the second truth of legends: interpretation. When DSS caseworker Jessica Patterson recounts stories about people making comments about the nice cars in the parking lot, she suggests there may be a story behind the story that runs counter to the standard assumption of fraud. She lists the options in short order: "They could've inherited that car from a family member that passed away. They could be borrowing that car from someone. Or they could've been working and making car payments and lost their job. They could've bought the car and got behind on their bills; that's why they're here. Their husband could've left or wife could've left." Each hypothetical possibility operates as a kernel narrative for the audience to fill in the rest.

Hypothetical scenarios and stories can also be used to confirm master narratives, providing detail and dialogue to what is typically imagined more theoretically and abstractly. The belief that unemployment is used as a vacation, for example, is cast into narrative by one of the businessmen during their Friday morning breakfast club.

> Well, in the case of unemployment, unemployment's great. It's needed. It needs to be there for the times we're in.
>
> But when we extend it to ninety-nine weeks, and I'm unemployed, I'm going to think, "Man, I've got ninety-nine weeks. I think I'll just sit on my butt for about eighty weeks and just do nothing." No incentive to work. Then maybe the last few weeks, I might start.
>
> We've incentivized people to take the work ethic out of it, just taken it out.

The line between imagination and reality is porous and, over time, can disappear altogether. What starts as a thought exercise can become a confirmed truth.[7] This is where the hypothetical traditionally lives: imagining "what if" and encouraging people to role play as a means of imagining the present.

Among aid recipients, the hypothetical narrative can also operate as a steam valve when imagining the future. Christie Huston considers what she would say if she could talk to President Barack Obama and the people in charge of the welfare system.

> The first thing I would ask them is, "Why am I less than you? Why do I even have to be made to feel like I'm less than you? Just because you live in the White House and you make choices, that don't make you no better than me, but you believe you better than me. You would come here, and you would shake my hand, and you would put a smile on your face, and you would talk to me, and as soon as you leave, you would wash your hands and be like, "Oh my goodness. Look where we're at. Hurry up and get us out of here."
>
> My family don't even like coming over here. How do you think that makes somebody feel? They don't even want to come to your house because they're like, "Oh, she live in the projects."
>
> If he came here, I would just ask . . . I'd probably tell him, "Please take me with you. Just please take me, please, with you. Come on, please. Look, I'll rake; I'll wash the dishes; I'll do whatever you need me to do. Just take us with you."
>
> It would just be real simple things, like, "Help me." I'm not asking nobody to give me nothing. I don't want you to give me nothing. Help me figure out how to get it on my own; that way you can't look back at me and be like, "I did this. I did that." I hate when people do that, because I don't do people like that: "I did this, I did that."

Christie imagines a conversation with President Obama and the life she could lead if she was treated as a fellow human being, no less nor more than anyone else. More often, however, aid recipients engage in thought exercises about future goals for themselves and their children. Jeanna Jarrett has brutally honest conversations with her sons about growing up as black men in the United States, with a clear goal in mind: "I want them to look back when they are twenty-five, twenty-six and be like, you know, 'My mom came from here, and she went here, and, you know, she done it. I can do it.'" Christie, a consummate storyteller, imagines her future as well.

> If I could have just the American dream, it would just be as simple as a house that's mine that I don't have to worry about nobody putting me out of, funds that can take care of me and my. . . . I don't want to be rich. I don't. I would never ask to be a rich woman, just enough to get by.
>
> If something breaks on my car . . . Some people, they got a wallet. They can open their wallet, and they can go to the mechanic, and they can get their car fixed.
>
> Oh no, not Christie. Oh no. Car broken? "Oh hell, what are we going to do?"
>
> I'm going to call somebody and beg somebody to please help me fix my car because I don't have it.
>
> That's what an American dream would be to me, simple things like that. Open a refrigerator: "Oh, we don't have a gallon of milk. Oh, just run down to the store and get us a five-dollar gallon of milk because I got five dollars."
>
> Oh no, it don't work like that. Do we got a dollar? Do we got a dollar? It's that serious.
>
> If it was possible for me, if I got lucky one day, I don't want to be rich; I just want to have simple necessities that people have every single day of their life. Some people don't ever have to do without stuff like that. When you go to the bathroom and you got to use a washrag because it ain't a roll of toilet paper in your house, that is not an American freaking dream! I just need basic necessities, and that would be the most perfect American dream for me.

Inevitably, the present comes crashing through, a foil to a hoped-for future. Like Betsy Maller, who imagines the ease with which middle-class families feed their families, Christie highlights the seemingly small but incredibly significant challenges that so many people take for granted. In fact, it is from the thought exercises of imagining life in the middle class that provides her the narrative of her imagined future.

THE CRUCIAL ROLE OF GENERALIZABILITY

The concept of generalizability in legends, generalized experience narratives, and hypothetical narratives proves to be a crucial concept in understanding how stories are used and interpreted. First, attending to the generalizability of legends helps direct attention to an underexamined area of narrative performance, where doubt can emerge. Second, the concept of generalizability more broadly highlights an important rhetorical move that allows people to challenge the meaning and importance of a story without calling the narrator a liar. Third, generalized experience narratives paradoxically highlight those places of greatest and least evidence. Fourth and finally, attending to the generalizability of narrative draws attention to the creative dimension of storytelling, where narrators craft the specific from the general and vice versa, drawing on personal experience as well as canonical narratives to fill crucial interpretive gaps.

ISIM: I SAW IT MYSELF

A doubt-centered approach to legend highlights the many places where audiences may question the truth of a story. Within the first truth of the accuracy of a story alone, doubt may be raised in a number of places, from whether the entire story has been fabricated to questions about a particular plot element or descriptive detail. But many definitions of the legend make clear that one area of doubt is assumed from the start: doubt about narrative distance.

Narrative distance refers to the distance between the storyteller and the events being recounted. That distance is shortest when someone tells a story of their own personal experience. It lengthens when a person tells someone else's personal experience narrative, making it a secondhand story. Whether narrative distance should be used to distinguish one genre from the next has been argued and challenged ever since Carl von Sydow proposed a generic distinction between the firsthand memorate and the second- or thirdhand fabulate (1948). As one of the most outspoken opponents to such a division, Linda Dégh has argued that the exact same story told in first person does not jump genres the minute it gets retold by someone else (1991). This rationale makes sense if the goal is archival sorting and tale-type indexing. But the field of folklore has a long tradition of recognizing emic genres, not just etic ones. Truth can shift as quickly as narrative distance in a story, perhaps even more quickly, as narrators choose to frame a story as fiction, nonfiction, or something in between. We do not suggest that the criterion of fact or fiction is inherently irrelevant to genre classification (if so, libraries and bookstores have their work cut out for them), so why do the same for narrative distance?

Edgar Slotkin has argued what seems commonsensical: that we hear a story differently when it is told in first person by an eyewitness than when we hear a story told second- or thirdhand (1988, 89–90). This was the case with narrative traditions of Latter-Day Saints, where a firsthand story was believed to be true and sacred, had the potential to evoke the Holy Ghost, and could edify all those who listened, while a thirdhand story was more likely to raise doubt and be dismissed, potentially doing more harm than good (Mould 2011a, 134–36). The question is whether we hear a story differently or we hear a different story.

By defining the legend as a story about someone else, legend scholars such as Jan Harold Brunvand, Bill Ellis, Gary Alan Fine, Bill Nicolaisen, and Donna Wycoff implicitly accept that a shift in narrative distance indicates a shift in genre (Brunvand 1981, 1986b; Fine 1979, 1992; Fine and Ellis 2010; Nicolaisen 1992; Wyckoff 1993). But not all shifts are created equal. The shift from first person to second is a game changer. But the shift from fifth to fourth to third is all part of the expectations for the legend, captured in the most famous acronym in the field of folklore: FOAF.

Coined by Rodney Dale in 1978 in his book *The Tumour in the Whale: A Collection of Modern Myths* and popularized by Jan Harold Brunvand in his series of collections of contemporary legends, FOAF, or friend of a friend, refers to the tendency for people to maintain relatively short narrative distance between themselves and the events of the story. We seem willing to share a story twice removed, but more than that becomes a memory exercise in attribution that undercuts any credibility for the story. So we move the story closer. Instead of a story from a coworker's sister's roommate's brother's barber, we tell a story of our coworker's sister or coworker's barber, balancing credibility with plausible deniability.

The question is whether we stop at stories twice removed. Might we reduce narrative distance even further? Are we willing, for example, to transform someone else's story into our own? Scattered evidence over the past fifty years suggests the answer is yes.

From the moment von Sydow defined memorates and fabulates, he recognized that the two could not always be distinguished from one another (1948). In 1959, Barbara Allen Woods echoed this possibility, noting that "the material of legends is very fluid and may shift in form from one category to another. The fabulat or ordinary legend may appear at times as a memorat" (1959, 11). But not until the 1960s, when A. J. M. Sykes talked to union members in the civil engineering industry, did we get proof.[8] "In every case," of their stories of heroic actions of trade union representatives against barbaric foremen, "the narrator was moved to indignation. When the active trade unionists told a story the narration would be most dramatic. The narrator would describe the incidents as though he were an eyewitness and as he told the story he would become more and more indignant" (Sykes 1965, 330). Although the majority of these incidents happened before the narrators were even born, they told the stories as if they had witnessed the events themselves.

In 1974, Linda Dégh and Andrew Vázsonyi provided English-language names to these stories, calling them pseudo-memorates and quasi-memorates. While they offered no examples of their own, they drew on the scholarship of such European scholars as K. V. Čistov, Juha Pentikäinen, Hermann Bausinger, and Will-Erick Peuckert, the last of whom "lists examples to illustrate how an experience that must have happened to a third party was converted into an 'I' and an 'us' story" (Dégh and Vázsonyi 1971, 228). In 1981, Georgina Smith picked up on this topic in her short but powerful article "Urban Legend, Personal Experience Narrative and Oral History," suggesting that such shifts are commonplace in oral histories. She mentions Sykes's work, as well as an example about the welfare system in England that echoes the welfare queen legends of the United States.

> In 1976, for example, stories about Social Security claimants being provided with colour televisions were particularly prevalent. Reporting the matter in *The Guardian* of the 3rd January, 1977, however, Michael Parkin noted: "One newspaper received a letter from a reader who said that her sister worked in a social security office and had signed the bill for a colour television set for someone on supplementary benefit. The newspaper sent a reporter hotfoot to Cardiff to interview the reader. 'Well,' she said, 'it was not really my sister who signed the bill, I just put that in my letter because it looked better. Actually, one of my friends ...'" (Smith 1981, 170)

The reader personalizes the story from a friend of a friend (FOAF) to her own sister. LeRoy Gruber does her one better by substituting himself into his story. In April 1980, Adeline Johnson was interviewing her father-in-law LeRoy Gruber for a school project when he told her a secondhand story of the death of a man in the mill whose ghost continued to haunt the mill to that day, describing the scene and the unnamed worker who found his colleague dead behind the engines. But when Adeline returned a month later to record the story again, this time with her mother-in-law (LeRoy's wife) and her foster son, Gruber told the story as if *he* had found the body (Slotkin 1988).

Darker examples exist as well. Beginning in the 1980s, Bill Ellis began documenting cases where legends prompted copycats, hoaxes, and misinterpretations that ranged from the fairly innocuous worlds of summer camp, school, and prom to threats of poisoned candy, satanic cults, and child sex abuse. Ellis discusses cases of people swearing they saw mutilated animals strung up from light poles during a cult panic in Jamestown, New York (2003, 163), much like the "scary clown" sightings that spread across the United States during the fall of 2016. Far worse, he found a case where children falsely claimed to have been sexually assaulted in ways that mirrored legends circulating at the time (232–35). These children seemed to be telling as personal experience narratives what many people told as third-person legends.

The most obvious reason for reducing narrative distance is based on the assumption that the closer a narrator is to the protagonist and eyewitness, the more believable the story.[9] Further, as analysis of the narrative tradition made clear, questioning the truth of a second- or thirdhand story is much easier than a firsthand one. Another reason for reducing narrative distance is to gain attention by making a personal connection to a compelling event (Ellis 2003, 163).

Other reasons have less to do with credibility, identity, or story content than with the aesthetics of a good narrative and the fallibility of memory. A few months after graduating from college, I found myself swapping stories with two college friends, Dick and Danny. As we shared stories both of the past and of new exploits, Danny told us about watching his high school friend try to pick up women by exploiting the fact that he had a glass eye. He would hide his eye in one hand and have one of his friends slap him on the back, only to reveal the eye as if it had shot out of his head, or slip the eye into women's drinks, saying, "I've got my eye on you." We laughed, Dick most of all. "You got to be kidding me. That was *my* friend. I told you that story in college." Danny thought for a bit and then laughed, remembering that Dick was probably right.

Danny likely began telling the story as his own not because having a friend with a glass eye was particularly prestigious or appealing but because maintaining a string of attributions can be clunky and distracting to a good story. Over time, however, memory fades. A vivid story can make us feel we were there. Over time, we can believe we actually were. The fact that Danny shared this story with the friend who first told him the story suggests that these shifts are not always conscious, intentional, or remembered. This may have been the case when Brian Williams recounted a story of being forced down in a helicopter under enemy fire in Iraq. This was true for one of the helicopters flying an hour ahead of him, but not the one he was in that followed. He reported the story accurately in 2003 when the event happened. By 2005 he suggested he witnessed the event himself, and by 2007 he described all of the helicopters being fired on, his included. The story became more descriptive and harrowing when he shared it as entertainment on late night talk shows. But when he shared it again in 2015 in his role as trusted news anchor on NBC's *Nightly News*, the uproar cost him his job.

In the welfare narrative tradition, the most common type of story told is an eyewitness story where someone observes fraud in a grocery store, luxury items in a free-clinic waiting room, or Cadillacs driving up to DSS, food pantries, or homeless shelters. In all of them, people aver, "I saw it myself." Such stories are virtually impossible to disprove, and no doubt some of the stories are true. But legend scholarship suggests many may not be, and some of the welfare narratives suggest how this may work.

Consider the story that launched this project, shared in chapter 1. After hearing Janet's story of watching a woman buy steak for her dog when she couldn't buy dog food with her food stamps, I noted my surprise and interest and asked her when and where this happened. Despite locating her story as happening "not long ago," she could not remember any of the details: not the store, the general time period, or the area of town. The details she remembered were the details of the classic welfare queen legend. She may have simply forgotten, but it is also possible that instead of localizing a story to a friend of a friend, she may have localized it much closer, to "I saw it myself."

Rarely, a person may backtrack on a story they personalized too closely, revealing this process more clearly. Ricky Thorne shared a story about a couple who committed welfare fraud.

> I know people that . . . I know this couple. They had a child, one child. And then she got pregnant again and found out it was going to be twins. So they—or she—went to the welfare office or whatever and gave them this sob story that she was separated, her husband didn't live at home. So they got welfare, food stamps; they paid for the medical part of the kids being born.
>
> But they don't check! The government or whatever does not check to see if all these things that they are being told are true.
>
> It wasn't true. She works. He works a job and mows on the side. So that's three incomes they got coming in, but they still got welfare, food stamps, and they got the medical free for those two kids.
>
> I know it for a fact. I know that it's true.

Jessica Elizondo, the Elon student who was talking with Ricky followed up: "But is this your friend, you said? How did you hear about this story?" Ricky's response is illuminating: "Yeah. Well, word of mouth through my wife. She was told, you know. I don't know, but it's true. We checked into it, and it's true."

Ricky admitted that he had never met the couple and suggested that neither had his wife. In other words, the story was already a FOAF by the time it got to him. But he felt comfortable shifting from knowing *of* a couple to knowing the couple directly and was adamant in stating, "I know it for a fact."

Eyewitness narratives are particularly well suited to such shifts in perspective. These narratives position the narrator as an observer rather than the protagonist. It would be difficult to plausibly place oneself into the story of the person who dipped his hand into a bucket of chicken and pulled out a fried rat or the person who woke up with "Welcome to the Wonderful World of Aids" on his bathroom mirror after a one-night stand, and it is doubtful anyone would want to. But with stories told from the perspective of an onlooker, observing something as common as grocery shopping, it is quite easy to slip into the story. The difference between *my friend saw this woman at the grocery* and *I saw this woman at the grocery* is problematic factually but hardly problematic to narrate and make plausible.

Eyewitness narratives dominate the narrative tradition, requiring their own distinct code to distinguish between personal *witness* or eyewitness narratives and personal *experience* narratives.[10]

It is impossible to determine how common "I saw it myself," or ISIM, stories are. Ricky Thorne is unusual in admitting that he did not know the couple personally after averring that he did. Confounding efforts to identify ISIM stories is the social science research in psychology and sociology that suggests when challenged, we are more likely to double down on our claims to save face than admit we are wrong (chap. 12).

Both FOAF and ISIM raise doubts about the accuracy of a story. Such manipulation can be troubling in terms of taking a story at face value but equally troubling for the ethnographic enterprise and the kinds of warnings scholars must make to each other from time to time about not assuming that we know better than our participants or that our participants are either misinformed, naive, delusional, or lying.

REVISITING LEGENDS

Stories deemed legends can be true, but it is the doubt they evoke, along with traditional elements and multiple variations, that distinguishes them from other stories told as true. Stories shared second- or thirdhand often raise doubt with the recognition that transmission can be imperfect, making them particularly susceptible to questioning. Firsthand stories may raise similar doubts, at any of the three areas where truth is levied: about the event, the interpretation, or the generalizability. Accordingly, while personal experience narratives and legends may be viewed as different genres emically by those who share these stories, subsuming both under the umbrella of legend analysis is not only possible but in many cases necessary.

Stories that mirror widespread legends should be attended to carefully, whether as scholar, citizen, or neighbor, particularly when those stories further stereotype and stigmatize already marginalized peoples. Some people will transform unsubstantiated legends into personal experience narratives to increase credibility, and some audiences will interpret personal experience narratives as legends because they do not trust the source. The result is that legend analysis cannot rule out stories told as personal experiences. At least emically, the legend exists in the eye of the beholder.

Such attention to how stories are heard and interpreted is particularly important as we consider in the final chapter the ways in which people have attempted to change perceptions, stereotypes, and opinions about aid recipients and aid programs in the United States through the stories they tell.

NOTES

1. *BTW* stands for *by the way, b/f* for *boyfriend*, and *CZ* for *cubic zirconia* (a common manufactured diamond substitute that costs a fraction of the price of a real diamond). The comment was posted by Strpenta.

2. Such social truths fit a consensus model of truth, as developed by Jürgen Habermas (1979).

3. Although the article remains, the comments have been removed. The former editor of the newspaper Madison Taylor believes they were inadvertently dropped when the newspaper switched from a Facebook-based system to a third-party vendor in 2015 (personal correspondence). Fortunately, I printed out the comments when I accessed the article in 2014.

4. See Bell citing scholars of both critical race theory and discourse analysis (2003, 4), and Marchevsky and Theoharris (2006, 7–8).

5. The term *generalized experience narrative* is in flux and understudied. Gary Butler appears to have coined the term "generalized experience narrative," though his definition seems more apt to what we might call a hypothetical narrative: narratives that "express what, in the past, all inhabitants believed would happen under certain circumstances or in certain areas of the community and its immediate vicinity. Such narratives contain no character per se" (1992, 53n2). Livia Polanyi uses the term "generic narrative" to describe a narrative not located in time but describing habitual actions (1989, 16), though this is complicated by the fact that Amy Shuman uses the same term to refer to stock stories (2005, 58). Pauline Greenhill employs the term "generalization narratives" to describe narratives that describe the past in general rather than specific terms, pitting them against personal experience narratives (1992, 240). Neal Norrick refers to "generalized recurrent experience," which he describes as "narrative-like representation of a recurrent shared past experience in generalized form without reference to any specific instance" (2000, 151). Labov and Waltezky weigh in as well, arguing that such utterances are not narratives at all (1967, 29). Psychologists have also studied these types of narratives, distinguishing between single event memory narratives and summary event memory narratives (e.g., Singer and Moffitt 1992).

6. Two of the three of these uses parallel what Greg Myers found in his analysis of hypothetical reported discourse: propose counterarguments and engage in thought experiments. His third, to model possible responses, was used by leaders of focus groups to suggest the kinds of answers they were looking for (1999, 579).

7. Compare to how this works with the creation of prophecy, where conjecture about what might happen in the future can become what will likely happen and then what *will* happen (Mould 2003, 139–43).

8. This is the first published instance I have been able to find. Research in other fields may well have turned up others, particularly in oral history, as Georgina Smith suggests (1981).

9. The reasons for distancing oneself further from the story are less obvious and likely less common. Georgina Smith suggests such moves can be understood as a signal of "psychological discomfort with the content of the legend or the setting of its performance" (1981, 172), a tendency similar to the "my friend has this problem" move to distance oneself from the stigmatizing or embarrassing topic noted earlier in the text.

10. See Mould (2020) for a more in-depth discussion of how eyewitness narratives influence stories about public assistance, particularly in the context of recall, narrative completion, and narrative distance.

TWELVE

—⁄⁄⁄—

OVERTHROWING THE QUEEN

IN 1995, AS POLITICAL RHETORIC about changing welfare as we know it was moving into full swing, the Jewish Council on Urban Affairs in Illinois organized a Welfare Truth Squad. The seven men on the squad were former aid recipients who had lost their benefits in recent cutbacks. Professional storytellers were brought in to help the men tell their stories in ways that would be most persuasive to their audiences (Terry 1995). Around the same time in Maine, the Women's Economic Security Project began efforts to counter the antiwelfare rhetoric that had become so pervasive during welfare reform debates in Congress. One of their events was to pair legislators with aid recipients for a Walk-a-Mile project. A Republican legislator who was against expanding public assistance was paired with a young woman who was struggling to complete her college degree. After the walk, the legislator became a supporter of removing TANF's restrictions on higher education, which ultimately led to progressive legislation in Maine to promote education and skills training (Price 2005, 92–94). More recently but farther away, the Facebook group We Are Beneficiaries began providing a platform for aid recipients in New Zealand to share their stories of living with the help of public assistance. The stories have gone viral on social media and have inspired national debates with an eye toward reform.[1]

While the Truths Squad's impact is anecdotal, the We Are Beneficiaries campaign is affecting national conversations, and the Walk-a-Mile program helped lead to legislative change.[2] Cutting out the middleman can be effective. The legislator in Maine had surely heard stories of aid recipients before from government administrators and directors of nonprofits, but it was when he talked directly to an aid recipient that he began to shift his perspective. Similarly, the only success stories aid recipients shared were from other recipients, not aid providers (chap. 6).

Of course, aid recipients do not wait for aid providers and researchers to provide the opportunity to tell their stories. Delia Taylor regularly tells her story about living with public assistance to coworkers who dismiss all aid recipients as lazy. Carla Robinson shares hers with her church group. Still others enter the volatile virtual worlds of online and social media (chap. 10 and 11). Overall, however, there is general dearth of personal experience stories shared by aid recipients themselves. Lorraine Higgins and Lisa Brush explored this phenomenon in the context of welfare and public debate, arguing that marginalized or "subordinated" groups rarely have access to public platforms, and when they do, they are often dismissed by "experts" (2006, 695).

This is not to say that aid recipients are not engaged in resistance, however. As Patricia Ewick and Susan Silbey document, some aid recipients work around the system, as when one aid recipient responded to court-ordered community service by simply counting the work she was already doing with her church. Such strategies are powerful for the individual—often meaning the difference between making ends meet and having one's utilities turned off or getting evicted. But as the authors note, "Successful dodges, ruses, and feints such as these rarely leave a structural imprint" (1998, 13).

There are other weapons however.

Some of these weapons are wielded by aid recipients, others by aid providers and volunteers, and still others by concerned community members. Researchers also have an arsenal of resources that can and should be deployed to help create a public discourse that challenges rather than trades in stereotypes and spurious legends. This chapter explores many of these varied resources and draws on relevant scholarship in folklore, anthropology, psychology, rhetoric, and strategic communication to examine and provide strategies for ensuring that our understanding of welfare is shaped by a more inclusive narrative tradition than the one that often dominates public discourse.

LEGENDS AND PARODY AS WEAPONS OF THE FOLK

After Hurricane Katrina, evacuees in the Ninth Ward who felt abandoned by the government told stories of how the government dynamited the levees that protected their homes so that they could stop the rising floodwaters from damaging the homes of the wealthy (Lindahl 2012, 149). When the surgeon general issued warnings about cigarettes, African Americans shared rumors about tobacco companies owned by the KKK targeting the black community with menthol cigarettes that would speed up the development of lung cancer (Turner 1992, 431,438). When unhealthy fast-food restaurants moved into poor, largely black neighborhoods, people began telling stories of fried chicken restaurants sterilizing black men with their food and corporate offices run by racists (Turner 1992, 438).

The legend is a powerful tool of the folk. Like the biblical story of David and Goliath, underdogs can rise up to challenge more powerful foes when armed with small, simple, but powerful weapons. Of course, those weapons can be wielded against the disempowered and destitute as well. One counterresponse is the antilegend that operates as antidote through parody.[3] A classic example emerged in 1994 just as personal computers and the internet were exploding into homes across the United States. Fears of the uncharted and mostly unknown world of the World Wide Web, created two years earlier, were ripe for exploitation. Into this fertile landscape came the Good Times email virus.

> FYI, a file, going under the name "Good Times" is being sent to some internet users who subscribe to on-line services (Compuserve, Prodigy and America On Line). If you should receive this file, do not download it! Delete it immediately. I understand that there is a virus included in that file, which if downloaded to your personal computer, will ruin all of your files. (Jones 1998)

The message was a hoax; the damage of the virus was that it automatically emailed itself to all the user's contacts, flooding the system with longer and longer strings of data. As word spread that the message was bogus, antilegends emerged. Some borrowed lines from the popular St. Jude charity chain letter, others from the "Lights Out" gang initiation legend, but in all variations, the warnings were either hyperdramatic ("The instructions in this message must be followed exactly or an ill fate will destroy you!") or ludic ("My sysop's mother got one of these messages, opened it, and her Kaypro exploded! She is still sweeping up the pieces off her living room floor").[4] The email was still well enough known that ten years later, a full-blown parody emerged called "Bad Times" that threatened to demagnetize your credit cards, recalibrate your freezer so your ice cream melts, give your new phone number to ex-boyfriends and ex-girlfriends, and "drink all your beer and leave its socks out on the coffee table when company comes over" (Christensen 2018).

Welfare legends have spawned some of their own antilegends as well. Of the nine examples shared from social media, there were two folk treatises, five memes (figs. 12.1–12.7), one cartoon (fig. 12.8), and one narrative (discussed later in this chapter). The treatises, memes, and cartoon were all cast with a negative valence, skewering or satirizing conservatives, the wealthy, and corporations. Two of the examples can be traced to Someecards, an online company brokering in humorous greeting card memes. Someecards is not fighting the progressive fight, however, but serving a market. Of the five Someecard examples I received from email and Facebook, the other three were clearly antiwelfare, addressing some of the standard complaints about drugs tests, iPhones, and taxes for lazy aid recipients (chap. 9). I happened upon an eighth example online: a blogger said he found the trick-or-treat cartoon circulating on social media as a pair, where the original had been edited to provide a counterargument (Stevens 2012) (fig. 12.8).

I'm tired of paying for lazy idiots on welfare!

I'm tired of paying the salary of Supreme Court Justice who has a vested interest in success of Monsanto. I I'm tired of paying for the health care of Wal-Mart workers because Wal-Mart won't pay its employees living wage or provide insurance. I'm tired of paying Israel $8 million a day. I'm tired paying oil industry $22 Million a day.

And I am REALLY tired of hearing all the problems in the country being blamed on people who are struggling to make it through one more day. The vast majority of whom are themselves tired of being on welfare and would give anything to be self-sufficient.

Mary Elizabeth Grey

Storm is Coming

Figure 12.1. "I'm tired of paying for lazy idiots on welfare!"

Last year, 44 Americans were shot by Muslim terrorists.

By comparison, 52 Americans were shot by toddlers.

Which raises the question: Why isn't the government doing more to protect us from toddlers?

Think about it. They don't share our values. They barely speak English. They steal our welfare. They have no marketable skills. They're prone to angry outbursts. Worst of all? Most of them aren't even Christians. How long until we say enough is enough and deport these free-loading parasites once and for all???

Figure 12.2. Toddlers: freeloading parasites.

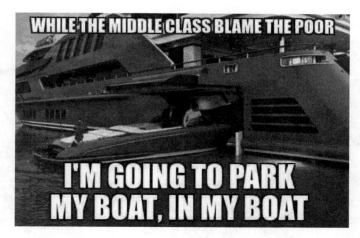

I suspect there is an even
bigger boat to park that boat.

Figure 12.3. Meme: blaming the poor.

Figure 12.4. Meme: corporate welfare.

Figure 12.5. Meme: corporate
welfare tax complaint.

Figure 12.6. Meme: "Conservative
Jesus" refuses to feed the hungry.[5]

Figure 12.7. Meme: "Conservative
Jesus" demands self-sufficiency.

Figure 12.8. Trick-or-treating parody cartoon.

In the grand scheme of things, however, these antilegends paled in comparison to the hegemonic narratives on social media critiquing welfare and its recipients, with only 9 pro-welfare examples out of the 130 examples of welfare lore shared on social media (see chap. 9). Considering that the political range of the family, friends, colleagues, and students who sent me examples skewed heavily to the political Left, we cannot blame this imbalance on a sample size that ignored liberals, progressives, and Democrats.

Expanding beyond social media to the internet, more antilegends can be found, but existence online does not equate to viewership or a shared folk tradition, and again, the overwhelming majority reinforce rather than challenge the stereotypes.[6] So while there are people creating memes and jokes that speak against the welfare queen legends and stereotypes, they are in the minority, and their work appears to be falling on deaf ears. One reason may be the deep ideologies about race and class that underlie these stories.[7] Unlike the Good Times legend that fed on anxieties over computer hacking that were (1) relatively new, (2) confined to a specific aspect of computer use, and (3) depersonalized, stories of welfare fraud are (1) long-standing, (2) extend to broader issues of poverty, employment, and morality, and (3) challenge constructions of identity not just of "the other" but of ourselves.

As Fine and Turner have argued, there are three ways that rumors and legends disappear: boredom, saturation, or intervention (2001, 69–71). If the fears and anxieties become irrelevant to us, we can be expected to bore of the stories and no longer tell them, rendering them dormant if not dead. More controversial is the assumption that legends thrive on novelty, so once everyone has heard them, the topic becomes saturated, the interest sated, and the story disappears. So far, however, fears of people gaming the system remain, and decades of welfare queen stories do not appear to have exhausted our interest in them. For the moment, then, we are left with intervention as an active strategy to counter welfare legends.

INTERVENTION

Uniting targets of legends can create strange bedfellows. Aligning the poor who are maligned by welfare queen legends with CEOs and politicians who are accused of racism and corruption seems to flip the world on its head, especially since legends about racist companies and government conspiracies often emerge as responses to threats perceived by *minority* groups while legends about welfare queens emerged as responses to threats perceived by *majority* ones. Yet there are lessons to be learned from how companies and politicians have fought back against unsubstantiated legends and rumors that can be useful in considering ways to overthrow the stereotype of the welfare queen.

The range of responses extends from silence to showy public denials, with most cases falling somewhere in between. In her research of rumors and legends about corporations shared within African American communities, Patricia Turner contacted the corporations for information about what they had done to respond to these stories (1993). Cigarette companies like Philip Morris seem to have done little to counter the rumors that they were owned by the KKK. Church's Fried Chicken was similarly silent in the face of rumors that their chicken was injected with chemicals that would sterilize black men, a plot explained by the company's presumed ties to the KKK. Yet when rumors of ties to the KKK spread to Popeye's Fried Chicken—this time in the form of stories about campaign donations to KKK Grand Dragon David Duke—the company responded forcefully with a press conference and flyers distributed throughout the community offering a "$25,000 cash reward for information which results in the successful criminal prosecution of the instigator of this lie." When the makers of Tropical Fantasy faced similar rumors about sterilizing black men, they went to court, a tactic used by other companies, such as Proctor and Gamble in the face of accusations of devil worship. Both companies had compelling evidence that while the rumors may not have been started by the competition, they were fueled by them. Both companies also enlisted community leaders to speak out against the rumors.[8]

Rebuttal not only feels justified—righteously countering false claims and attacks—it often seems necessary. US government officials certainly felt so when they created a rumor-management clinic during World War II (Turner 1993, 1) or more recently when the State Department International Information Program issued a statement in response to false rumors that Jews did not report to work at the World Trade Center on September 11, 2001, because they were responsible for the terrorist attack (Goldstein 2009, 23–40). Politicians regularly face this dilemma. John Kerry has been criticized for not responding to the bogus stories created by the Swift Boat Veterans for Truth sooner, suggesting his response was too little, too late to save his presidential campaign. Barack Obama's efforts to combat the so-called birthers who question the validity of his Hawaiian birth certificate has been evaluated more positively. His actions combined (1) a forceful rebuttal with humor to highlight the ridiculousness of the claim, (2) limited direct mention of the rumor to avoid creating another news cycle repeating the legend, and (3) a website with the facts for those seeking such information (Turner 2018).

Even churches have entered the fray. When rumors emerged in the 1960s that the president of the Church of Jesus Christ of Latter-Day Saints, John Taylor, prophesied in 1885 that the church would be ruined at the hands of black men, the church issued a formal denunciation, though not until the 1970s after the rumors had become widespread. They did the same in 2008 when old legends about Mormon youth having served as generals in heaven before being born resurfaced when President Gordon B. Hinckley died. Local church leaders have attempted similar, small-scale interventions when rumors circulate among their ward or congregation (Mould 2011a, 18–20).

In the end, however, a road map built from case studies remains hazy. General consensus among strategic communications scholars is that organizations should "fight rumors aggressively to prevent problems such as those experienced by Proctor & Gamble's connection to the devil" (Coombs 1995, 459), recommending aggressive denial strategies to do so (Coombs 2015, 152). Yet while Newsom, Kirk, and Kruckeberg concur that "when rumors do start, you need to act immediately to control or counteract them," they also point out that when rumors start from "rogue websites," "engaging the operator of the site might not only be ineffective and a waste of time, but what you say could be distorted and used against you" (2012, 330). Reflecting on decades of research into rumors and legends about corporations, the folklorists Gary Alan Fine and Patricia Turner declared that formal rumor control does not seem to do any harm; it just may not do any good (2001, 70–71).

So is rebuttal better than silence? If so, is a particular method of rebuttal more successful than another? It is tempting to create a neat and tidy story from the Church's and Popeye's examples by pointing out that the company that stayed silent lost sales and was ultimately bought out by Popeye's, the company that spoke out. Perhaps not surprisingly, the PR firm handling the Popeye's rumor declared their rebuttal strategy a success, though they also admitted that the rumor could appear again the next time David Duke ran for office (Turner 1992, 429). But correlation is not causation. And without a clear control group, it is impossible to say. Experiments are needed.

BELIEF

Psychologists have led the charge in creating experiments to understand how we respond to rumor and legend. Surveying the past half century of research and conducting additional experiments of their own, Nicholas DiFonzo and Prashant Bordio developed recommendations for rumor management.[9] First and foremost, except in rare cases where the person denying a rumor or legend is not seen as honest and credible, a company should always rebut a false rumor or legend and the sooner the better. Further, the rebuttal should come from someone viewed as neutral, honest, and appropriately positioned to make the rebuttal. A conciliatory rather than inflammatory tone helps ensure the rebuttal is effective. Finally, the rebuttal should include sufficient context of the original rumor or legend so that people who have not heard the rumor will not become suspicious and distrustful of a claim of innocence in the absence of an accusation. These strategies should not only reduce belief in the rumor or legend but also decrease anxiety about the fears underlying them (DiFonzo and Bordia 2007, 102–3, 205–27).

While compelling, these findings are challenged by an extensive body of research that suggests our brains trick us into confirming what we already believe and ignoring the rest. Under such circumstances, even the best laid plans at refuting a rumor or legend may fall on deaf ears.

The first shot across the bow came in 1960 when the psychologist Paul Wason asked participants to consider the numbers 2, 4, and 6 and identify the pattern. Each participant was to offer up their own three numbers, after which the researcher would indicate whether the numbers conformed to the pattern or not. Once the participant thought they had figured out the pattern, they were to write it down. Out of the twenty-nine participants, six reached the correct conclusion the first time they tried (with the fastest doing it after offering only five sets of numbers) and ten with their second guess. After that, success tapered off dramatically. Only four participants found the correct rule on their third guess, and none of the remaining nine were able to find the correct answer.

One might imagine that the results were determined by the participant's knowledge of mathematics, but the sophistication of the guesses by participants who guessed incorrectly defies such a conclusion. Rather, what Wason found was that the students who did not succeed rarely if ever attempted to disprove their original hypothesis. Further, over half of those who did not initially succeed kept trying *not* by throwing out the initial hypothesis but by trying new numbers that would help them refine it. That is, they assumed their original hypothesis was correct but was either too specific or not specific enough.

Since then, scholars have tested the tendency to confirm one's initial assumptions rather than attempt to falsify them, identifying a dizzying array of mental gymnastics that we go through to uphold early conclusions. One of the most relevant was a study at Stanford University that took forty-eight students, half of whom were strongly in favor of the death penalty, half of whom were against. They were given two sets of data, one that supported the death penalty as a deterrent, one that refuted it. Consistently, participants accepted data that fit their argument and picked apart data that did not, confirming their original beliefs and, in 23 percent of the cases, becoming even more convinced of their stance (Lord, Ross, and Lepper 1979, 2105).

That tendency to become more convinced of one's argument in the face of competing evidence—what has become known as confirmation bias—became even more disturbing when the results of a series of experiments published in 2010 made it clear that not only are we more likely to believe new information that confirms what we already believe and dismiss information that we do not, but we may become more convinced we are right in the face not just of competing evidence but of *clear evidence to the contrary.*

The political scientists Brendan Nyhan and Jason Reiffler developed four experiments to find out what happens when efforts are made to correct false or unsubstantiated beliefs about a political issue. Unlike previous studies, they used realistic modes of communication, presenting participants with news stories that provided the correction to the false or unsubstantiated information. For people who did not hold strong beliefs one way or the other, the correction was often effective. However, for people with strong beliefs that a story was true, corrective information that showed it was not was either ignored or strengthened their original beliefs (2010).

Three years later, Nyhan and Reiffler along with Peter Ubel revisited the question with the topic of health care (2013). Specifically, they wanted to know whether a news story that corrected Sarah Palin's statements about death panels was effective in combating the false information. One group read a story with Palin's false accusations. Another group read a story that included Palin's false accusations but immediately provided evidence to refute her claims. Once again, he found confirmation bias, where people who were opposed to Palin or liked Palin but had little political knowledge were more likely to believe the correction. But politically knowledgeable Palin supporters did not just *not* believe the correction; they became even more convinced that death panels were real. They called this the backfire effect.

Confirmation bias and the backfire effect lend weight to the popular belief that in some cases denials can keep a story in the news cycle long after it would have naturally died away, cement the story in people's minds, spread it farther afield, and introduce it to people who had not yet encountered it, thereby not just proving ineffective but making the problem worse. These theories also suggest that belief systems may have little to do with facts and more to do with the identities bound up in one position or another. Climate change deniers, for example, may refuse to entertain scientific evidence because to do so would align them with liberals rather than conservatives, in the same way that pro-choice advocates may refuse to consider ethical and religious arguments about life because to do so would signal a similar shift in political identity.

Content poses one challenge; source, another. If the source is already suspect, denials may serve as confirmation rather than alleviation of guilt (Turner 1993). The same may be true not just for specific companies but for the mass media more generally. "If one's distrust of the 'lamestream media' is great enough, such debunking only confirms the story in question" (Frank 2015, 328). In an era of "alternative facts" and "fake news," distrust is easily sewn and applied liberally to fact and fiction alike (see Frank 2018 and Lowthorp 2018). At best, however, research into belief and trust is only half the picture. Any clear path toward understanding how to address misleading, biased, or simply false rumors or legends requires consideration of another, particularly tricky variable: memory.

MEMORY

In his book *An Epidemic of Rumor*, John Lee reviewed some of the experiments about memory and recall related to correcting widespread misperceptions (2014). Those studies revealed that we are more likely to remember familiar statements as true. Within spans as short as thirty minutes, people went from correctly identifying a statement as false to remembering it as true. Importantly, the reverse was not the case. People did not misremember true information as false. Repetition breeds trust; repeating false information, therefore, even to debunk it, risks spreading it as the truth.

Another study found that using language that has a clear opposite was helpful for memory. People are more likely to correctly remember "not smart" than "not responsible" since "not smart" has an obvious synonym unrelated to the parent word—"dumb"—whereas "not responsible" does not. The result is that people are more likely to drop the "not" and remember the characteristic as simply "responsible." From these studies, Lee developed a set of rules that suggest a normative approach to dealing with rumor and legend: "(1) if we naturally assume that familiar statements are true and (2) we tend to misremember false statements as true and (3) if bi-polar descriptions are better remembered than their uni-polar counterparts, then (4) accurate, oft-repeated, positive descriptions are superior to efforts made in rehashing narratives only to deny their veracity" (2014, 178). I say "normative" because as the case studies show, different groups, different key actors, and different messages affect the degree to which one strategy will work better than another.

SYNTHESIS

Returning to the central question "To rebut or not to rebut," belief studies say yes; memory studies say no. Belief studies suggest we can alter belief for those who are not already committed when the message comes from a trustworthy source, but these studies rarely account for the passage of time. Memory studies, on the other hand, recognize that rumors and legends cycle back to us days, weeks, months, even years later, suggesting that we may remember false information as true, despite clear evidence to the contrary. Adding one more layer of complication is the backfire effect, where rebuttals can force ideologically committed people to double down on beliefs that are unsupported by evidence. If some form of rebuttal is deemed useful, belief studies suggest it should include the rumor itself as context. From the perspective of memory and recall, however, repeating false information should be avoided at all costs. With such fundamental contradictions, a one-size-fits-all approach to combatting false or misleading rumors and legends is clearly impossible. Finding a reasonable approach for a specific rumor or legend, however, may not be.

IMPLICATIONS FOR THE WELFARE QUEEN

Stories of welfare queens differ from many rumors and legends in having found a comfortable niche in American thought, operating more like a deep-seated stereotype than a flash-in-the-pan rumor or legend with a relatively short shelf life. By virtue of these stories having been around for over forty years and having antecedents that extend back much further, immediate rebuttal is no longer an option. Further, it is unclear how effective such an option would have been. After all, mainstream media outlets in the 1970s *did* accuse Reagan of embellishment from the moment he began telling his story. The problem was that the real case of Linda Taylor was also capturing headlines, along with other isolated cases of welfare fraud, which confirmed Reagan's story conceptually if not specifically for many readers.

Further, these legends tap into deep-seated ideologies about race, class, the economy, morality, and the American dream. As such, welfare stories are particularly susceptible to confirmation bias. Like the study about Obamacare and death panels, the topic of welfare is a similarly politicized hot-button issue that evokes strong emotions. Counternarratives and "corrections" to the welfare queen legend could be effective for those who identify as liberal or progressive or who have low political knowledge about issues of poverty and public assistance and therefore are not already committed one way or the other. But for those who believe the legends, who are convinced that aid recipients are lazy and commit fraud, well-supported rebuttals may backfire and drive people even further into their corners.

Another important difference for welfare legends is that they compose a corpus of stories that as often as not are shared as secondhand or even firsthand experiences with thousands of culprits. There is not one company or politician or celebrity to point a finger at. The power and danger of the welfare queen legend is that she is everywhere. Debunk one story, and a person merely needs to pivot to another. This is no doubt one reason why pointing out the discrepancies in Reagan's story about Linda Taylor had little effect on belief in the larger "truth" of his story. Another is the fact that some of the stories *are* true. Linda Taylor did commit fraud, and much worse. The same is true for Barbara Jean Williams and Dorothy Woods (chap. 7). And there continue to be cases of egregious welfare fraud. It is not that the individual story is not true but rather that one story can spawn hundreds of others that get localized in new places, making the single case appear widespread.

The clear black-and-white divide of truth from fiction in stories about satanic rituals for Proctor and Gamble or fried chicken that sterilizes African American men can be denounced as unambiguously false. These companies can make clear, declarative statements about what is true and not true about their product. That luxury is not open to advocates fighting against a more complex corpus of legends, such as those surrounding welfare in the United States. Overthrowing the queen, then, is less about trying to prove welfare fraud does not exist than that fraud is rare enough that a dramatically different story is needed.

Figuring out what that story should be or how to deploy it is far from simple. Responding to a person's welfare queen story with a counternarrative is likely to have little effect on its own, resulting in each party agreeing there are many types of aid recipient but leaving assured that their story is more generalizable and valid. More troubling is the maxim about legends: that as long as the fear and anxiety exist, so too will the legends that provide a means to discuss them. A strategy that addresses the symptom but not the cause would appear doomed to failure. Rather than this final dictum rendering any concerted efforts to overthrow the queen impossible, however, it provides a strategy for finding a better story to tell.

EMPATHY AND COHERENCE

In their book *Made to Stick*, Chip Heath and Dan Heath describe a series of studies that tested the effect of stories and statistics on people's willingness to donate to an international charity for impoverished children. In the first study, participants who were given statistics about world hunger gave at a rate of 22 percent, but those who were given a story about a young girl suffering malnutrition gave at a rate of 47 percent, more than double the statistics group. In the second experiment, participants were given both the story and the statistics to determine whether the combination of the specific emotional story with the scale of the statistics would encourage even greater giving. It did not. In fact, participants gave only 28 percent, barely more than the statistics-only group. A story buttressed with statistics and facts was not just less effective but much less (almost 20 percent less). In the third and final experiment, participants were asked questions that would put them in either an analytical frame of mind or an emotional one.[10] Then both groups were given the story of the young girl. Those primed to think about feelings gave at a rate similar to the initial group who read her story (46 percent), but those who were primed to think analytically gave at 25 percent, only 3 percent more than the initial group that only got statistics. In other words, the same story was met with dramatically different results simply by the degree to which people were encouraged to think analytically or emotionally (Heath and Heath 2007, 165–67).

Statistics were found to be similarly impotent in a study conducted about perceptions of welfare. Participants were given an unflattering story of a woman with three children who had been on welfare for thirteen years. Half of the participants were also given statistics that made the amount of time the woman was receiving aid appear either typical (fifteen years, which was not true) or atypical (two years, which was true). The statistics had no impact on the participants. Both groups generalized from the story to the entire group so that a single negative story, despite data to the contrary, was used to define all aid recipients (Hamill, Wilson, and Nisbett 1980). Once again, stories trumped statistics.

The strategy for encouraging people to view aid recipients more charitably, then, would seem to be to toss statistics out the window and focus on emotions, something stories are particularly effective at doing. Such an approach appears to be supported by research in confirmation bias, including a study by political scientists who found that providing facts about welfare had either no impact or at best a transitory one on correcting misinformation and reshaping opinion (Kuklinski et al. 2000).

The critics of a strategy that tosses facts by the wayside can be heard shouting as far back as the Enlightenment and even earlier to ancient Greece. Reason was supposed to replace emotion and religion. Storytelling too often played on the emotions of its listeners, manipulating them to the will of the storyteller and leading them to faulty conclusions. The famed educator Horace Mann similarly warned that reading novels caused the mind to surrender itself "to the interest and excitement of the story, while the powers by which we discern tendencies and balance probabilities, are discarded" (cited by Smith 1998, 367). Although he was speaking specifically of novels, his concerns echo complaints levied against any kind of storytelling, due to the belief that storytelling encourages artifice and manipulation in the service of entertainment.

And yet, as Walter Fisher has argued, reason and narrative need not sit opposed. Rather, stories establish their own degrees of reason and logic. Arguing against a rational-world paradigm, Fisher claims people evaluate the stories they hear based on their own experiences and values. He termed this process of evaluation "narrative rationality" (1989). Fisher says we typically do not use classical logic and reason when communicating; Kimberly Smith goes one step farther, arguing not only that we do not but also that we need not:

> Contemporary anxiety about racism, sexism and other judgment-impairing moral faults continues to undermine our faith in the politics of reason; such biases, we fear, may distort even the most rationalized decision making processes. Storytelling is a potential solution to this problem. Stories, as the abolitionists recognized, can give us access to alternative perspectives and provide moral exemplars, influencing our moral reasoning by addressing the emotive, noncognitive bases of moral judgment. In this sense, stories are less a supplement to rational argument than a replacement for it; we tell stories precisely because argument has failed, because we need some other means to influence judgment. (Smith 1998, 377)

Key to this effectiveness, however, is coherence. Fisher notes that people are more likely to believe a story if it has narrative, structural, material, and char-acterological coherence (1989, 47). In other words, effective stories must appear not only externally valid to the listener but internally valid as well. This can be a tall order; good storytelling is an art and skill. Yet it is an even taller order for aid recipients whose stories so often recount physical, emotional, and psychological trauma that can result in gaps, breaks, silences, and nonlinear structures difficult to follow (see Goldstein 2012).

There are dozens of other criteria that people use to evaluate effective narra-tives, many of which are both story specific and culture specific. Empathy and coherence are simply two characteristics that are particularly useful in consid-ering the effectiveness of political stories at the macro level when deciding the general parameters of a persuasive story. Storytellers have to consider the range of additional criteria as they prepare to share a story in a particular context with a particular audience, recognizing that even empathy is not unproblematic, ironi-cally risking alienation by preserving a distance between people who receive aid and those who do not (see Shuman 2005, 144–45). But with an eye trained on the macro level, there are three key steps for identifying effective stories about welfare in order to overthrow the legends of the welfare queen: (1) identify the canonical narratives, (2) identify the fears and anxieties, and (3) identify alternative narra-tives that sidestep or alleviate those fears and counter the canonical narratives.

DEVELOPING AN EFFECTIVE COUNTERNARRATIVE

Identify the Canonical Narratives

Canonical narratives describe those stories that have come to dominate the narrative tradition within a society. The welfare queen legend is the obvious contender for one of the major canonical narratives about welfare, operating also as a hegemonic narrative that reinforces the status quo. These narratives are framed by fraud. However, there are other canonical narratives in welfare debates including well-honed counternarratives. Foremost among these is the counternarrative of the welfare mom who pulled herself out of poverty. These stories are framed by independence and hard work. These are the "welfare success stories" heralded by Bill Clinton as evidence that his welfare reform was a success and repeated by George W. Bush of women who traded "a welfare check for a paycheck" (Marchevsky and Theoharis 2005, 9; see also Carcusson 2006). Both stories promote a similar story line, one where success depends not on systemic or structural issues but on individuals. The first runs counter to the American dream and is censored; the second upholds the American dream and is rewarded. Both miss the boat. In the first, the poor can be ignored because of their shortcomings, in the second, because the system works, and no further effort is necessary. Demonized or lionized, the poor end up marginalized. The canonical narratives about welfare provide little room for stories that present a more complicated picture.

Part of the reason is that institutional settings often restrict the range of narratives that can be heard. As Amy Shuman and Carol Boehmer found, refugees seeking asylum in the United States had to abandon their own cultural norms for storytelling and, in many cases, abandon their personal reactions to their trauma, to tell a story that fit bureaucratic expectation in order to be effective (2004). Francesca Polletta found the same in her review of the stories told in court during sex discrimination cases. Judges were receptive to stories that either women are just like men and want high-paying jobs too, or women are not like men and don't want high-paying jobs, but not that women are different than men and want high-paying jobs (2006, 15). Those more complicated, nuanced, divergent, and subversive stories either fell on deaf ears or were heard within the narrow range of the two dominant canonical stories. The same was true for battered women: "Lawyers, judges, and scholars hear the stories that battered women tell. But they hear them through familiar plot lines with stock characters. A battered woman tells her story of abuse and is heard as a passive, powerless, incapacitated victim, incapable of reasoned action. Or she is heard as unapologetic and provocative, hardly a victim" (124). Rarely is she heard as an individual, both victim and survivor.[11]

Identify the Fears

The stories told about welfare recipients in chapter 3 and the chapters in section 3 reveal a number of anxieties and fears held by nonrecipient storytellers that the most effective counternarratives will have to address, key among them

- fear of working hard and receiving little while others work little and receive lots,
- fear of immigrants taking what is "ours,"
- fear that the American dream does not work,
- fear that if poverty is not about individual failing, then it could happen to me, and
- fear that public aid is a disincentive to work.

These fears can further be understood within political ideologies that guide self-professed liberals and conservatives in the United States. Research in moral foundations theory suggests that liberals are more likely to hold values of fairness and protection from harm, while conservatives are more likely to hold values of loyalty, respect for authority, and purity (Graham et al. 2009; Haidt and Graham 2007). Accordingly, one might expect liberals to be particularly anxious about working hard while others do not, while conservatives might be particularly anxious about immigrants and fraud. Related research in moral reframing suggests that by evoking the values most likely to be held by audiences, speakers have a significantly greater chance of shifting opinion in the arguments and stories they share (Feinberg and Willer 2015; Voelkel and Feinberg 2018). Considering audiences and the types of values and fears they may harbor is crucial to whether a particular story will find purchase and shift perspectives and opinions.

Identify Alternative Narratives

On April 27, 1953, Dwight D. Eisenhower signed Executive Order 10450. While it never mentioned homosexuality specifically, it ordered the firing of government workers engaged in "sexual perversion" and other immoral acts. The result was that thousands of LGBTQ employees lost their jobs and thousands more were barred from federal employment. The order was in lockstep with how homosexuality was framed in legislation and popular discourse at the time: as criminally and morally deviant.

Almost exactly one year later, the Supreme Court desegregated schools in *Brown v. Board of Education,* a decision that would serve as a powerful clarion call of the civil rights movement. The civil rights movement articulated a clear narrative of equal rights for all. It was a story that was not written specifically for the LGBTQ community, but gay rights activists embraced the story of civil rights as a relevant master narrative that could transform a story about morality into a story about justice. The move was a powerful one, helping the gay rights movement initially win major legal battles and eventually win popular opinion so that by 2018, 75 percent of Americans thought gay or lesbian relations between consenting adults should be legal, up from just 36 percent in 1986 (Niedwiecki 2014; Gallup 2018).

A similar strategy was used even earlier. In the first half of the nineteenth century, abolitionists were wringing their hands. Reasoned arguments to slavery proponents about the immorality of slavery had fallen on deaf ears, and emotional appeals were viewed suspiciously as manipulative. The abolitionists' solution was to reframe the issue by borrowing one of the most effective and widespread narrative types of the time: Christian conversion narratives. Conversion narratives were identifiable and familiar. Slavery proponents would not only have heard these stories in church; they would have had their own narrative as well. Telling slave stories like conversion stories allowed slavery proponents to see themselves in the story from the perspective of slaves, thereby creating space for empathy. Like conversion narratives that did not wallow in the sinful past but focused on the path to redemption, so too did these new slave narratives. Counterintuitively, they created empathy not by focusing on the horrors of slavery but by depicting a familiar journey to freedom and liberty (Smith 1998).

Both the abolitionists and the gay rights activists found a new way to tell their story. They did so by finding a familiar cultural narrative already well established within society and applying it to a new topic. In doing so, they reframed the conversation.

That is one strategy.

There is another, one that begins in familiar territory, initially recapitulating the canonical narrative but then diverging from expectations by suggesting a new conclusion. For this strategy to work, the story must cohere with what Walter Fisher would refer to as "narrative rationality" (1989). In other words, the new ending has to make sense and even appear obvious when the end has been reached.

Both strategies exploit the familiar to challenge expectations. The danger of the first is that it risks running parallel to the hegemonic narrative, allowing both to exist. In such a landscape, the new narrative has an uphill battle trying to unseat the hegemonic narrative already well known and trusted by listeners. The danger of the second strategy is that by initially evoking a familiar narrative and then subverting it, one risks a defensive response from the listener who is asked to revise their canonical narrative to allow for a different conclusion. As studies in confirmation bias make clear, such efforts can have disastrous effects, making matters worse rather than better. No solution is perfect, but both offer promising paths forward.

A NEW NARRATIVE

When Bad Things Happen to Good People

"I was a CNA at Moses Cone," Diane Clemens begins.

First I went to White Oak Manor. I worked there for ten years, and I left there and went part-time for White Oak for seven. Then I went to Greensboro for twenty.

And I had got really sick on the job, then, you know, didn't know, had no idea. They didn't have no idea what it was, but I went blind. And so, while I was blind in the hospital, they had diagnosed me with type 2 diabetes. And the doctor had said that's probably why my eyesight had . . . I had lost my eyesight coming from the diabetes.

I had to stay in the hospital for like five weeks because my sugar was so . . . It was like, it wouldn't register; it had went off the meter. And they couldn't get it to, back to normal, so I had to stay five weeks to, so they could try medicine, see what type of medicine I was going to be on and to control it, to get it down. And then they got it down to where I could go home and be on insulin and sugar pills.

I didn't go back to nursing because they was saying that I had to do a lot of walking. You know, nursing, you had to walk back and forward, back and forward, and it had . . . The diabetes had messed up this leg of mine where I couldn't. It was swelling a lot when I walked, and it started . . . Fluid started draining out of it. And then they didn't know where that was coming from. Then I ended up . . . They sent me to Chapel Hill for that. And when I went to Chapel Hill, they said it was a disease called edema. Something from . . . trigger from diabetes.

And the doctor down there said that I probably wouldn't be able to . . . I could function in my job but by then it swelled so much that he would refer me to come out my job and draw disability.

And it was devastating for me because I like to work with people. And then I didn't want to . . . At my age, I didn't want to be at home all the time, constantly just being at home with nothing to do. So I was really upset and angry. I got, went into a deep depression while I was out of work, and I had to go to therapy for that. And I just couldn't handle it that well. Just, it was just, because I was eating healthy and I was just wanting answers. Why I had to get diabetes? I was exercising every day, and I couldn't understand. And the doctor said it was in my genes because my mother has it, and she have three siblings that have it, and her mother has it.

The story fits a master narrative that became part of the cultural zeitgeist in 1978 when Harold Kushner published his book *When Bad Things Happen to Good People*. The narrative speaks directly against the idea that people should be blamed for their lot in life. But that story of blame is not easily overturned. When folklorists, literary scholars, Jungian psychologists, and script writers compile their lists of archetypal stories, one is notably absent: a story where bad things happen for no apparent reason. Rather, stories of tragedy are brought into an ordered and rational world by identifying a cause. The classic tragedy is precipitated by "the fatal flaw." In classical Greek drama, the flaw was hubris. Those flaws have expanded since then, but in all cases, the tragic end is made meaningful by individual failing. At the heart of this master narrative is the concept of a just world, often employed to explain poverty by blaming the poor.[12] Prosperity theology depends on the same master narrative. The righteous will be rewarded, not just spiritually but monetarily. The corollary is clear: to be poor is punishment for immorality.

So when bad things happen to good people, we look for answers. Our stories have taught us to do so. But those answers may be few and far between. A two-thousand-year-old Chinese folktale is often pressed into service to provide solace.

> A Chinese farmer gets a horse, which soon runs away. A neighbor says, "That's bad news." The farmer replies, "Good news, bad news, who can say?"
> The horse comes back and brings another horse with him. Good news, you might say.
> The farmer gives the second horse to his son, who rides it, then is thrown and badly breaks his leg. "So sorry for your bad news," says the concerned neighbor. "Good news, bad news, who can say?" the farmer replies.
> In a week or so, the emperor's men come and take every able-bodied young man to fight in a war. The farmer's son is spared. (Theiss 2009)

The story is often interpreted as a message of hope. What may seem bad right now may have a silver lining we cannot yet see. We should not be surprised by this interpretation. Research into canonical narratives suggests we will force new stories to fit familiar ones. But perhaps we should take the farmer at his word: Who can say? In the end, there really may be no rhyme or reason to our good fortune.

At first glance, such an option for an alternative narrative for welfare might seem a poor one, with too many deeply entrenched narratives to fight against. But direct opposition can be a strength, confronting head on the dominant narrative that the only obstacles to one's success are those of one's own making. This was, after all, the primary assumption in almost 70 percent of the personal experience narratives shared in social media (chap. 9). Further, personal experience is a powerful resource for how we make decisions, and "Why me?" is a question most of us ask but rarely answer satisfactorily. Finally, there is no shortage of such stories of good people who have been laid low. Cutbacks at work, unforeseen illnesses, complicated pregnancies, learning disabilities, abusive spouses, and impoverished parents all provide viable narratives to counter welfare legends (chap. 3).

The narrative tradition is rife with stories of when bad things happen to good people; they may just need more explicit framing.

Redemption Narratives

One downside to "when bad things happen to good people" stories is that they fit comfortably within the master narrative of the deserving and undeserving poor. The deserving poor can prove their circumstances are outside their control. Without such evidence, a person is cast as undeserving. But what about when bad things happen to regular people? What about people who, like all of us, make mistakes sometimes? Like the strategy used by abolitionists to combat slavery, conversion narratives with redemption at their core provide one answer. While the United States professes a clear separation between church and state, the country is predominantly Christian, and our political leaders are often expected to be as well. While "born again" stories will resonate more with fundamentalists, Baptists, and Pentecostals, more generic conversion narratives will be recognizable to most Christians. It was a classic story of redemption that George W. Bush told as he ran for the White House. A hard drinker and business failure, Bush turned to Jesus, gave up alcohol, married, and committed himself to a life of public service (see McAdams 2011).

Redemption stories provide avenues for imperfect people to avoid being cast aside, ignored, or discredited. In this narrative frame, Mary Barker can be heard as a mother struggling to keep her job and provide for her children, not as a drug addict to be ignored. Further, many recipients have in fact turned to religion for help (see chaps. 3 and 7) and, like Lilly Gibbs, recount their stories as redemption narratives. Already a part of the narrative tradition, these stories are simply waiting to be shared more widely.

Structural Injustice Narratives

In her book *Responsibility for Justice*, Iris Young identifies the reasons someone may find themselves in need, distinguishing among a person's own actions, the actions of others, bad luck, and structural injustice (2013).[13] The first three are fairly self-explanatory, with the first laying blame at the feet of the poor, the second laying blame at the feet of bad actors and bad policies, and the third laying blame at the feet of fate, God, or some other inexplicable, unseen force. "When bad things happen to good people" stories typically fall into the bad luck category. But as Young argues, many of the challenges faced by the poor are predictable, based on social structures that disadvantage some groups over others, including the poor. Chapter 1 explored some of these structures, including access to education, capital, and employment. Many of the challenges were results from bad actors and bad policies, but larger economic processes were at play as well, including the steady decrease in real income that has led to a shrinking of the middle class and a decline in jobs that provide a living wage. Young addresses the issue of affordable housing and details just how long this list of factors can be, including policies of the court system, the banking industry, housing associations, real estate agencies, federal government agencies such as the Federal Reserve, and local agencies such as zoning boards (2013, 48–50). Even with all of these agencies and individuals operating ethically, constraints remain for the poor.

For example, a person may not be able to seek the lowest-priced housing because it is not on a bus line that can get them to work or not be able to accept a job because it is too far from home. Michael Caster got a job at a local fast-food chain, but with no public transportation, he was often late to work. He was fired. Ayanna Spencer has been trying to finish her college degree so she can earn a living wage, but the only childcare option near her home that had availability was literally falling down. Bradley Jewell is a military veteran with a college degree but still cannot find a match between his skill set and job openings, told again and again that he is either too qualified or not qualified enough. Tabatha Tucker, also a military vet, heard the same thing. She was ultimately able to relocate and find a job, but moving is expensive, and without family help, she would not have been able to do it. No bad actors, no obvious bad policies, but structures and systems in place that make success difficult to achieve. Once again, the stories are there; they simply need to be highlighted and disseminated.

CONVERSATIONAL COUNTERNARRATIVES

The ideal counternarrative (1) retells the story of welfare in a way that is more accurate, fair, and humane; (2) treats aid recipients not as a homogenous, monolithic group demonized for the sins of a few but as individuals within a heterogeneous group with life experiences that highlight social problems that make traditional standards of success difficult to attain; and (3), most difficult of all, persuades audiences to adopt these stories as the dominant image of welfare in place of stories of fraud. This is the long game. In conversation, however, there may be counternarratives that are rhetorically effective in the short term that chip away at specific parts of the hegemonic narratives about welfare even if they do not reframe the core narrative.

Fallacy of Scale

Concerning the issue of scale, for example, one might highlight the fallacy of using one bad example to discredit an entire group by substituting occupations or group identities held or valued by audience members. To friends in business, one can tell the story of Enron as a clear example that all business employees are crooks. To lawyer friends, one can tell the story of the hundreds of lawyers in Wisconsin convicted of fraud, corruption, sex offenses, drugs, drunk driving, and battery who are still practicing law, many of whom did not even lose their license while they were in jail (Spivak and Poston 2011). To doctor friends, one can tell the stories of the ten physicians named to the Insurance Fraud Hall of Shame for signing off on treatments they never provided and sanctioning medical clinics that did not exist (Crane 2017). Similar lurid stories can be found for any occupation, white or blue collar. In telling these stories, the satire must be clear, the fallacy of such argument explicit.

Corporate Welfare

For the issue of the general concept of aid, one might point out the hypocrisy of demonizing aid recipients but not corporations, banks, CEOs, and farmers who receive billions in subsidies and tax breaks. In fact, this is the major theme of the few examples of antilegends that show up in the folk tradition on social media (figs. 12.1–12.5, noted earlier). In figure 1, part of the critique is leveled against Walmart, whose profits depend on hidden government subsidies by paying low wages and denying many employees full-time work to avoid having to offer health insurance.[14] In figures 12.4 and 12.5, people are reminded not only that corporations get handouts too but at a rate exponentially higher than what is paid to the poor, a point the aid recipient Rick Banks makes as well:

> People think that people are just depending too much on government to get
> their needs taken care of, but welfare is only a tiny fraction of government spend
> out really. You really look at the overall picture, it's only a small percentage.
> Organizations like Lockheed Martin that build planes and the weapons and
> whatnot, those are the real welfare recipients. They get billions. So my little twenty-
> four dollars a month is nothing compared to what Lockheed Martin is getting.[15]

Congressional representatives, columnists, and op-ed writers have made similar arguments over the years, highlighting the fact that not only do major corporations and the wealthiest individuals in the country get massive aid from the government, but they exploit tax loopholes that allow them to pay little to no taxes while the poor are asked to pay a larger and larger share. In 2010, the Republican senator from Oklahoma Tom Coburn began publishing an annual "Wastebook" report, documenting wasteful spending in the government. His 2011 report made headlines such as "Welfare for Millionaires" and included damning statistics: "From unemployment payments to subsidies and tax breaks on luxury items like vacation homes and yachts, Americans earning more than $1 million collect more than $30 billion in government largesse each year" (Stone and Colarusso 2011). In the wake of the Panama Papers scandal that revealed the widespread use of offshore tax havens to hide money and avoid taxes, Oxfam compiled a study of the top fifty US companies that revealed that for each $1 these companies paid in federal taxes, they received $27 back in government support. Lobbying helps. For every $1 spent on lobbying, these corporations received $130 back in tax breaks and $4,000 back in subsidies from the US government (Oxfam International 2016). A watchdog group in Illinois found the benefits from all federal grants, loans, direct payments, and insurance subsidies to Fortune 100 companies from 2000 to 2012 totaled $1.2 trillion.[16] In 2014, Matt Taibbi published *The Divide: American Injustice in the Age of the Wealth Gap*, detailing both the scope and the scale of government bailouts, tax breaks, subsidies, and fraud that is rampant within the corporate and banking worlds and hides in plain sight.

> Legally, there's absolutely no difference between a woman on welfare who falsely declares that her boyfriend no longer lives in the home and a bank that uses a robo-signer to cook up a document swearing that he has kept regular records of your credit card account. But morally and politically, they're worlds apart. When the state brings a fraud case against a welfare mom, it brings it with disgust, with rage, because in addition to committing the legal crime, she's committed the political crime of being needy and an eyesore.
>
> Banks commit the legal crime of fraud wholesale; they do so out in the open, have entire departments committed to it, and have employees who've spent years literally doing nothing but commit, over and over again, the same legal crime that some welfare mothers go to jail for doing once. But they're not charged, because there's no political crime. The system is not disgusted by the organized, mechanized search for profit. It's more like it's impressed by it. (Taibbi 2014, 384)

The poor become our focal point for disgust and righteous anger so that when rich and poor are accused of similar crimes, one is demonized while the other is virtually ignored. In a 1995 survey just before the passing of the Personal Responsibility and Work Opportunity Reconciliation Act of 1996, 40 percent of Americans said it was worse that some poor people get welfare they did not deserve than it was for the rich not to pay taxes. Only 20 percent said it was worse that the rich pay no taxes.[17] In other words, two times as many Americans felt it was worse for the poor to get undeserved welfare benefits than for the wealthy to get undeserved tax breaks.[18]

Stories of corporate welfare and fraud can be satisfying to tell and have the added benefit of addressing one of the key fears underlying so many welfare narratives: fear of being victims of injustice. Welfare legends blame the poor; corporate welfare stories blame the rich. Corporate welfare counternarratives face two key challenges in swaying popular opinion. The first is the deep-seated belief, fostered by the American dream, that one of the greatest moral shortcomings in the United States is the "crime" of being lazy. Such a view allows Americans to conclude that while both welfare recipients and business executives receive government aid, one is lazy, the other industrious. For many, therefore, comparing the two is a false analogy. Subsidies for corporations, business owners, and farmers are excused because they are supporting wage labor, while welfare is demonized for undermining it. The critique does not hold up, however. Farmers are sometimes paid *not* to plant a particular crop, just as corporations are often given subsidies that end up lining the pockets of CEOs and investors rather than employees and result in a loss of jobs rather than their creation. More importantly, welfare programs support people who work outside the home as well as inside it (see chap. 1).

The second problem is that while stories of corporate welfare highlight widespread hypocrisy, they do not necessarily rehabilitate the image of the aid recipient. When conversation returns to public assistance, the same critical stories focused on fraud remain. Welfare has gained a fellow scapegoat rather than exonerated the poor. Not only is this unhelpful; it risks feeding a narrative that government aid is inherently bad.

Immigration and Government Waste

People have also attempted to deploy counternarratives to address issues of immigration or government waste. Immigration has often been a central part of the American dream story, but in the contemporary political climate, immigration is too hot to touch. During our first discussion in 2011, when I met with half a dozen community members to start thinking about what a research project around the stories of welfare might look like, a few people suggested the project would be ignored or, worse, discredited if we talked about immigration. The rationale was that people became so fired up over the issue they could not hear anything else.

There is also the master narrative of government waste. If there is one thing most people can agree on, it is that the government does not work as efficiently as it should. Stories of the $600 government hammer abound and even spawned a Hammer Award to recognize effective and efficient examples of government programs.[19] Pointing out that welfare programs have no more waste on average than other large government programs seems helpful, but reframing the issue as a bureaucratic one risks being consumed by policy debates that allow deflection from the underlying assumptions about the poor. When fraud and waste have been addressed in the welfare system, the response has been to cut funding. As a short-term response to set the record straight, normalizing public assistance with military spending, for example, can be helpful but ultimately reifies rather than subverts the assumption that welfare and fraud go hand in hand.

OLD STORY, NEW ENDING
Story Behind the Story

"Some people!" snorted a man standing behind me in the long line at the grocery store.

"You would think the manager would pay attention and open another line," said a woman.

I looked to the front of the line to see what the hold up was and saw a well-dressed, young woman trying to get the machine to accept her credit card. No matter how many times she swiped it, the machine kept rejecting it.

"It's one of them welfare card things. Damn people need to get a job like everyone else," said the man standing behind me.

The young woman turned around to see who had made the comment.

"It was me," he said, pointing to himself.

The young lady's face began to change expression. Almost in tears, she dropped the welfare card onto the counter and quickly walked out of the store. Everyone in the checkout line watched as she began running to her car. Never looking back, she got in and drove away.

After developing cancer in 1977 and having had to use food stamps, I had learned never to judge anyone without knowing the circumstances of their life. This turned out to be the case today.

Several minutes later a young man walked into the store. He went up to the cashier and asked if she had seen the woman. After describing her, the cashier told him that she had run out of the store, got into her car, and drove away.

"Why would she do that?" asked the man. Everyone in the line looked around at the fellow who had made the statement.

"I made a stupid comment about the welfare card she was using. Something I shouldn't have said. I'm sorry," said the man.

"Well, that's bad, real bad, in fact. Her brother was killed in Afghanistan two years ago. He had three young children and she has taken on that responsibility. She's twenty years old, single, and now has three children to support," he said in a very firm voice.

"I'm really truly sorry. I didn't know," he replied, shaking both his hands about.

The young man asked, "Are these paid for?" pointing to the shopping cart full of groceries.

"It wouldn't take her card," the clerk told him.

"Do you know where she lives?" asked the man who had made the comment.

"Yes, she goes to our church."

"Excuse me," he said as he made his way to the front of the line. He pulled out his wallet, took out his credit card and told the cashier, "Please use my card. PLEASE!" The clerk took his credit card and began to ring up the young woman's groceries.

"Hold on," said the gentleman. He walked back to his shopping cart and began loading his own groceries onto the belt to be included. "Come on people. We got three kids to help raise!" he told everyone in line.

Everyone began to place their groceries onto the fast moving belt. A few customers began bagging the food and placing it into separate carts. "Go back and get two big turkeys," yelled a heavyset woman, as she looked at the man.

"NO," yelled the man. Everyone stopped dead in their tracks. The entire store became quiet for several seconds. "Four turkeys," yelled the man. Everyone began laughing and went back to work.

When all was said and done, the man paid a total of $1,646.57 for the groceries. He then walked over to the side, pulled out his check book, and began writing a check using the bags of dog food piled near the front of the store for a writing surface. He turned around and handed the check to the young man. "She will need a freezer and a few other things as well," he told the man.

The young man looked at the check and said, "This is really very generous of you."

"No," said the man. "Her brother was the generous one."

Everyone in the store had been observing the odd commotion and began to clap. And I drove home that day feeling very American.

The story sounds familiar. A woman in the checkout line holding up the rest of the shoppers as she attempts to use her EBT card. People in line grumble. But then the story takes a twist. By a turn of events that strains narrative coherence and believability, her backstory is discovered, and she is revealed to be one of the rare deserving aid recipients.

The story was circulating via email in July 2008 with a number of different titles, including "And We Have Problems?," "Never Judge," "Never Judge Anyone," and "Think Before We Speak," though never, apparently, with the title it was originally published under, "The Generous One."[20]

The fact that the story was picked up by people and emailed widely to friends and family bodes well for an audience willing to entertain the idea that not all is as it seems when judging welfare recipients. As an exemplar, however, it holds the bar incredibly high for what it takes to be viewed as a deserving aid recipient. One hopes that more humble stories of daily struggle against a lifetime of small setbacks would also encourage empathy, even if not the outpouring of generosity that this story describes.

Interviews with aid recipients make clear that those humbler stories exist. There was Davey Cannon, who could be seen smoking cigarettes outside the homeless shelter. He knows they are not good for him, but they provide comfort as he faces permanent disability and the possibility that he may never walk again thanks to a degenerative joint disease that went undiagnosed for too long.

Or Keira Tapper, who could be seen in the grocery story, dressed immaculately, with carefully coiffed hair and manicured nails, using food stamps. She relied on food stamps for four months while she was going through a divorce, moving homes, and trying to find a job in a new city, all as a newly single parent raising two children. Her clothing and appearance reflected not only the life she had recently led but the jobs she was aggressively applying for.

Lilly Gibbs walks her dog every day, rain or shine, even when she was homeless. It would be easy to judge her. Should a person who can't pay her bills have a pet? Not long ago, Lilly had her own thriving Avon business, when she realized that if she stayed with the man she was living with, she might not survive. She escaped but found herself in a new town with no money, no home, no family, and no job. With the help of public assistance and her church, she got a job and car. She is still struggling mentally and financially, but her dog provides important comfort for her as she continues to move towards self-sufficiency.

This project has provided a warehouse of "story behind the story" narratives to tell. But everyone can work to create their own stories by getting to know their neighbors who receive public assistance, learning people's backstories, and sharing those stories, if not with names, then with the compelling, compassionate details that provide a more human, humane, and honest glimpse of what welfare looks like in the United States.

Salvaging the American Dream

Story-behind-the-story narratives provide one avenue for taking a familiar story and rerouting it toward a new ending. American dream stories ironically provide another. At first this seems a perverse suggestion. American dream stories have been applied in the most grotesque way to welfare by painting aid recipients as mirror opposites of the Horatio Alger hero (chap. 3). However, today we tend to ignore a crucial part of those foundational American dream stories: the role of the benefactor. In those early stories by Alger, the young protagonist worked hard but faced challenges again and again that only with the help of others was he able to overcome.

Despite how deeply embedded the assumption of independence is in the cultural fabric of American society generally and the American dream specifically, stories can reclaim and recognize the degrees to which people depend on one another for their success. American dream stories can also be retold with new endings where success is not guaranteed. Ellie Fitzer's story about her favorite client does both. Asked if she knows any "success stories," Ellie responds, "There are lots." And then by way of introduction, she adds, "This is a different success."

> There is a guest . . . and he's one of my all-time favorite guests. I can't say names. He's one of my all-time favorite guests at Allied Churches. And he was a guest last year. And he was an ex-offender.
>
> And it's very hard. I don't know how familiar you are, but it's very hard. A lot of places have rules where they will not hire ex-offenders, so it's very hard to get a job and get on your feet, and it's harder to get assistance and all kinds of things.
>
> And so he was in a ninety-day program, but he was working really hard, working with the system, working with some other programs, never stopped working. So we gave him an extension for a while, like a couple of months extra after the three months. I think he ended up staying for maybe six or seven months. And then he left, and he didn't have an apartment. With another organization, he could get small jobs on the weekends where he could move out someone's furniture after someone passed away or something, so he would receive hourly money for a day but was living on a friend's couch.
>
> He said from the support we gave him—and he was part of another organization, Sustainable Alamance—and he said that having me and having some of the other employees and some of the people at Sustainable Alamance, we were the first people who ever cared about him and that he didn't want, not only did he not want to let himself down, but he didn't want to let other people down because never in his life had he had other people pulling for him.
>
> And so he's been out of the shelter now since the summer, I think since June. Hasn't had a place to live, and he just got his first apartment, and he came to the shelter last week [to tell us.] He's still on probation—his PO [parole officer] came—but just kept trying. And when things are very hard, like the systems in Alamance County there's high poverty, there's no transportation, there's not employment, but the fact that he was able to keep trying . . .
>
> And I'm not saying he's not going to be receiving assistance because he probably will. But the fact that he kept trying and using his resources and doing little things and focusing on himself, and he's able to get an apartment and didn't give up on himself. And it would have been so much easier to commit another crime, go back to jail. That's the easiest thing to do, and he didn't, and that's a major success.

Such stories remind people that hard work is rarely enough to ensure success. Nor is operating in isolation. It takes a village. But such a strategy only works if people are willing to consider the invisible networks and supports that make the American dream possible. Such remediation may first require retelling well-known American dream stories of historical leaders and contemporary celebrities to make visible the support the current American dream narrative tradition has increasingly omitted.

SHARING THE STORY

Addressing Fears

The counternarratives that challenge canonical narratives by reframing welfare either with recognizable cultural narratives new to welfare or old welfare stories with new endings address some fears and anxieties better than others. "When bad things happen to good people" stories help relieve fears of working hard while others do nothing by providing stories of people who face challenges unenviable by any and receive help that pales in comparison. Such stories may do little to allay fears that such hardships can happen to them, that poverty may be a paycheck away, and that the American dream is fundamentally flawed, but the stories directly address the fear of working hard and receiving little while others work little and receive lots and can evoke empathy while doing so.

Structural injustice narratives have the same strengths and weaknesses of stories of bad things happening to good people but push the needle even further by not just removing the blame from the individual but shifting it to societal structures that undermine the American dream. Such stories are riskier but have a bigger payoff.

Redemption narratives face a particularly difficult rhetorical challenge, relying on a message fundamental to Christian thought but often antithetical to human nature: to provide second chances. Such stories should help address if not relieve the fear of working hard while others do not, reducing the us-versus-them dichotomy by reminding audiences we are all sinners and deserve grace and pushing audiences to be more empathetic than they might naturally be. Further, redemption narratives provide hope for the promise of the American dream that depends on opportunity, not closed doors.

Salvaging the American dream stories addresses the fear that the American dream does not work by suggesting we return to its original form and recognize the social contract at its foundation. Generous benefactors, good luck, and, most of all, people working together to support one another are crucial criteria for predictable success. Such stories should also address fears of immigration since the American dream has a distinct application to past and present immigration to the United States.

Corporate welfare stories have the potential to address the fear that public aid is a disincentive to work, but the larger problem is that this fear is not unfounded, just not for the reasons people often think. Welfare is not a disincentive because the benefits are so generous but because its benefit structure makes it incredibly difficult to work outside the home as a single parent or save money as people gain small raises.

Getting Involved

When the utterly false legends of Proctor and Gamble's ties to Satanism began circulating in the 1990s, the company was horrified. They were also incredibly proactive. It seemed they had little choice. For months, the company received five hundred calls a day about its ties to devil worship. In response, the company mailed "truth kits" to each caller, enlisted the help of prominent religious leaders, targeted towns where the legend was emerging, and developed a national ad campaign (DiFonzo and Bordia 2007, 295). Proctor and Gamble could do this because they are the largest product company in the world, with a net worth of $68 billion.[21] The targets of welfare legends are hardly so well off or so well organized. While formal ad campaigns by the government agencies that oversee TANF, food stamps, and SSI could be developed, there appears little political will to do so.

There is a more modest approach, however, one that adheres to the research to strike as soon as the rumors and legends start. Nationally, a new media "welfare queen" emerges fairly rarely.[22] But local examples emerge from time to time. In these situations, the new story reanimates the legend. Aid providers, politicians, and people who have committed to working on issues of poverty and public assistance should have stories at their fingertips, whether for interviews, op-eds, or letters to the editors. Scholars can help ensure that allies can join aid recipients with stories that are easily accessible and constructed and shared in ways most likely to be heard.

The long game, however, requires that the public take up the heavy lifting as well. While much of the blame for the welfare queen can be laid at the feet of politicians and the mass media, the oral tradition of the general public has not only ensured those more public performances find purchase but also perpetuated a robust antiwelfare narrative tradition of its own. Further, as research has shown, denials from officials who may be seen as biased or untrustworthy may cause more harm than good (Turner 1993). Stories from trusted sources—friends, family, neighbors, and coworkers—have a greater chance at turning the tides of public sentiment, especially as these stories make their way into political speech. Although memetics suggests that positive stories cannot compete with those that disgust us (chap. 9), we know trickle-up storytelling can happen. It is, after all, how the welfare queen got started in the first place.

As one prepares to enter the fray, it is important never to bring a knife to a gunfight. Eileen Collins complained about trying to have a productive conversation with family members: "Facts really get in the way of the story. For some people the facts are not really helpful, or they don't really believe factual information." Eileen's problem is that she brought a knife to a gunfight. Her relative tells a story;

she counters with facts. But facts fare poorly against a good story. Responding with a counternarrative when we *know* the backstory rather than just imagine it can be effective if the response shifts the frame from an analytical to an emotional one. Using rhetorical questions to encourage audiences to imagine themselves in the aid recipient's shoes is a good start. And folk wisdom can help provide responses to welfare queen stories when we do not know the backstory. The ideas of innocent until proven guilty, the benefit of the doubt, tie goes to the runner, and, of course, don't judge a book by its cover remind us to consider the second truth of legends and make the same rhetorical move that guides our storytelling in the first place: apply the familiar to a new context, and encourage a new conclusion.

Aid Recipients

Despite the height of the hurdles, some of the most effective storytelling is done by aid recipients themselves. Asking people to speak who are struggling to meet basic needs and who are deeply stigmatized in society is a tall order. But aid agencies should continue to identify recipients who have found the time and unfathomable courage to stand up and speak out and provide platforms for them to speak directly to politicians, community groups, and the general public.

While it may be tempting to want to step in and coach these storytellers, as the Jewish Council on Urban Affairs did with the Welfare Truth Squad, it is far more important that when aid recipients get their moment to speak directly to audiences, they get to tell their story the way they choose.[23] The prescriptive suggestions for storytelling in this chapter, on the other hand, are for welfare advocates seeking strategies for engaging friends, family, and coworkers, as well as the larger public. These approaches need not exclude aid recipients, but they are intended as options for a public that does not have a wellspring of their own experiences and narratives to draw upon.

Of course, the stories in this book cannot substitute for hearing stories directly from aid recipients. As Fisher's narrative rationality theory suggests, if people evaluate stories based on their own experiences, then people need an opportunity to have more experiences with people making ends meet with the help of public assistance (1989). Gordon Allport's contact theory also supports such an approach, as long as those experiences are positive (1954). And it explains why the Walk-a-Mile program in Maine was successful. Politicians were able to hear stories directly from the people receiving assistance, stories that could evoke empathy as well as sympathy by literally placing people side by side to talk.

A New Storyteller

In the final weeks of 2014, the scientific community was stunned by new research that seemed poised to upend long-held beliefs about social persuasion and bias reduction. Published in the preeminent academic journal *Science*, the study showed that a ten-minute conversation with a person who identifies as LGBTQ could significantly reduce prejudice against LGBTQ people not just for the moment but for months afterward, affecting voting decisions on marriage equality legislation. The mass media quickly picked up the story as extraordinary and paradigm shifting with results almost too good to believe.

But within months, researchers conducting similar research began to find inconsistencies in the study and began to investigate. By May it was clear: the study was bogus, the data fabricated, the conclusions invalid. A retraction was made; the study and scholars, discredited. The results *were* too good to be true.

Or so it seemed. But those researchers conducting similar research completed their study and found, much to the surprise of a wary scientific and mass media community, that key findings of the fabricated study held up. Specifically, they found that a ten-minute conversation using an active perspective-taking strategy had profound and lasting effects at reducing prejudice against transgender people and increased support for a nondiscrimination law to protect them (Broockman and Kalla 2016). Unlike the fabricated study, the identity of the researcher holding the conversation did not matter; members and nonmembers of the transgender community were both successful.

The key was the active perspective-taking conversational strategy, also called analog perspective taking. Research in lab settings has suggested for some time that "brief messages can durably change individuals' attitudes when individuals engage in active, effortful, processing (known as 'System 2' processing) of those messages" (Broockman and Kalla 2016, 220, citing Petty, Haugtvedt, and Smith 1995). Encouraging people to imagine the world from another person's perspective can help bypass stereotypical thinking and biases common to system 1 processing. The researchers did this by asking people to first think of a time when they were judged negatively for being different. They then encouraged them to consider how this experience related to how transgender people are treated (221). The technique reduced prejudice significantly, holding steady even three months later. The strategy parallels research in the rhetorical power of empathy in storytelling. Getting people to see themselves in the stories of discredited and stigmatized others is powerful in changing views.

Although the focus of this chapter has been on how non-aid recipients and aid recipients alike can tell stories to overthrow the stereotype of the welfare queen, encouraging family, friends, neighbors, and coworkers to tell their own stories first may be a powerful, even crucial first step in doing so. Such a strategy has the benefit of creating both empathy and coherence, as well as allowing people to frame the conversation through their own personal experience first, mitigating against the chance of the backfire effect.

Even in the most optimistic scenario, however, limitations remain. First, Broockman and Kalla's study needs to be replicated with other issues; as they point out, views about transgender people may not be as deeply ingrained as racial bias, for example, a major factor in stereotypes about the poor and public assistance (2016). Second, for people with their own stories of economic need who have not received or been eligible for public assistance, such personal narratives could exacerbate the problem. As we saw in chapter 8, many people are already telling their stories of when they feel they have been discriminated against or unfairly treated, cultivating animosity rather than empathy toward aid recipients because the discrimination was related to their own denied applications for aid. Active perspective taking through personal narrative may be effective only when the experiences of the two groups are clearly different.

In the end, there is no single magic bullet to eliminate the stereotype and stigma associated with welfare in the United States. Every counternarrative that promises a new image of welfare has an Achilles' heel that tempers immediate success. But the folk traditions of narrative and online lore provide an arsenal of weapons. Different audiences require different strategies. But success will be determined as much by our will as by our message. We have the weapons; we just need to decide to use them.

NOTES

1. For an article describing the initiative and the power for stories for social change, see Saltemarsh (2018).

2. The *New York Times* article included interviews with two women in the audience of one of the Welfare Squad's evening storytelling sessions: one woman remained skeptical; another left with lots to think about (Terry 1995).

3. John Vlach coined the term in 1971, applying it to humorous horror stories. Linda Dégh and Andrew Vázsonyi expanded the definition to include any story that attacks a legend and works to destroy it, initially assuming this process existed outside the legend "ecosystem" (1973) but revising their assessment to include jokes and humorous stories that operated symbiotically with legends (1995). For one of the most thorough discussions of the antilegend, see Ellis (2005).

4. "Sysop" is short for systems operator; "Kaypro" was a brand of home computer in the 1980s. These examples are from Ellis (1995, 5). The St. Jude chain letter promises good luck to the sender if they pass along the letter (or forward the email) to others, while the "Lights Out" gang initiation legend warn drivers not to flash their lights at cars driving at night without their lights on because gangs used this as a way to identify their next victim (see Ellis 2005, 129–30).

5. There were four "conservative Jesus" memes shared together on Facebook. The other two also parodied conservative politics: one referenced health care; the other, tax breaks for the wealthy.

6. All Google searches will be different based on past search histories, but the link here reflects my Google search on January 25, 2018, for "welfare queen meme": https://www.google.com/search?q=welfare+queen+meme&sa=X&tbm=isch&tbo =u&source=univ&ved=oahUKEwjz15PboLbXAhUK7yYKHavaDgMQsAQIJw &biw=962&bih=765#imgrc=.

7. John Lee hypothesizes that antilegends have little chance of succeeding when facing "deep-seated distrust and strong emotions" and narratives "that espouse racism and xenophobia," which may be too entrenched in a person's worldview to be overturned by parody or ridicule (2014, 174–75).

8. All of these legends can be found in Turner (1993). The reward flyer is reproduced on page 89. Additional details about the cases can be found in Turner's *Journal of American Folklore* article that came out the previous year (1992).

9. Many of their conclusions are specific to internal rumors—rumors that spread within a company. I have focused on their research related to external rumors and legends that spread throughout the public and threaten a company's brand.

10. The approach aligns with Jerome Bruner's concept of paradigmatic and narrative modes of thinking, where the paradigmatic looks for universal truths while the narrative focuses on the particular as a way of making meaning (2009).

11. This chapter focuses on counternarratives employing the more specific definition of narrative that folklorists typically use, as distinct from looser definitions that include any coherent discourse (see chap. 2). For scholars who have attempted counter discourses about welfare, see Cassiman, who focuses on the trauma of poverty (2006), and Rich, who focuses on challenging fundamental assumptions about wage labor, parenting, self-sufficiency, and privacy (2016).

12. For a discussion of the just-world hypothesis, see Montada and Lerner (1998).

13. Young defines structural injustice as follows: "Structural injustice is a kind of moral wrong distinct from the wrongful action of an individual agent or the repressive policies of a state. Structural injustice occurs as a consequence of many individuals and institutions acting to pursue their particular goals and interests, for the most part within the limits of accepted rules and norms" (2013, 52).

14. The documentary film *Wal-Mart: The High Cost of Low Prices* explores this system in great detail (Greenwald 2005).

15. Rick Banks is exactly right. Lockheed Martin was the largest beneficiary of government aid, with $392 billion between 2000 and 2012 (Moore 2014).

16. Open the Books is a government watchdog nonprofit (https://www .openthebooks.com/). These stats were reported in the *National Review* (Moore 2014).

17. "What's a bigger problem for this country right now: rich people not paying their fair share of taxes, or people on welfare getting benefits they don't deserve?" (*Los Angeles Times* 1995).

18. Reasons for this belief can be found throughout the book, particularly in chap. 8, and include the distinction between employed and unemployed (noted in the text here), as well as the injustice felt by working-class people, who are more apt to see parallels between themselves and aid recipients rather than business executives. The fraudulent aid recipient is getting ahead in ways that are possible and understandable for themselves as well, while the fraud committed by bankers and CEOs are often neither. A more charitable interpretation of these statistics, however, is the common belief that if aid is given to an undeserving person, less will go to a deserving one. Coupled with a shortsighted view of how taxes work, some may see welfare fraud as harming the poor, while tax fraud harms only the government.

19. Variously $400, $200, or another amount depending on the variant of the story. For analysis of this story, see Roberts (1984) and Freedberg (1998). For a record of the Hammer Award, see Barry (1998).

20. The first record of the story appears to be in Roger Dean Kiser's self-published book *Helping Our Fellowman* (D. Mikkelson 2015a). Perhaps not surprisingly, the description of the book credits the author as a regular contributor to the *Chicken Soup for the Soul* book series.

21. For information about some of the lawsuits, see "Procter & Gamble Awarded $19.25 Million in Satanism Lawsuit" (Fox News 2007). Note also that this is the marginally "pro-welfare" narrative referenced earlier in the chapter.

22. The most recent example is probably Jason Greenslate, dubbed by Fox News as "the Food Stamp Surfer" from 2013 (chap. 3).

23. This is a key thesis of the folklorist Kate Parker Horigan's recent book *Consuming Katrina*, which documents how personal narratives from survivors get transformed from powerful statements of autonomy into abbreviated recapitulations of stereotypical images of victims (2018).

EPILOGUE

THE SCORES OF PEOPLE WE met at the shelter are gone now. Time limits ensure that there is a constant turnover. People leave with no forwarding address, no permanent phone number, difficult to track down. Life remains unstable, housing transitory, support networks shallow.

Even many of the families in public housing have moved. Pat Jackson's health took another turn for the worse, and she was forced to leave Burlington and move in with her daughter in Greensboro. It has been almost ten years since April Ayers's husband was deported. She has faced the fact that she needs to move on, figuratively and literally. Recently, she moved her family to High Point to live with a friend, but health problems continue to plague her and her children, and she regularly posts calls for payers on Facebook.

Jeffrey Thornton moved out of public housing into his girlfriend's home. She is confined to a wheelchair, as is his brother; he serves as primary caregiver for both, as well as for one child and two grandchildren. But his own health is not good; he has asthma, emphysema, COPD, congestive heart failure, social anxiety, and depression but has not been able to get disability aid. His dreams of a vacation, even for just a few days, seem further out of reach these days.

Diane Clemens remains, relying on her faith to guide her and continuing to help in her community, whether by serving as a foster mother or representing her community on the resident advisory board at Burlington Housing Authority. Delia Taylor is still working her way toward a Habitat for Humanity house but has found building sufficient savings to be difficult with reduced hours at work and growing daughters whose expenses have only gotten larger.

Ayanna Spencer got married and is raising her two children in her own home, no longer reliant on family whose interest in helping her have blown hot and cold. The same is true for Marilyn Sanchez, whose husband's work has been steady and sufficient for a life that no longer teeters on the poverty line. Etta Washington continues to make ends meet doing hair and working at fast-food restaurants. Her hopes of starting a candy business with her friend Karraha amicably evaporated when Karraha and Justin Shepard moved, but they remain friends.

Justin and Karraha have moved out of public housing and are renting a single-family home in High Point with a volleyball net in the backyard and room to plant a garden. They have a fuel-efficient car and friendly neighbors. Both are heavily involved in church and devoted to raising their daughter, Lotus, who continues to thrive, both precocious and kind. In addition, now that Lotus is in school, Karraha has picked up a job as a barista, while Justin has continued to work full time in catering. Both are also working on completing college degrees—Justin in animation and business, Karraha in computer technology—while Karraha continues to earn extra money sewing and fixing up cast-off furniture, lawn equipment, and other household goods to provide a comfortable home on a lean budget. Justin's parents come by regularly to watch Lotus so that Justin and Karraha can exercise or have a date night.

By all accounts, their story is a success story. But their success should not distract from the ongoing challenges they face or that are faced by others who have not been so lucky—others who still have not found work, do not have loving partners to support them, do not have parents in town who can help with childcare, and do not have solid high school educations that can be built on with advanced degrees. Nor should their success be cast as evidence of the viability of the American dream for all. Both Justin and Karraha are often exhausted at the end of the day, balancing so much to ensure a productive and fulfilling life with hopes for a promising future. Further, while Karraha's health has improved dramatically, health insurance remains unaffordable, and the worry of another illness or complications from her Bell's palsy looms as a constant threat.

But their story provides hope, which can often be in short supply among the millions of people who rely on public assistance in the United States today. As Makayla Stirling says, "It takes a village." That village includes not only our families and neighbors but also our public officials and community leaders. It includes the informal acts of kindness and generosity all of us can undertake daily as well as the formal programs that provide sustained and reliable help to provide basic needs and much-needed stability. The historical record is clear: in the beginning, the American dream depended not on the solitary work of the individual but the network of people who came together to support each other. The stories in this book told by the people who are still working toward their own dreams provide new stories to guide us, stories that need to be told not alongside the American dream but as part of it, as a renewed story that more honestly captures the complex world in which we live.

APPENDIXES

Key to Sources

1. ABC News Poll, January 1995.
2. ABC News Poll, April 1996.
3. ABC News/Washington Post Poll, February 1981.
4. ABC News/Washington Post Poll, January 1986.
5. ABC News/Washington Post Poll, October 1991.
6. ABC News/Washington Post Poll, 1980s early.
7. American Enterprise Institute/Los Angeles Times Poverty Survey, June 2016.
8. American National Election Study (Post-Election), November 1980.
9. American National Election Study (Post-Election), November 1984.
10. American National Election Study (Post-Election), November 1988.
11. American National Election Study (Post-Election), November 1994.
12. Anti-Semitism in the United States Survey, October 1964.
13. Associated Press/Gfk Knowledge Networks Poll, August 2012.
14. Associated Press/Knowledge Networks Poll, December 2009.
15. Associated Press/Yahoo Poll, August 2008.
16. CBS News Poll, March 1996.
17. CBS News Poll, October 1996.
18. CBS News Poll, January 1997.
19. CBS News/New York Times Poll, August 1976.
20. CBS News/New York Times Poll, October 1976.
21. CBS News/New York Times Poll, July 1977.
22. CBS News/New York Times Poll, June 1978.
23. CBS News/New York Times Poll, November 1980.
24. CBS News/New York Times Poll, January 1986.
25. CBS News/New York Times Poll, June 1986.

26. CBS News/New York Times Poll, December 1994.
27. CBS News/New York Times Poll, January 1994.
28. CBS News/New York Times Poll, April 1995.
29. CBS News/New York Times Poll, December 1995.
30. CBS News/New York Times Poll, February 1995.
31. CBS News/New York Times Poll, early 1980s.
32. Data Black Survey, September 1980.
33. Elon Poll, September 2013.
34. For-Profit and Not-for-Profit Health Care Organizations Survey, October 1997.
35. Fox News/Opinion Dynamics Poll, June 1999.
36. Gallup Poll, August 1989.
37. Gallup Poll, February 1992.
38. Gallup Poll (AIPO), November 1964.
39. Gallup Poll (AIPO), December 1978.
40. Gallup/CNN/USA Today Poll, July 1993.
41. Gallup/CNN/USA Today Poll, April 1994.
42. Gallup/Newsweek Poll, August 1985.
43. Gallup/Newsweek Poll, February 1988.
44. General Social Survey, February 1986.
45. General Social Survey, February 1990.
46. Harris Poll, December 1994.
47. Harris Poll, February 1995.
48. Harris Poll, May 2000.
49. Harris Survey, September 1964.
50. Harris Survey, February 1976.
51. Harris Survey, June 1976.
52. Harris Survey, September 1977.
53. Health Policy Survey, June 1996.
54. Kaiser/Harvard Survey on Welfare Reform, December 1994.
55. Los Angeles Times Poll, April 1981.
56. Los Angeles Times Poll, April 1985.
57. Los Angeles Times Poll, October 1992.
58. Los Angeles Times Poll, June 1993.
59. Los Angeles Times Poll, April 1994.
60. Los Angeles Times Poll, October 1995.
61. Los Angeles Times Poll, early 1980s.
62. Merit Report, January 1982.
63. National Conference Survey on Inter-group Relations, August 1993.
64. National Hispanic Media Coalition/Latino Decisions: The Impact of Media Stereotypes on Opinions and Attitudes Towards Latinos Survey, March 2012.

65. NBC News Poll, June 1995.
66. NBC News/Associated Press Poll, September 1981.
67. NBC News/Wall Street Journal Poll, May 1992.
68. NBC News/Wall Street Journal Poll, January 1994.
69. NBC News/Wall Street Journal Poll, June 1994.
70. NBC News/Wall Street Journal Poll, September 1994.
71. NBC News/Wall Street Journal Poll, April 1995.
72. NBC News/Wall Street Journal Poll, June 2014.
73. New York Times Poll, May 1992.
74. Nixon Poll, May 1971.
75. NPR/Kaiser/Kennedy School—Poverty in America Survey, January 2001.
76. ORC Public Opinion Index, March 1969.
77. People & the Press—Mood of America Survey, March 1994.
78. Pew Forum on Religion & Public Life/Pew Research Center for the People & the Press Survey, February 2002.
79. Pew Hispanic Center Immigration Poll, February 2006.
80. Pew News Interest Index Poll, April 1997.
81. PRRI Kids' Wellbeing Survey, April 2017.
82. PRRI/The Atlantic Survey, September 2016.
83. Public Religion Research Institute Hispanic Values Survey, August 2013.
84. Racial Attitudes and Consciousness Exam, August 1989.
85. Rasmussen Reports, July 2011.
86. Roper Report 83-2, January 1983.
87. Roper Report 86-10, October 1986.
88. Social Capital Community Benchmark Survey, July 2000.
89. Social Capital Community Survey, January 2006.
90. Social Security Reform Survey, June 1996.
91. Taking America's Pulse II Survey, January 2000.
92. Taking America's Pulse III—Intergroup Relations Survey, January 2005.
93. Time/CNN/Yankelovich Clancy Shulman Poll, March 1992.
94. Time/CNN/Yankelovich Clancy Shulman Poll, May 1992.
95. Time/CNN/Yankelovich Clancy Shulman Poll, September 1993.
96. Time/CNN/Yankelovich Clancy Shulman Poll, February 1994.
97. Time/CNN/Yankelovich Clancy Shulman Poll, May 1994.
98. Time/CNN/Yankelovich Clancy Shulman Poll, September 1994.
99. Time/CNN/Yankelovich Partners Poll, May 1994.
100. Time/Yankelovich, Skelly & White Poll, March 1974.
101. Time/Yankelovich, Skelly & White Poll, January 1976.
102. Time/Yankelovich, Skelly & White Poll, April 1985.
103. Washington Post/Kaiser Family Foundation/Harvard Americans on Values Survey, July 1998.

104. Washington Post/Kaiser Family Foundation/Harvard University Follow-
     up Latinos Survey, August 1999.
105. What Americans Want from Welfare Reform Survey, December 1995.
106. Women's Equality Poll, March 1995

*All polls found through i-Roper or Harris Poll.

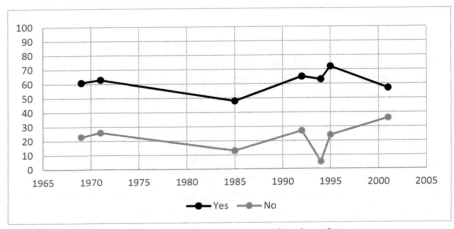

Chart A1.1. Do women have more babies to increase their benefits?
Data drawn from 54, 56, 59, 60, 69, 73, 74, 75, 76.

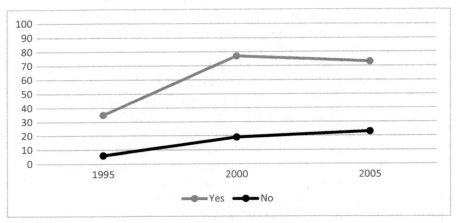

Chart A1.2. Do welfare recipients suffer greater discrimination
than other Americans? Data drawn from 91, 92, 105.

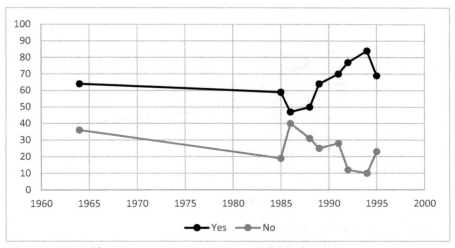

Chart A1.3. Is welfare a disincentive to work? Data drawn from
5, 36, 43, 44, 49, 56, 59, 68, 69, 71, 93, 94, 97, 105.

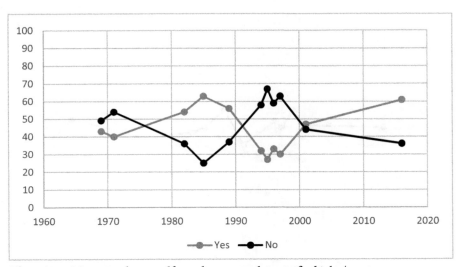

Chart A1.4. Most people on welfare who can work try to find jobs/want
to be employed. Data drawn from 1, 2, 3, 7, 17, 18, 26, 27, 28, 30, 36, 48, 54,
56, 69, 74, 76, 105, 106. Related data from 12, 45, 49, 50, 62, 63, 73.

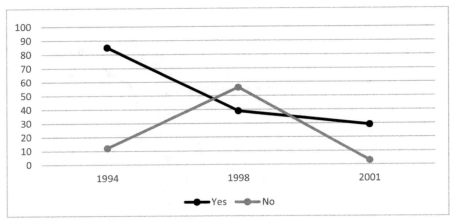

Chart A1.5. Are people on welfare because of lower moral values? Data drawn from 54, 75, 103.

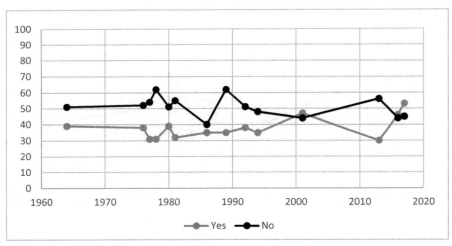

Chart A1.6. Do aid recipients really need help? Data drawn from 4, 12, 19, 20, 21, 22, 23, 24, 27, 27, 32, 41, 51, 52, 54, 66, 67, 75, 81, 82, 84, 84, 93, 94, 96, 99. Related data from 13, 14, 15, 56, 74, 76, 83.

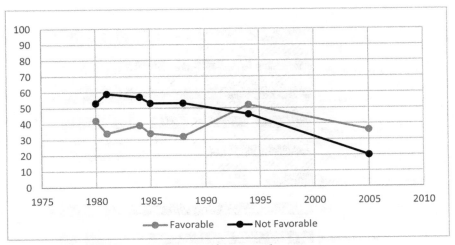

Chart A1.7. Feelings about people on welfare. Data drawn from 8, 9, 10, 11, 42, 55, 103. Relevant data: 105.

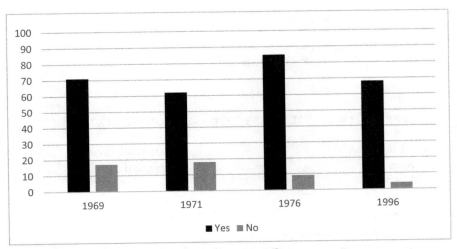

Chart A1.8. Do people on welfare cheat the system? Data drawn from 51, 74, 76, 106. Relevant data: 39, 89, 107.

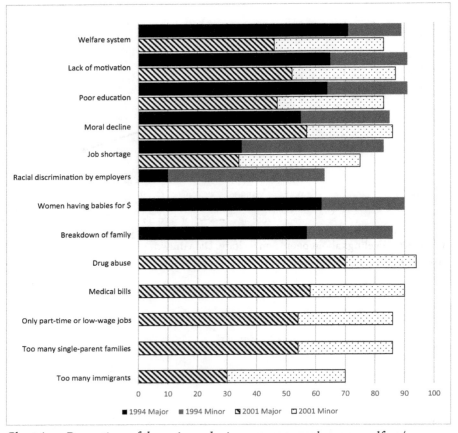

Chart A1.9. Perceptions of the major and minor reasons people are on welfare/in poverty. Data drawn from 54, 75. Relevant data: 26, 67, 69, 70, 72.

APPENDIX 2: CODE LIST FOR LORE ON SOCIAL MEDIA

- Title
- Summary
- Variant
- Citation
- Date shared
- Date of previous receipt
- Transmission data
- Number of forwards
- Additions/Revisions
- Narrative distance
- Contextual data
- Notes
- Genre
- Medium
- Valence
- Told as true/false
- Actually true/false
- Author identity

- Contributor identity
- Pathos
- Ethos
- Logos
- Credibility
- Believability
- Aesthetics

- Formula
- Assumptions
- Political orientation
- Themes
- Motifs
- Scapegoats
- Framing

APPENDIX 3: RECORDED INTERVIEWS

Note: all interviewers, except for the author, were Elon University students.

- Allen, Sharise. Interviewed by Hannah Hyatt on March 7, 2013.
- Allison, Linda. Interviewed by Heather Cassano on October 10, 2012.
- Ayers, April. Interviewed by Kristen Bryar on July 8, 2013.
- Ayers, April. Interviewed by Tom Mould on January 7, 2016.
- Bailey, Darren. Interviewed by Hannah Hyatt on March 7, 2013.
- Banks, Rick. Interviewed by Gloria So on October 15, 2012.
- Bardwell, Neil. Interviewed by Ben Waldon on November 9, 2012.
- Barker, Mary. Interviewed by Tom Mould on March 26, 2013.
- Bassi, Ruth. Interviewed by Ben Waldon on October 21, 2012.
- Beasley, Matt. Interviewed by Chessa Simpson on October 21, 2012.
- Bennett, Andrew. Interviewed by Hannah Hyatt on April 30, 2013.
- Bennett, Andrew. Interviewed by Tom Mould on October 7, 2015.
- Borden, Serena. Interviewed by Heather Cassano on November 13, 2012.
- Bowman, Jimmy. Interviewed by Greg Honan on October 30, 2012.
- Brock, Mark. Interviewed by Chessa Simpson on October 21, 2012.
- Bryant, James. Interviewed by Laura Lee Sturm on November 15, 2012.
- Buckley, Chad. Interviewed by Hannah Hyatt on April 30, 2013.
- Burke, Lynn. Interviewed by Tom Mould on April 17, 2013.
- Cannon, Davey. Interviewed by Hannah Hyatt on April 30, 2013.
- Carlton, Peyton. Interviewed by Tom Mould on March 26, 2013.
- Carter, Lorrie. Interviewed by Jamie Albright on November 7, 2012.
- Carter, Terrell. Interviewed by Hannah Hyatt on March 7, 2013.
- Carter, Luke. Interviewed by Jamie Albright on November 24, 2012.
- Caster, Michael. Interviewed by Tom Mould on March 20, 2013, and October 7, 2015.

- Chance, Bethany. Interviewed by Kristen Bryar on June 27, 2013.
- Clemens, Diane. Interviewed by Kristen Bryar on June 28, 2013.
- Clemens, Diane. Interviewed by Tom Mould on September 30, 2015.
- Coachman, Gail. Interviewed by Whittni Holland on October 30, 2015.
- Collins, Eileen. Interviewed by Greg Honan on November 16, 2012.
- Colton, Ashley. Interviewed by Laura Lee Sturm on November 13, 2012.
- Cook, Maggie. Interviewed by Kit Connor on October 30, 2012.
- Currier, Andrew. Interviewed by Laura Lee Sturm on November 18, 2012.
- Danell, Reggie. Interviewed by Gloria So on October 8, 2012.
- Dartmouth, Bob. Interviewed by Jessica Elizondo on November 9, 2012.
- Dean, Tamera. Interviewed by Rihana Spinner on October 15, 2015.
- Dedrick, Callahan. Interviewed by Jessica Elizondo on November 20, 2012.
- Douglas, Gary. Interviewed by Tom Mould on November 18, 2012.
- Duggins, Gary. Interviewed by Laura Lee Sturm on November 18, 2012.
- Dunn, Elliott. Interviewed by Jamie Albright on November 14, 2012.
- Ellis, Frank. Interviewed by Jessica Elizondo on November 9, 2012.
- Endicott, Lizzie. Interviewed by Greg Honan on October 18, 2012.
- Evered, Christine. Interviewed by Hannah Hyatt on April 9, 2013.
- Faulkner, Kate. Interviewed by Chessa Simpson on October 21, 2012.
- Fitzer, Ellie. Interviewed by Laura Lee Sturm on November 12, 2012.
- Ford, Wanda. Interviewed by Whittni Holland on October 2, 2015.
- Forester, Leslie. Interviewed by Hannah Hyatt on April 30, 2013.
- Franklin, Josh. Interviewed by Greg Honan on November 16, 2012.
- Frisson, Sally. Interviewed by Kit Connor on October 30, 2012.
- Fulton, Leanna. Interviewed by Whittni Holland on November 30, 2015.
- Garland, Lynne. Interviewed by Ben Waldon on November 9, 2012.
- Garnett, Kate. Interviewed by Tom Mould on March 8, 2012; June 13, 2012; and October 31, 2013.
- Gibbons, Alice. Interviewed by Jamie Albright on October 21, 2012.
- Gibbs, Lilly. Interviewed by Jamie Albright on November 19, 2012.

- Giles, Lizzy. Interviewed by Kit Connor on October 24, 2012.
- Glover, Terry. Interviewed by Caroline Miller on November 2, 2012.
- Griffin, Sophie. Interviewed by Alex Sherry on November 13, 2012.
- Hall, Latawnya. Interviewed by Heather Cassano on October 25, 2012.
- Hancock, Leslie. Interviewed by Jessica Elizondo on October 21, 2012.
- Harper, Jill. Interviewed by Gloria So on October 22, 2012.
- Harris, Lorena. Interviewed by Heather Cassano on October 21, 2012.
- Harris, Kimberly. Interviewed by Tom Mould on March 26, 2013.
- Herman, Terrence. Interviewed by Kristen Bryar on September 20, 2013.
- Hewitt, Emma. Interviewed by Tom Mould on April 7, 2012.
- Hicks, Wilt. Interviewed by Jessica Elizondo on November 17, 2012.
- Howard, Louise. Interviewed by Tom Mould and Sophie Rupp on November 4, 2013.
- Huston, Christie. Interviewed by Sara Blough and Emily Thomas on October 7, 2015.
- Huston, Christie. Interviewed by Tom Mould on June 14, 2016.
- Ingram, Parthenia. Interviewed by Tom Mould on March 27, 2013.
- Jackson, Pat. Interviewed by Tom Mould and Kristen Bryar on March 2, 2013.
- Jackson, Pat. Interviewed by Kristen Bryar June 1, 2013, and October 14, 2013.
- Jackson, Pat. Interviewed by Tom Mould on May 17, 2013, and October 3, 2015.
- Jakeman, Andrea. Interviewed by Gloria So on October 15, 2012.
- Jami, Abdul. Interviewed by Ben Waldon on November 11, 2012.
- Jarrett, Jeanna. Interviewed by Kristen Bryar on November 6, 2013.
- Jewell, Bradley. Interviewed by Hannah Hyatt on April 9, 2013.
- Johnson, Paul. Interviewed by Tom Mould on October 11, 2013.
- Johnson, Wanda. Interviewed by Heather Cassano on November 6, 2012.
- Kingston, Jashanna. Interviewed by Vashti Shiwmangal and Anna Rice on September 9, 2015, and April 18, 2016.
- Kingston, Jashanna. Interviewed by Vashti Shiwmangal on October 25, 2015.
- Lacy, Delois. Interviewed by Gloria So on October 8, 2012.
- Lacy, Delois. Interviewed by Tom Mould on September 9, 2018.

- Langdon, Maura. Interviewed by Kit Connor on October 30, 2012.
- Larson, Crystal. Interviewed by Tom Mould on March 18, 2012.
- Macy, Sharlene. Interviewed by Kristen Bryar on October 4, 2013.
- Maller, Betsy. Interviewed by Tom Mould on October 31, 2013.
- Matthews, Silas. Interviewed by Caroline Miller on November 24, 2012.
- McMurry, Ethan. Interviewed by Ben Waldon on November 18, 2012.
- Moore, Latrice. Interviewed by Kristen Bryar on October 23, 2013.
- Morales, Martina. Interviewed by Citlaly Mora on October 5, 2015; October 25, 2015; and May 18, 2016.
- Morton, Sara. Interviewed by Gloria So on October 8, 2012.
- Mynatt, Sonya. Interviewed by Alex Sherry on October 22, 2012.
- Nguyen, Eliza. Interviewed by Anna Rice on October 12, 2015, and October 24, 2015.
- Nguyen, Eliza. Interviewed by Anna Rice and Vashti Shiwmangal on April 16, 2016.
- Nielson, Gina. Interviewed by Hannah Hyatt on April 9, 2013.
- North, Tamara. Interviewed by Caroline Miller on November 16, 2012.
- Osborne, Susan. Interviewed by Alex Sherry on November 6, 2012.
- Palmisano, Daniel. Interviewed by Greg Honan on November 16, 2012.
- Patterson, Jessica. Interviewed by Alex Sherry on November 13, 2012.
- Phillips, Susan. Interviewed by Sara Blough and Emily Thomas on October 21, 2015, and October 28, 2015.
- Phillips, Susan. Interviewed by Tom Mould on June 14, 2016.
- Poole, Michelle. Interviewed by Alex Sherry on November 29, 2012.
- Porter, Richard. Interviewed by Kit Connor on October 30, 2012.
- Pound, Brenna. Interviewed by Heather Cassano on November 13, 2012.
- Powell, Cindy. Interviewed by Jessica Elizondo on November 15, 2012.
- Putnam, Matt. Interviewed by Hannah Hyatt on March 29, 2013.
- Reed, Lamar. Interviewed by Gloria So on October 8, 2012.
- Reston, Sarah. Interviewed by Kit Connor on October 25, 2012.
- Richardson, Tiffany. Interviewed by Kristen Bryar on June 14, 2013.
- Roberts, Henry. Interviewed by Kit Connor on October 31, 2012.

- Robinson, Carla. Interviewed by Kristen Bryar on July 13, 2013.
- Rowe, Christy. Interviewed by Jamie Albright on November 26, 2012.
- Russell, Dylan. Interviewed by Chessa Simpson on October 21, 2012.
- Rutherford, Tracie. Interviewed by Noah Rossen and Shenandoah Lucero-Keniston on October 9, 2015.
- Rutherford, Tracie. Interviewed by Noah Rossen on November 2, 2015.
- Sadler, Martha. Interviewed by Jamie Albright on November 9, 2012.
- Salisbury, Tracy. Interviewed by Caroline Miller on October 24, 2012.
- Salisbury, Tracy. Interviewed by Tom Mould on January 25, 2014.
- Sanchez, Marilyn. Interviewed by Kristen Bryar on November 5, 2013.
- Sands, Sharleen. Interviewed by Noah Rossen on November 7, 2015.
- Schmidt, Julie. Interviewed by Hannah Hyatt on May 7, 2013.
- Seward, Karen. Interviewed by Laura Lee Sturm on October 21, 2012.
- Shaw, Patrice. Interviewed by Hannah Hyatt on March 7, 2013.
- Shepard, Justin, and Karraha Shepard. Interviewed by Jamie Fleishman and Tim Kitslaar on October 2, 2015, and October 29, 2015.
- Shepard, Justin, and Karraha Shepard. Interviewed by Sara Blough and Emily Thomas on May 5, 2016.
- Shepard, Justin, and Karraha Shepard. Interviewed by Tom Mould on June 7, 2016, and August 9, 2017.
- Simcox, Jeff. Interviewed by Jessica Elizondo on November 9, 2012.
- Simmons, Mike. Interviewed by Ben Waldon on November 12, 2012.
- Solomon, Tia. Interviewed by Heather Cassano on November 13, 2012.
- Spencer, Ayanna. Interviewed by Jeremy Revelise on October 9, 2015, and November 10, 2015.
- Spencer, Ayanna. Interviewed by Tom Mould on June 24, 2016.
- Stark, Derick. Interviewed by Alex Sherry on November 13, 2012.
- Steeple, Bill. Interviewed by Jessica Elizondo on November 9, 2012.
- Stirling, Makayla. Interviewed by Kristen Bryar on October 27, 2013.

- Strogue, Matt. Interviewed by Jessica Elizondo on November 9, 2012.
- Sutton, Tim. Interviewed by Greg Honan on November 8, 2012.
- Sutton, Tim. Interviewed by Tom Mould on October 1, 2012.
- Tapper, Keira. Interviewed by Tom Mould on June 23, 2016.
- Taylor, Delia. Interviewed by Tim Kitslaar and Jamie Fleishman on October 15, 2015, and November 13, 2015.
- Taylor, Delia. Interviewed by Tom Mould on November 7, 2017.
- Thorne, Ricky. Interviewed by Jessica Elizondo on November 5, 2012.
- Thornton, Jeffrey. Interviewed by Kristen Bryar on June 20, 2013.
- Thornton, Jeffrey. Interviewed by Tom Mould on September 29, 2015.
- Tylor, Jim. Interviewed by Ben Waldon on November 9, 2012.
- Vertis, Dan. Interviewed by Jessica Elizondo on November 9, 2012.
- Vetter, Sara. Interviewed by Alyssa Potter and Citlaly Mora on October 3, 2015, and October 17, 2015.
- Vetter, Sara. Interviewed by Alyssa Potter on November 12, 2015.
- Vetter, Sara. Interviewed by Tom Mould on June 14, 2016.
- Vincent, Laurie. Interviewed by Caroline Miller on November 12, 2012.
- Wade, Eddie. Interviewed by Jessica Elizondo on October 26, 2012.
- Washington, Etta. Interviewed by Rihana Spinner and Osca Opoku on September 27, 2015, and May 3, 2016.
- Washington, Etta. Interviewed by Rihana Spinner on October 31, 2015.
- Washington, Etta. Interviewed by Tom Mould on October 13, 2016.
- Waterman, Lisa. Interviewed by Gloria So on October 8, 2012.
- Webb, Deidra. Interviewed by Gloria So on October 8, 2012.
- Webb, Jaye. Interviewed by Whittni Holland on October 2, 2015.
- Whittle, Bertha. Interviewed by Olivia Musgrave on November 8, 2015.
- Whittle, Jada. Interviewed by Olivia Musgrave on October 22, 2015.
- Wilmer, Shannon. Interviewed by Jamie Albright on October 24, 2012.
- Wyatt, Becky. Interviewed by Alex Sherry on November 23, 2012.

WORKS CITED

Abromovitz, Mimi. 1996. *Regulating the Lives of Women: Social Welfare Policy from Colonial Times to the Present*. Boston: South End.

Adair, Vivyan. 2000. *From Good Ma to Welfare Queen: A Genealogy of the Poor Woman in American Literature, Photography and Culture*. New York: Garland.

Adams, James Truslow. (1931) 1941. *The Epic of America*. New York: Triangle Books.

Alamance County Community Assessment. 2011. http://www.alamance communityassessment.com/.

Allied Churches of Alamance County. 2017. "Portraits of Hope." http://www .alliedchurches.org/portraits-hope.

Allport, Gordon W. 1954. *The Nature of Prejudice*. Reading, PA: Addison Wesley.

Auto Remarketing Staff. 2011. "African-American Buyers?" *Auto Remarketing*. April 27, 2011. https://www.autoremarketing.com/content/trends/which -brands-most-attract-african-american-buyers.

Bachrach, Judy. 1982. "Sen. Bob Packwood Is the Republican Gadfly Who Keeps Stinging the President." *People*, March 22, 1982. http://people.com/archive /sen-bob-packwood-is-the-republican-gadfly-who-keeps-stinging-the-president -vol-17-no-11/.

Bal, Mieke. (1985) 2009. *Narratology: Introduction to the Theory of Narrative*. 3rd ed. Toronto: University of Toronto Press.

Bargh, John A., Katelyn Y. A. McKenna, and Grainne M. Fitzsimons. 2002. "Can You See the Real Me? Activation and Expression of the 'True Self' on the Internet." *Journal of Social Issues* 58 (1): 33–48.

Barrett, Margaret S., and Sandra L. Stauffer. 2009. "Narrative Inquiry: From Story to Method." In *Narrative Inquiry in Music Education: Troubling Certainty*, edited by Margaret S. Barrett and Sandra L. Stauffer, 7–17. New York: Springer.

Barry, Dan. 1998. "Snubbed by Giuliani, Vice President Will Send Police Award." *New York Times*, April 23, 1998. https://www.nytimes.com/1998/04/23/nyregion /snubbed-by-giuliani-vice-president-will-send-police-award.html.

Bartels, Larry M. 2016. *Unequal Democracy: The Political Economy of the New Gilded Age*. Princeton, NJ: Princeton University Press.

Basso, Keith H. 1979. *Portraits of the "Whiteman": Linguistic Play and Cultural Symbols among the Western Apache*. Cambridge: Cambridge University Press.

Bausinger, Hermann. 1968. *Formen Der "Volkspoesie."* Vol. 6. Berlin: E. Schmidt.

Bauman, Richard. 1977. *Verbal Art as Performance*. Long Grove, IL: Waveland Press.

———. 1986. *Story, Performance, and Event: Contextual Studies of Oral Narrative*. Cambridge: Cambridge University Press.

———. 2004. *A World of Others' Words: Cross-Cultural Perspectives on Intertextuality*. Malden, MA: Blackwell.

Baumeister, Roy F., Ellen Bratslavsky, Catrin Finkenauer, and Kathleen D. Vohs. 2001. "Bad Is Stronger Than Good." *Review of General Psychology* 5 (4): 323–70.

Baxter, Vern Kenneth, and Peter Marina. 2008. "Cultural Meaning and Hip-Hop Fashion in the African-American Male Youth Subculture of New Orleans." *Journal of Youth Studies* 11 (2): 93–113.

Baynham, Mike. 2000. "Narrative as Evidence in Literacy Research." *Linguistics and Education* 11 (2): 99–117.

Beemgee. 2018. "Story vs. Narrative." Accessed November 13, 2019. https://www.beemgee.com/blog/story-vs-narrative/.

Bell, Lee Anne. 2003. "Telling Tales: What Stories Can Teach Us about Racism." *Race Ethnicity and Education* 6 (1): 3–28.

Ben-Amos, Dan. 1971. "Toward a Definition of Folklore in Context." *Journal of American Folklore* 84 (331): 3–15.

Benedict, Ruth. 1935. *Zuni Mythology*. New York: Columbia University Press.

Bennett, Gillian, and Paul Smith. 2007. *Urban Legends: A Collection of International Tall Tales and Terrors*. Westport, CO: Greenwood.

———. (1996) 2011. *Contemporary Legend: A Reader*. New York: Routledge.

Bernstein, David. 2014. "Revisiting Krugman on Reagan and Race Part II." *Volokh Conspiracy*. January 8, 2014. http://volokh.com/2014/01/08/revisiting-krugman-reagan-race-part-ii/.

Best, Joel, and Kathleen A. Bogle. 2014. *Kids Gone Wild: From Rainbow Parties to Sexting, Understanding the Hype over Teen Sex*. New York: New York University Press.

Black, Kerrigan. 1996. "Afro-American Personal Naming Traditions." *Names* 44 (2): 105–25.

Blake, John. 2012. "Return of the 'Welfare Queen.'" CNN.com. January 23, 2012. http://www.cnn.com/2012/01/23/politics/weflare-queen/index.html.

Blank, Trevor J. 2013. *The Last Laugh: Folk Humor, Celebrity Culture, and Mass-Mediated Disasters in the Digital Age*. Madison: University of Wisconsin Press.

Bliss, George. 1974. "'Welfare Queen' Jailed in Tucson." *Chicago Tribune*, October 12, 1974.

Blumenfeld, Warren J. 2016. "God and Natural Disasters: It's the Gays' Fault?" *HuffPost*, February 2, 2016. https://www.huffingtonpost.com/warren-j-blumenfeld/god-and-natural-disasters-its-the-gays-fault_b_2068817.html.

Bock, Sheila. 2012. "Contextualization, Reflexivity, and the Study of Diabetes-Related Stigma." *Journal of Folklore Research* 49 (2): 153–78.

Boris, Eileen. 2007. "On Cowboys and Welfare Queens: Independence, Dependence, and Interdependence at Home and Abroad." *Journal of American Studies* 41 (3): 599–621.

Briggs, Charles L. 1988. *Competence in Performance: The Creativity of Tradition in Mexicano Verbal Art*. Philadelphia: University of Pennsylvania Press.

Briggs, Charles L., and Richard Bauman. 1992. "Genre, Intertextuality, and Social Power." *Journal of Linguistic Anthropology* 2 (2): 131–72.

Broockman, David, and Joshua Kalla. 2016. "Durably Reducing Transphobia: A Field Experiment on Door-to-Door Canvassing." *Science* 352 (6282): 220–24.

Bruner, Jerome S. (1986) 2009. *Actual Minds, Possible Worlds*. Boston: Harvard University Press.

Brunvand, Jan Harold. 1981. *The Vanishing Hitchhiker: American Urban Legends and Their Meanings*. New York: W. W. Norton.

———. 1984. *The Choking Doberman and Other "New" Urban Legends*. New York: W. W. Norton.

———. 1986a. *The Mexican Pet: More "New" Urban Legends and Some Old Favorites*. New York: W. W. Norton.

———. 1986b. *The Study of American Folklore*. 3rd ed. New York: W. W. Norton.

———. 1988. *The Mexican Pet: More "New" Urban Legends and Some Old Favorites*. New York: W. W. Norton.

———. 1989. *Curses, Broiled Again! The Hottest Urban Legends Going*. New York: W. W. Norton.

———. 2001a. "Folklore in the News (and, Incidentally, on the Net)." *Western Folklore* 60 (1): 47–66.

———. 2001b. *Encyclopedia of Urban Legends*. Santa Barbara, CA: ABC-CLIO.

Bump, Philip. 2015. "48% of Millennials Think the American Dream Is Dead. Here's Why." 2015. *Washington Post*, December 10, 2015. https://www.washington post.com/news/the-fix/wp/2015/12/10/48-percent-of-millennials-think-the -american-dream-is-dead-heres-why/?utm_term=.e8cfc9e98665.

Butler, Gary. 1992. "Indexicality, Authority, and Community in Traditional Narrative Discourse." *Journal of American Folklore* 105:34–56.

Campion-Vincent, Véronique. 2005. *Organ Theft Legends*. Jackson: University of Mississippi Press.

Carcasson, Martin. 2006. "Ending Welfare as We Know It: President Clinton and the Rhetorical Transformation of the Anti-Welfare Culture." *Rhetoric and Public Affairs* 9 (4): 655–92.

Carnevale, Anthony P., Stephen J. Rose, and Ban Cheah. 2011. *The College Payoff: Education, Occupations, Lifetime Earnings*. Washington, DC: Center on Education and the Workforce.

Carr, Howie. 2018. "Rep's Sign Complaint Is Latest Example of Cluelessness." March 19, 2018. https://howiecarrshow.com/2018/03/19/reps-sign-complaint-is-latest -example-of-cluelessness/.

Cash, Johnny, and Patrick Carr. 1997. *Cash: The Autobiography*. New York: Harper Collins.

Cashman, Ray. 2016. *Packy Jim: Folklore and Worldview on the Irish Border*. Madison: University of Wisconsin Press.

Cassiman, Shawn A. 2006. "Of Witches, Welfare Queens, and the Disaster Named Poverty: The Search for a Counter-Narrative." *Journal of Poverty* 10 (4): 51–66.

Caswell, Julie A., and Ann L. Yaktine, eds. 2013. *Supplemental Nutrition Assistance Program: Examining the Evidence to Define Benefit Adequacy*. Institute of Medicine and National Research Council. Washington, DC: National Academies.

CBS Houston. 2015. "Oklahoma GOP Chairman Compares Food-Stamp Recipients to Animals." July 14, 2015. http://houston.cbslocal.com/2015/07/14/oklahoma-gop-chairman-compares-food-stamp-recipients-to-animals/.

Cesca, Bob. 2017. "Keep Your Goddamn Government Hands off My Medicare!" *HuffPost*, December 6, 2017. https://www.huffingtonpost.com/bob-cesca/get-your-goddamn-governme_b_252326.html.

Chetty, Raj, Nathaniel Hendren, Maggie R. Jones, and Sonya R. Porter. 2018. "Race and Economic Opportunity in the United States: An Intergenerational Perspective." No. w24441, National Bureau of Economic Research. https://www.nber.org/papers/w24441.pdf.

Christensen, Brett M. 2016. "Badtimes Spoof Makes Fun of Old 'Good Times' Virus Hoax." Hoax-Slayer. July 16, 2016. https://www.hoax-slayer.net/badtimes-spoof-makes-fun-old-good-times-virus-hoax/.

Cho, Sumi, Kimberlé Williams Crenshaw, and Leslie McCall. 2013. "Toward a Field of Intersectionality Studies: Theory, Applications, and Praxis." *Signs: Journal of Women in Culture and Society* 38 (4): 785–810.

Čistov, K. V. 1967. "Das Problem Der Kategorien Mündlicher Volksprosa Nicht-Märchenhaften Charakters." *Fabula* 9 (1–3): 27–40.

Clark, Gregory. 2014. *The Son Also Rises: Surnames and the History of Social Mobility*. Princeton, NJ: Princeton University Press.

Clawson, Rosalee A., and Rakuya Trice. 2000. "Poverty as We Know It: Media Portrayals of the Poor." *Public Opinion Quarterly* 64 (1): 53–64.

Connolly, Deborah R. 2000. *Homeless Mothers: Face to Face with Women and Poverty*. Minneapolis: University of Minnesota Press.

Coombs, W. Timothy. 2015. *Ongoing Crisis Communication: Planning, Managing, and Responding*. 4th ed. Thousand Oaks, CA: Sage.

Corak, Miles. 2013. "Inequality from Generation to Generation: The United States in Comparison." In *The Economics of Inequality, Poverty, and Discrimination in the 21st Century*, edited by Robert Rycroft, 107–26. Santa Barbara, CA: ABC-CLIO.

Corman, Steven R. 2013. "The Difference between Story and Narrative." Arizona State University, Center for Strategic Communication. March 21, 2013. http://csc.asu.edu/2013/03/21/the-difference-between-story-and-narrative/.

cotletdude [pseud.]. 2010. "Italian Auction." August 16, 2010. YouTube video, Aspirin Cardio commercial, 0:46. https://www.youtube.com/watch?v=camvoWdQsZs.

Cottom, Tressie Mcmillan. 2013. "Why Do Poor People 'Waste' Money on Luxury Goods?" Talking Points Memo. November 1, 2013. https://talkingpointsmemo .com/cafe/why-do-poor-people-waste-money-on-luxury-goods.

Couch, Robbie. 2017. "Donald Trump Jr. Tweeted about Candy and 'Socialism.' It Backfired." Upworthy.com. November 1, 2017. http://www.upworthy.com /donald-trump-jr-tweeted-about-candy-and-socialism-it-backfired?c=ufbo&s=p.

Coughlin, Richard M. 1989. "Welfare Myths and Stereotypes." In *Reforming Welfare: Limits, Lessons, and Choices*, edited by Richard M. Coughlin, 79–106. Albuquerque: University of New Mexico Press.

Covert, Bryce, and Josh Israel. 2017. "States Spend Millions to Drug Test the Poor, Turn Up Few Positive Results." *Think Progress*, April 17, 2017. https://thinkprogress .org/states-spend-millions-to-drug-test-the-poor-turn-up-few-positive-results -81f826a4afb7/.

Crane, Mark. 2017. "Doctors Named to 'Fraud Hall of Shame.'" *Medscape*, January 20, 2017. https://www.medscape.com/viewarticle/874737.

Cray, Ed. 1980. *Chrome Colossus: General Motors and Its Times*. New York: McGraw-Hill.

Cullen, Jim. 2004. *The American Dream: A Short History of an Idea That Shaped a Nation*. New York: Oxford University Press.

Cunha, Darlene. 2014. "This Is What Happened When I Drove My Mercedes to Pick Up Food Stamps." *Washington Post*, July 8, 2014. https://www.washington post.com/posteverything/wp/2014/07/08/this-is-what-happened-when -i-drove-my-mercedes-to-pick-up-food-stamps/?utm_term=.2c9e2af60796 #comments.

Dance, Daryl Cumber. 1978. *Shuckin' and Jivin': Folklore from Contemporary Black Americans*. Bloomington: Indiana University Press.

———. 1998. *Honey, Hush! An Anthology of African American Women's Humor*. New York: W. W. Norton.

Darrow, Ryan. 2017. "The Porter Wagoner Show." Tennessee Encyclopedia of History and Culture. October 8, 2017. http://tennesseeencyclopedia.net/entry.php?rec=1680.

Davis, Liane V., and Jan L. Hagen. 1996. "Stereotypes and Stigma: What's Changed for Welfare Mothers." *Affilia* 11 (3): 319–37.

Dégh, Linda. 1991. "What Is a Legend after All?" *Contemporary Legend* 1:11–38.

———. 1994. *Folklore and the Mass Media*. Bloomington: Indiana University Press.

———. 1995. *Narratives in Society: A Performer-Centered Study of Narration*. Folklore Fellows' Communications (Ffc): 255. Helsinki: Suomalainen Tiedeakatemia.

———. 2001. *Legend and Belief: Dialectics of a Folklore Genre*. Bloomington: Indiana University Press.

Dégh, Linda, and Andrew Vázsonyi. 1971. "Legend and Belief." *Genre* 4 (3): 281–304.

———. 1973. *The Dialectics of the Legend*. Vol. 1. Bloomington, IN: Folklore Publications Group.

———. 1974. "The Memorate and the Proto-Memorate." *Journal of American Folklore* 87 (345): 225–39.

———. 1983. "Does the Word 'Dog' Bite? Ostensive Action: A Means of Legend-Telling." *Journal of Folklore Research* 20 (1): 5–34.

Delaney, Arthur. 2013. "Jason Greenslate, Food Stamp Surfer, Responds to the Haters." *HuffPost*, September 22, 2013. https://www.huffingtonpost.com/2013/09 /20/jason-greenslate-food-stamp_n_3960737.html.

Delgado, Richard. 1995. "Legal Storytelling: Storytelling for Oppositionists and Others: A Plea for Narrative." In *Critical Race Theory: The Cutting Edge*, edited by Richard Delgado and Jean Stefancic, 64–74. Philadelphia: Temple University Press.

Deloitte Consulting. 2016. "Fighting Waste, Fraud and Error in Government Programs." May 11, 2016. https://www2.deloitte.com/etc/insights-lists/interactives /fighting-waste-fraud-error-government-programs/index.html.

Dempsey, Bobbi D. 2018. "Poor People Deserve Better Than Food in a Box." *New York Times*, February 14, 2018. https://www.nytimes.com/2018/02/14/opinion /trump-food-stamps-box.html?emc=edit_tnt_20180215&nlid=66024070 &tntemailo=y.

DeNavas-Walt, Carmen, Bernadette D. Proctor, and Jessica C. Smith. 2012. "Income, Poverty, and Health Insurance Coverage in the United States: 2011." US Census Bureau. September 2012. http://www.census.gov/prod/2012pubs/p60-243.pdf.

Derrida, Jacques. 1982. *Positions*. Chicago: University of Chicago Press.

DiFonzo, Nicholas, and Prashant Bordia. 2007. *Rumor Psychology: Social and Organizational Approaches*. Washington, DC: American Psychological Association.

Dorson, Richard M. 1964. *Buying the Wind: Regional Folklore in the United States*. Chicago: University of Chicago Press.

———. 1983. *Handbook of American Folklore*. Bloomington: Indiana University Press.

Drake, Guy. 1970. "Guy Drake—Welfare Cadillac." YouTube video, 2:39, posted by TEDodd [pseud.], December 24, 2007. https://www.youtube.com/watch?v= pRKOmAPejNQ.

DuBois, W. E. B. 1903. *The Souls of Black Folk*. New York: Penguin.

Dundes, Alan. 1964. *The Morphology of North American Indian Folktales*. Helsinki: Suomalainen Tiedeakatemia.

———. 1972. *Mother Wit from the Laughing Barrel: Readings in the Interpretation of Afro-American Folklore*. Englewood Cliffs, NJ: Prentice-Hall.

Dundes, Alan, and Carl R. Pagter. (1975) 1992. *Work Hard and You Shall Be Rewarded: Urban Folklore from the Paperwork Empire*. Detroit: Wayne State University Press.

E-Net News. 2013. "Elon Poll: In North Carolina, Mixed Approval for New State Laws." Elon University. September 20, 2013. http://www.elon.edu/e-net/Article/78285.

Edin, Kathryn, and Laura Lein. 1997. *Making Ends Meet: How Single Mothers Survive Welfare and Low-Wage Work*. New York: Russell Sage Foundation.

Edin, Kathryn J., and H. Luke Shaefer. 2015. *$2.00 a Day: Living on Almost Nothing in America*. New York: Houghton Mifflin Harcourt.

Edsall, Thomas Byrne, and Mary D. Edsall. 1991. *Chain Reaction: The Impact of Race, Rights, and Taxes on American Politics*. New York: W. W. Norton.

Edwards, George C. 2006. *On Deaf Ears: The Limits of the Bully Pulpit*. New Haven, CT: Yale University Press.

Ellis, Bill. 1995. "'Good-Times Cathy' Computer Virus." *FOAFtale News* 36:4–5.

———. 2003. *Aliens, Ghosts, and Cults: Legends We Live*. Jackson: University Press of Mississippi.

———. 2005. "Legend/Antilegend: Humor as an Integral Part of the Contemporary Legend Process." In *Rumor Mills: The Social Impact of Rumor and Legend*, edited by Gary Alan Fine, Véronique Campion-Vincent, and Chip Heath, 123–40. New Brunswick, NJ: Transaction.

———. 2009. "Whispers in an Ice Cream Parlor: Culinary Tourism, Contemporary Legends, and the Urban Interzone." *Journal of American Folklore* 122 (483): 53–74.

———. 2018. "Contemporary Legendry: A Fundamentally Political Act." *Contemporary Legend* 3 (7): 1–19.

Ellison-Potter, Patricia, Paul Bell, and Jerry Deffenbacher. 2001. "The Effects of Trait Driving Anger, Anonymity, and Aggressive Stimuli on Aggressive Driving Behavior." *Journal of Applied Social Psychology* 31 (2): 431–43.

Ewick, Patricia, and Susan S. Silbey. 1995. "Subversive Stories and Hegemonic Tales: Toward a Sociology of Narrative." *Law and Society Review* 29 (2): 197–226.

———. 1998. *The Common Place of Law: Stories from Everyday Life*. Chicago: University of Chicago Press.

Examining the Means-Tested Welfare State: 79 Programs and $927 Billion in Annual Spending: Committee on the Budget, US House of Representatives. 2012. Testimony of Robert Rector, April 17, 2012.

Fader, Carole. 2012. "Fact Check: Did Woman Really Buy a Grape with a Food Stamp Card and Get $24 Cash Back?" Jacksonville.com. October 20, 2012. http://jacksonville.com/news/metro/2012-10-20/story/fact-check-did-woman-really-buy-grape-food-stamp-card-and-get-24-cash.

FAIR. 1995. "Five Media Myths about Welfare." Fair.org. May 1995. https://fair.org/extra/five-media-myths-about-welfare/.

Falk, Gene. 2016. "Temporary Assistance for Needy Families (TANF): Size and Characteristics of the Cash Assistance Caseload." Congressional Research Service. January 29, 2016. https://fas.org/sgp/crs/misc/R43187.pdf.

Feinberg, Matthew, and Robb Willer. 2015. "From Gulf to Bridge: When Do Moral Arguments Facilitate Political Influence?" *Personality and Social Psychology Bulletin* 41 (12): 1665–81.

Fine, Gary Alan. 1979. "Cokelore and Coke Law: Urban Belief Tales and the Problem of Multiple Origins." *Journal of American Folklore* 92 (366): 477–82.

———. 1985. "The Goliath Effect: Corporate Dominance and Mercantile Legends." *Journal of American Folklore* 98:63–84.

———. 1992. *Manufacturing Tales: Sex and Money in Contemporary Legends.* Knoxville: University of Tennessee Press.

Fine, Gary Alan, and Bill Ellis. 2010. *The Global Grapevine: Why Rumors of Terrorism, Immigration, and Trade Matter.* New York: Oxford University Press.

Fine, Gary Alan, and Barry O'Neill. 2010. "Policy Legends and Folklists: Traditional Beliefs in the Public Sphere." *Journal of American Folklore* 123 (488): 150–78.

Fine, Gary Alan, and Patricia A. Turner. 2001. *Whispers on the Color Line: Rumor and Race in America.* Berkeley: University of California Press.

Fine, Michelle, Lois Weis, Susan Weseen, and Loonmun Wong. 2003. "For Whom? Qualitative Research, Representations, and Social Responsibilities." In *The Landscape of Qualitative Research,* edited by Norman K. Denzin and Yvonna S. Lincoln, 167–207. Thousand Oaks, CA: Sage.

Fisher, Walter R. 1989. *Human Communication as Narration: Toward a Philosophy of Reason, Value, and Action.* Columbia: University of South Carolina Press.

Fox News. 2007. "Procter & Gamble Awarded $19.25 Million in Satanism Lawsuit." March 20, 2007. http://www.foxnews.com/story/2007/03/20/procter-gamble -awarded-125-million-in-satanism-lawsuit.html.

Fox News Insider. 2016. "NY Bill: Food Stamps Can't Be Used for Lobster, Steak, Energy Drinks." February 23, 2016. http://insider.foxnews.com/2016/02/23 /ny-bill-food-stamps-cant-be-used-lobster-steak-energy-drinks.

Frank, Russell. 2009. "The Forward as Folklore: Studying E-mailed Humor." In *Folklore and the Internet: Vernacular Expression in a Digital World,* edited by Trevor J. Blank, 98–122. Logan: Utah State University Press.

———. 2011. *Newslore: Contemporary Folklore on the Internet.* Jackson: University Press of Mississippi.

———. 2015. "Caveat Lector: Fake News as Folklore." *Journal of American Folklore* 128 (509): 315–32.

———. 2018. "Fake News vs. 'Foke' News: A Brief, Personal, Recent History." *Journal of American Folklore* 131 (522): 379–87.

Freedberg, Sydeney J., Jr. 1998. "The Myth of the $600 Hammer." *Government Executive,* December 7, 1998. http://www.govexec.com/federal-news/1998/12 /the-myth-of-the-600-hammer/5271/.

Freytag, Gustav. (1863) 1968. *Technique of the Drama: An Exposition of Dramatic Composition and Art.* New York: Johnson Reprint.

Friedman, Howard Steven. 2011. "Reagan's Welfare Queen Has Morphed into the Health Care Queen." *HuffPost,* May 25, 2011. https://www.huffington post.com/howard-steven-friedman/reagans-welfare-queen-has_b _733747.html.

Gallup. 2018. "Gay and Lesbian Rights." Accessed November 13, 2019. http://news
.gallup.com/poll/1651/gay-lesbian-rights.aspx.

Gans, Herbert J. 1990. "Deconstructing the Underclass: The Term's Dangers as a
Planning Concept." *Journal of the American Planning Association* 56 (3): 271–77.

———. 1996. *The War against the Poor.* New York: Basic Books.

Gantz, Harry, and Joe Gantz. 2013. *American Winter.* HBO.

Genius. n.d. "Guy Drake—Welfare Cadillac." Accessed April 2, 2018. https://genius
.com/Guy-drake-welfare-cadillac-lyrics.

Georges, Robert A. 1971. "The General Concept of Legend: Some Assumptions to Be
Reexamined and Reassessed." In *American Folk Legend: A Symposium,* edited by
Wayland D. Hand, 1–19. Berkeley: University of California.

Gergen, David. 2001. *Eyewitness to Power: The Essence of Leadership, Nixon to Clinton.*
New York: Simon and Schuster.

Gilbert, Daniel T., and Patrick S. Malone. 1995. "The Correspondence Bias."
Psychological Bulletin 117 (1): 21–38.

Gilens, Martin. 1996. "Race and Poverty in America: Public Misperceptions and the
American News Media." *Public Opinion Quarterly* 60:515–41.

———. 1999. *Why Americans Hate Welfare: Race, Media, and the Politics of Anti-
Poverty Policy.* Chicago: University of Chicago Press.

———. 2012. *Affluence and Influence: Economic Inequality and Political Power in
America.* Princeton, NJ: Princeton University Press.

Gilliam, Franklin D., Jr. 1999. "The 'Welfare Queen' Experiment: How Viewers React
to Images of African-American Mothers on Welfare." *Nieman Reports* 53 (2): 49–52.

Goffman, Erving. 1963. *Stigma: Notes on the Management of Spoiled Identity.*
Englewood Cliffs, NJ: Prentice-Hall.

———. 1972. "On Face-Work: An Analysis of Ritual Elements in Social Interaction."
In *Communication in Face-to-Face Interaction,* edited by John Laver and Sandy
Hutcheson, 319–46. Harmondsworth, UK: Penguin.

Goldstein, Diane E. 2004. *Once upon a Virus: Aids Legends and Vernacular Risk
Perception.* Logan: Utah State University Press.

———. 2009. "The Sounds of Silence: Foreknowledge, Miracles, Suppressed
Narratives, and Terrorism—What Not Telling Might Tell Us." *Western Folklore*
68:235–55.

———. 2012. "Rethinking Ventriloquism: Untellability, Chaotic Narratives, Social
Justice, and the Choice to Speak for, about, and Without." *Journal of Folklore
Research* 49 (2): 179–98.

Goldstein, Diane E., and Amy Shuman. 2012. "The Stigmatized Vernacular: Where
Reflexivity Meets Untellability." *Journal of Folklore Research* 49 (2): 113–26.

Gordon, John Steele. 2009. "The May Who Saved the Cadillac." *Forbes,* May 1, 2009.
https://www.forbes.com/2009/04/30/1930s-auto-industry-business-cadillac.html.

Gordon, Linda. 1994. *Pitied but Not Entitled: Single Mothers and the History of Welfare
1890–1935.* New York: Free Press.

Graham, Jesse, Jonathan Haidt, and Brian A. Nosek. 2009. "Liberals and Conservatives Rely on Different Sets of Moral Foundations." *Journal of Personality and Social Psychology* 96 (5): 1029–46.

Graham, Joe. 1981. "The Caso: An Emic Genre of Folk Narrative." In *"And Other Neighborly Names": Social Processes and Cultural Image in Texas Folklore,* edited by Richard Bauman and Roger D. Abrahams, 11–43. Austin: University of Texas Press.

Gray, Kelsey Farson, Sarah Fisher, and Sarah Lauffer. 2016. "Characteristics of Supplemental Nutrition Assistance Program Households: Fiscal Year 2015." US Department of Agriculture, Food and Nutrition Service, Office of Policy Support. November 14, 2016. https://www.fns.usda.gov/snap/characteristics -supplemental-nutrition-assistance-households-fiscal-year-2015.

Green, Mark, and Gail MacColl. 1983. *There He Goes Again: Ronald Reagan's Reign of Error.* New York: Pantheon Books.

Greenhill, Pauline. 1992. "English Immigrants' Narratives of Linguistic and Cultural Confusion: Examples of Ethnic Expression from Ontario." *Ethnic and Racial Studies* 15 (2): 236–65.

Greenidge, Kaitlyn. 2016. "My Mother's Garden." *New York Times,* March 26, 2016. https://www.nytimes.com/2016/03/27/opinion/sunday/my-mothers-garden.html.

Greenwald, Robert. 2005. *Wal-Mart: The High Cost of Low Prices.* Brave New Films.

Gurbrium, Jaber F., and James A. Holstein. 1999. "At the Border of Narrative and Ethnography." *Journal of Contemporary Ethnography* 28 (5): 561–73.

Guerin, Bernard, and Yoshihiko Miyazaki. 2006. "Analyzing Rumors, Gossip, and Urban Legends through Their Conversational Properties." *Psychological Record* 56:23–34.

Gustafson, Kaaryn S. 2011. *Cheating Welfare: Public Assistance and the Criminalization of Poverty.* New York: New York University Press.

Habermas, Jürgen. 1979. *Communication and the Evolution of Society.* Translated by Thomas McCarthy. Boston: Beacon.

Haidt, Jonathan, and Jesse Graham. 2007. "When Morality Opposes Justice: Conservatives Have Moral Intuitions That Liberals May Not Recognize." *Social Justice Research* 20 (1): 98–116.

Hall, Edward T. 1976. *Beyond Culture.* Garden City, NY: Anchor Books.

Hall, Judy. 2013. "Witness to Wasteful Purchase Was Astonished." *Times News,* July 23, 2013. http://www.thetimesnews.com/article/20130723/News/307239918.

Halverson, Jeffry R. 2011. "Why Story Is Not Narrative." Arizona State University, Center for Strategic Communication. December 8, 2011. http://csc.asu.edu/2011/12 /08/why-story-is-not-narrative/.

Halverson, Jeffry, Steven Corman, and H. Lloyd Goodall. 2011. *Master Narratives of Islamist Extremism.* New York: Palgrave Macmillan.

Hamill, Ruth, Timothy D. Wilson, and Richard E. Nisbett. 1980. "Insensitivity to Sample Bias: Generalizing from Atypical Cases." *Journal of Personality and Social Psychology* 39 (4): 578–89.

Hancock, Ange-Marie. 2004. *The Politics of Disgust: The Public Identity of the Welfare Queen*. New York: New York University Press.

Handler, Joel F., and Yeheskel Hasenfeld. 2007. *Blame Welfare, Ignore Poverty and Inequality*. New York: Cambridge University Press.

Harris-Perry, Melissa V. 2011. *Sister Citizen: Shame, Stereotypes, and Black Women in America*. New Haven, CT: Yale University Press.

Harvard University Institute of Politics. 2015. "Survey of Young American's Attitudes towards Politics and Public Service." 28th ed. October 30–November 9. Accessed March 12, 2018. http://www.iop.harvard.edu/sites/default/files_new/pictures /151208_Harvard_IOP_Fall_2015_Topline.pdf.

Hays, Sharon. 2003. *Flat Broke with Children: Women in the Age of Welfare Reform*. New York: Oxford University Press.

Heath, Chip, Chris Bell, and Emily Sternberg. 2001. "Emotional Selection in Memes: The Case of Urban Legends." *Journal of Personality and Social Psychology* 81 (6): 1028–41.

Heath, Chip, and Dan Heath. 2007. *Made to Stick: Why Some Ideas Survive and Others Die*. Hardcover ed. New York: Random House.

Henry J. Kaiser Family Foundation. 2001. "National Survey on Poverty in America." April 29, 2001. Poll conducted by National Public Radio, Kaiser Family Foundation and Kennedy School of Government. https://www.kff.org/medicaid /poll-finding/national-survey-on-poverty-in-america/.

Higgins, Lorraine D, and Lisa D Brush. 2006. "Personal Experience Narrative and Public Debate: Writing the Wrongs of Welfare." *College Composition and Communication* 57 (4): 694–729.

Hodges, Adam. 2011. *The "War on Terror" Narrative: Discourse and Intertextuality in the Construction and Contestation of Sociopolitical Reality*. New York: Oxford University Press.

Horigan, Kate Parker. 2018. *Consuming Katrina: Public Disaster and Personal Narrative*. Jackson: University Press of Mississippi.

Hurwitz, Jon, and Mark Peffley. 2005. "Playing the Race Card in the Post-Willie Horton Era: The Impact of Racialized Code Words on Support for Punitive Crime Policy." *Public Opinion Quarterly* 69 (1): 99–112.

Hymes, Dell H. 1981. *"In Vain I Tried to Tell You": Essays in Native American Ethnopoetics*. Philadelphia: University of Pennsylvania Press.

Iceland, John. 2006. *Poverty in America: A Handbook*. Berkeley: University of California Press.

Jacobson, Louis. 2014. "Social Media Meme Says 75 Have Joined Food Stamp Rolls for Every Job Created by Barack Obama." Politifact.com. May 28, 2014. http://www.politifact.com/truth-o-meter/statements/2014/may/28 /facebook-posts/social-media-meme-says-75-have-joined-food-stamp-r/.

Jacobs, Ken. 2006. "The Hidden Cost of Jobs without Health Care Benefits." *Perspectives on Work* 10 (2): 14–17.

Jaffe, Harry Joe. 1975. "The Welfare Letters." *Western Folklore* 34 (2): 144–48.

Jarman, Rufus. 1949. "Detroit Cracks Down on Relief Chiselers." *Saturday Evening Post*, December 10, 1949, 19.

Jemie, Onwuchekwa. 2003. *Yo Mama! New Raps, Toasts, Dozens, Jokes, and Children's Rhymes from Urban Black America*. Philadelphia: Temple University Press.

Jet Magazine. 1974. "Alleged 'Welfare Queen' Is Accused of $154,000 Ripoff." December 19, 1974.

Jones, Edward E., and Richard E. Nisbett. 1972. "The Actor and the Observer: Divergent Perceptions of the Causes of Behavior." In *Attribution: Perceiving the Causes of Behavior*, edited by Edward E. Jones, David Kanouse, Harold Kelley, Stuart Valins, and Bernard Weiner, 79–94. New York: General Learning.

Jones, Les. 1998. "Good Times Virus Hoax: Frequently Asked Questions." December 12, 1998. http://fgouget.free.fr/goodtimes/goodtimes.html.

Kaestner, Robert. 1998. "Drug Use and AFDC Participation: Is There a Connection?" *Journal of Policy Analysis and Management* 17 (3): 495–520.

Kalčik, Susan. 1975. "'. . . Like Ann's Gynecologist or the Time I Was Almost Raped': Personal Narratives in Women's Rap Groups." *Journal of American Folklore* 88 (347): 3–11.

Kantrowitz, Mark. 2011. "The Distribution of Grants and Scholarships by Race." Finaid.org. Accessed March 30, 2018. http://www.finaid.org/scholarships/20110902racescholarships.pdf.

Katz, Michael B. 1993. *The "Underclass" Debate: Views from History*. Princeton, NJ: Princeton University Press.

———. 1989. *The Undeserving Poor: From the War on Poverty to the War on Welfare*. New York: Pantheon Books.

———. 2013. *The Undeserving Poor: America's Enduring Confrontation with Poverty; Fully Updated and Revised*. Oxford: Oxford University Press.

Kelly, Michael. 1993. "Words and Deeds: The Guinier Affair Aggravates Clinton's Credibility Problem." *New York Times*, June 6, 1993. https://www.nytimes.com/1993/06/06/weekinreview/words-and-deeds-the-guinier-affair-aggravates-clinton-s-credibility-problem.html.

Kibby, Marjorie D. 2005. "Email Forwardables: Folklore in the Age of the Internet." *New Media and Society* 7 (6): 770–90.

Kiesler, Sara, Jane Siegel, and Timothy W. McGuire. 1984. "Social Psychological Aspects of Computer-Mediated Communication." *American Psychologist* 39 (10): 1123–34.

Kitta, Andrea. 2011. *Vaccinations and Public Concern in History: Legend, Rumor, and Risk Perception, Routledge Studies in the History of Science, Technology and Medicine*. New York: Routledge.

Kochhar, Rakesh, Richard Fry, and Paul Taylor. 2011. "Wealth Gaps Rise to Record Highs between Whites, Blacks and Hispanics." Pew Research Center. July 26, 2011. https://www.pewsocialtrends.org/2011/07/26/wealth-gaps-rise-to-record-highs-between-whites-blacks-hispanics/.

Kohler-Hausmann, Julilly. 2015. "Welfare Crises, Penal Solutions, and the Origins of the 'Welfare Queen.'" *Journal of Urban History* 41 (5): 756–71.

———. 2017. *Getting Tough: Welfare and Imprisonment in 1970s America*. Princeton, NJ: Princeton University Press.

Kuklinski, James H., Paul J. Quirk, Jennifer Jerit, David Schwieder, and Robert F. Rich. 2000. "Misinformation and the Currency of Democratic Citizenship." *Journal of Politics* 62 (3): 790–816.

Kruger, Justin, Nicholas Epley, Jason Parker, and Zhi-Wen Ng. 2005. "Egocentrism over E-mail: Can We Communicate as Well as We Think?" *Journal of Personality and Social Psychology* 89 (6): 925–36.

Kushner, Harold S. 1981. *When Bad Things Happen to Good People*. New York: Random House.

Labov, William, and Joshua Waletzky. 1967. "Narrative Analysis: Oral Versions of Personal Experience." In *Essays on the Verbal and Visual Arts*, edited by June Helm, 12–44. Seattle: American Ethnological Society.

Langlois, Janet L. 2005. "'Celebrating Arabs': Tracing Legend and Rumor Labyrinths in Post-9/11 Detroit." *Journal of American Folklore* 118 (468): 219–36.

Lauder, Thomas Suh, and David Lauter. 2016. "Views on Poverty: 1985 and Today." *Los Angeles Times*, August 14, 2016. http://www.latimes.com/projects/la-na-pol-poverty-poll-interactive/.

Lauffer, Sarah. 2017. "Characteristics of Supplemental Nutrition Assistance Program Households: Fiscal Year 2016," US Department of Agriculture, Food and Nutrition Service, Office of Policy Support. November 28, 2017. https://www.fns.usda.gov/snap/characteristics-supplemental-nutrition-assistance-program-households-fiscal-year-2016.

Lawinski, Terese. 2010. *Living on the Edge in Suburbia: From Welfare to Workfare*. Nashville: Vanderbilt University Press.

Lea, Martin, Tim O'Shea, Pat Fung, and Russell Spears. 1992. "'Flaming' in Computer-Mediated Communication: Observations, Explanations, Implications." In *Contexts of Computer-Mediated Communication*, edited by Martin Lea, 89–112. Hertfordshire, UK: Harvester Wheatsheaf.

Lee, John D. 2014. *An Epidemic of Rumors: How Stories Shape Our Perceptions of Disease*. Logan: Utah State University Press.

Levin, Josh. 2013. "The Welfare Queen." *Slate*, December 19, 2013. http://www.slate.com/articles/news_and_politics/history/2013/12/linda_taylor_welfare_queen_ronald_reagan_made_her_a_notorious_american_villain.html.

Lewis, Oscar. 1959. *Five Families: Mexican Case Studies in the Culture of Poverty*. New York: Mentor Books.

Liasson, Mara. 2017. "Republicans Talk of Changes to Welfare Next." NPR. December 22, 2017. https://www.npr.org/2017/12/22/572791731/republicans-talk-of-changes-to-welfare-next.

Lieber, Andrea. 2010. "Domesticity and the Home(Page): Blogging and the Blurring of Public and Private among Orthodox Jewish Women." In *Jews at Home: The Domestication of Identity*, edited by Simon Bronner, 258–82. Oxford: Littman Library of Jewish Civilization.

Lieberson, Stanley, and Kelly S. Mikelson. 1995. "Distinctive African American Names: An Experimental, Historical, and Linguistic Analysis of Innovation." *American Sociological Review* 60 (6): 928–46.

Lindahl, Carl. 2011. "Series Editor's Preface." In *Contemporary Legends: A Reader*, edited by Gillian Bennett and Paul Smith, xi–xviii. New York City: Routledge.

———. 2012. "Legends of Hurricane Katrina: The Right to Be Wrong, Survivor-to-Survivor Storytelling, and Healing." *Journal of American Folklore* 125 (496): 139–76.

Linde, Charlotte. 1986. "Private Stories in Public Discourse: Narrative Analysis in the Social Sciences." *Poetics* 15:183–202.

Lino, Mark, Kevin Kuczynski, Nestor Rodriguez, and TusaRebecca Schap. 2017. "Expenditures on Children by Families, 2015." Miscellaneous Publication No. 1528–2015. US Department of Agriculture, Center for Nutrition Policy and Promotion.

Living Wage Action Coalition. n.d. "What's a Living Wage?" Accessed March 18, 2018. http://www.livingwageaction.org/resources_lw.htm.

Living Wage Calculator. n.d. "Living Wage Calculation for Alamance County, North Carolina." Accessed February 8, 2018. http://livingwage.mit.edu/counties /37001[1].

Livingston, Gretchen. 2015. "Family Size among Mothers." Pew Research Center Social and Demographic Trends. May 7, 2015. http://www.pewsocialtrends.org /2015/05/07/family-size-among-mothers/.

López, Ian Haney. 2014. "The Racism at the Heart of the Reagan Presidency." *Salon*, January 11, 2014. https://www.salon.com/2014/01/11/the_racism_at_the_heart _of_the_reagan_presidency/.

———. 2015. *Dog Whistle Politics: How Coded Racial Appeals Have Reinvented Racism and Wrecked the Middle Class*. Oxford: Oxford University Press.

Lord, Charles G., Lee Ross, and Mark R. Lepper. 1979. "Biased Assimilation and Attitude Polarization: The Effects of Prior Theories on Subsequently Considered Evidence." *Journal of Personality and Social Psychology* 37 (11): 2098–109.

Lowthorp, Leah. 2015. "#CRISPRfacts, Gene Editing, and Joking in the Twittersphere." *Journal of American Folklore* 131 (522): 482–92.

Lubiano, Wahneema. 1992. "Black Ladies, Welfare Queens, and State Minstrels: Ideological War by Narrative Means." In *Race-ing Justice, En-gendering Power: Essays on Anita Hill, Clarence Thomas, and the Construction of Social Reality*, edited by Toni Morrison, 323–63. New York: Pantheon.

Lyotard, Jean-François. 1984. *The Postmodern Condition: A Report on Knowledge*. Translated by Geoff Bennington and Brian Massumi. Vol. 10, *Theory and History of Literature*. Minneapolis: University of Minnesota Press.

M15 to South Ferry. 2005. "It Didn't Take Long for the Waste to Start." Subchat.com. October 17, 2005. http://www.subchat.com/otchat/readflat.asp?Id=68119&p=1 #68637.

Macdougall, Curtis D. (1940) 1958. *Hoaxes.* New York: Dover.

MacLeod, Laurie, Darrel Montero, and Alan Speer. 1999. "America's Changing Attitudes toward Welfare and Welfare Recipients, 1938–1995." *Journal of Sociology and Social Welfare* 26:175–86.

Maher, Bill. 2014. *Real Time with Bill Maher.* "Overtime." Aired June 20, 2014. https://www.real-time-with-bill-maher-blog.com/index/2014/6/24/overtime -june-20-2014.

Main, David, and Sandy Hobbs. 2007. "The Substitute Personal Experience Narrative in Contemporary Legends." *Contemporary Legend: The Journal of the International Society for Contemporary Legend Research* 10:38–51.

Marchevsky, Alejandra, and Jeanne Theoharis. 2006. *Not Working: Latina Immigrants, Low-Wage Jobs, and the Failure of Welfare Reform.* New York: New York University Press.

Martin, Douglas. 2012. "James R. Dumpson, a Defender of the Poor, Dies at 103." *New York Times,* November 9, 2012. http://www.nytimes.com/2012/11/09/nyregion /james-r-dumpson-a-defender-of-the-poor-dies-at-103.html?_r=0.

McAdams, Dan P. 2010. *George W. Bush and the Redemptive Dream: A Psychological Portrait.* Oxford: Oxford University Press.

McKee, Heidi. 2002. "'Your Views Showed True Ignorance!!!': (Mis)Communication in an Online Interracial Discussion Forum." *Computers and Composition* 19: 411–34.

McKee, Robert J. 2014. *Community Action against Racism in West Las Vegas: The F Street Wall and the Women Who Brought It Down.* Boulder, CO: Lexington Books.

McKinnon, Ian. 1988. "Xeroxlore: Sentences from Welfare Letters." Memorial University of Newfoundland Folklore and Language Archives. Accession number 88-075.

McLaughlin, Nancy. 2015. "Greensboro Program Seeks to Break Cycle of Poverty." *Greensboro News and Record,* April 10, 2015. https://www.greensboro.com /news/local_news/greensboro-program-seeks-to-break-cycle-of-poverty /article_1bcbf220-df04-11e4-881e-434f8c79c28d.html.

———. 2017. "'A Light of Opportunity': Unique United Way Program Offers an Escape from Poverty." *Greensboro News and Record,* May 20, 2016. http://www .greensboro.com/news/local_news/a-light-of-opportunity-unique-united-way -program-offers-an/article_8abf0b69-5f85-5b41-8f3c-d81c7f3b06c7.html.

McNeill, Lynne S. 2009. "The End of the Internet: A Folk Response to the Provision of Infinite Choice." In *Folklore and the Internet: Vernacular Expression in a Digital World,* edited by Trevor J. Blank, 80–97. Logan: Utah State University Press.

McPherson, Miller, Lynn Smith-Lovin, and James M. Cook. 2001. "Birds of a Feather: Homophily in Social Networks." *Annual Review of Sociology* 27 (1): 415–44.

Merlan, Anna. 2012. "Rick Perry and State Senator Jane Nelson Want Texas to Drug Test Welfare Recipients." *Dallas Observer*, November 13, 2012. http://www.dallasobserver.com/news/rick-perry-and-state-senator-jane-nelson -want-texas-to-drug-test-welfare-recipients-7142725.

Metsch, Lisa R., and Harold A. Pollack. 2005. "Welfare Reform and Substance Abuse." *Milbank Quarterly* 83 (1): 65–99.

Michelmore, Molly. 2012. *Tax and Spend: The Welfare State, Tax Politics, and the Limits of American Liberalism.* Philadelphia: University of Pennsylvania Press.

Mikkelson, Barbara. 2007. "Welfare Applications." Snopes.com. June 29, 2007. https://www.snopes.com/fact-check/welfare-applications/.

Mikkelson, David. 2012. "An Obama Administration Program Provides Free Cell Phones and Cellular Service to Welfare Recipients?" Snopes.com. October 10, 2012. https://www.snopes.com/fact-check/phone-home/.

———. 2013. "Death Spiral." Snopes.com. December 14, 2013. https://www.snopes .com/fact-check/death-spiral/.

———. 2014. "Muslim Men Can Have 4 Wives on Welfare in Michigan?" Snopes .com. September 18, 2014. https://www.snopes.com/fact-check/muslim-men -can-4-wives-welfare-michigan/.

———. 2015a. "The Generous One." Snopes.com. April 13, 2015. https://www.snopes .com/fact-check/the-generous-one/.

———. 2015b. "I Could Careless." Snopes.com. June 4, 2015. https://www.snopes .com/fact-check/i-could-careless/.

Miller, Carolyn R. 2015. "Genre as Social Action (1984), Revisited 30 Years Later (2014)." *Letras and Letras* 31 (3): 56–72.

Miller, Peggy, Grace E. Cho, and Jeana R. Bracey. 2005. "Working-Class Children's Experience through the Prism of Personal Storytelling." *Human Development* 48:115–35.

Miller, Warren B. 1994. "Reproductive Decisions: How We Make Them and How They Make Us." *Advances in Population* 2:1–27.

Miller, Warren B., and David J. Pasta. 1994. "The Psychology of Child Timing: A Measurement Instrument and a Model." *Journal of Applied Social Psychology* 24 (3): 218–50.

Mink, Gwendolyn. 1995. *The Wages of Motherhood: Inequality in the Welfare State, 1917–1942.* Ithaca, NY: Cornell University Press.

Mink, Gwendolyn, and Rickie Solinger. 2003. *Welfare: A Documentary History of US Policy and Politics.* New York: New York University Press.

Mink, Louis O. 1978. "Narrative Form as Cognitive Instrument." In *The Writing of History: Literary Form and Historical Understanding,* edited by Robert H. Canary and Henry Kozicki, 129–40. Madison: University of Wisconsin Press.

Minow, Martha. 2008. "Stories in Law." In *Telling Stories to Change the World,* edited by Rickie Solinger, Madeline Fox, and Kayhan Irani, 249–63. New York: Routledge.

Miskimmon, Alister, Ben O'Loughlin, and Laura Roselle. 2014. *Strategic Narratives: Communication Power and the New World Order.* Vol. 3. New York: Routledge.

Montada, Leo, and Melvin J. Lerner. 1998. *Responses to Victimizations and Belief in a Just World.* New York: Plenum.

Moore, Stephen. 2014. "Corporate-Welfare Queens." *National Review,* March 27, 2014. https://www.nationalreview.com/2014/03/corporate-welfare-queens -stephen-moore/.

Mould, Tom. 2003. *Choctaw Prophecy: A Legacy of the Future, Contemporary American Indian Studies.* Tuscaloosa: University of Alabama Press.

———. 2004. *Choctaw Tales.* Jackson: University Press of Mississippi.

———. 2008. "Genre and the Intratextuality of Personal Experience Narratives." *Midwestern Folklore* 34 (1): 3–22.

———. 2011a. *Still, the Small Voice: Narrative, Personal Revelation, and the Mormon Folk Tradition.* Logan: Utah State University Press.

———. 2011b. "A Backdoor into Performance." In *The Individual in Tradition,* edited by Ray Cashman, Tom Mould, and Pravina Shukla, 126–43. Bloomington: Indiana University Press.

———. 2014. "Collaborative-Based Research in a Service-Learning Course: Reconceiving Research as Service." *Partnerships: A Journal of Service-Learning and Civic Engagement* 5 (1): 1–21.

———. 2016. "The Welfare Legend Tradition in Online and Off-Line Contexts." *Journal of American Folklore* 129 (514): 381–412.

———. 2018. "A Doubt-Centered Approach to Contemporary Legend and Fake News." *Journal of American Folklore* 131 (522): 413–20.

———. 2020. "Welfare, Politics, and Folklore." *Journal of Folklore Research* 57 (2).

Mullainathan, Sendhil, and Eldar Shafir. 2013. *Scarcity: Why Having Too Little Means So Much.* New York: Macmillan.

MyBiggestComplaint.com. 2009. "My Biggest Complaint about Taxpayers Money Spent on Welfare Luxuries." Accessed November 13, 2019. https:// web.archive.org/web/20121109113545/http:/mybiggestcomplaint.com:80 /taxpayers-money-spent-on-welfare-luxuries/.

Myers, Greg. 1999. "Unspoken Speech: Hypothetical Reported Discourse and the Rhetoric of Everyday Talk." *Text* 19 (4): 571–90.

Nass, Clifford Ivar, and Corina Yen. 2010. *The Man Who Lied to His Laptop: What Machines Teach Us about Human Relations.* New York: Current.

NBC News. 2014. "Poll: Fewer Americans Blame Poverty on the Poor." June 20, 2014. https://www.nbcnews.com/feature/in-plain-sight/poll-fewer-americans-blame -poverty-poor-n136051.

NC Department of Health and Human Services, Division of Social Services. 2013. "North Carolina's Temporary Assistance for Needy Families State Plan." March 28, 2013. https://www.ncdhhs.gov/document/temporary-assistance -needy-families-state-plan.

———. n.d. "Work First Eligibility and Income Requirements." Accessed December 18, 2019. https://www.ncdhhs.gov/divisions/social-services/work -first-family-assistance/work-first-eligibility-and-income.

Neubeck, Kenneth J., and Noel A. Cazenave. 2001. *Welfare Racism: Playing the Race Card against America's Poor*. New York: Routledge.

Newsom, Doug, Judy Turk, and Dean Kruckeberg. 2012. *Cengage Advantage Books: This Is PR; The Realities of Public Relations*. Boston: Wadsworth Cengage Learning.

New York Times. 1976a. "'Welfare Queen' Becomes Issue in Reagan Campaign." Special report from the *Washington Star*, February 15, 1976. https://www.nytimes .com/1976/02/15/archives/welfare-queen-becomes-issue-in-reagan-campaign -hitting-a-nerve-now.html.

———. 1976b. "'Welfare Queen' Loses Her Cadillac Limousine." February 29, 1976. https://www.nytimes.com/1976/02/29/archives/welfare-queen-loses-her-cadillac -limousine.html.

———. 1978. "'Queen of Welfare' Ordered Jailed in $239,500 Fraud." http://www .nytimes.com/1978/12/29/archives/around-the-nation-safe-containing-test -drugs-is-recovered-in.html.

———. 1982. "Reagan's Concept of America Hurts Party, Packwood Says." March 2, 1982. https://www.nytimes.com/1982/03/02/us/reagan-s-concept-of-america -hurts-party-packwood-says.html.

NHSDA Report. 2002. "Substance Use among Persons in Families Receiving Government Assistance." April 19, 2002. https://web.archive.org/web /20041108173833/http:/www.oas.samhsa.gov/2k2/GovAid/GovAid.pdf.

Nickerson, Raymond S. 1998. "Confirmation Bias: A Ubiquitous Phenomenon in Many Guises." *Review of General Psychology* 2 (2): 175.

Nicolaisen, William F. H. 1992. "Contemporary Legends: Narrative Texts versus Summaries." *Contemporary Legend: The Journal of the International Society for Contemporary Legend Research* 2:71–91.

Niedwiecki, Anthony S. 2013. "Save Our Children: Overcoming the Narrative That Gays and Lesbians Are Harmful to Children." *Duke Journal of Gender Law and Policy* 21:125–75.

Nordheimer, Jon. 1976. "Reagan Is Picking His Florida Spots." *New York Times*, February 5, 1976.

Norrick, Neal R. 2000. *Conversational Narrative: Storytelling in Everyday Talk*. Vol. 203. Philadelphia: John Benjamins.

NPR Online. 2001. "Poverty in America." Accessed December 18, 2019. https://www .npr.org/programs/specials/poll/poverty/results4.html.

Nyhan, Brendan, and Jason Reifler. 2010. "When Corrections Fail: The Persistence of Political Misperceptions." *Political Behavior* 32:303–30.

Nyhan, Brendan, Jason Reifler, and Peter A. Ubel. 2013. "The Hazards of Correcting Myths about Health Care Reform." *Medical Care* 51 (2): 127–32.

On the Media. 2013. "The Real Story of the Welfare Queen." WNYC Radio. December 20, 2013. https://www.wnyc.org/story/real-story-welfare-queen/.

Oring, Elliott. 1990. "Legend, Truth, and News." *Southern Folklore* 47 (2): 163–77.

———. 1992. *Jokes and Their Relations*. Lexington: University Press of Kentucky.

———. 2008. "Legendry and the Rhetoric of Truth." *Journal of American Folklore* 121 (480): 127–66.

———. 2012. "Jokes on the Internet: Listing toward Lists." In *Folk Culture in the Digital Age: The Emergent Dynamics of Human Interaction*, edited by Trevor J. Blank, 98–118. Boulder: University Press of Colorado.

Ortiz, Ana Teresa, and Laura Briggs. 2003. "The Culture of Poverty, Crack Babies, and Welfare Cheats: The Making of the 'Healthy White Baby Crisis.'" *Social Text* 21 (3): 39–57.

O'Toole, Garrison. 2017. "A Lie Can Travel Halfway around the World While the Truth Is Putting on Its Shoes." QuoteInvestigator.com. February 11, 2017. https://quoteinvestigator.com/2014/07/13/truth/.

Oxfam International. 2016. "Fifty Biggest Global US Companies Stash $1.3 trillion offshore." April 14, 2016. https://www.oxfam.org/en/pressroom/pressreleases/2016-04-14/fifty-biggest-global-us-companies-stash-13-trillion-offshore.

Oxford English Dictionary. 2014. s.v. "welfare." Oxford University Press. Accessed October 14, 2014. http://www.oed.com/view/Entry/226968.

Page, Benjamin I., Larry M. Bartels, and Jason Seawright. 2013. "Democracy and the Policy Preferences of Wealthy Americans." *Perspectives on Politics* 11 (1): 51–73. http://faculty.wcas.northwestern.edu/~jnd260/cab/CAB2012%20-%20Page1.pdf.

Page, Benjamin I., and Robert Y. Shapiro. 1992. *The Rational Public: Fifty Years of Trends in Americans' Policy Preferences*. Chicago: University of Chicago Press.

Parkin, Michael. 1977. "The Benefit of the Doubt." *The Guardian*, January 3, 1977.

Pattillo, Mary. 2003. "Extending the Boundaries and Definition of the Ghetto." *Ethnic and Racial Studies* 26 (6): 1046–57.

Paustian, P. Robert. 1978. "The Evolution of Personal Naming Practices among American Blacks." *Names* 26 (2): 177–91.

PaymentAccuracy.gov. n.d. "Frequently Asked Questions: Are All Improper Payments Fraud?" Accessed January 22, 2018. https://paymentaccuracy.gov/faq/#5.

Pear, Robert. 1982a. "Reagan Unverified on Fraud Stories." *New York Times*, March 25, 1982.

———. 1982b. "Reagan's Social Impact." *New York Times*, August 25, 1982. https://www.nytimes.com/1982/08/25/us/reagan-s-social-impact-news-analysis.html?pagewanted=all.

Pentikäinen, Juha. 1970. "Quellenanalytische Probleme Der Relgiösen Überlieferung." *Temenos* 6.

———. 1980. "Life History: A Neglected Folklore Genre." In *Folklore on Two Continents: Essays in Honor of Linda Dégh*, edited by Carl Lindahl and Nikolai Burlakoff, 150–59. Bloomington, IN: Trickster.

Petty, Richard E., Curtis P. Haugtvedt, and Stephen M. Smith. 1995. "Elaboration as a Determinant of Attitude Strength: Creating Attitudes That Are Persistent, Resistant, and Predictive of Behavior." In *Attitude Strength: Antecedents and*

Consequences, edited by Richard E. Petty and Jon A. Krosnick, 93–130. New York: Psychology Press.

Peuckert, Will-Erich. 1965. *Sagen: Geburt Und Antwort Der Mythischen Welt*. Vol. 1. Berlin: Erich Schmidt.

Pew Research Center. 2014. "Does Hard Work Lead to Success?" January 23, 2014. http://www.people-press.org/2014/01/23/most-see-inequality-growing -but-partisans-differ-over-solutions/1-23-2014_05/.

Pfeiffer, Robert S. 2018. "U.S. Welfare Programs." Federal Safety Net. Accessed January 15, 2018. http://federalsafetynet.com/us-welfare-programs.html.

Polanyi, Livia. 1989. *Telling the American Story*. Cambridge: MIT Press.

Politizane [pseud.]. 2012. "Welfare Inequality in America." November 20, 2012. YouTube video, 6:23. https://www.youtube.com/watch?v=QPKKQnijnsM.

Pollack, Harold A., Sheldon Danziger, Rukmalie Jayakody, and Kristin S. Seefeldt. 2002. "Drug Testing Welfare Recipients—False Positives, False Negatives, Unanticipated Opportunities." *Women's Health Issues* 12 (1): 23–31.

Polletta, Francesca. 2006. *It Was Like a Fever: Storytelling in Protest and Politics*. Chicago: University of Chicago Press.

———. 2008. "Storytelling in Politics." *Contexts* 7 (4): 26–31.

Popik, Barry. 2006. "Welfare Queen." April 11, 2016. http://www.barrypopik.com /index.php/new_york_city/entry/welfare_queen/.

Population Reference Bureau. 2002. "American Attitudes about Poverty and the Poor." May 30, 2002. https://www.prb.org/americanattitudesaboutpovertyandthe poor/.

Positively Republican! 2012. "The $50 Lesson." Facebook. June 26, 2012. https://www .facebook.com/positivelyrepublican/posts/10150904809701733.

Postmes, Tom, Russell Spears, and Martin Lea. 1998. "Breaching or Building Social Boundaries? Side-Effects of Computer-Mediated Communication." *Communications Research* 25 (6): 689–715.

Powell, Benjamin F. 2015. "Family Success Center to Open in GSO, Promises #2EndPoverty." *USA Today*, March 25, 2015. https://www.usatoday.com/story /news/local/2015/03/25/greensboro-family-success-center/70458984/.

Price, Charles. 2005. "Reforming Welfare Reform Postsecondary Education Policy: Two State Case Studies in Political Culture, Organizing, and Advocacy." *Journal of Sociology and Social Welfare* 32:81–106.

Quadagno, Jill S. 1994. *The Color of Welfare: How Racism Undermined the War on Poverty*. New York: Oxford University Press.

Raines, Howell. 1980. "Reagan Words Often Conflict with Strategy." *New York Times*, July 13, A12.

Rakesh, Kochhar, Richard Fry, and Paul Taylor. "Wealth Gaps Rise to Record Highs between Whites, Blacks, Hispanics." Pew Research Center, July 2011. Data is from the Survey on Income and Program Participation. Review 99, no. 2 (2009): 41–44.

Rank, Mark R. 1989. "Fertility among Women on Welfare: Incidence and Determinants." *American Sociological Review* 54 (2): 296–304.

Rasmussen Reports. 2011. "53% Support Automatic Drug Testing for Welfare Applicants." July 20, 2011. http://www.rasmussenreports.com/public_content /politics/general_politics/july_2011/53_support_automatic_drug_testing_for _welfare_applicants.

Reagan, Ronald. 1964. "A Time for Choosing." Reagan Foundation. Radio address, aired October 27, 1964. Accessed December 18, 2019. https://www.reagan foundation.org/reagan-institute/scholarship/essay-series-on-presidential -principles-and-beliefs/a-time-for-choosing-address-october-27-1964/.

Reason, Peter, and Hilary Bradbury. 2008. *The Sage Handbook of Action Research: Participative Inquiry and Practice*. Thousand Oaks, CA: Sage.

Reginal, Travis. 2015. "To Become a Bridge." *New York Times*, April 8, 2015. https:// www.nytimes.com/2015/04/12/education/edlife/to-become-a-bridge.html.

Reutter, Linda I., Miriam J. Stewart, Gerry Veenstra, Rhonda Love, Dennis Raphael, and Edward Makwarimba. 2009. "'Who Do They Think We Are, Anyway?': Perceptions of and Responses to Poverty Stigma." *Qualitative Health Research* 19 (3): 297–311.

Rich, Camille Gear. 2016. "Reclaiming the Welfare Queen: Feminist and Critical Race Theory Alternatives to Existing Anti-Poverty Discourse." *Southern California Interdisciplinary Law Journal* 25:257–88.

Roberts, Steven V. 1984. "Congress: The Provocative Saga of the $400 Hammer." *New York Times*, June 13, 1984. http://www.nytimes.com/1984/06/13/us /congress-the-provacative-saga-of-the-400-hammer.html.

Robinson, John A. 1981. "Personal Narratives Reconsidered." *Journal of American Folklore* 94 (371): 58–85.

Ronald Reagan Radio Commentary Sound Recordings. 1976. "Manchester, New Hampshire, 28 January 1976." Box 4. Hoover Institution Archives.

———. 1976. "Ronald Reagan Radio Series Recording." 76–03. October 18. Hoover Institution Archives.

Rosnow, Ralph L. 1991. "Inside Rumor: A Personal Journey." *American Psychologist* 46 (5): 484–96.

Ross, Lee. 1977. "The Intuitive Psychologist and His Shortcomings: Distortions in the Attribution Process." *Advances in Experimental Social Psychology* 10:173–220.

Rucker, Philip. 2009. "Sen. DeMint of S.C. Is Voice of Opposition to Health-Care Reform." *Washington Post*, July 28, 2009. http://www.washingtonpost .com/wp-dyn/content/article/2009/07/27/AR2009072703066.html?sid= ST2009072703107.

Saltmarshe, Ella. 2018. "Using Story to Change Systems." *Stanford Social Innovation Review*, February 20, 2018. https://ssir.org/articles/entry/using_story_to_change _systems.

Santana, Arthur D. 2014. "Virtuous or Vitriolic: The Effect of Anonymity on Civility in Online Newspaper Reader Comment Boards." *Journalism Practice* 8 (1): 18–33.

Sawhill, Isabel V. 1995. "Welfare Reform: An Analysis of the Issues." Urban Institute. May 1, 1995. http://www.urban.org/publications/306620.html#chap11f3.

Sawin, Patricia. 2004. *Listening for a Life: A Dialogic Ethnography of Bessie Eldreth through Her Songs and Stories*. Logan: Utah State University Press.

Schneider, William. 2002. *So They Understand: Cultural Issues in Oral History*. Logan: Utah State University Press.

Schwarz, Norbert, Lawrence J. Sanna, Ian Skurnik, and Carolyn Yoon. 2007. "Metacognitive Experiences and the Intricacies of Setting People Straight: Implications for Debiasing and Public Information Campaigns." *Advances in Experimental Social Psychology* 39:127–61.

Scott, James C. 1990. *Domination and the Arts of Resistance: Hidden Transcripts*. New Haven, CT: Yale University Press.

Seccombe, Karen. (1999) 2011. *"So You Think I Drive a Cadillac?": Welfare Recipients' Perspectives on the System and Its Reform*. 3rd ed. Boston: Allyn and Bacon.

Shapiro, Robert Y., and John T. Young. 1989. "Public Opinion and the Welfare State: The United States in Comparative Perspective." *Political Science Quarterly* 104 (1): 59–89.

Shapiro, Thomas, Tatjana Meschede, and Sam Osoro. 2013. "The Roots of the Widening Racial Wealth Gap: Explaining the Black-White Economic Divide." *Research and Policy Brief: Institute on Assets and Social Policy*, February 2013, 1–7.

Shropshire, Terry. 2013. "Don Butler Tells How Blacks Helped Save Cadillac from Extinction during ABFF Festival." Rollingout.com. June 22, 2013. http://rollingout.com/2013/06/22/don-butler-tells-how-blacks-helped-save-cadillac-from-extinction-during-abff-festival/2/#.

Shuman, Amy. 2005. *Other People's Stories: Entitlement Claims and the Critique of Empathy*. Urbana: University of Illinois Press.

Shuman, Amy, and Carol Bohmer. 2004. "Representing Trauma: Political Asylum Narrative." *Journal of American Folklore* 117 (466): 394–414.

Singer, Jefferson, and Kathie Halbach Moffitt. 1992. "An Experimental Investigation of Specificity and Generality in Memory Narratives." *Imagination, Cognition and Personality* 11 (3): 233–57.

Slotkin, Edgar M. 1988. "Legend Genre as a Function of Audience." In *Monsters with Iron Teeth*, edited by Gillian Bennett and Paul Smith, 89–111. Sheffield, UK: Sheffield Academic.

Small, Mario Luis, David J. Harding, and Michèle Lamont. 2010. "Reconsidering Culture and Poverty." *Annals of the American Academy of Political and Social Science* 629 (1): 6–27.

Smith, Georgina. 1981. "Urban Legend, Personal Experience Narrative and Oral History: Literal and Social Truth in Performance." *ARV Nordic Yearbook of Folklore* 37:167–73.

Smith, Kimberly K. 1998. "Storytelling, Sympathy and Moral Judgment in American Abolitionism." *Journal of Political Philosophy* 6 (4): 356–77.

Smith, Paul. 1989. "Contemporary Legend: A Legendary Genre?" In *The Questing Beast*, edited by Gillian Bennett and Paul Smith, 91–101. Vol. 4, *Perspectives on Contemporary Legend.* Sheffield, UK: Sheffield Academic.

———. "'Read All Bout It! Elvis Eaten by Drug-Crazed Giant Alligator': Contemporary Legend and the Popular Press." *Contemporary Legend: The Journal of the International Society for Contemporary Legend Research* 2:41–70.

Social Security Administration, Office of Retirement and Disability Policy. 2017a. "Annual Statistical Supplement to the Social Security Bulletin, 2016." May 2017. https://www.ssa.gov/policy/docs/statcomps/supplement/2016/index.html.

———. 2017b. "SSI Annual Statistical Report, 2016." November, 2017. https://www.ssa.gov/policy/docs/statcomps/ssi_asr/.

Spivak, Cary, and Ben Poston. 2011. "Convicted Attorneys Are Still Practicing." *Journal Sentinel*, January 29, 2011. http://archive.jsonline.com/watchdog/114879194.html/.

Stanford, Joseph B., Rachel Hobbs, Penny Jameson, M. Jann DeWitt, and Rachel C. Fischer. 2000. "Defining Dimensions of Pregnancy Intendedness." *Maternal and Child Health Journal* 4 (3): 183–89.

Statistical Abstracts of the United States. 2015. "Population." ProQuest.

Stempel, Jonathan. 2014. "U.S. Appeals Court Voids Florida Welfare Drug Testing Law." Reuters. December 3, 2014. https://www.reuters.com/article/us-usa-drugs-florida/u-s-appeals-court-voids-florida-welfare-drug-testing-law-idUSKCN0JH2CS20141203.

Stevens, Greg. 2012. "Complete List of Political Trick-Or-Treat Jokes." October 31, 2012. https://gregstevens.com/2012/10/31/complete-list-of-political-trick-or-treat-jokes/.

Stone, Daniel, and Laura Colarusso. 2011. "Coburn Report: Welfare for Millionaires." *Newsweek*, November 14, 2011, 23. http://www.newsweek.com/coburn-report-welfare-millionaires-66375.

Strand, Kerry J., Nicholas Cutforth, Randy Stoecker, Sam Marullo, and Patrick Donohue. 2003. *Community-Based Research and Higher Education: Principles and Practices.* San Francisco: Jossey-Bass.

Strauss, Valerie. 2015. "Are Our Rights 'Inalienable' or 'Unalienable'?" *Washington Post*, July 4, 2015. https://www.washingtonpost.com/news/answer-sheet/wp/2015/07/04/are-our-rights-inalienable-or-unalienable/?utm_term=.d2fba9c6a09e.

Sykes, A. J. M. 1965. "Myth and Attitude Change." *Human Relations* 18 (4): 323–37.

Taibbi, Matt. 2014. *The Divide: American Injustice in the Age of the Wealth Gap.* New York: Spiegel & Grau.

Takersley, Jim. 2017. "A 'Main Street' Tax Speech Becomes a Trump Riff on the Rich." *New York Times*, November 29, 2017. https://www.nytimes.com/2017/11/29/us/politics/a-main-street-tax-speech-becomes-a-trump-riff-on-the-rich.html.

Tangherlini, Timothy R. 2008. "The Beggar, the Minister, the Farmer, His Wife and the Teacher: Legend and Legislative Reform in Nineteenth-Century Denmark." In

Legends and Landscape, edited by Terry Gunnell, 171–95. Reykjavik: University of Iceland Press.

Tanner, Michael. 2012. "The American Welfare State: How We Spend Nearly $1 Trillion a Year Fighting Poverty—and Fail." *Policy Analysis* 694:1–24. https://object.cato.org/pubs/pas/PA694.pdf.

Terry, Don. 1995. "Lost in Land of Welfare: Some Travelers' Tales." *New York Times*, November 16, 1995. http://www.nytimes.com/1995/11/16/us/lost-in-land-of-welfare-some-travelers-tales.html.

Theiss, Eveyln. 2009. "Parable of a Chinese Farmer: How an Ancient Story Resonates in Today's Hard Times." Cleveland.com. February 13, 2009. http://www.cleveland.com/living/index.ssf/2009/02/parable_of_a_chinese_farmer_ho.html.

Thompsen, Philip A. 1994. "An Episode of Flaming: A Creative Narrative." *ETC: A Review of General Semantics* 51:51–72.

Titon, Jeff Todd. 1980. "The Life Story." *Journal of American Folklore* 93 (369): 276–92.

Tollison, Duane. 2012. "Our Smoking Habit." *New York Times*, June 15, 2012. https://www.nytimes.com/2012/06/17/magazine/our-smoking-habit.html.

Trattner, Walter I. 1974. *From Poor Law to Welfare State: A History of Social Welfare in America*. New York: Free Press.

TruthorFiction.com. 2015. "People Getting Cash Back by Using Food Stamp/EBT Cards with Minimum Purchase at Gainesville Publix Store—Fiction!" March 17, 2015. https://www.truthorfiction.com/ebt-2-penny-grapes/.

Tucker, Elizabeth. 2007. *Haunted Halls: Ghostlore of American College Campuses*. Jackson: University of Mississippi Press.

Turner, Patricia A. 1987. "Church's Fried Chicken and the Klan: A Rhetorical Analysis of Rumor in the Black Community." *Western Folklore* 46 (4): 294–306.

———. 1992. "Ambivalent Patrons: The Role of Rumor and Contemporary Legends in African-American Consumer Decisions." *Journal of American Folklore* 105 (418): 424–41.

———. 1993. *I Heard It through the Grapevine: Rumor in African-American Culture*. Berkeley: University of California Press.

———. "Respecting the Smears: Anti-Obama Folklore Anticipates Fake News." *Journal of American Folklore* 131 (522): 421–25.

Urban Dictionary. n.d. "Hoochie Mama." Accessed January 8, 2018. https://www.urbandictionary.com/define.php?term=hoochie%20mama.

USA Today. 2017. "State-by-State." November 1, 2017. https://www.pressreader.com/usa/usa-today-us-edition/20171101/281663960270740.

US Census Bureau. 2015. "21.3 Percent of U.S. Population Participates in Government Assistance Programs Each Month." May 28, 2015. https://www.census.gov/newsroom/press-releases/2015/cb15-97.html.

———. 2016. "Quick Facts." Accessed November 13, 2019. https://www.census.gov/quickfacts/fact/table/US/PST045216.

————. 2018. "Poverty Thresholds." Last updated January 19, 2018. https://www
.census.gov/data/tables/time-series/demo/income-poverty/historical
-poverty-thresholds.html.

US Department of Agriculture, Food and Nutrition Service. 2011. "Supplemental
Nutrition Assistance Program: Households: Fiscal Year 2010." https://www.fns
.usda.gov/pd/supplemental-nutrition-assistance-program-snap.

US Department of Health and Human Services, Office of the Assistant Secretary
for Planning and Evaluation. 2011. "2011 Poverty Guidelines, Federal Register
Notice." January 20, 2011. https://aspe.hhs.gov/2011-poverty-guidelines
-federal-register-notice.

US Department of Health and Human Services, Centers for Medicare and
Medicaid Services. 2015. *2015 CMS Statistics*. https://www.cms.gov/Research
-Statistics-Data-and-Systems/Statistics-Trends-and-Reports/CMS-Statistics
-Reference-Booklet/Downloads/2015CMSStatistics.pdf#page=22.

US Department of Health and Human Services, Office of Family Assistance. 2010.
"Characteristics and Financial Circumstances of TANF Recipients, Fiscal Year
2009." August 24, 2010. https://www.acf.hhs.gov/ofa/resource/character/fy2009
/tab30.

————. 2012. "Characteristics and Financial Circumstances of TANF Recipients,
Fiscal Year 2010." August 8, 2012. https://www.acf.hhs.gov/ofa/resource/character
/fy2010/fy2010-chap10-ys-final.

————. 2016. "Characteristics and Financial Circumstances of TANF Recipients,
Fiscal Year 2015." August 18, 2016. https://www.acf.hhs.gov/ofa/resource
/characteristics-and-financial-circumstances-of-tanf-recipients-fiscal-year-2015.

US Department of Health and Human Services, Office of Inspector General. 2017.
"Medicaid Fraud Control Units Fiscal Year 2016 Annual Report." May 2017.
https://oig.hhs.gov/oei/reports/oei-09-17-00210.asp.

US Department of Health and Human Services, Substance Abuse and Mental
Health Services Administration. 2012. "Results from the 2011 National Survey
on Drug Use and Health: Summary of National Findings." September 2012.
https://www.samhsa.gov/data/sites/default/files/Revised2k11NSDUH
SummNatFindings/Revised2k11NSDUHSummNatFindings/NSDUH
results2011.htm.

————. 2013. "National Survey of Substance Abuse Treatment Services, 2012: Data
on Substance Abuse Treatment Facilities." December, 2012. https://wwwdasis
.samhsa.gov/dasis2/nssats/2012_nssats_rpt.pdf.

US Department of Housing and Urban Development. 2018. "Resident Characteristics
Report." Accessed January 8, 2018. https://www.hud.gov/program_offices/public
_indian_housing/systems/pic/50058/rcr.

US Department of Labor. 2016. "BLS Information: Glossary." Bureau of Labor
Statistics. June 7, 2016. https://www.bls.gov/bls/glossary.htm.

US Government Accountability Office. 2016. *Supplemental Nutrition Assistance Program: Policy Changes and Calculation Methods Likely Affect Improper Payment Rates, and USDA Is Taking Steps to Help Address Recipient Fraud: House of Representatives, Committee on Agriculture.* Statement of Kay E. Brown, Director, Education, Workforce and Income Security Issues. July 6, 2016. https://www.gao.gov/products/GAO-16-708T.

VanArsdale, Daniel W. 2015. "The Paper Chain Letter Archive—Annotated Index." Accessed March 31, 2018. http://www.silcom.com/~barnowl/chain-letter/archive/%21content.html.

van Dijk, Teun A. 1975. "Action, Action Description, and Narrative." *New Literary History* 6 (2): 273–94.

———. 1993. *Elite Discourse and Racism.* Vol. 6. Thousand Oaks, CA: Sage.

van Doorn, Bas W. 2015. "Pre- and Post-welfare Reform Media Portrayals of Poverty in the United States: The Continuing Importance of Race and Ethnicity." *Politics and Policy* 43 (1): 142–62.

Vlach, John M. 1971. "One Black Eye and Other Horrors: A Case for the Humorous Anti-Legend." *Indiana Folklore* 4:95–140.

Voelkel, Jan G., and Matthew Feinberg. 2018. "Morally Reframed Arguments Can Affect Support for Political Candidates." *Social Psychological and Personality Science* 9 (8): 917–24.

Voices of Welfare. 2014a. "Causes of Generational Poverty." Accessed March 30, 2018. https://blogs.elon.edu/voicesofwelfare/causes-of-generational-poverty/.

———. 2014b. "Voices of Welfare." March 4, 2014. http://blogs.elon.edu/voicesofwelfare/.

von Sydow, Carl Wilhelm. 1948. "Kategorien Der Prosa-Volksdichtung." In *Selected Papers on Folklore*, edited by Carl Wilhelm von Sydow, 11–43. Copenhagen: Rosenkilde and Bagger.

Vosoughi, Soroush, Deb Roy, and Sinan Aral. 2018. "The Spread of True and False News Online." *Science* 359 (6380): 1146–51.

Wacquant, Loïc J. D. 1997. "Three Pernicious Premises in the Study of the American Ghetto." *International Journal of Urban and Regional Research* 21 (2): 341–53.

Walker, Robert H. 1983. "Rags to Riches." In *Handbook of American Folklore*, edited by Richard M. Dorson, 67–72. Bloomington: Indiana University Press.

Warr, Deborah J. 2005. "Social Networks in a 'Discredited' Neighbourhood." *Journal of Sociology* 41 (3): 285–308.

Washington Post. 1973. "Charles Town Race Charts." September 1, 1973.

———. 1978. "Woman Guilty of $240,000 Welfare Fraud." December 2, 1978. https://www.washingtonpost.com/archive/politics/1978/12/02/woman-guilty-of-240000-welfare-fraud/5f30ed75-1d8c-4488-9b75-9bcf452a2209/?utm_term=.bc7bc732d6a3.

Wason, Peter C. 1960. "On the Failure to Eliminate Hypotheses in a Conceptual Task." *Quarterly Journal of Experimental Psychology* 12 (3): 129–40.

We Are Beneficiaries. n.d. Facebook Group. Accessed November 13, 2019. https://
www.facebook.com/pg/WeAreBeneficiaries/about/?ref=page_internal.

West, Laurel Parker. 2002. "Soccer Moms, Welfare Queens, Waitress Moms, and
Super Moms: Myths of Motherhood in State Media Coverage of Child Care."
MARIAL Working Papers, Emory University.

WFMY News. 2013. "North Carolina Is Committed to Cutting out Food Stamp
Fraud." February 21, 2013. http://www.wfmynews2.com/article/news/local_state
/article.aspx?storvid=27055?storvid=27055.

———. 2017. "Fraud Hotline to Report Misuse of Food Stamps and Other
Programs." January 3, 2017. http://www.wfmynews2.com/article/news/crime
/fraud-hotline-to-report-misuse-of-food-stamps-and-other-programs/381662531.

Whitaker, Morgan. 2014. "GOP Candidate Compares Food Stamp Recipients to
Wild Animals." MSNBC. May 1, 2014. http://www.msnbc.com/politicsnation
/gop-candidate-compares-food-stamp-recipients-wild-animals.

Whyte, William Foote. 1943. *Street Corner Society: The Social Structure of an Italian
Slum*. Chicago: University of Chicago Press.

Wilson, William A. 1989. "The Study of Mormon Folklore: An Uncertain Mirror for
Truth." *Dialogue* 22:95–110.

Woods, Barbara Allen. 1959. *The Devil in Dog Form: A Partial Type-Index of Devil
Legends*. Vol. 11. Berkeley: University of California Press.

Woollcott, Alexander. 1934. *While Rome Burns*. New York: Viking.

Wyckoff, Donna. 1993. "Why a Legend? Contemporary Legends as Community
Ritual." *Contemporary Legend: The Journal of the International Society for
Contemporary Legend Research* 3:1–36.

Yahoo Answers. 2010. "Do the People on Unemployment Really Need It?" Accessed
December 16, 2016. https://answers.yahoo.com/question/index;_ylt=AwrCowx5
Yg1epWAADkFPmolQ;_ylu=X3oDMTByOHZyb21tBGNvbG8DYmYxBHBvcw
MxBHZoaWQDBHNlYwNzcg--?qid=20100315105341AAcrsSu.

———. 2012. "Unemployment Foodstamps and WIC?" Accessed December 16, 2016.
https://answers.yahoo.com/question/index;_ylt=AwrCiC1gHrJXEVEA7
.lPmolQ;_ylu=X3oDMTEybzcob2RqBGNvbG8DYmYxBHBvcwMoBHZoa
WQDQjliNTdfMQRzZWMDc2M-?qid=20100328181933AACKvru.

Young, Iris Marion. 2013. *Responsibility for Justice*. Oxford: Oxford University Press.

INDEX

health care, 3–4, 260 (*see also* Obamacare); cost of, 24, 215–16; lack of, 15, 146
Heath, Chip, 65, 204, 291
Heath, Dan, 65, 291
Hicks, Witt, 156
Higgins, Lorraine, 280
Hispanic, 22, 25–27, 146, 195–96, 207. *See also* Latino
homelessness, 62, 72–73, 77, 81, 86, 89, 91, 101, 103, 109, 122, 136, 138, 171–72, 232, 235, 249–50. *See also* housing
homeless shelter, 6, 8, 84, 101, 104, 137–38, 154–55, 171, 238, 249–51, 274, 306, 315
Honan, Greg, 241n9
housing, 270, 300; assistance, 18–19, 23, 32, 258; lack of, 73, 80, 85–86, 116, 121–28; in narrative, 72, 86, 89–91, 103, 106–7, 117, 126–27, 129, 136–39, 176, 178, 224, 230, 258, 262, 265; public, 18, 80, 107, 109, 116–17, 122–30, 139–41, 176, 178, 186, 224, 262, 265, 315–16. *See also* homelessness; homeless shelter
Howard, Louise, 86, 94, 98, 103–4, 173
Huelskamp, Tim, 59
Hurricane Katrina, 38, 196, 202, 206, 280
Huston, Christie, 90–91, 94, 98, 105, 108, 120–22, 126–28, 262, 269–70

independent, 62, 64, 65, 80, 105, 162, 235, 294, 306. *See also* self-sufficiency
immigration, 25, 58, 61–62, 92, 108, 166, 195–96, 295, 303–4, 308. *See also* welfare legend stock characters: immigrants
immorality. *See* morality: lack of
inequalities, structural, 20, 24, 32, 280, 308, 313n13
Ingram, Parthenia, 136, 151, 155, 160, 168, 236
intersectionality, 108–9
intertextuality, 256
inverse identity theory. *See* theory: inverse identity
I saw it myself (ISIM) narratives. *See* narrative types: I saw it myself

Jackson, Pat, 87, 94, 128–32, 315
jail and prison, 107, 302; in narrative, 51, 82, 85–90, 102, 130–31, 186, 307
Jarman, Rufus, 51

Jarratt, Mary C., 52
Jarrett, Jeanna, 270
Jewell, Bradley, 86, 94, 179, 268, 300
jewelry, 64, 156, 166, 198, 218, 222, 242–43, 255–57
jobs. *See* employment
Johnson, Lyndon B., 54, 227
Johnson, Paul, 166–67
jokes, 107, 149, 152–53, 159, 182–84, 186–87, 193, 196, 197, 200–201, 204–7, 253, 268, 284

Kalla, Joshua, 311–12
Katz, Michael, 161
kernel story, 15, 51, 220, 227, 269
Kerry, John, 286
Kingston, Jashanna, 9, 91, 98, 122, 133–34
Kohler-Hausmann, Julilly, 54

Lacy, Delois, 137
Larson, Crystal, 235
Latino, 22–24, 54, 108, 151, 254. *See also* Hispanic
lazy. *See* work ethic, lack of
Lee, John, 289
legend: analytical approach to, 242–59; characteristics, 204–5; contemporary, 35–36, 184–85, 204, 244–46, 257, 273, 280, 291; definitions, 34–36, 244, 246, 256; function, 61, 204–5, 256–57, 281–85; vs. personal experience narratives, 12, 92, 135, 182–86, 273–76. *See also* antilegend; I saw it myself
Letterman, David, 190
Lewis, Drew, 48
Lewis, Oscar, 24
LGBTQ, 109, 295–96, 311
Lifeline, 201. *See also* Obama phone
life stories, 81–82, 136, 236
Lindahl, Carl, 256–57
lists, 21; as folklore, 184, 190, 193, 196–97, 204
lobster, 10, 59, 148, 156
logical fallacies, 203, 300–301, 303
lottery tickets, 53, 154, 198–99, 243
Low Income Home Energy Assistance Program (LIHEAP), 18, 177
luck, bad, 92–93

making ends meet, 116–35; strategies for, 120–23. *See also* aid recipient narrative types: making ends meet

Maller, Betsy, 91, 94, 133, 235, 267, 270

mass media, 12, 36, 49, 175, 311; bias in, 48, 161; critique of, 199, 289, 309; and the folk tradition, 47, 160, 170; public assistance discussed in, 12, 15, 17, 44–46, 58–59, 154, 217–18, 252. *See also* public assistance fraud: in the media; welfare queen: in the media

Matthews, Silas, 47–48, 145–48, 160–62, 167, 172

McCoy, Gary, 191

McLuhan, Marshall, 16

Medicaid, 14–15, 18–19, 23–24, 32, 43, 130, 152, 176, 235; cuts to, 58–59; eligibility, 71, 117, 121, 215–16, 260

medical field, 83, 103, 116–17, 136–37, 146, 151–52, 297

Medicare, 17, 19, 47

memes, 183–84, 187–88, 193, 197–209

memetics, 204, 309

memory, 135, 263, 272–74, 289–90; social, 6

methodology, 5–10, 37–38, 183–84

microaggressions, 112

Miller, Caroline, 47

Morales, Martina, 108, 118, 121, 134, 171–72, 254

moral foundations theory. *See* theory: moral foundations

morality, 5, 36, 61–65, 93, 165, 175, 284, 290, 293, 302–3; lack of, 5, 15, 20, 22, 24, 29, 38, 47, 53, 154, 160, 162, 172, 198, 205, 298; in narrative, 216, 220, 227, 295–96

Moynihan Report, 24, 48

Muslim, 196–98, 203, 246

myth, 35, 61, 64, 155, 232, 246

narrative: coherence, 114, 291–93, 305; completion, 83–84; definitions, 33–34; distance, 135, 137, 174, 183, 207–8, 221, 228, 248, 265, 271–76, 291 (*see also* secondhand stories); evaluation of, 293; rationality, 293, 296, 310; structure, 97–98, 103, 135, 263. *See also* storytelling

narrative types, 16; canonical, 12, 34, 225, 253–54, 271, 293–98, 308; counter, 34, 38, 73, 178, 221–22, 246–47, 254, 285–86, 290–91, 294–95, 300–304, 308–12;

crystallized, 97; cultural, 253, 256, 296, 308; eyewitness, 32, 110, 173, 195, 198–202, 209, 239, 271–76; generalized experience narratives, 13, 97, 120, 177, 220, 228, 258–66, 270–71; hegemonic, 34, 38, 179–80, 221, 284, 294, 296, 300, 302; hypothetical narratives, 265–70; I saw it myself (ISIM), 271–76; local, 66; master, 12, 34, 66, 264, 269, 295, 297–99, 303; personal narratives (*see* personal narratives); short shelf-life, 97, 125–26. *See also* aid recipient narrative types; welfare legend types

New Deal, 64

news: fake, 13, 289; lore, 184

Nguyen, Eliza, 92, 98, 123

Nicolaisen, Bill, 272

Nielson, Gina, 122

Nixon, Richard M., 43, 45, 48, 55

North, Tamara, 252, 254

Nowak, Ben, 183–84

Nyhan, Brendan, 288

Obama, Barack, 3, 60, 145, 184, 188–89, 191, 195, 200–202, 269–70; birth certificate, 246–47, 286

Obamacare, 4, 32, 290. *See also* Affordable Care Act

Obama phone, 201, 226

O'Connor, John E., 51

official documents as folklore, 184, 186, 196, 200, 207

Open Door Clinic (ODC), 6–7, 71, 135, 171, 215, 238

Oring, Elliott, 35–36, 190, 202, 224, 244–45

Osborne, Susan, 230–31, 234, 238

Packwood, Bob, 51–53

Palin, Sarah, 288

Palmisano, Daniel, 151

parenting: single, 14, 22, 24, 27–29, 31, 54, 57, 82, 85–90, 96–97, 99–100, 107, 117, 134, 306, 308. *See also* family

parody, 150, 183, 186, 192–93, 280–85

Parton, Dolly, 147

Patterson, Jessica, 268

Pentikäinen, Juha, 273

personal narratives, 66, 183–85, 195–201, 205–8, 221, 264, 312; personal experience narratives, 36, 66, 85–86, 92, 133, 193, 220,

TOM MOULD is Professor of Anthropology and Folklore at Butler University. He is author of *Still, the Small Voice: Narrative, Personal Revelation, and the Mormon Folk Tradition, Choctaw Prophecy: A Legacy of the Future,* and *Choctaw Tales.*